PLANETARY

CROSSING WORLDS

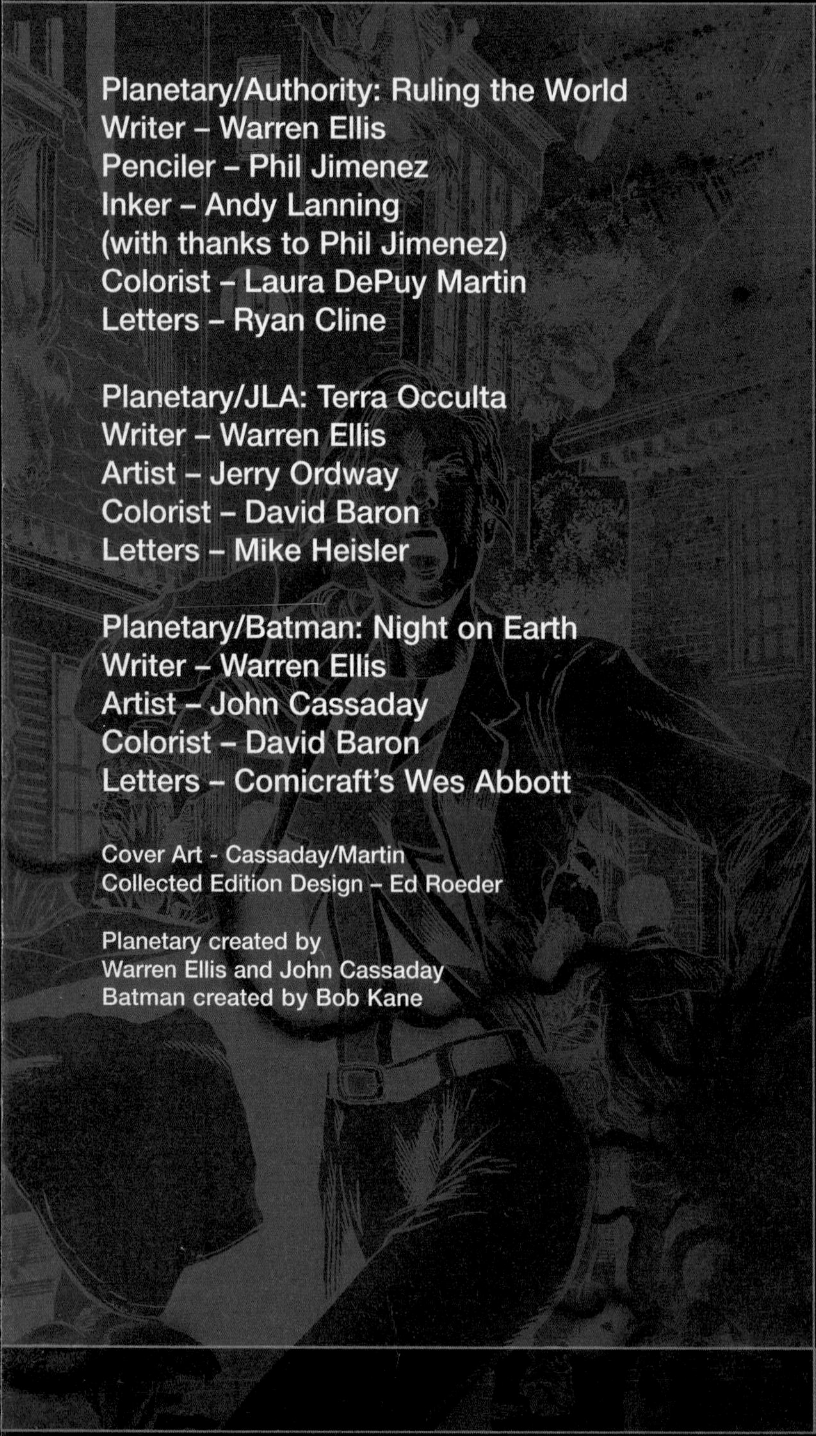

Planetary/Authority: Ruling the World
Writer – Warren Ellis
Penciler – Phil Jimenez
Inker – Andy Lanning
(with thanks to Phil Jimenez)
Colorist – Laura DePuy Martin
Letters – Ryan Cline

Planetary/JLA: Terra Occulta
Writer – Warren Ellis
Artist – Jerry Ordway
Colorist – David Baron
Letters – Mike Heisler

Planetary/Batman: Night on Earth
Writer – Warren Ellis
Artist – John Cassaday
Colorist – David Baron
Letters – Comicraft's Wes Abbott

Cover Art - Cassaday/Martin
Collected Edition Design – Ed Roeder

Planetary created by
Warren Ellis and John Cassaday
Batman created by Bob Kane

Planetary/Batman honors several versions of Batman from past eras and should be taken in the context of the time each represents. The Batman holding a gun on page 146 is the same as depicted in DETECTIVE COMICS #32 from 1939.

PLANETARY: CROSSING WORLDS published by WildStorm Productions. 888 Prospect St. #240, La Jolla, CA 92037. Cover and compilation copyright © 2004 DC Comics. All Rights Reserved. WildStorm and logo, all characters, the distinctive likenesses thereof and all related elements are trademarks of DC Comics. Originally published in single magazine form as PLANETARY/AUTHORITY: RULING THE WORLD, PLANETARY/JLA: TERRA OCCULTA, and PLANETARY/BATMAN: NIGHT ON EARTH © 2000, 2002, 2003 DC Comics.
The stories, characters, and incidents mentioned in this magazine are entirely fictional. Printed on recyclable paper. WildStorm does not read or accept unsolicited submissions of ideas, stories or artwork. Printed in Canada. THIRD PRINTING. ISBN: 1-4012-0279-9   ISBN 13: 978-1-4012-0279-8

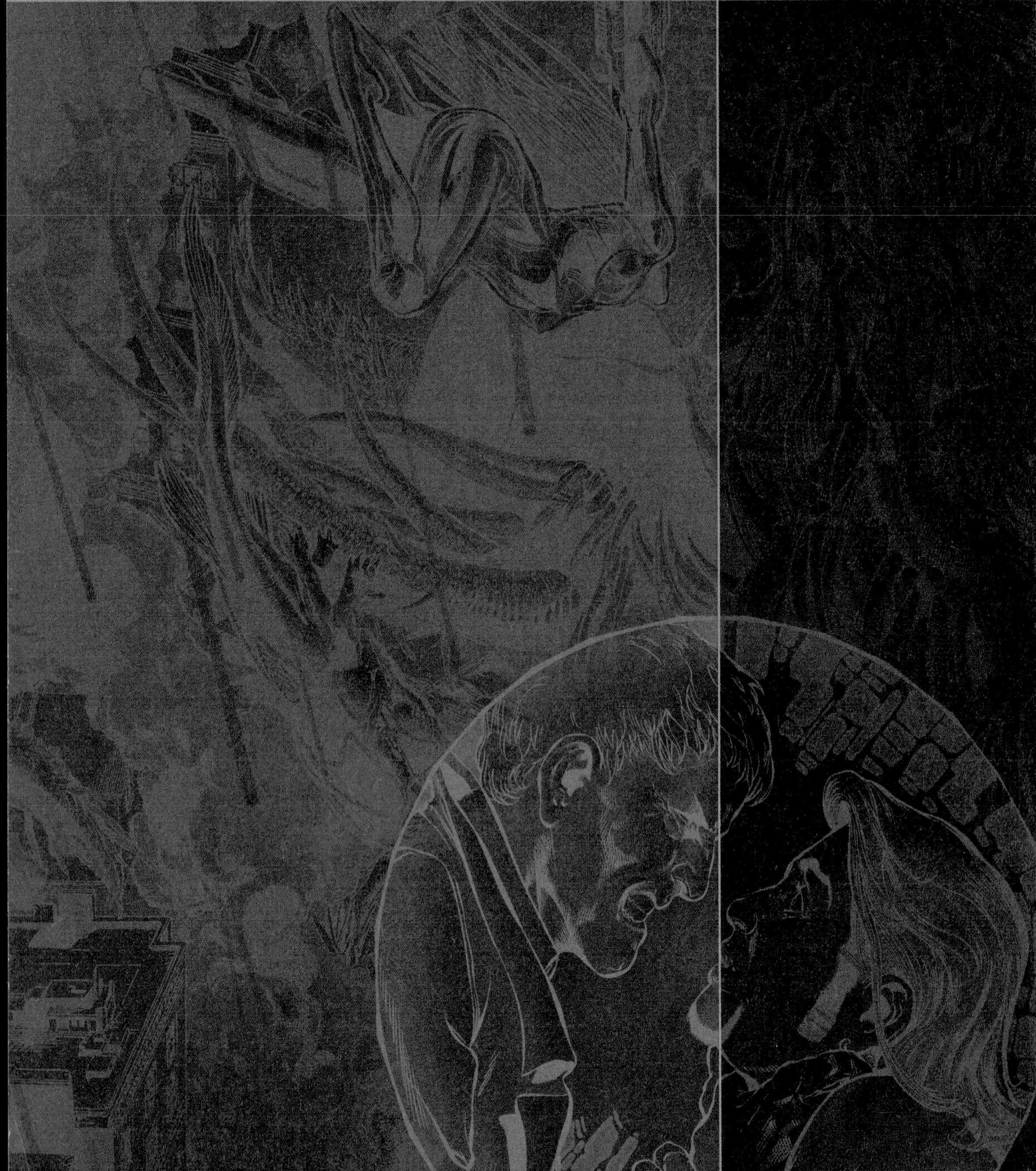

CHAPTER 1

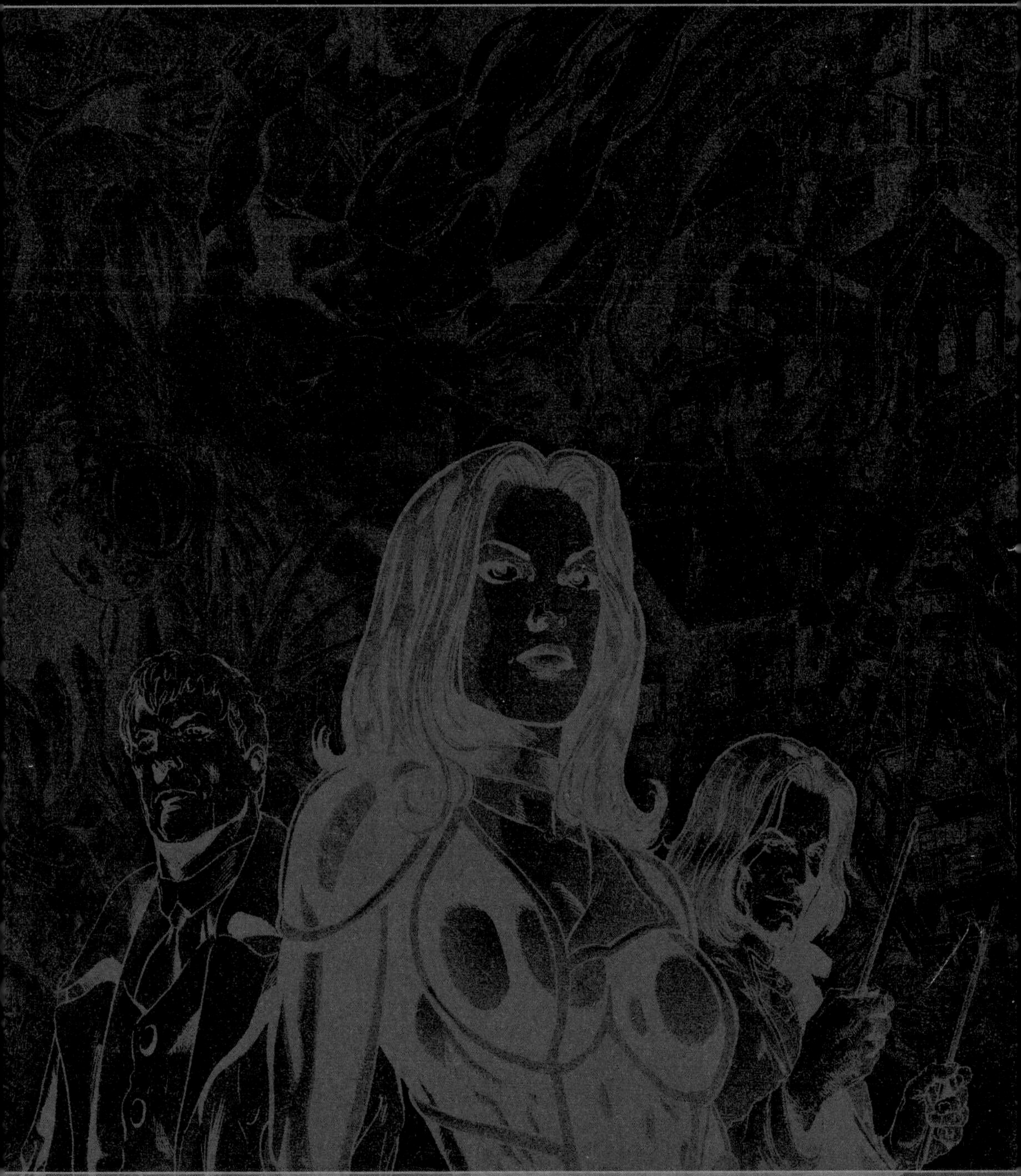

RULING THE WORLD

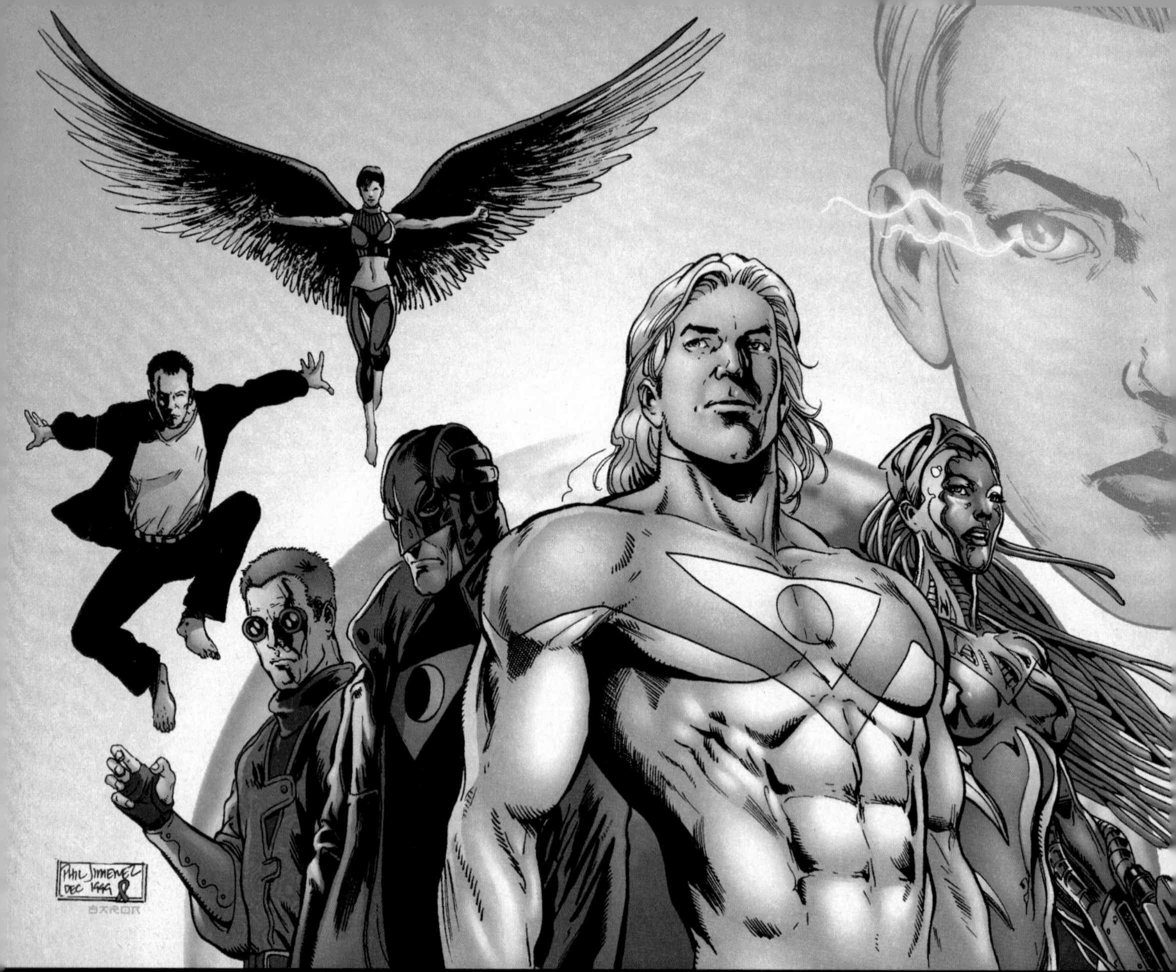
PHIL JIMENEZ
DEC 1999
BARON

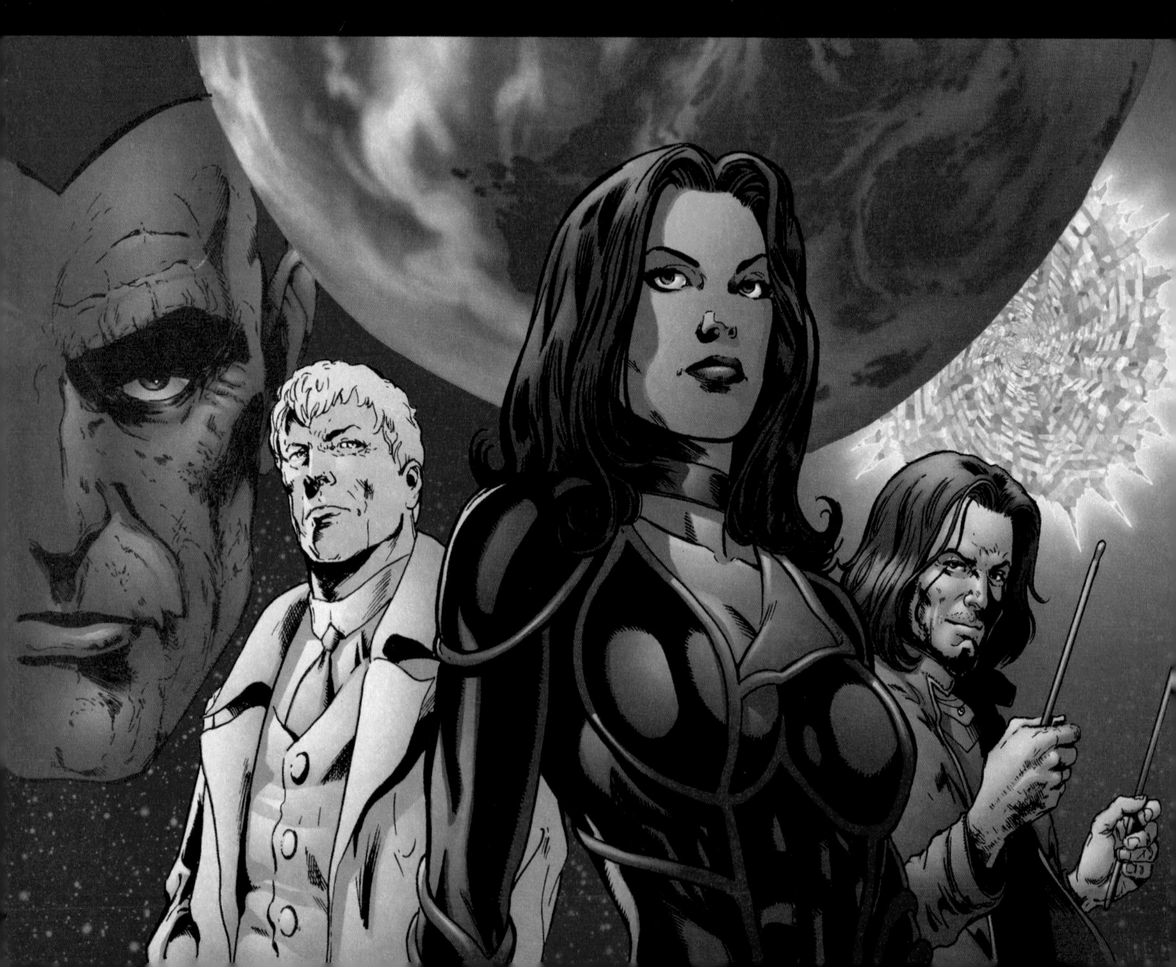

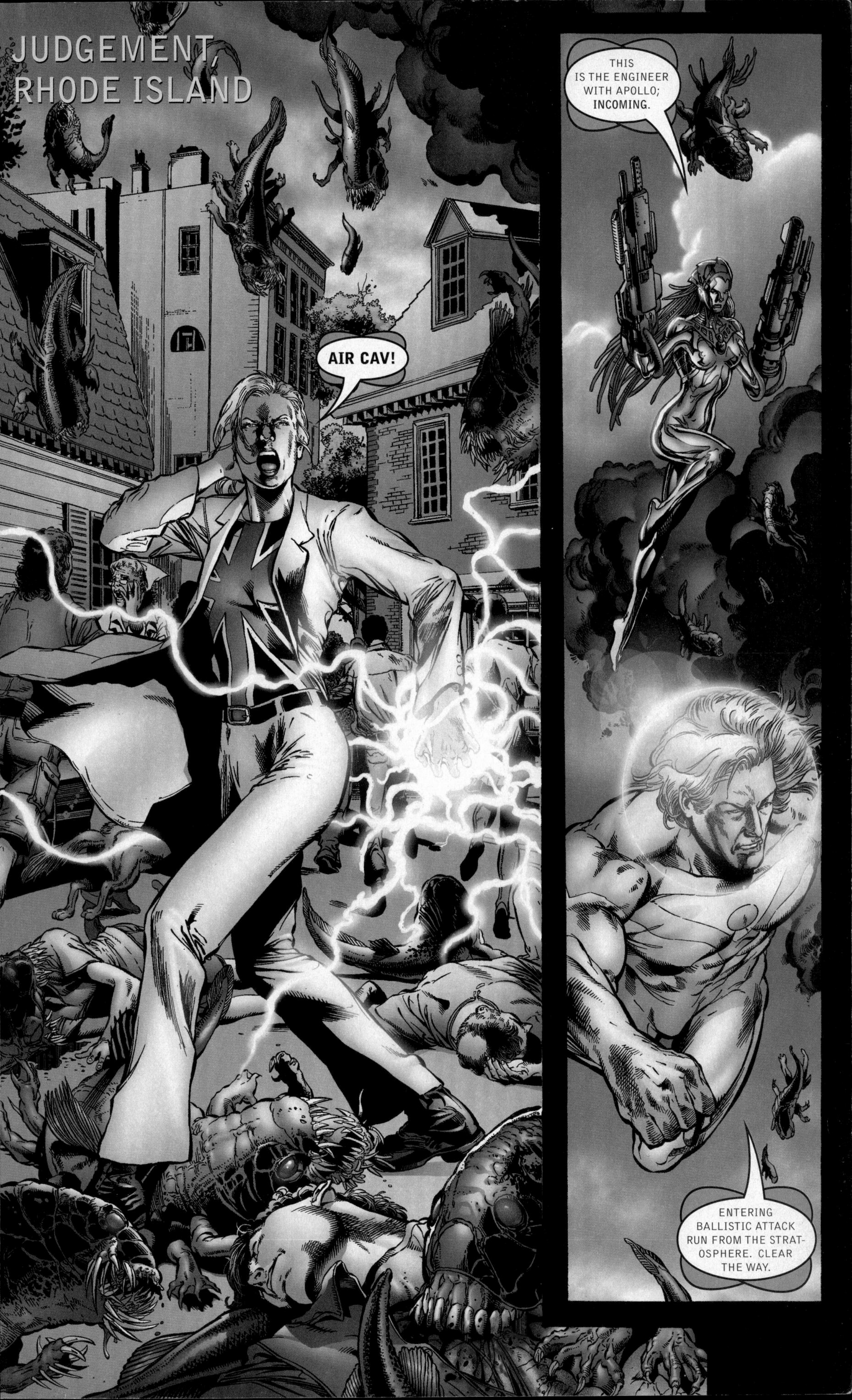
JUDGEMENT, RHODE ISLAND
AIR CAV!
THIS IS THE ENGINEER WITH APOLLO; INCOMING.
ENTERING BALLISTIC ATTACK RUN FROM THE STRAT-OSPHERE. CLEAR THE WAY.

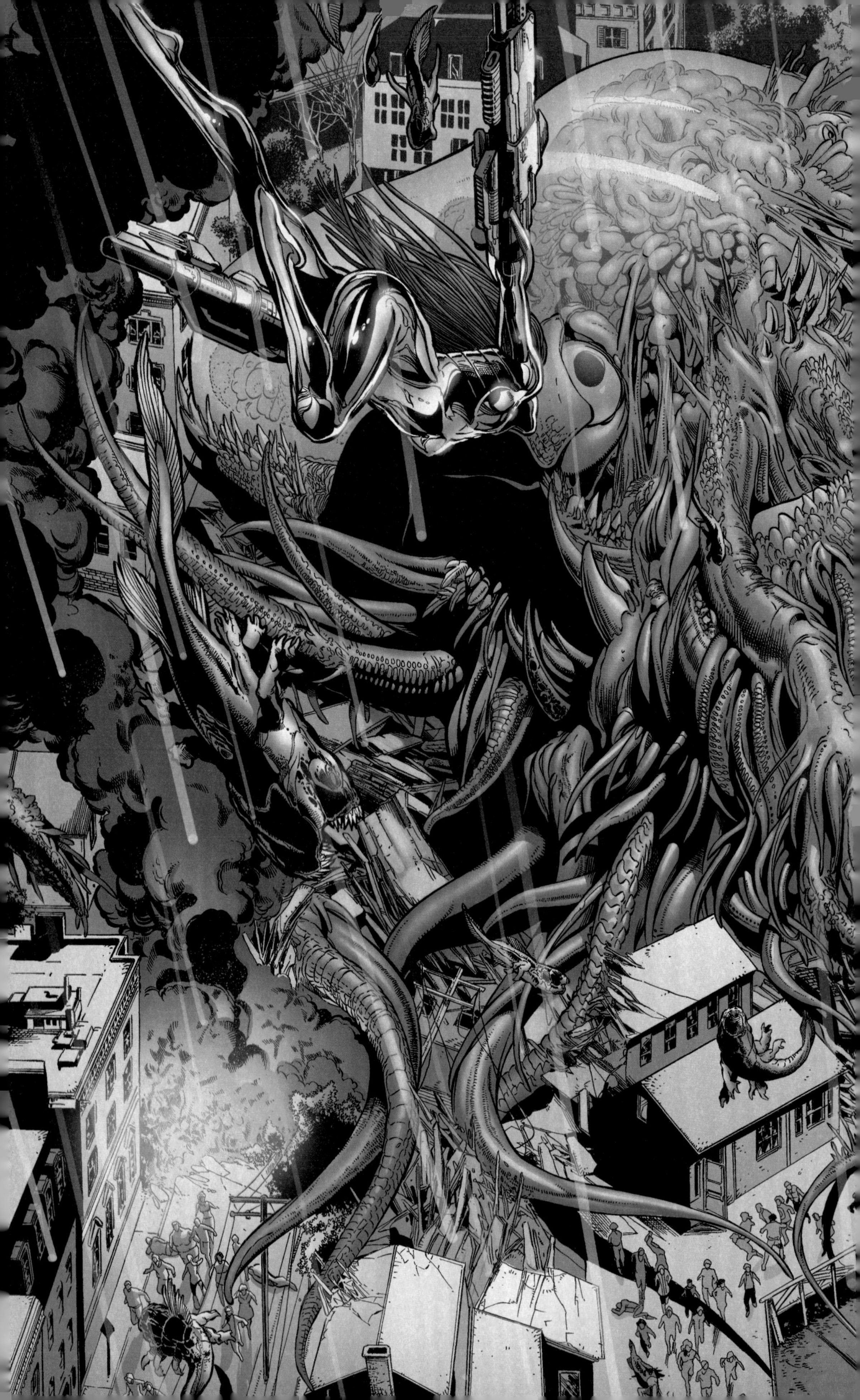

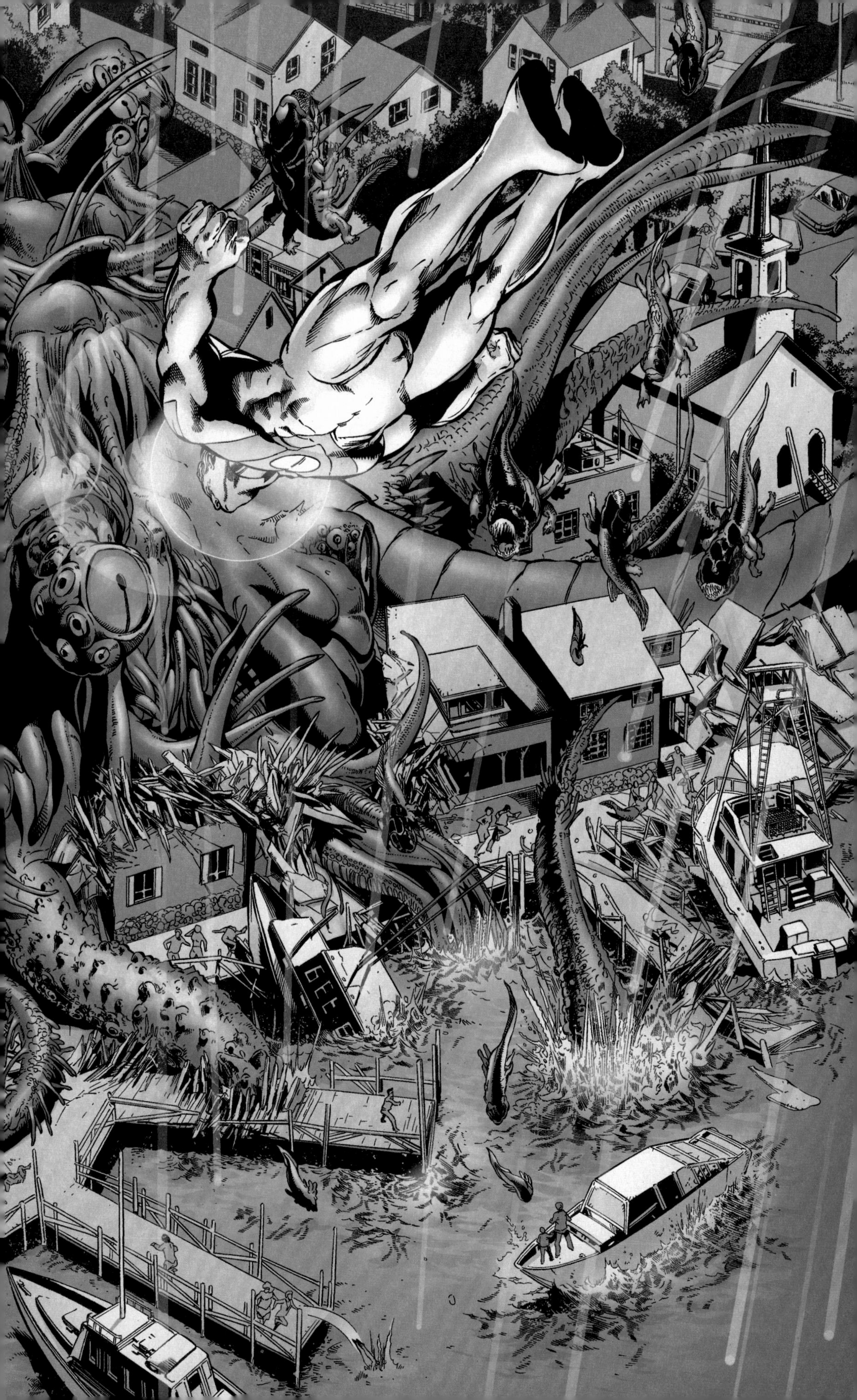

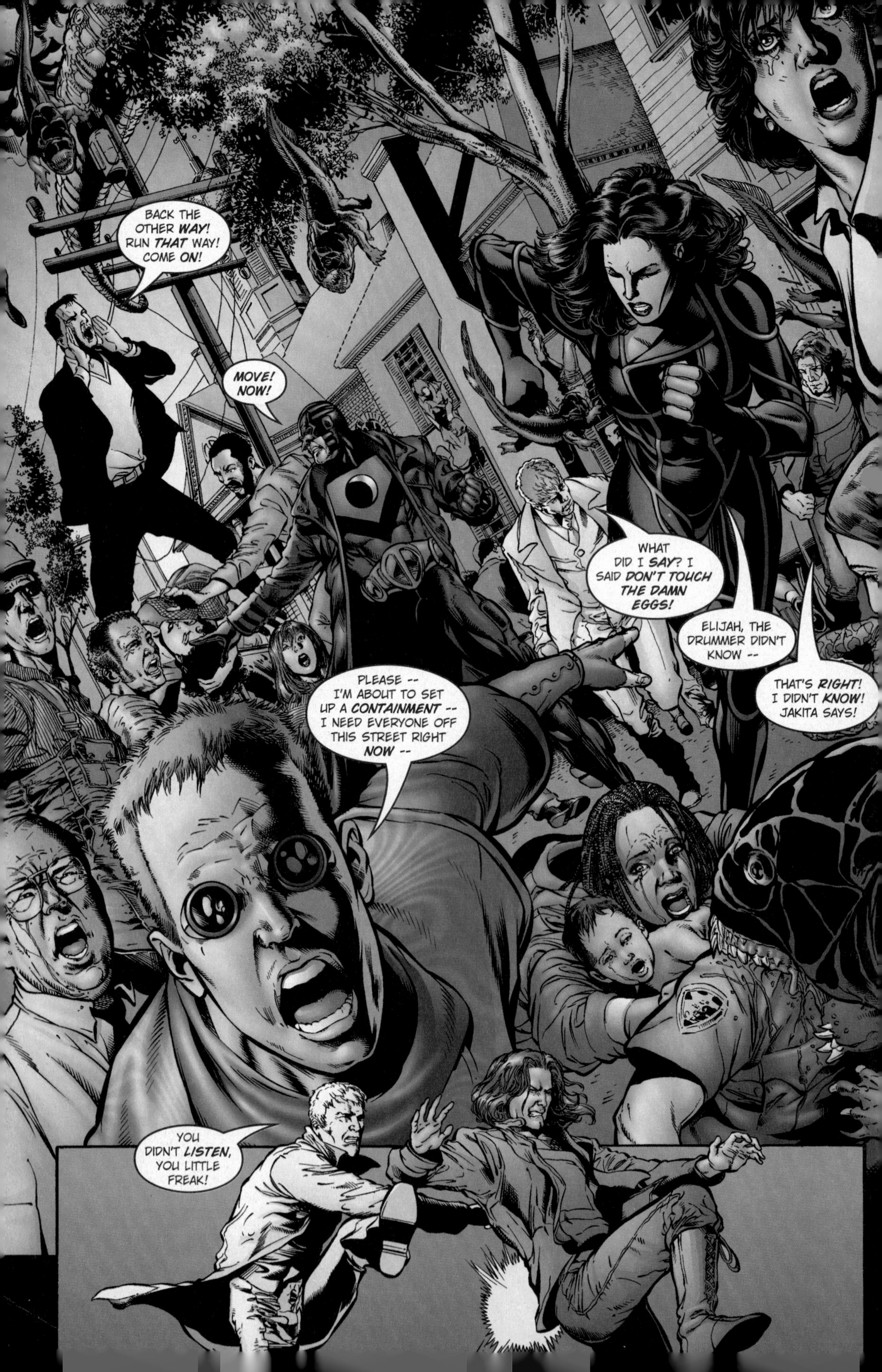
BACK THE OTHER WAY! RUN THAT WAY! COME ON!
MOVE! NOW!
WHAT DID I SAY? I SAID DON'T TOUCH THE DAMN EGGS!
ELIJAH, THE DRUMMER DIDN'T KNOW --
THAT'S RIGHT! I DIDN'T KNOW! JAKITA SAYS!
PLEASE -- I'M ABOUT TO SET UP A CONTAINMENT -- I NEED EVERYONE OFF THIS STREET RIGHT NOW --
YOU DIDN'T LISTEN, YOU LITTLE FREAK!

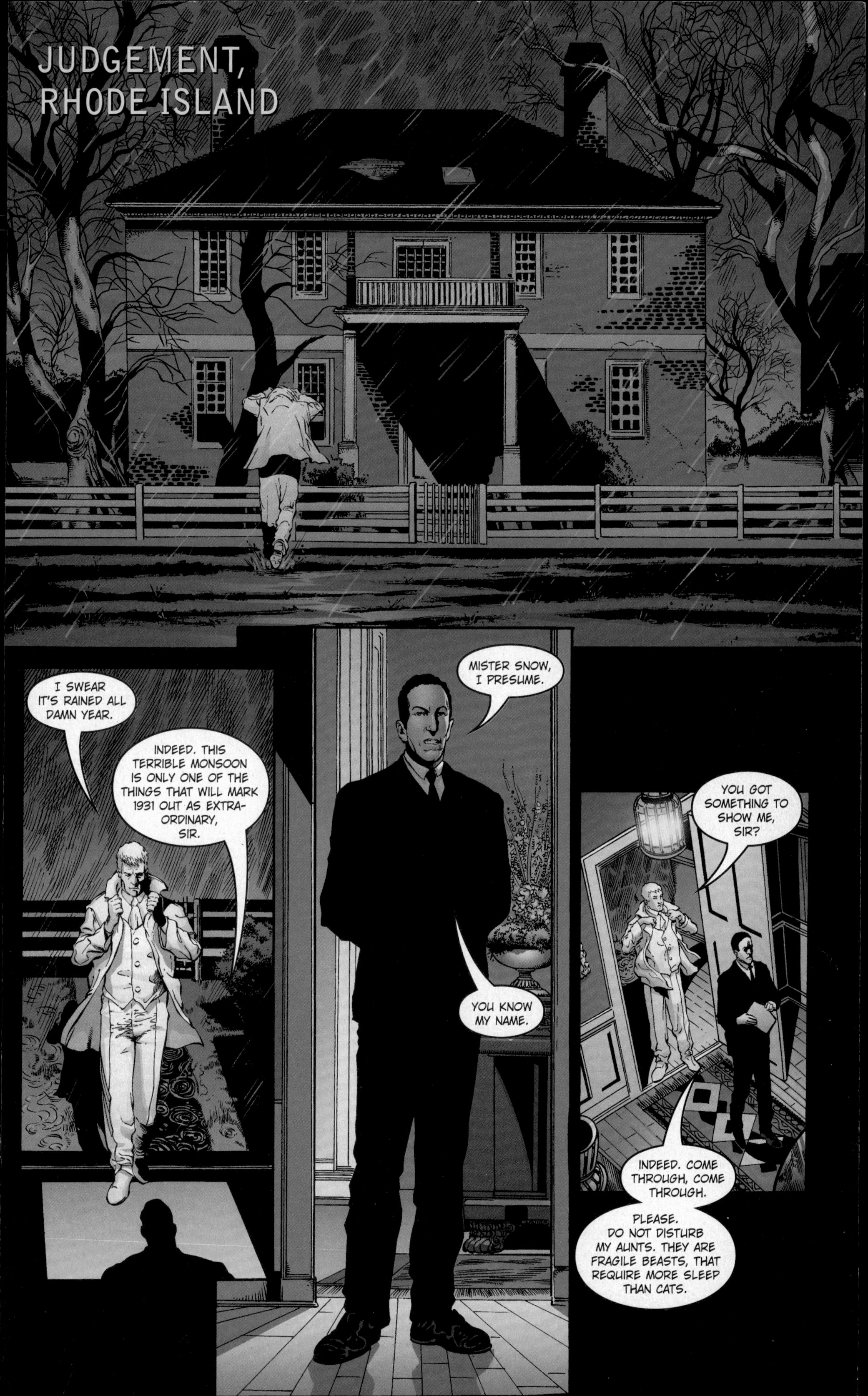
JUDGEMENT, RHODE ISLAND
I SWEAR IT'S RAINED ALL DAMN YEAR.
INDEED. THIS TERRIBLE MONSOON IS ONLY ONE OF THE THINGS THAT WILL MARK 1931 OUT AS EXTRA-ORDINARY, SIR.
MISTER SNOW, I PRESUME.
YOU KNOW MY NAME.
YOU GOT SOMETHING TO SHOW ME, SIR?
INDEED. COME THROUGH, COME THROUGH.
PLEASE. DO NOT DISTURB MY AUNTS. THEY ARE FRAGILE BEASTS, THAT REQUIRE MORE SLEEP THAN CATS.

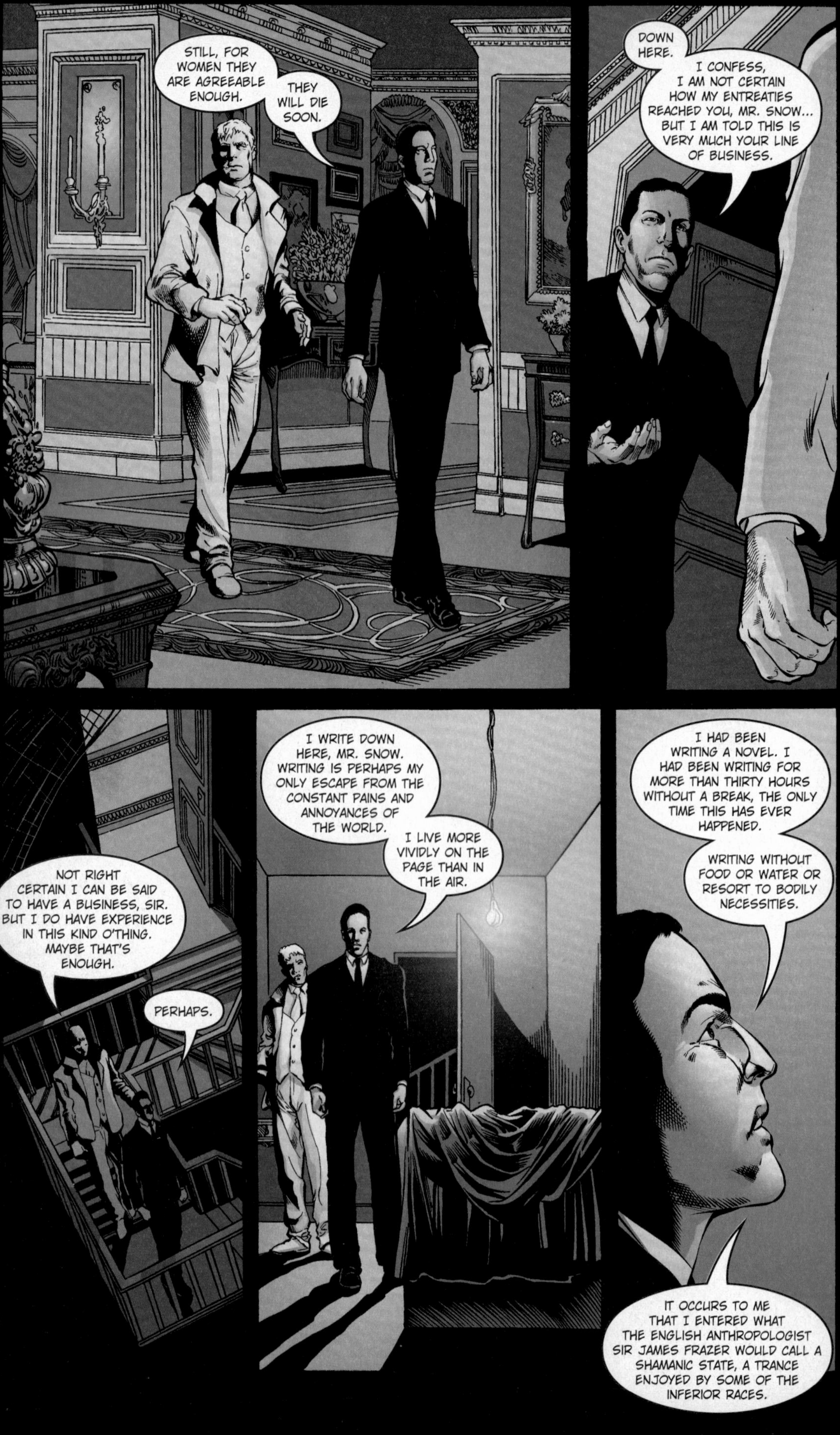
STILL, FOR WOMEN THEY ARE AGREEABLE ENOUGH.
THEY WILL DIE SOON.
DOWN HERE.
I CONFESS, I AM NOT CERTAIN HOW MY ENTREATIES REACHED YOU, MR. SNOW... BUT I AM TOLD THIS IS VERY MUCH YOUR LINE OF BUSINESS.
NOT RIGHT CERTAIN I CAN BE SAID TO HAVE A BUSINESS, SIR. BUT I DO HAVE EXPERIENCE IN THIS KIND O'THING. MAYBE THAT'S ENOUGH.
PERHAPS.
I WRITE DOWN HERE, MR. SNOW. WRITING IS PERHAPS MY ONLY ESCAPE FROM THE CONSTANT PAINS AND ANNOYANCES OF THE WORLD.
I LIVE MORE VIVIDLY ON THE PAGE THAN IN THE AIR.
I HAD BEEN WRITING A NOVEL. I HAD BEEN WRITING FOR MORE THAN THIRTY HOURS WITHOUT A BREAK, THE ONLY TIME THIS HAS EVER HAPPENED.
WRITING WITHOUT FOOD OR WATER OR RESORT TO BODILY NECESSITIES.
IT OCCURS TO ME THAT I ENTERED WHAT THE ENGLISH ANTHROPOLOGIST SIR JAMES FRAZER WOULD CALL A SHAMANIC STATE, A TRANCE ENJOYED BY SOME OF THE INFERIOR RACES.

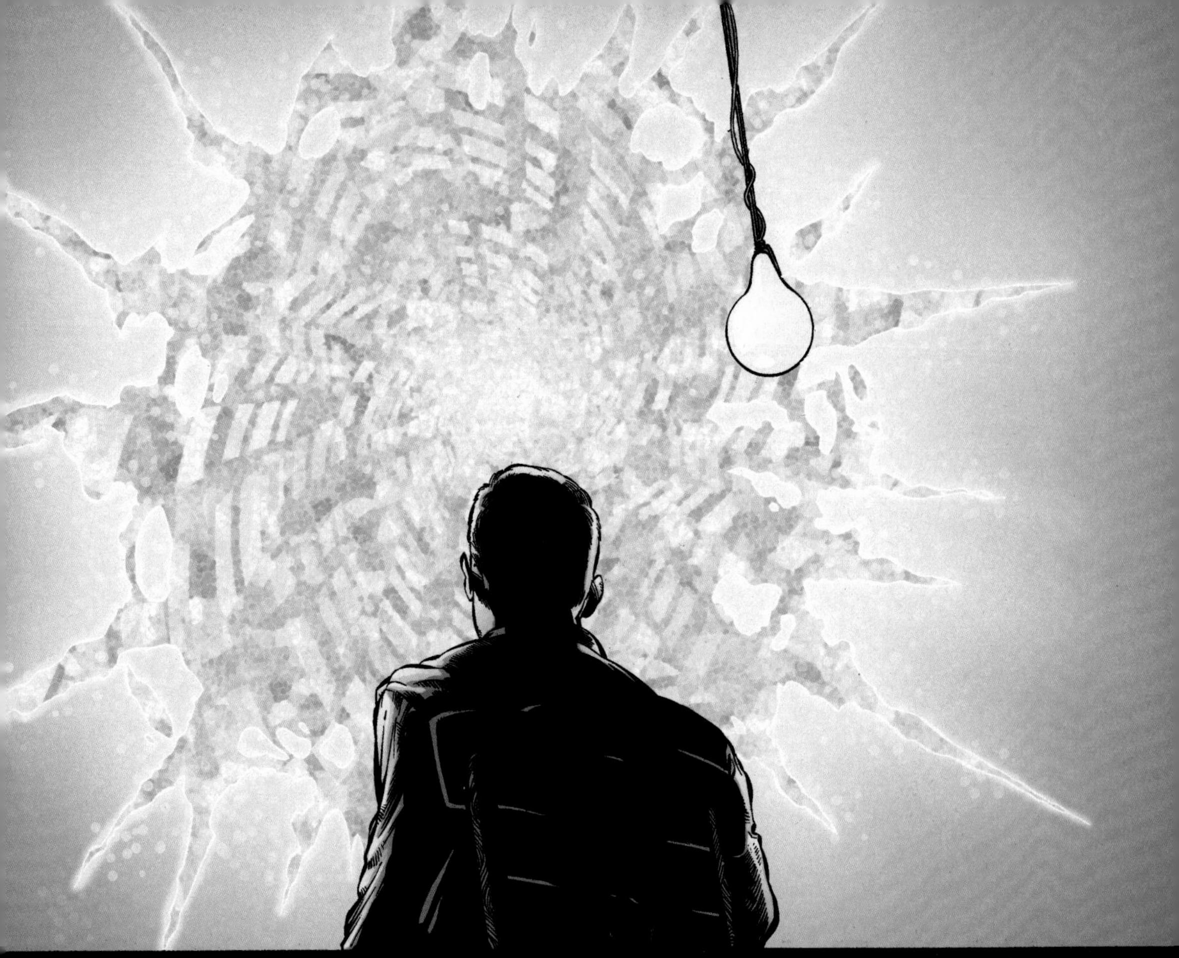

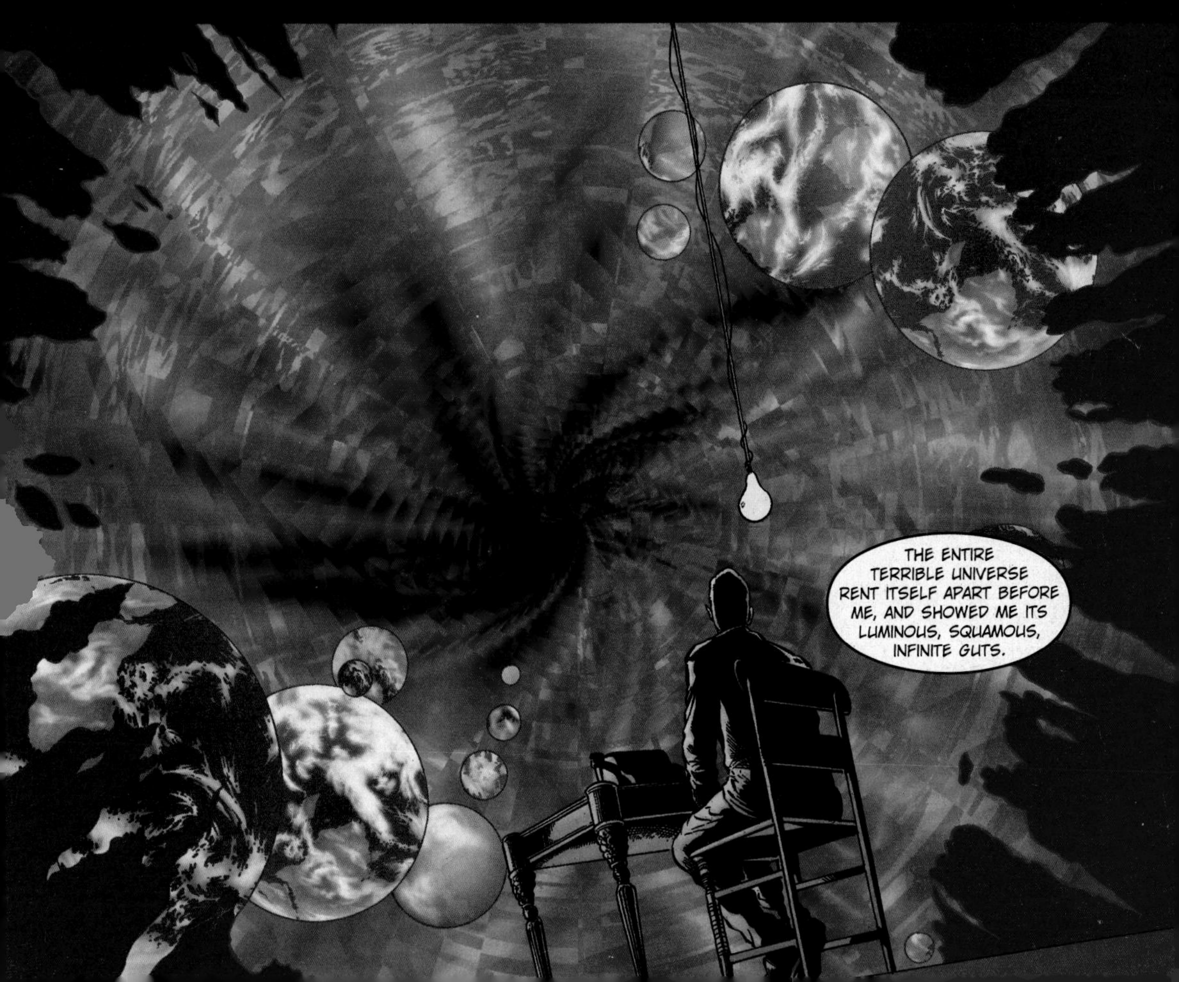
THE ENTIRE TERRIBLE UNIVERSE RENT ITSELF APART BEFORE ME, AND SHOWED ME ITS LUMINOUS, SQUAMOUS, INFINITE GUTS.

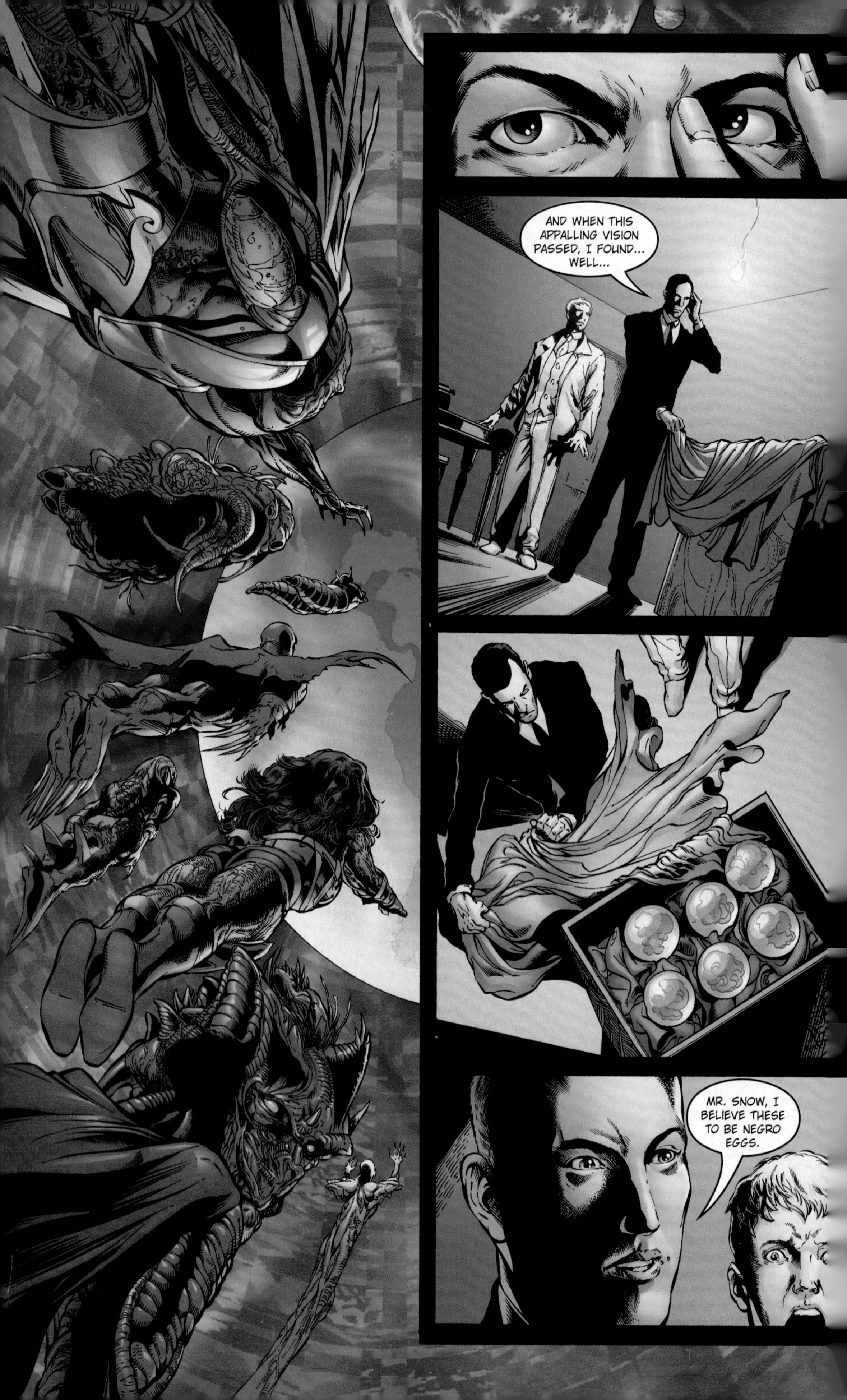
AND WHEN THIS APPALLING VISION PASSED, I FOUND... WELL...
MR. SNOW, I BELIEVE THESE TO BE NEGRO EGGS.

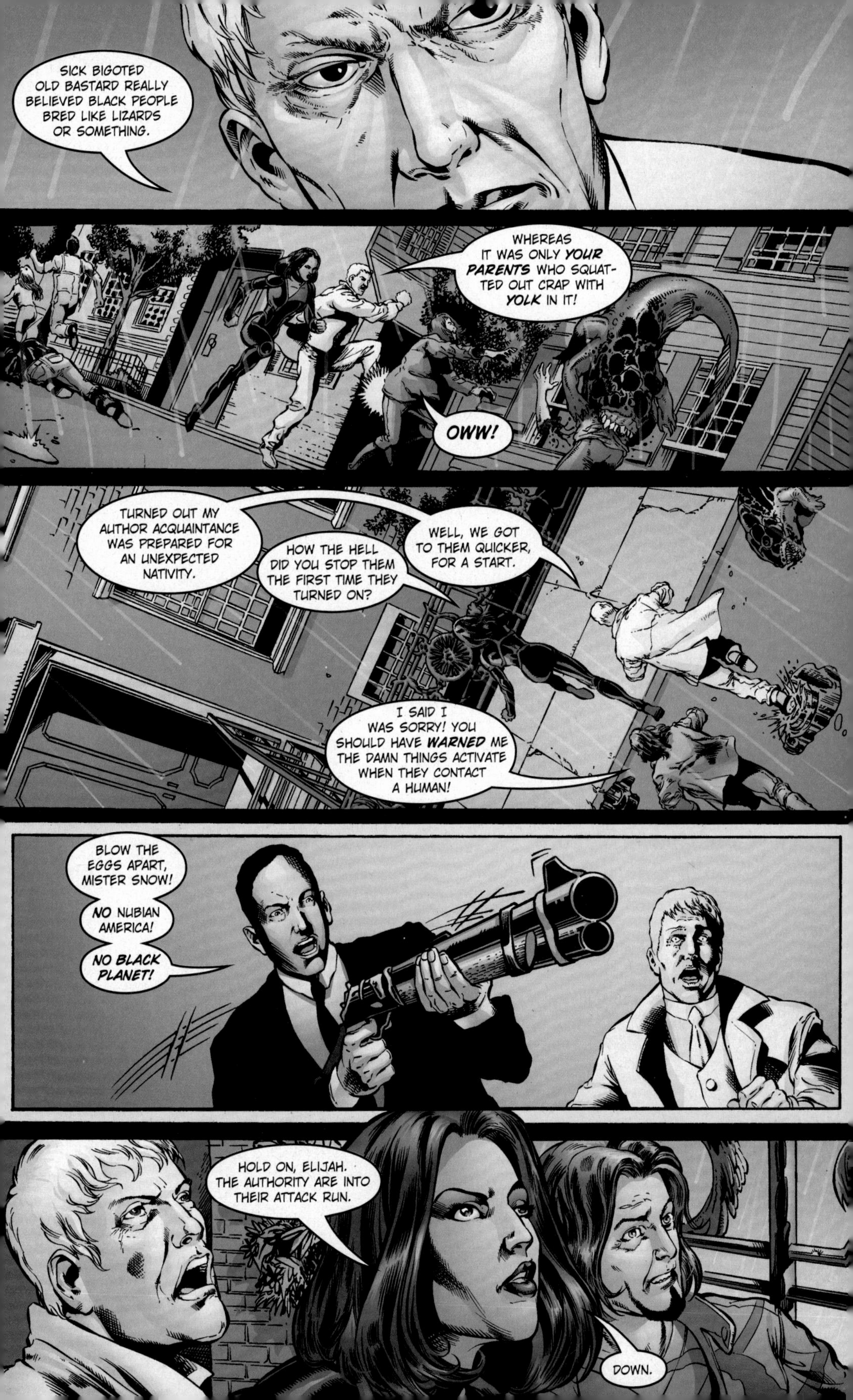

SICK BIGOTED OLD BASTARD REALLY BELIEVED BLACK PEOPLE BRED LIKE LIZARDS OR SOMETHING.
WHEREAS IT WAS ONLY YOUR PARENTS WHO SQUATTED OUT CRAP WITH YOLK IN IT!
OWW!
TURNED OUT MY AUTHOR ACQUAINTANCE WAS PREPARED FOR AN UNEXPECTED NATIVITY.
HOW THE HELL DID YOU STOP THEM THE FIRST TIME THEY TURNED ON?
WELL, WE GOT TO THEM QUICKER, FOR A START.
I SAID I WAS SORRY! YOU SHOULD HAVE WARNED ME THE DAMN THINGS ACTIVATE WHEN THEY CONTACT A HUMAN!
BLOW THE EGGS APART, MISTER SNOW!
NO NUBIAN AMERICA!
NO BLACK PLANET!
HOLD ON, ELIJAH. THE AUTHORITY ARE INTO THEIR ATTACK RUN.
DOWN.

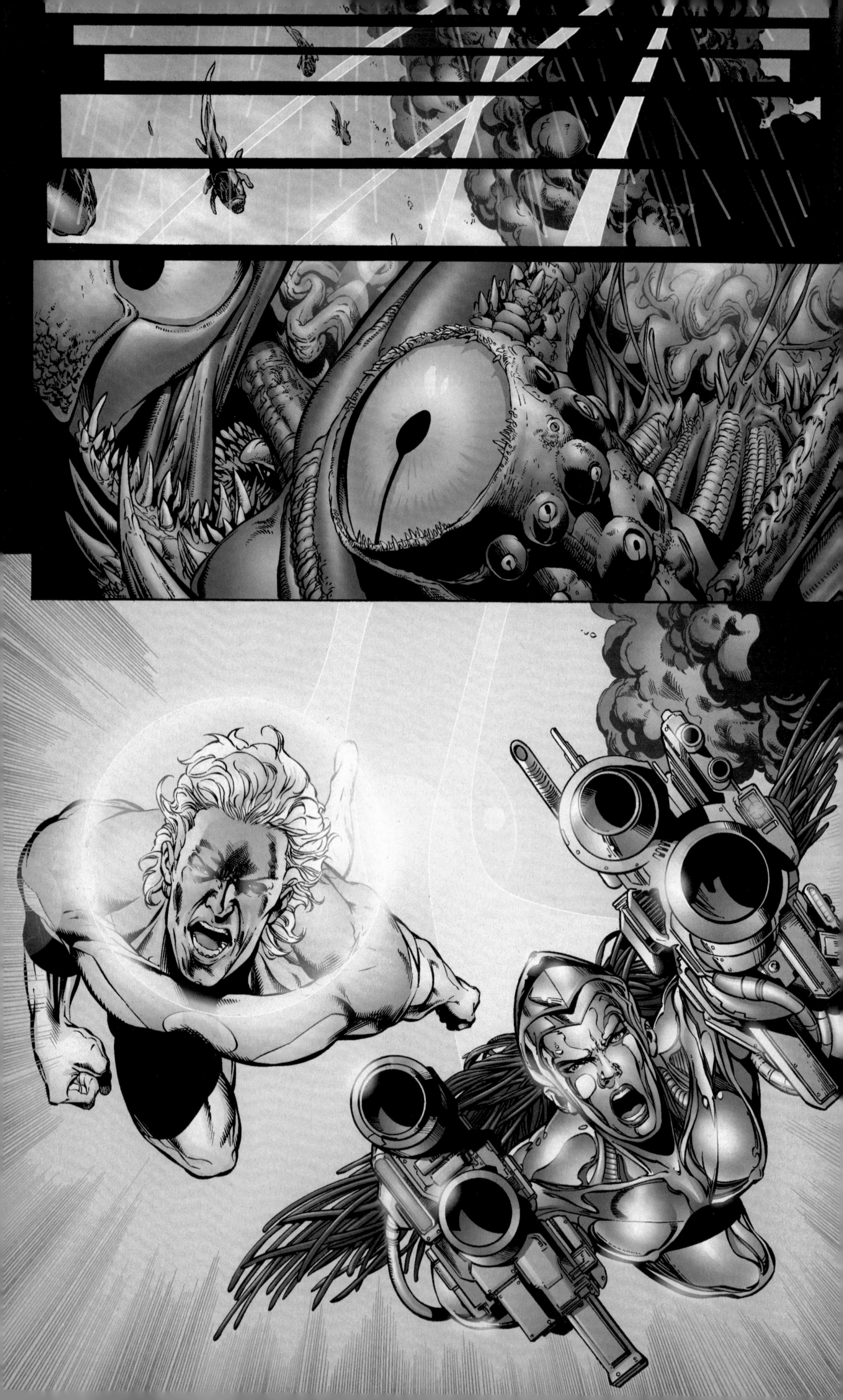

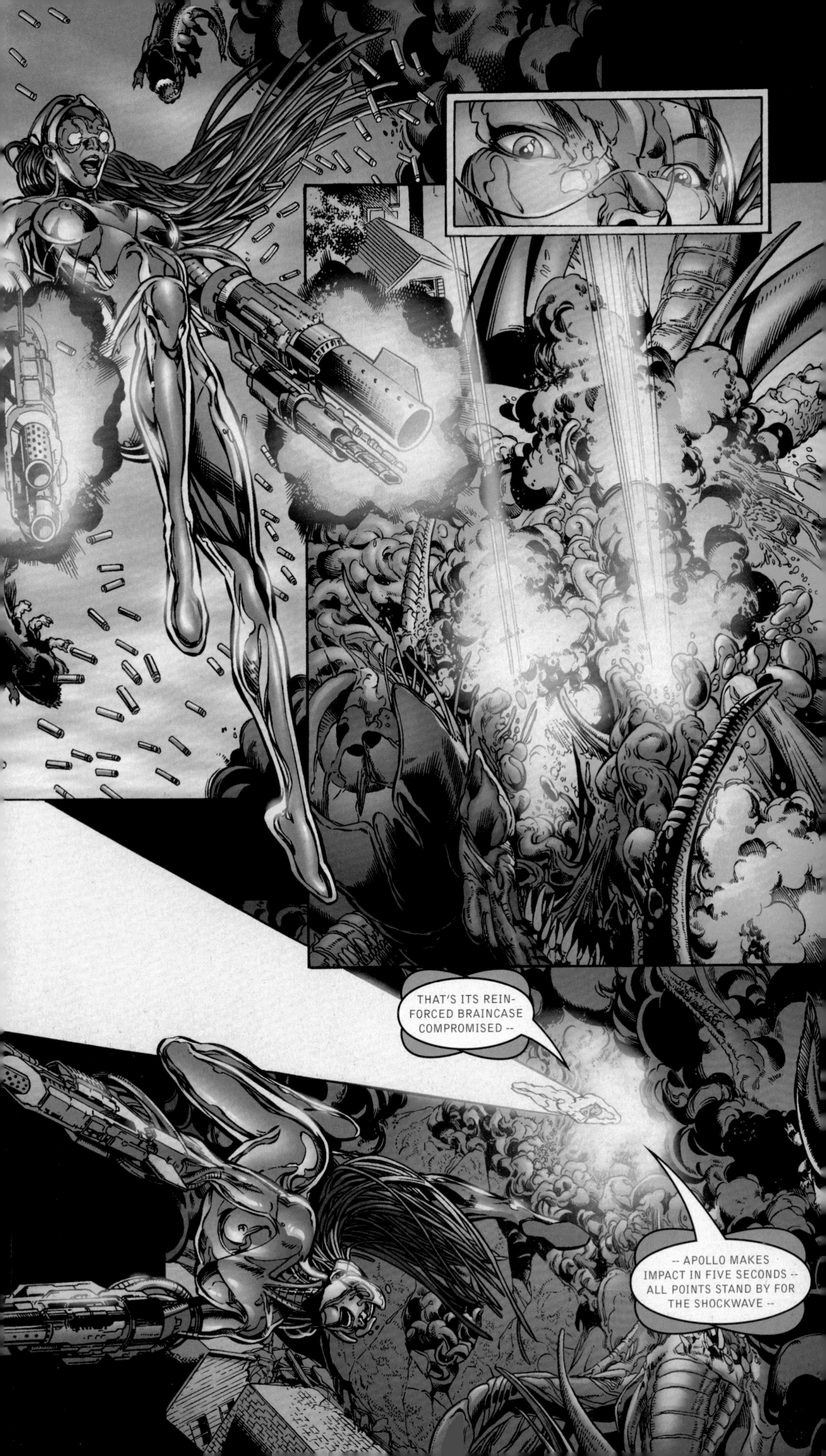
THAT'S ITS REIN-FORCED BRAINCASE COMPROMISED --
-- APOLLO MAKES IMPACT IN FIVE SECONDS -- ALL POINTS STAND BY FOR THE SHOCKWAVE --

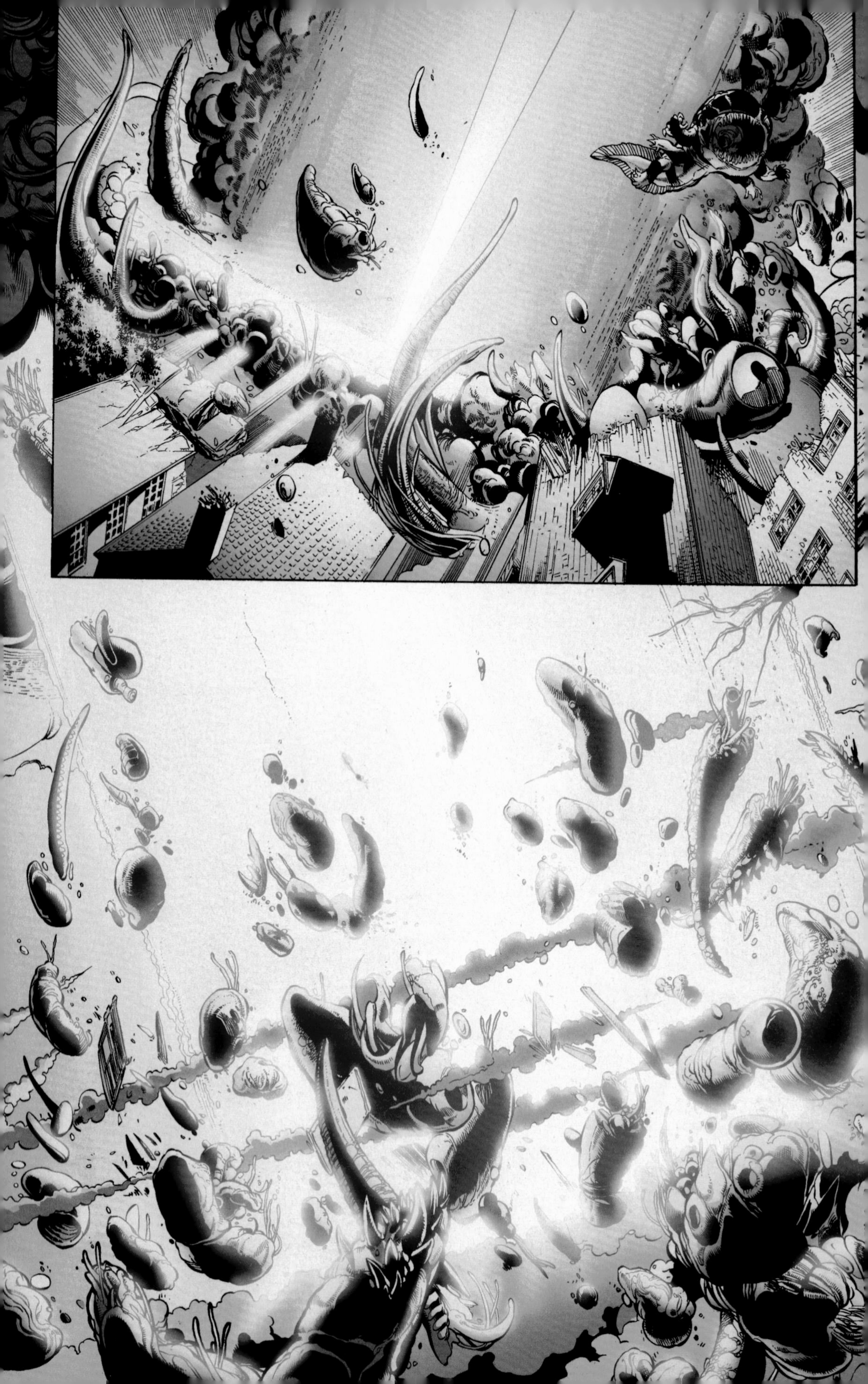

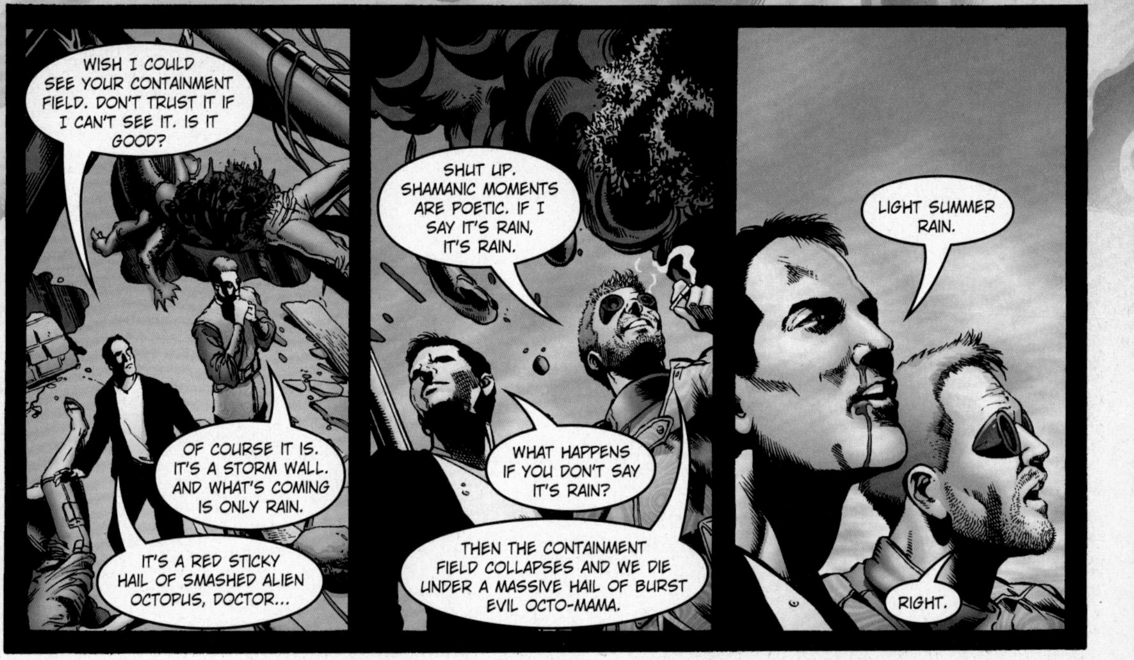
WISH I COULD SEE YOUR CONTAINMENT FIELD. DON'T TRUST IT IF I CAN'T SEE IT. IS IT GOOD?
OF COURSE IT IS. IT'S A STORM WALL. AND WHAT'S COMING IS ONLY RAIN.
IT'S A RED STICKY HAIL OF SMASHED ALIEN OCTOPUS, DOCTOR...
SHUT UP. SHAMANIC MOMENTS ARE POETIC. IF I SAY IT'S RAIN, IT'S RAIN.
WHAT HAPPENS IF YOU DON'T SAY IT'S RAIN?
THEN THE CONTAINMENT FIELD COLLAPSES AND WE DIE UNDER A MASSIVE HAIL OF BURST EVIL OCTO-MAMA.
LIGHT SUMMER RAIN.
RIGHT.

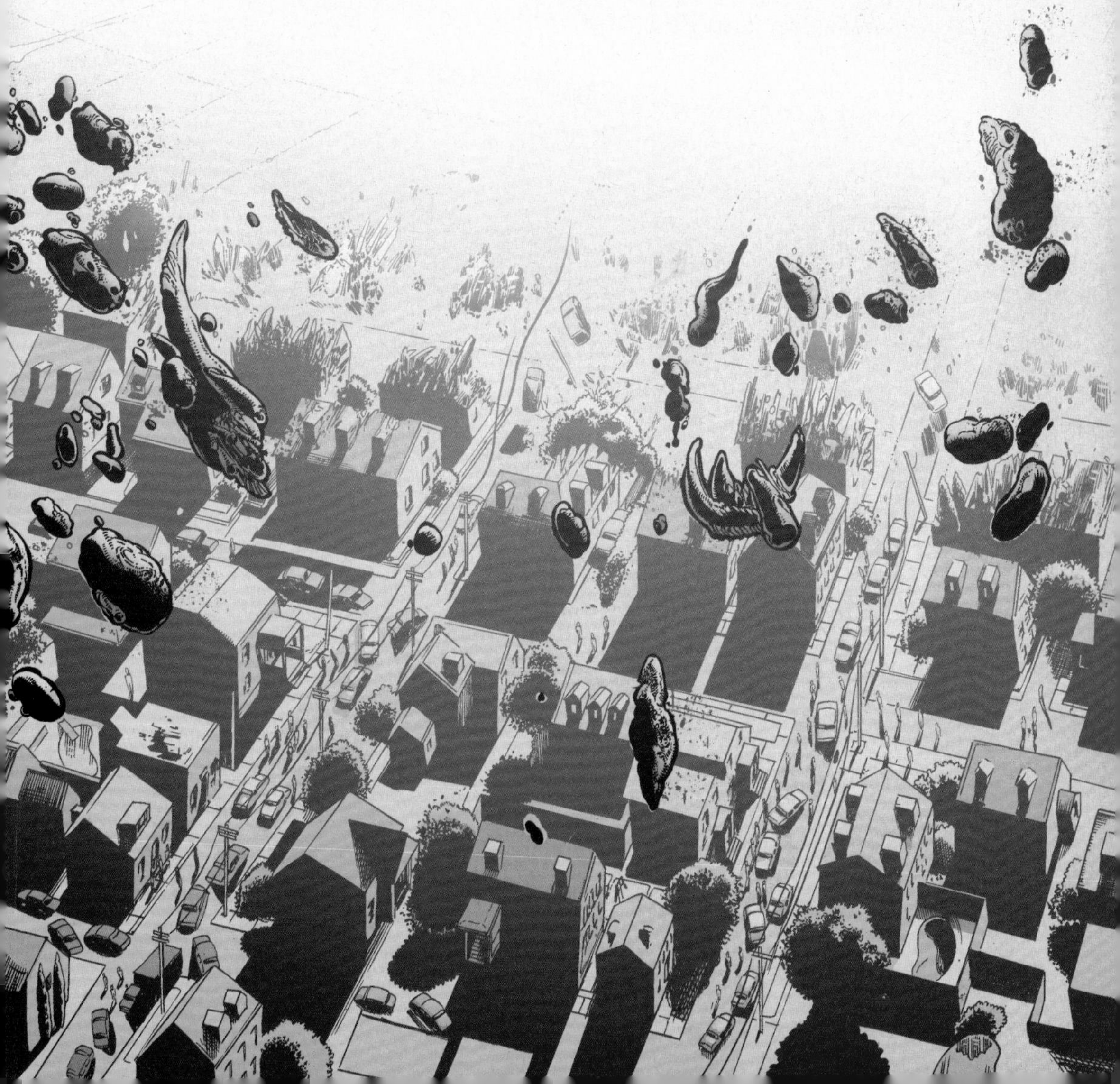

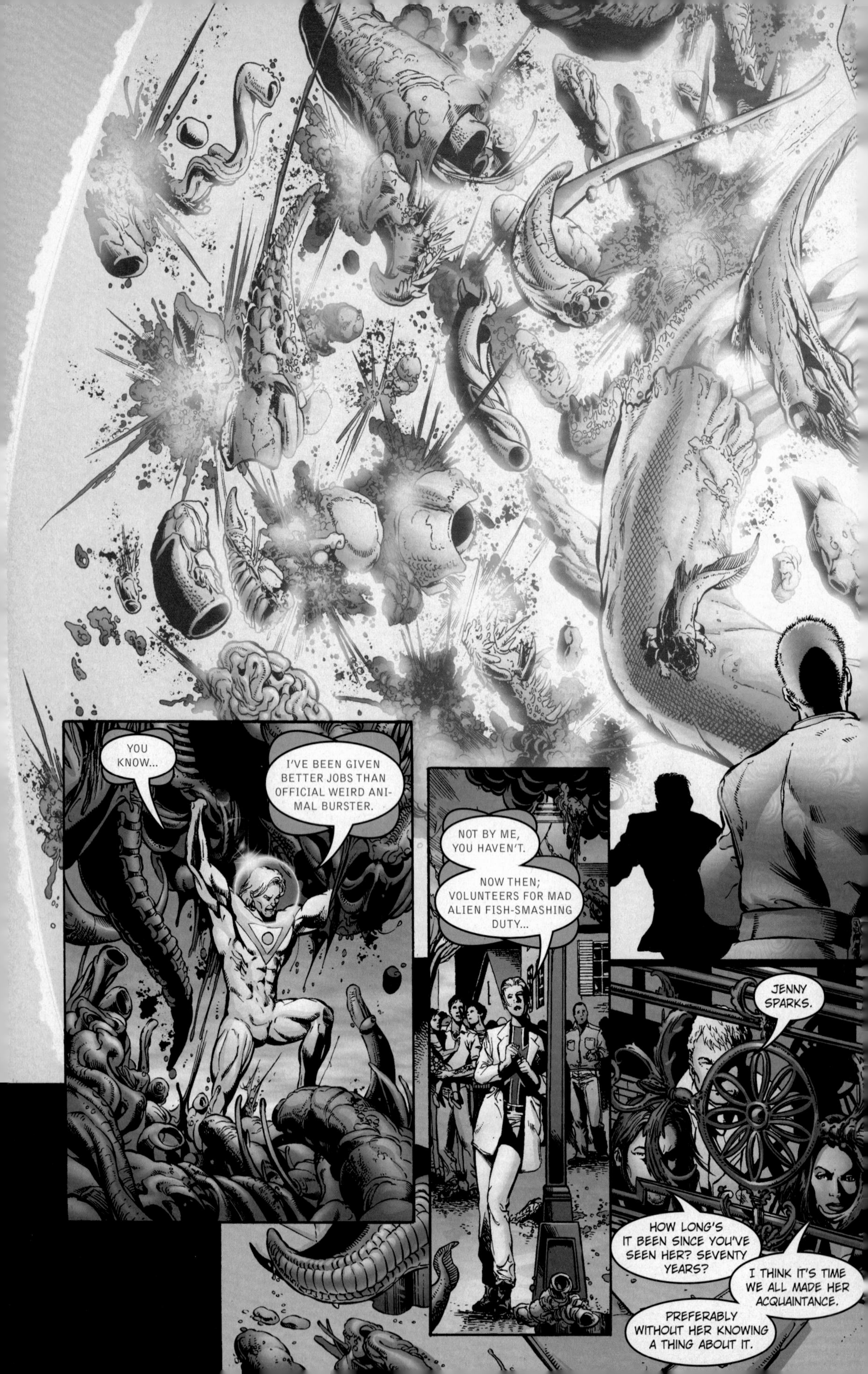
YOU KNOW...
I'VE BEEN GIVEN BETTER JOBS THAN OFFICIAL WEIRD ANI-MAL BURSTER.
NOT BY ME, YOU HAVEN'T.
NOW THEN; VOLUNTEERS FOR MAD ALIEN FISH-SMASHING DUTY...
JENNY SPARKS.
HOW LONG'S IT BEEN SINCE YOU'VE SEEN HER? SEVENTY YEARS?
I THINK IT'S TIME WE ALL MADE HER ACQUAINTANCE.
PREFERABLY WITHOUT HER KNOWING A THING ABOUT IT.

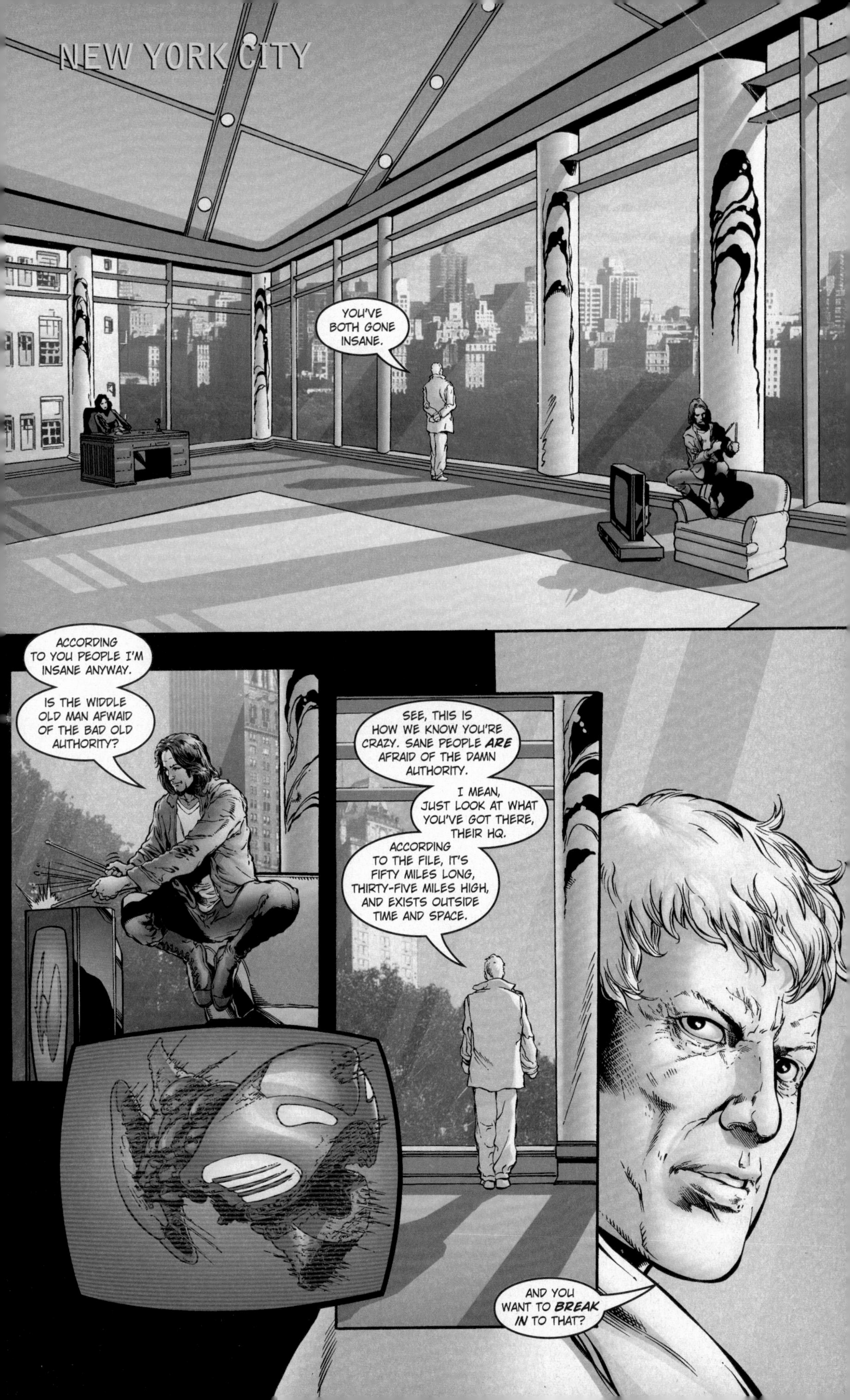
NEW YORK CITY
YOU'VE BOTH GONE INSANE.
ACCORDING TO YOU PEOPLE I'M INSANE ANYWAY.
IS THE WIDDLE OLD MAN AFWAID OF THE BAD OLD AUTHORITY?
SEE, THIS IS HOW WE KNOW YOU'RE CRAZY. SANE PEOPLE ***ARE*** AFRAID OF THE DAMN AUTHORITY.
I MEAN, JUST LOOK AT WHAT YOU'VE GOT THERE, THEIR HQ.
ACCORDING TO THE FILE, IT'S FIFTY MILES LONG, THIRTY-FIVE MILES HIGH, AND EXISTS OUTSIDE TIME AND SPACE.
AND YOU WANT TO ***BREAK IN*** TO THAT?

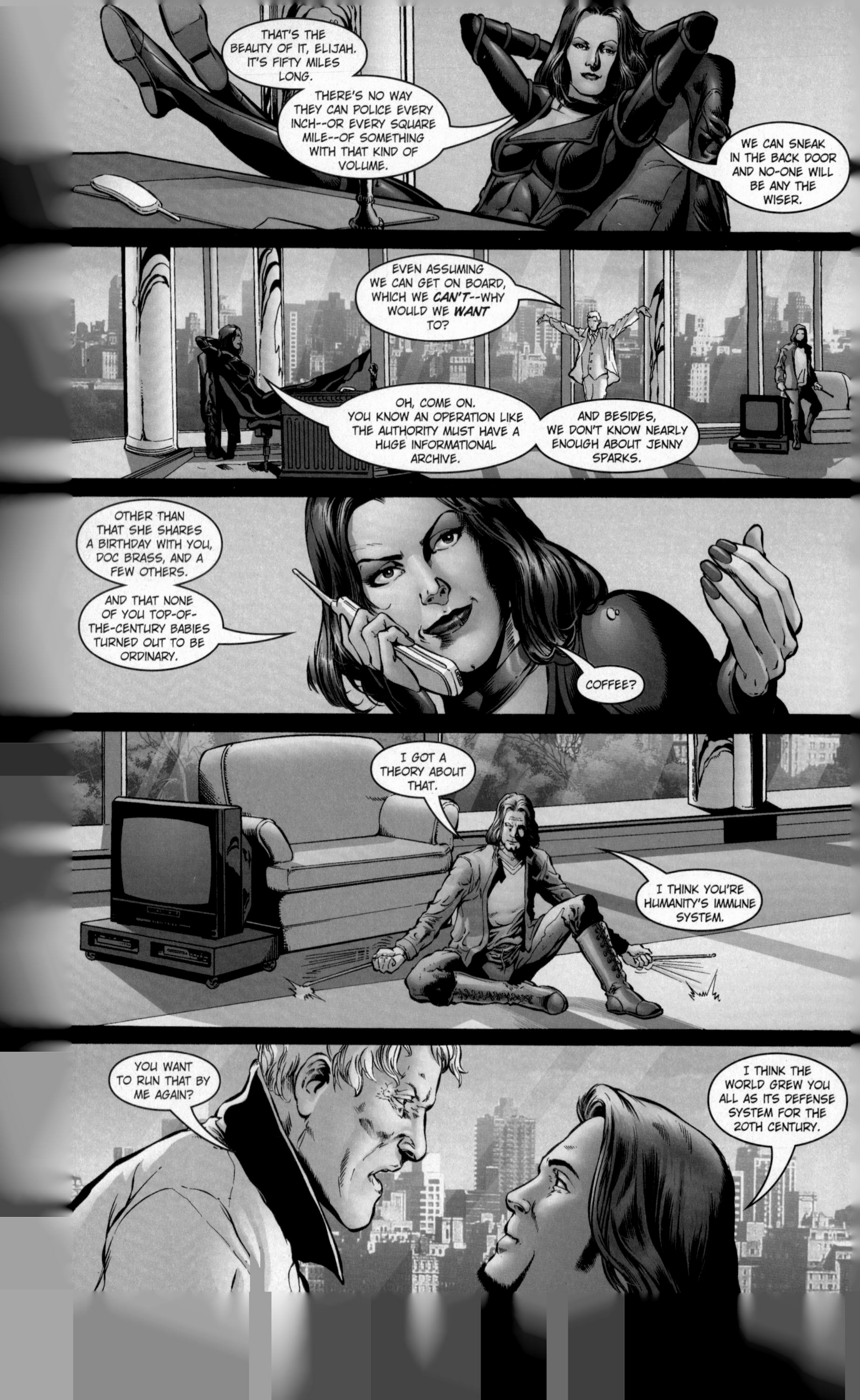
THAT'S THE BEAUTY OF IT, ELIJAH. IT'S FIFTY MILES LONG.
THERE'S NO WAY THEY CAN POLICE EVERY INCH--OR EVERY SQUARE MILE--OF SOMETHING WITH THAT KIND OF VOLUME.
WE CAN SNEAK IN THE BACK DOOR AND NO-ONE WILL BE ANY THE WISER.
EVEN ASSUMING WE CAN GET ON BOARD, WHICH WE CAN'T--WHY WOULD WE WANT TO?
OH, COME ON. YOU KNOW AN OPERATION LIKE THE AUTHORITY MUST HAVE A HUGE INFORMATIONAL ARCHIVE.
AND BESIDES, WE DON'T KNOW NEARLY ENOUGH ABOUT JENNY SPARKS.
OTHER THAN THAT SHE SHARES A BIRTHDAY WITH YOU, DOC BRASS, AND A FEW OTHERS.
AND THAT NONE OF YOU TOP-OF-THE-CENTURY BABIES TURNED OUT TO BE ORDINARY.
COFFEE?
I GOT A THEORY ABOUT THAT.
I THINK YOU'RE HUMANITY'S IMMUNE SYSTEM.
YOU WANT TO RUN THAT BY ME AGAIN?
I THINK THE WORLD GREW YOU ALL AS ITS DEFENSE SYSTEM FOR THE 20TH CENTURY.

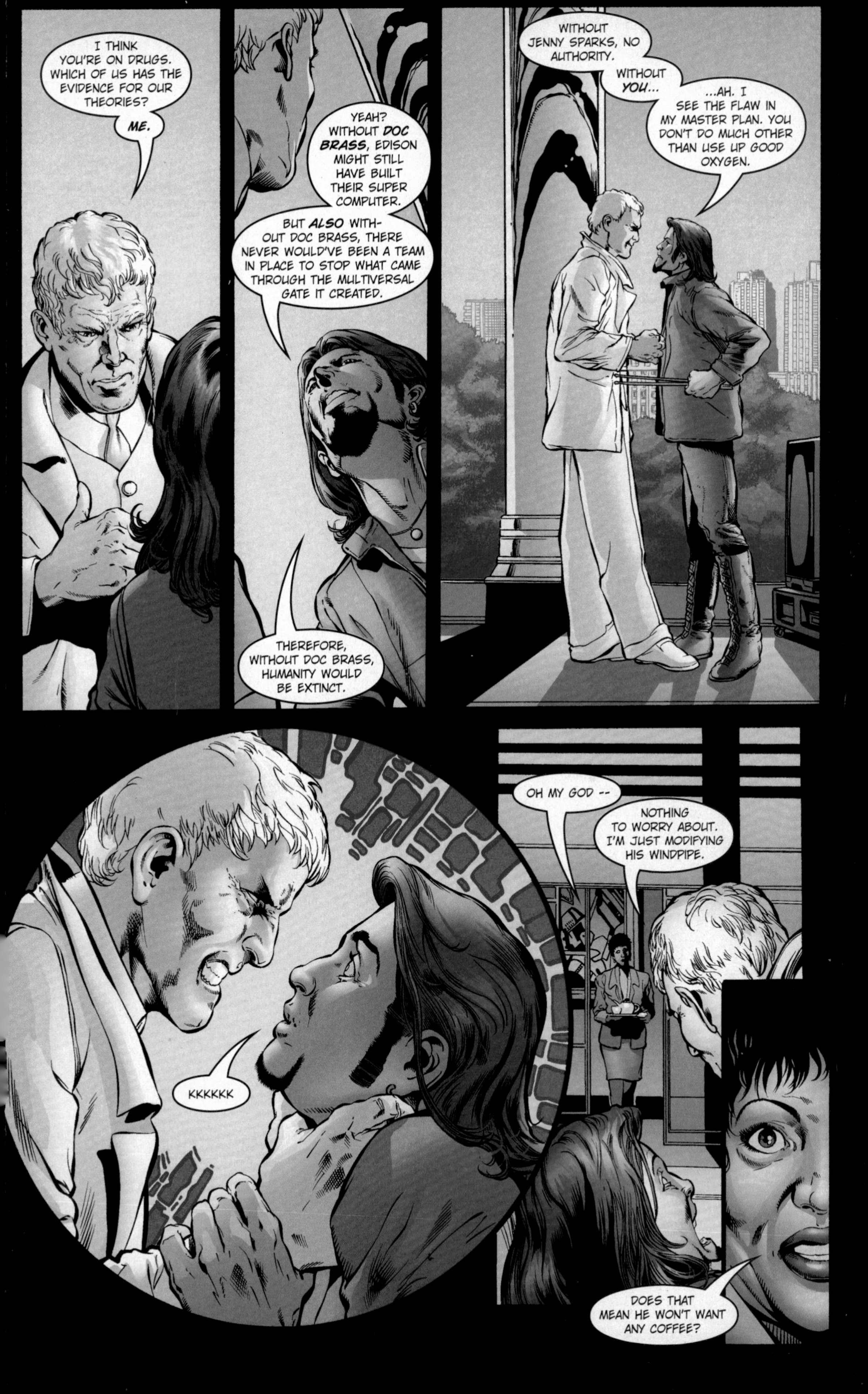
I THINK YOU'RE ON DRUGS. WHICH OF US HAS THE EVIDENCE FOR OUR THEORIES?
ME.
YEAH? WITHOUT DOC BRASS, EDISON MIGHT STILL HAVE BUILT THEIR SUPER COMPUTER.
BUT ALSO WITH-OUT DOC BRASS, THERE NEVER WOULD'VE BEEN A TEAM IN PLACE TO STOP WHAT CAME THROUGH THE MULTIVERSAL GATE IT CREATED.
THEREFORE, WITHOUT DOC BRASS, HUMANITY WOULD BE EXTINCT.
WITHOUT JENNY SPARKS, NO AUTHORITY.
WITHOUT YOU...
...AH. I SEE THE FLAW IN MY MASTER PLAN. YOU DON'T DO MUCH OTHER THAN USE UP GOOD OXYGEN.
KKKKKK
OH MY GOD --
NOTHING TO WORRY ABOUT. I'M JUST MODIFYING HIS WINDPIPE.
DOES THAT MEAN HE WON'T WANT ANY COFFEE?

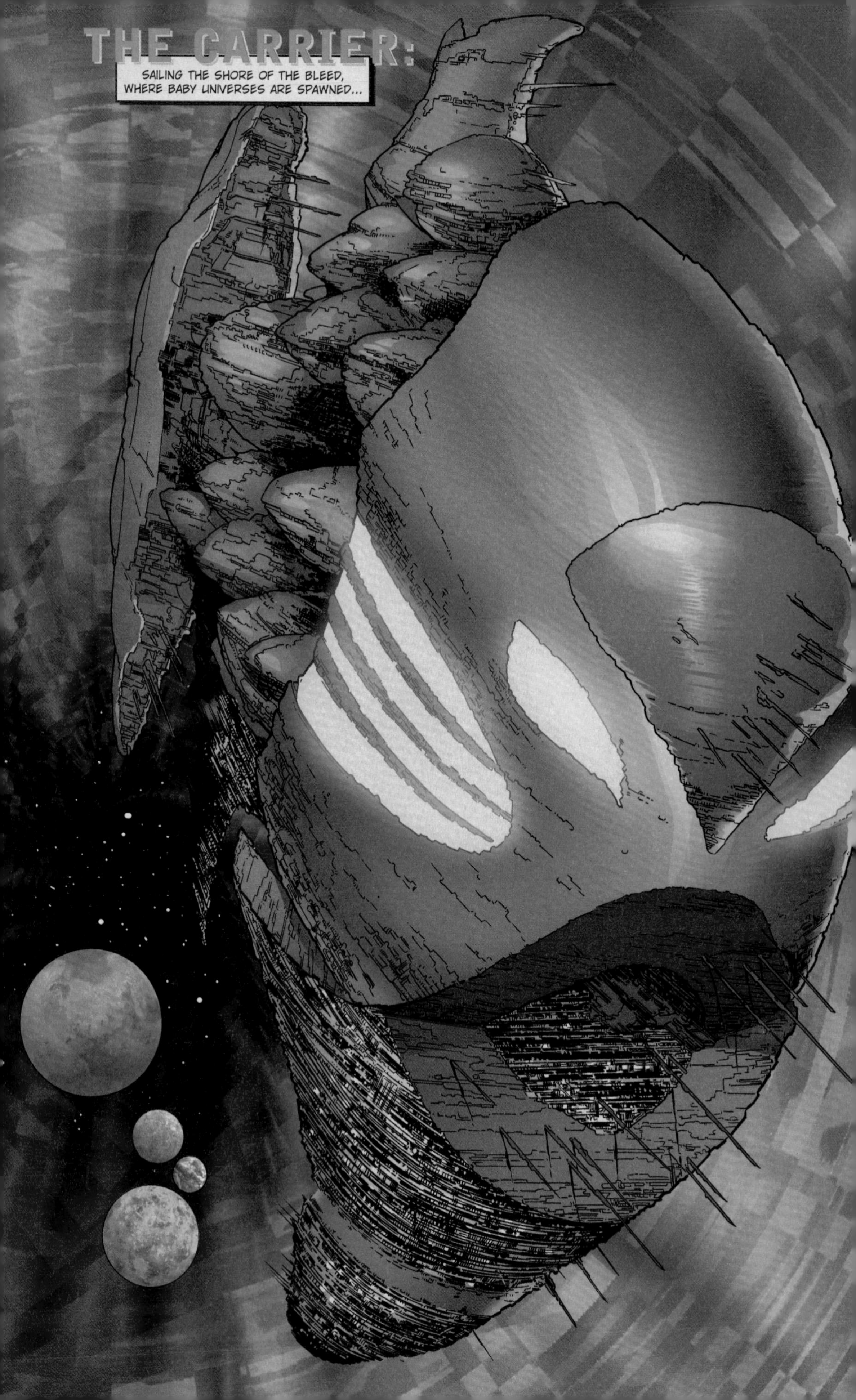
THE CARRIER:
SAILING THE SHORE OF THE BLEED, WHERE BABY UNIVERSES ARE SPAWNED...

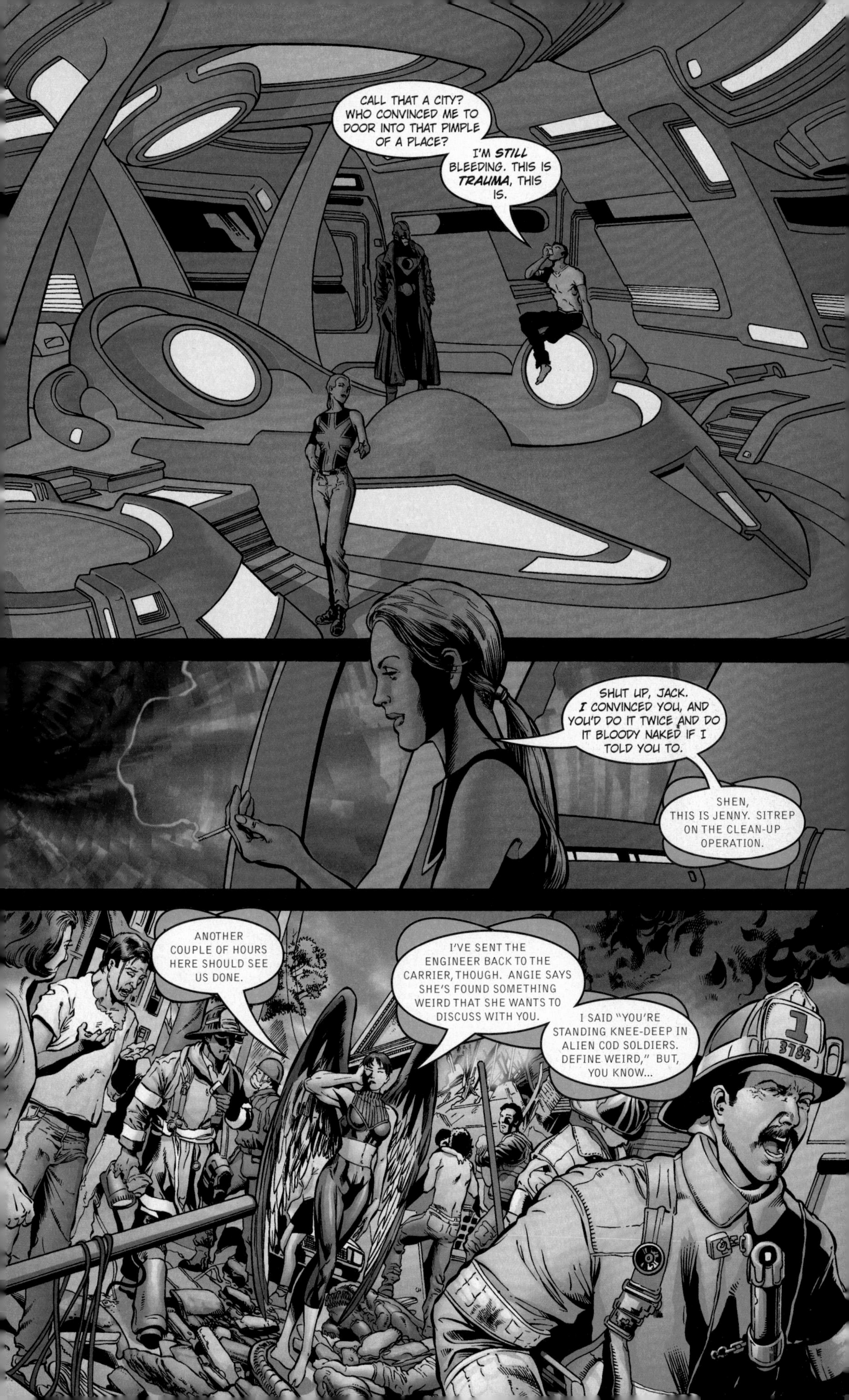
CALL THAT A CITY? WHO CONVINCED ME TO DOOR INTO THAT PIMPLE OF A PLACE?
I'M *STILL* BLEEDING. THIS IS *TRAUMA*, THIS IS.
SHUT UP, JACK. *I* CONVINCED YOU, AND YOU'D DO IT TWICE AND DO IT BLOODY NAKED IF I TOLD YOU TO.
SHEN, THIS IS JENNY. SITREP ON THE CLEAN-UP OPERATION.
ANOTHER COUPLE OF HOURS HERE SHOULD SEE US DONE.
I'VE SENT THE ENGINEER BACK TO THE CARRIER, THOUGH. ANGIE SAYS SHE'S FOUND SOMETHING WEIRD THAT SHE WANTS TO DISCUSS WITH YOU.
I SAID "YOU'RE STANDING KNEE-DEEP IN ALIEN COD SOLDIERS. DEFINE WEIRD," BUT, YOU KNOW...

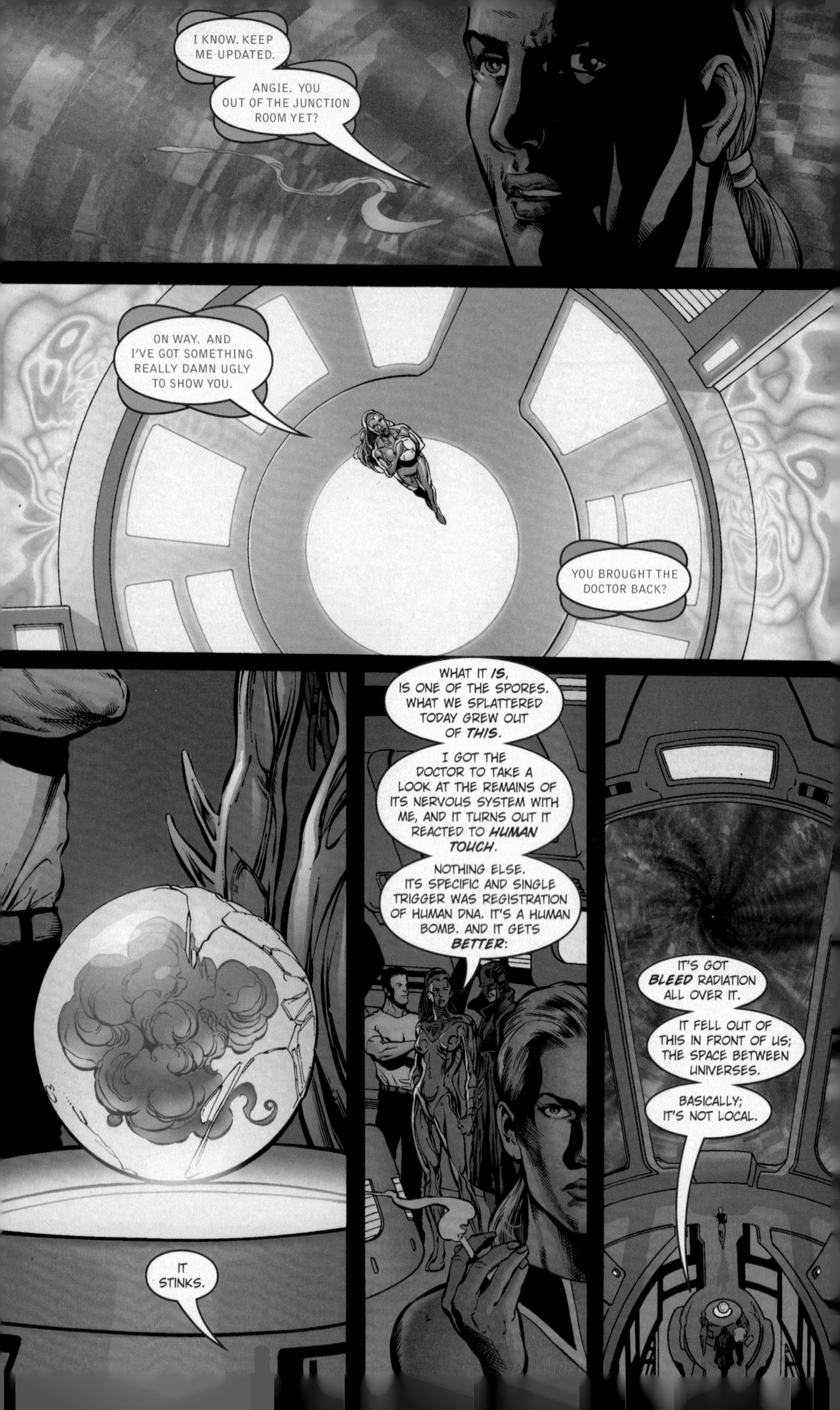
I KNOW. KEEP ME UPDATED.
ANGIE. YOU OUT OF THE JUNCTION ROOM YET?
ON WAY. AND I'VE GOT SOMETHING REALLY DAMN UGLY TO SHOW YOU.
YOU BROUGHT THE DOCTOR BACK?
IT STINKS.
WHAT IT *IS*, IS ONE OF THE SPORES. WHAT WE SPLATTERED TODAY GREW OUT OF *THIS*.
I GOT THE DOCTOR TO TAKE A LOOK AT THE REMAINS OF ITS NERVOUS SYSTEM WITH ME, AND IT TURNS OUT IT REACTED TO *HUMAN TOUCH*.
NOTHING ELSE. ITS SPECIFIC AND SINGLE TRIGGER WAS REGISTRATION OF HUMAN DNA. IT'S A HUMAN BOMB. AND IT GETS *BETTER*:
IT'S GOT *BLEED* RADIATION ALL OVER IT.
IT FELL OUT OF THIS IN FRONT OF US; THE SPACE BETWEEN UNIVERSES.
BASICALLY; IT'S NOT LOCAL.

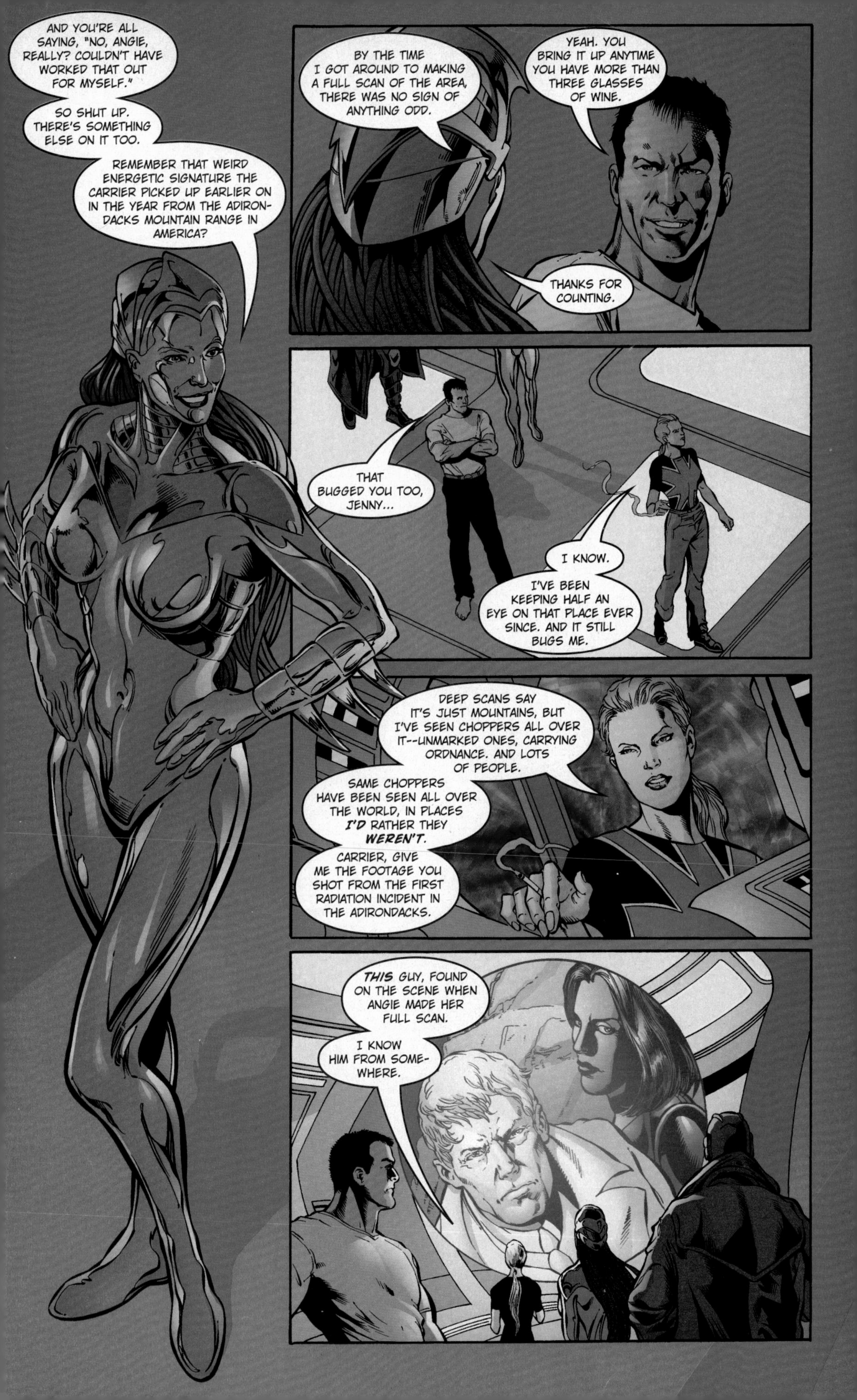
AND YOU'RE ALL SAYING, "NO, ANGIE, REALLY? COULDN'T HAVE WORKED THAT OUT FOR MYSELF."
SO SHUT UP. THERE'S SOMETHING ELSE ON IT TOO.
REMEMBER THAT WEIRD ENERGETIC SIGNATURE THE CARRIER PICKED UP EARLIER ON IN THE YEAR FROM THE ADIRONDACKS MOUNTAIN RANGE IN AMERICA?
BY THE TIME I GOT AROUND TO MAKING A FULL SCAN OF THE AREA, THERE WAS NO SIGN OF ANYTHING ODD.
YEAH. YOU BRING IT UP ANYTIME YOU HAVE MORE THAN THREE GLASSES OF WINE.
THANKS FOR COUNTING.
THAT BUGGED YOU TOO, JENNY...
I KNOW.
I'VE BEEN KEEPING HALF AN EYE ON THAT PLACE EVER SINCE. AND IT STILL BUGS ME.
DEEP SCANS SAY IT'S JUST MOUNTAINS, BUT I'VE SEEN CHOPPERS ALL OVER IT--UNMARKED ONES, CARRYING ORDNANCE. AND LOTS OF PEOPLE.
SAME CHOPPERS HAVE BEEN SEEN ALL OVER THE WORLD, IN PLACES ***I'D*** RATHER THEY ***WEREN'T***.
CARRIER, GIVE ME THE FOOTAGE YOU SHOT FROM THE FIRST RADIATION INCIDENT IN THE ADIRONDACKS.
THIS GUY, FOUND ON THE SCENE WHEN ANGIE MADE HER FULL SCAN.
I KNOW HIM FROM SOMEWHERE.

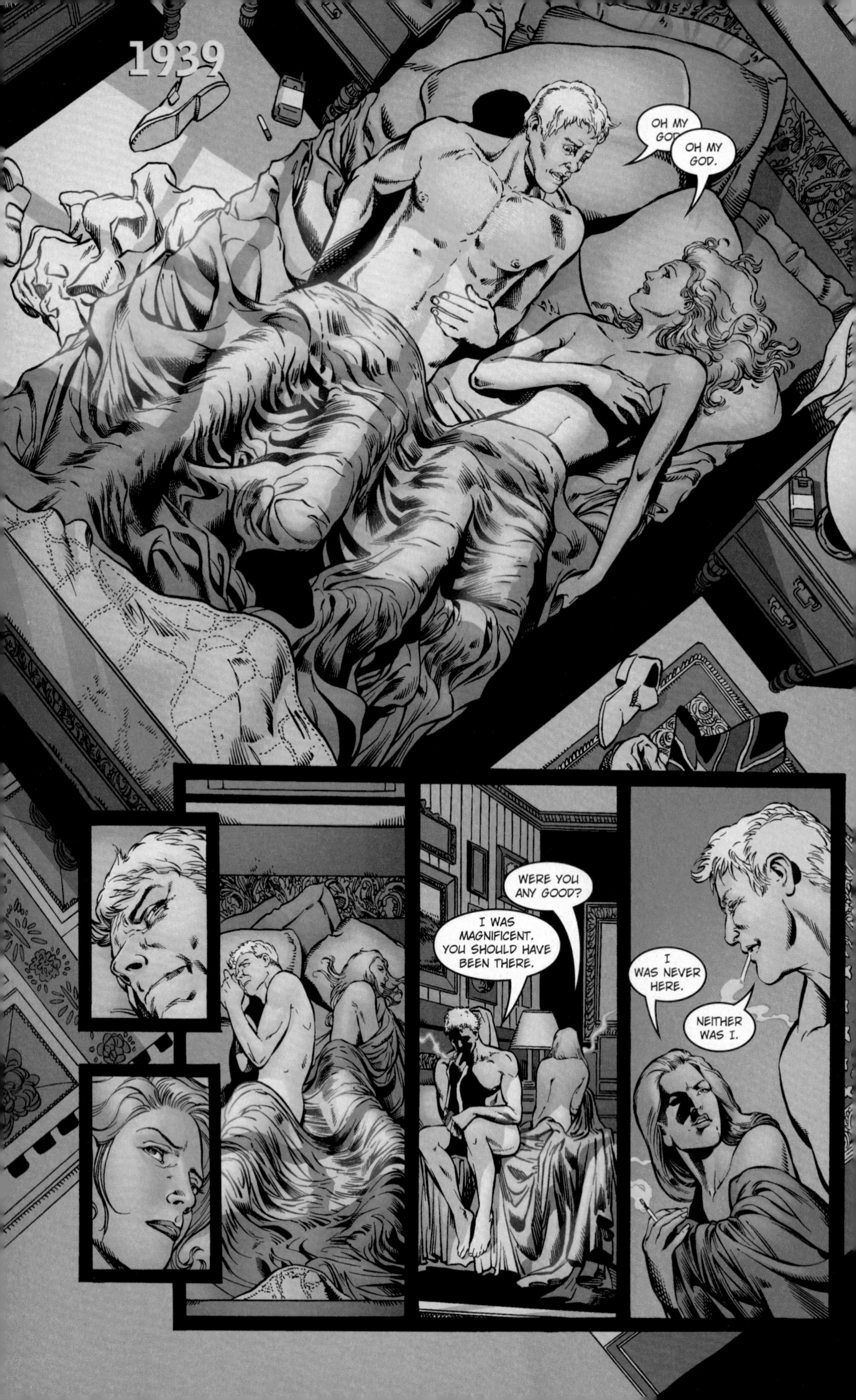
1939
OH MY GOD
OH MY GOD.
WERE YOU ANY GOOD?
I WAS MAGNIFICENT. YOU SHOULD HAVE BEEN THERE.
I WAS NEVER HERE.
NEITHER WAS I.

I KNOW THE BASTARD'S FACE FROM SOMEWHERE.

CARRIER; SHOW ME MY FAVORITE SPOT IN THE ADIRONDACKS.

NOTHING THERE. JUST CHOPPERS.

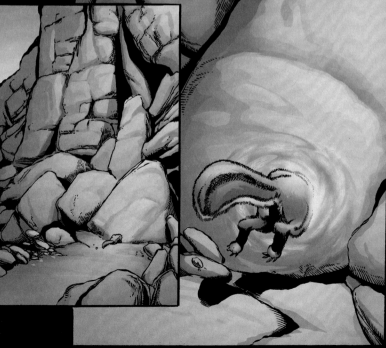

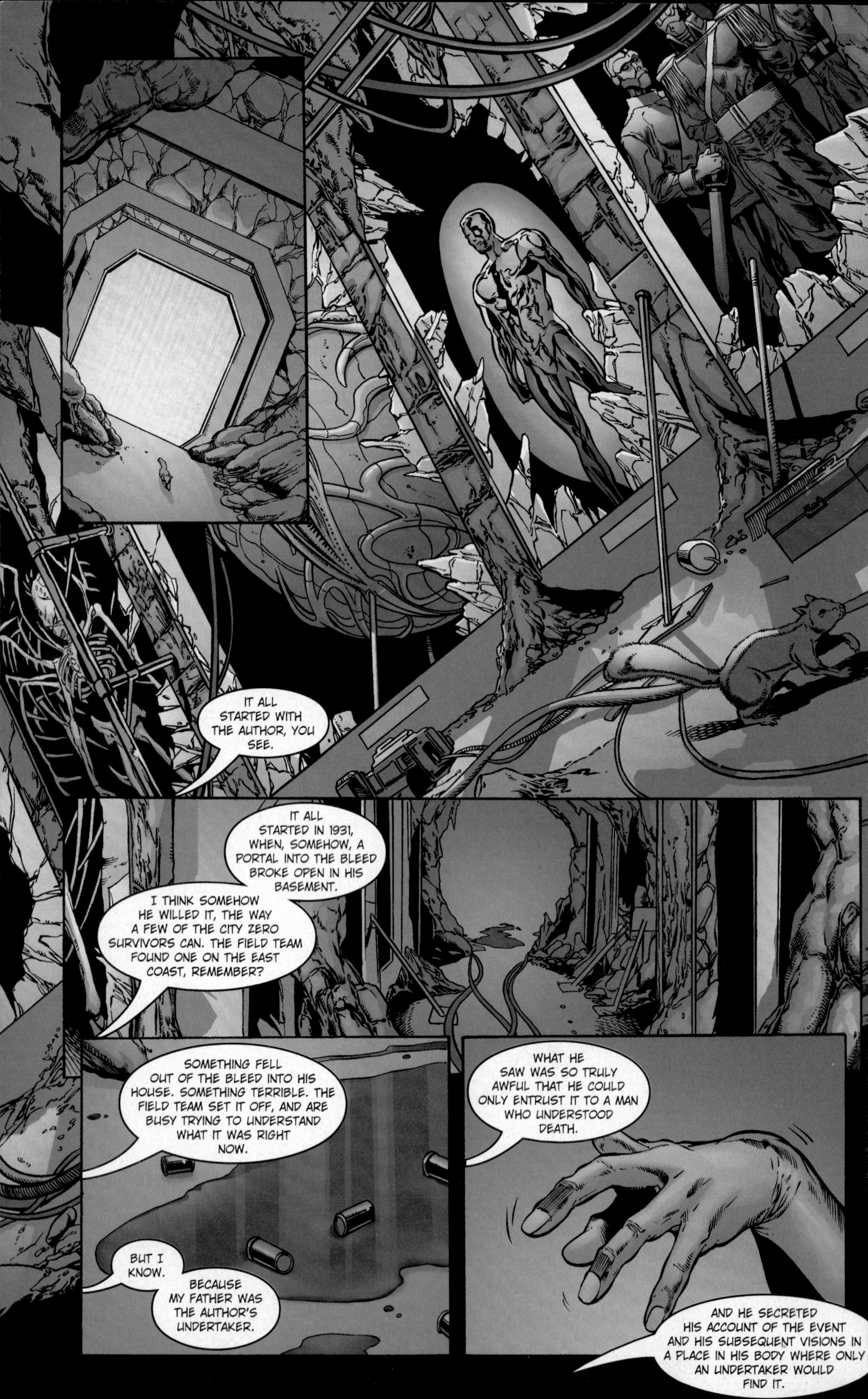
IT ALL STARTED WITH THE AUTHOR, YOU SEE.
IT ALL STARTED IN 1931, WHEN, SOMEHOW, A PORTAL INTO THE BLEED BROKE OPEN IN HIS BASEMENT.
I THINK SOMEHOW HE WILLED IT, THE WAY A FEW OF THE CITY ZERO SURVIVORS CAN. THE FIELD TEAM FOUND ONE ON THE EAST COAST, REMEMBER?
SOMETHING FELL OUT OF THE BLEED INTO HIS HOUSE. SOMETHING TERRIBLE. THE FIELD TEAM SET IT OFF, AND ARE BUSY TRYING TO UNDERSTAND WHAT IT WAS RIGHT NOW.
BUT I KNOW.
BECAUSE MY FATHER WAS THE AUTHOR'S UNDERTAKER.
WHAT HE SAW WAS SO TRULY AWFUL THAT HE COULD ONLY ENTRUST IT TO A MAN WHO UNDERSTOOD DEATH.
AND HE SECRETED HIS ACCOUNT OF THE EVENT AND HIS SUBSEQUENT VISIONS IN A PLACE IN HIS BODY WHERE ONLY AN UNDERTAKER WOULD FIND IT.

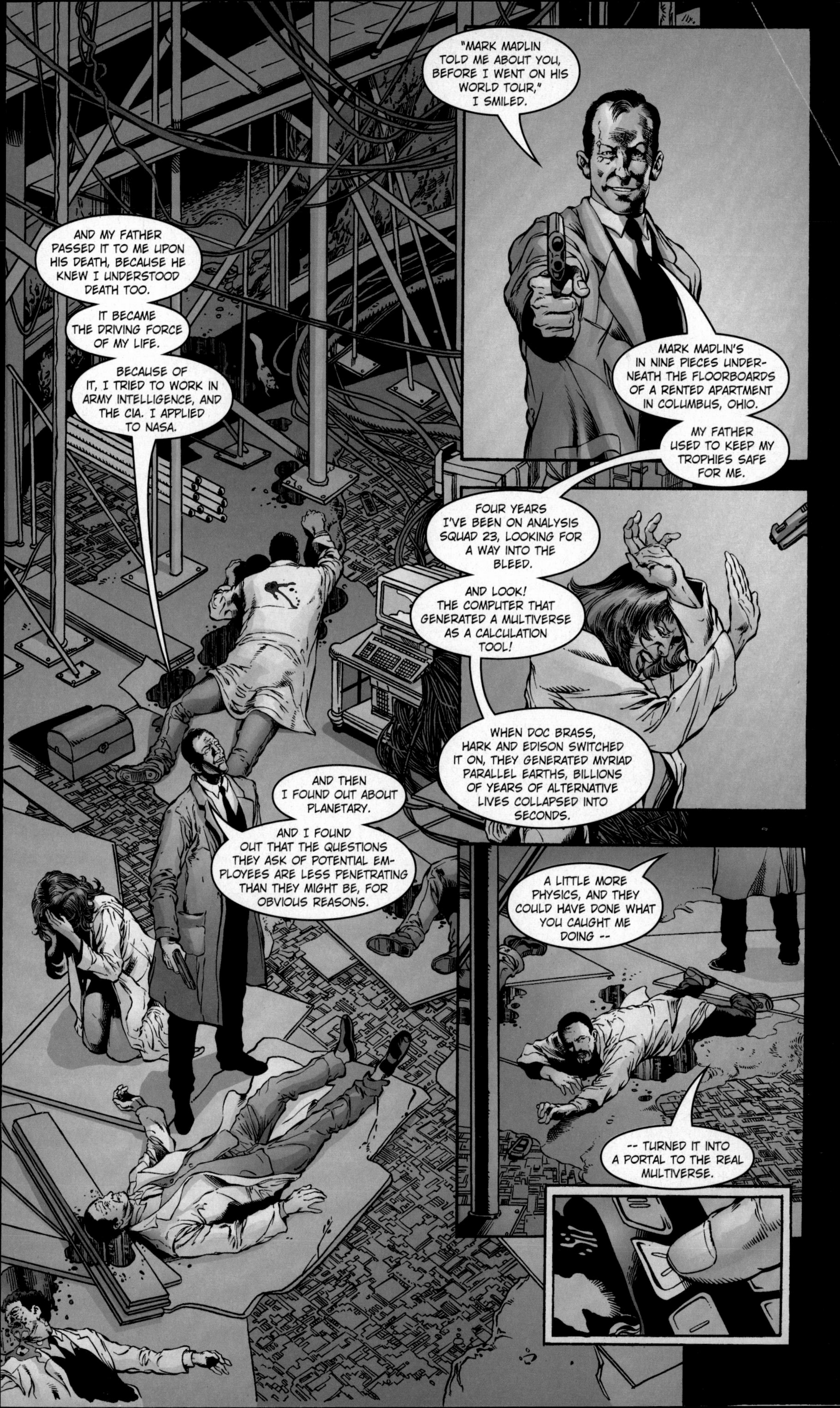
"MARK MADLIN TOLD ME ABOUT YOU, BEFORE I WENT ON HIS WORLD TOUR," I SMILED.
AND MY FATHER PASSED IT TO ME UPON HIS DEATH, BECAUSE HE KNEW I UNDERSTOOD DEATH TOO.
IT BECAME THE DRIVING FORCE OF MY LIFE.
BECAUSE OF IT, I TRIED TO WORK IN ARMY INTELLIGENCE, AND THE CIA. I APPLIED TO NASA.
MARK MADLIN'S IN NINE PIECES UNDER-NEATH THE FLOORBOARDS OF A RENTED APARTMENT IN COLUMBUS, OHIO.
MY FATHER USED TO KEEP MY TROPHIES SAFE FOR ME.
FOUR YEARS I'VE BEEN ON ANALYSIS SQUAD 23, LOOKING FOR A WAY INTO THE BLEED.
AND LOOK! THE COMPUTER THAT GENERATED A MULTIVERSE AS A CALCULATION TOOL!
WHEN DOC BRASS, HARK AND EDISON SWITCHED IT ON, THEY GENERATED MYRIAD PARALLEL EARTHS, BILLIONS OF YEARS OF ALTERNATIVE LIVES COLLAPSED INTO SECONDS.
AND THEN I FOUND OUT ABOUT PLANETARY.
AND I FOUND OUT THAT THE QUESTIONS THEY ASK OF POTENTIAL EM-PLOYEES ARE LESS PENETRATING THAN THEY MIGHT BE, FOR OBVIOUS REASONS.
A LITTLE MORE PHYSICS, AND THEY COULD HAVE DONE WHAT YOU CAUGHT ME DOING --
-- TURNED IT INTO A PORTAL TO THE REAL MULTIVERSE.

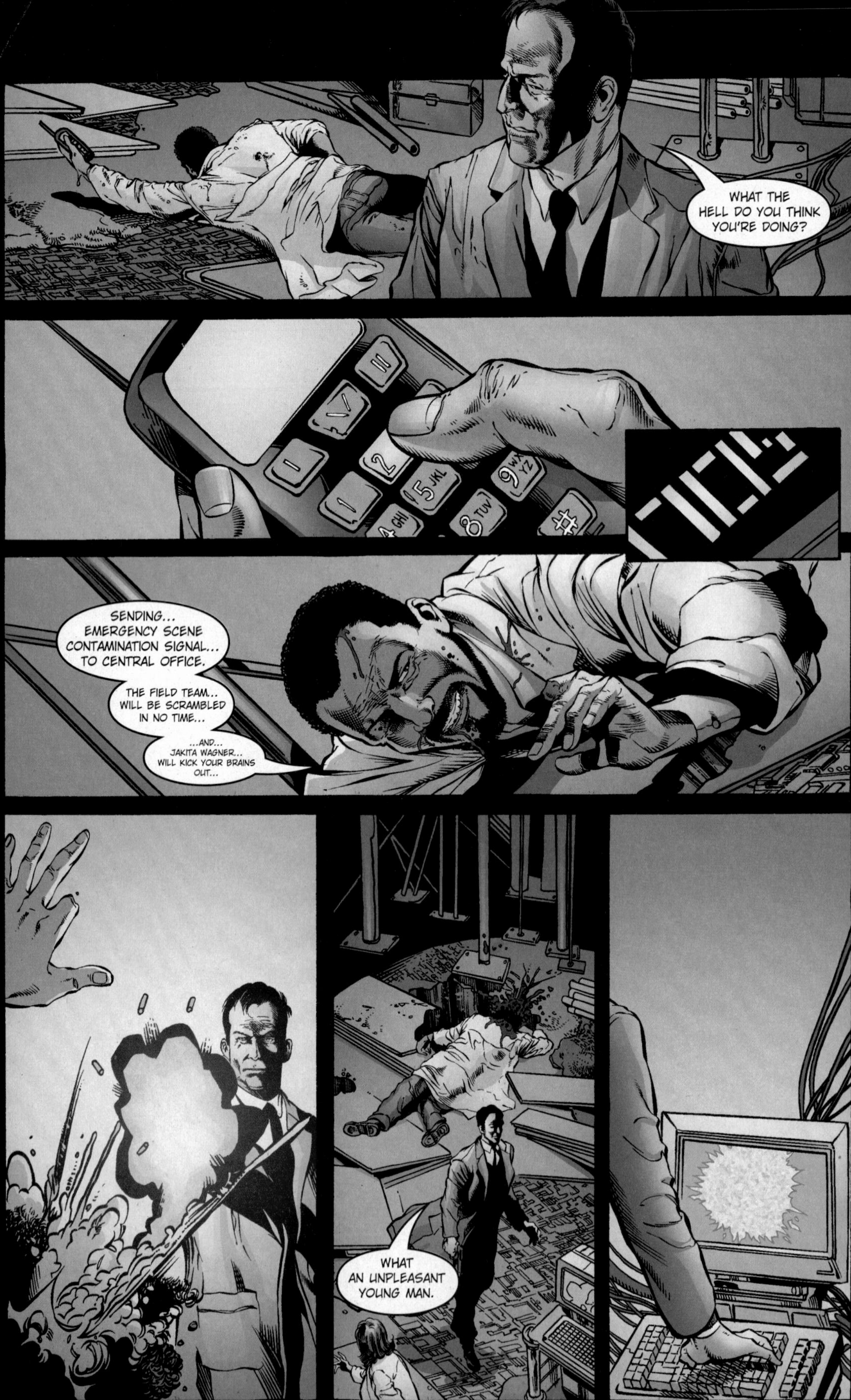
WHAT THE HELL DO YOU THINK YOU'RE DOING?
SENDING... EMERGENCY SCENE CONTAMINATION SIGNAL... TO CENTRAL OFFICE.
THE FIELD TEAM... WILL BE SCRAMBLED IN NO TIME...
...AND... JAKITA WAGNER... WILL KICK YOUR BRAINS OUT...
WHAT AN UNPLEASANT YOUNG MAN.

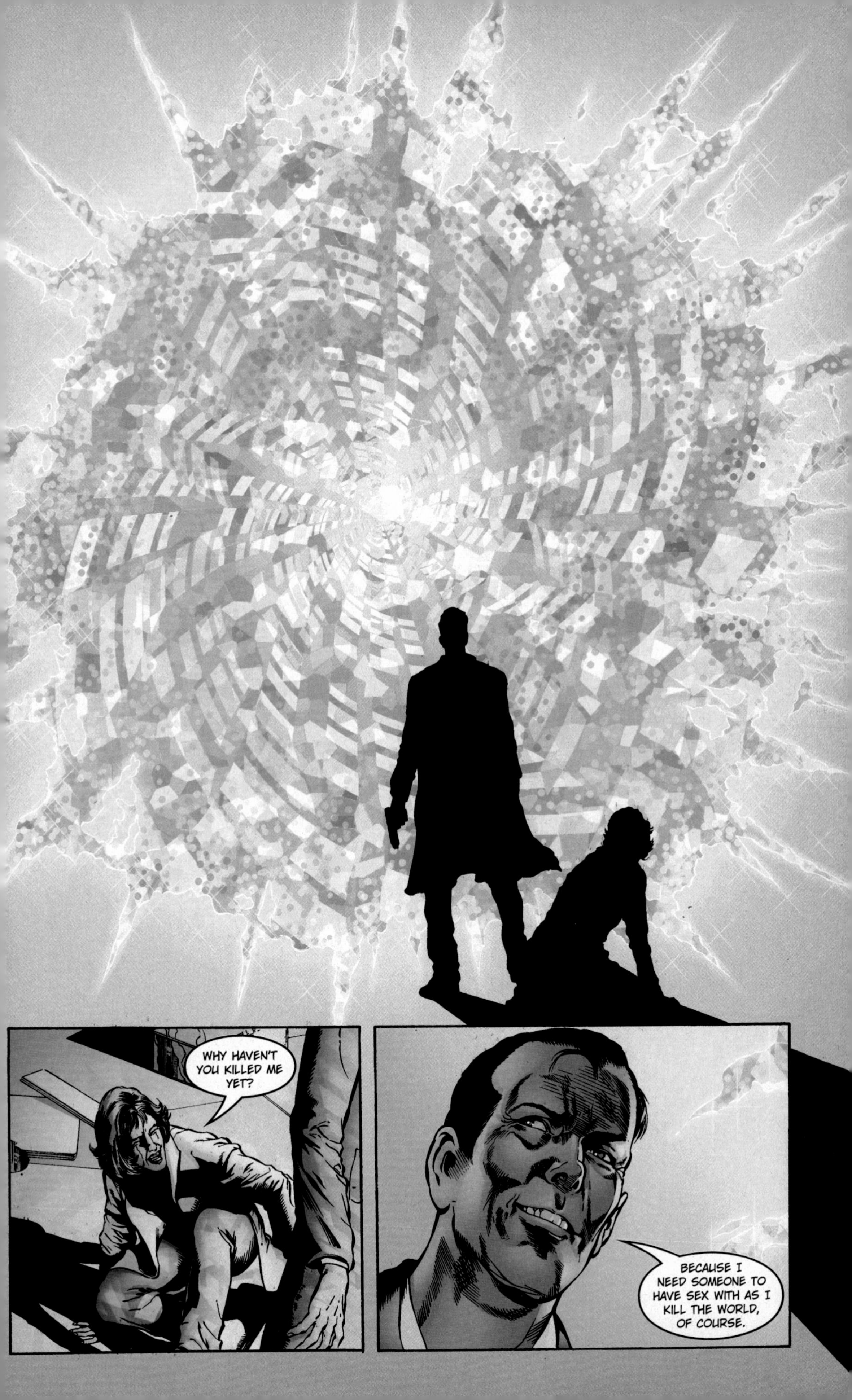
WHY HAVEN'T YOU KILLED ME YET?
BECAUSE I NEED SOMEONE TO HAVE SEX WITH AS I KILL THE WORLD, OF COURSE.

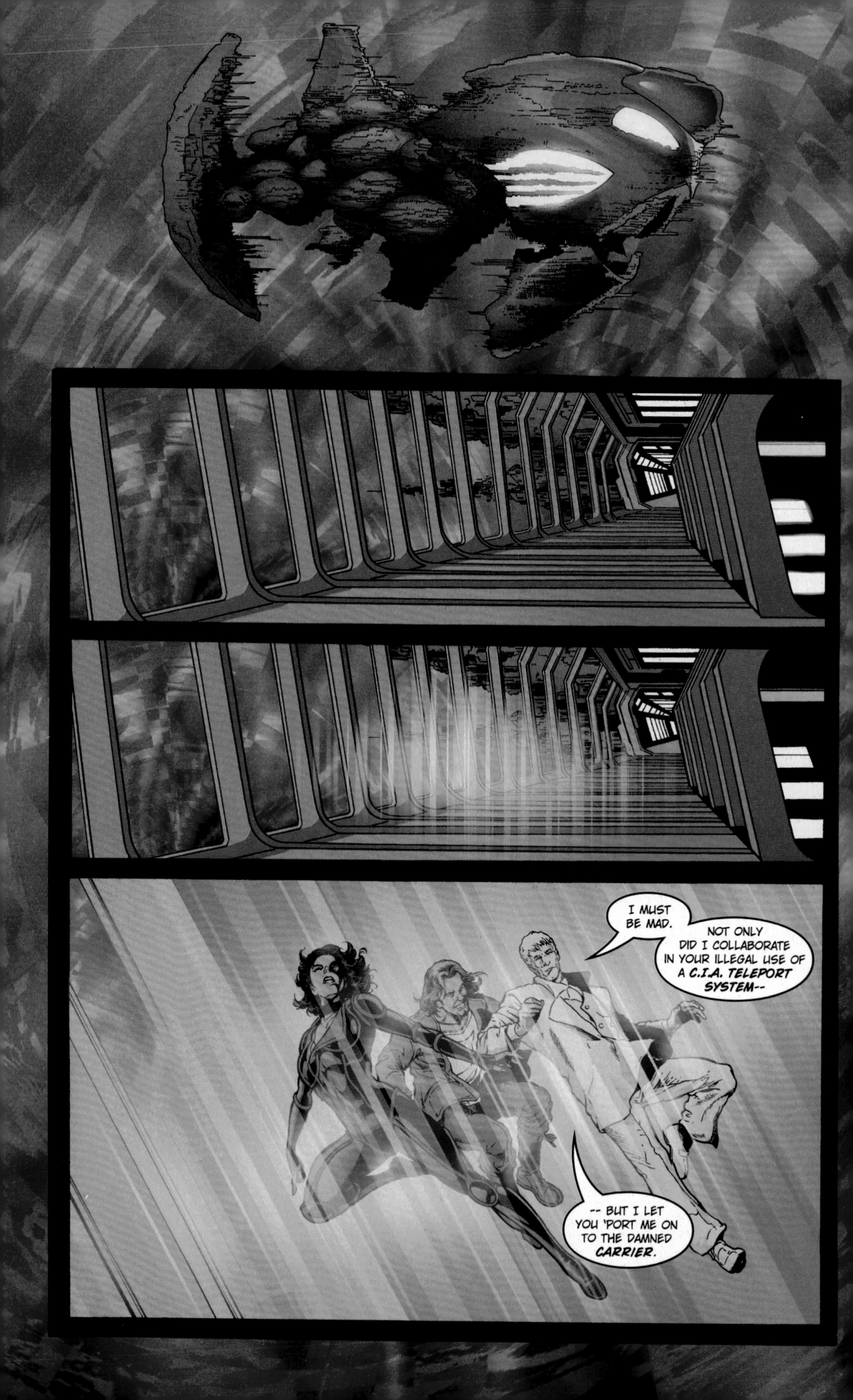
I MUST BE MAD.
NOT ONLY DID I COLLABORATE IN YOUR ILLEGAL USE OF A C.I.A. TELEPORT SYSTEM--
-- BUT I LET YOU 'PORT ME ON TO THE DAMNED CARRIER.

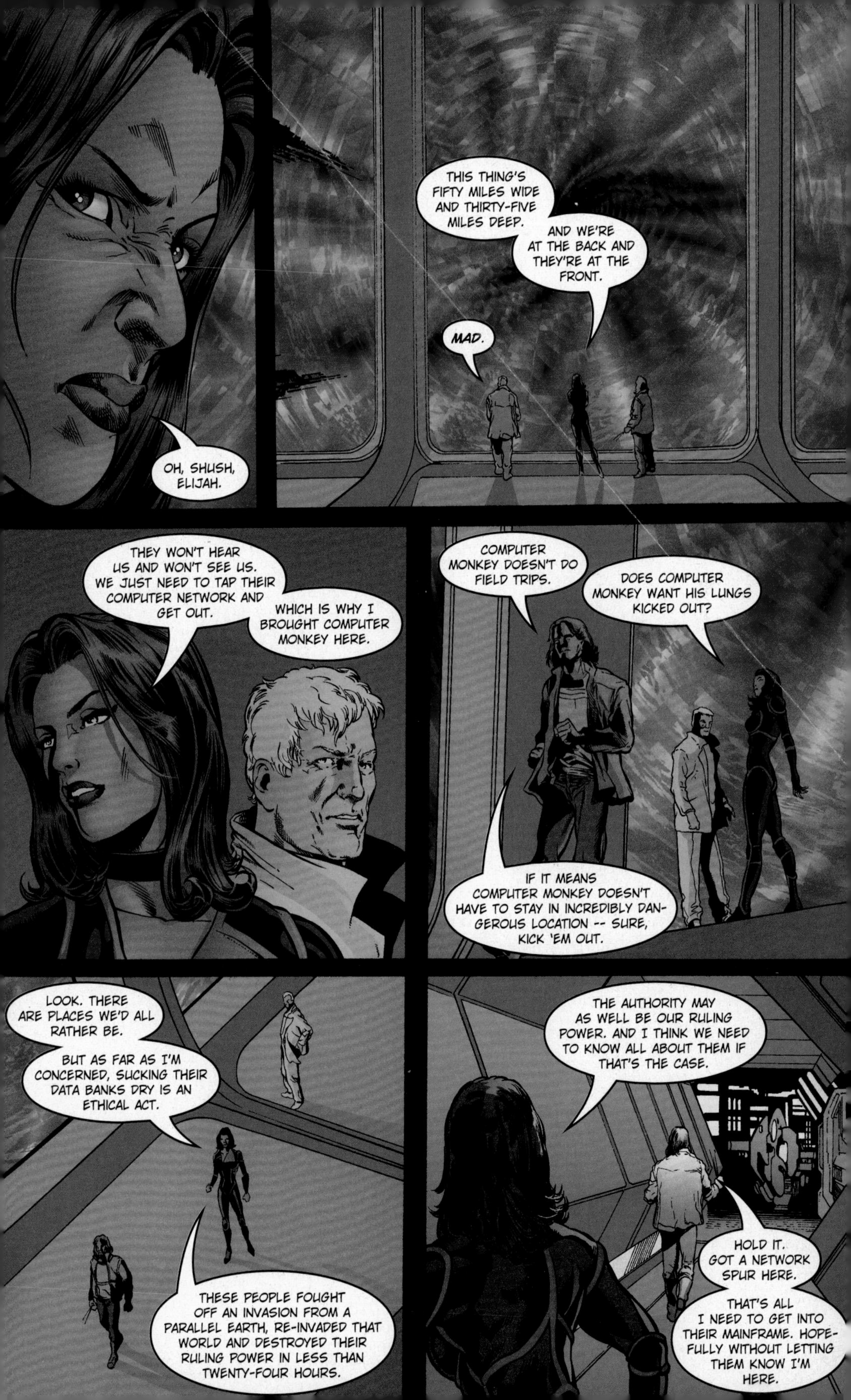
THIS THING'S FIFTY MILES WIDE AND THIRTY-FIVE MILES DEEP.
AND WE'RE AT THE BACK AND THEY'RE AT THE FRONT.
MAD.
OH, SHUSH, ELIJAH.
THEY WON'T HEAR US AND WON'T SEE US. WE JUST NEED TO TAP THEIR COMPUTER NETWORK AND GET OUT.
WHICH IS WHY I BROUGHT COMPUTER MONKEY HERE.
COMPUTER MONKEY DOESN'T DO FIELD TRIPS.
DOES COMPUTER MONKEY WANT HIS LUNGS KICKED OUT?
IF IT MEANS COMPUTER MONKEY DOESN'T HAVE TO STAY IN INCREDIBLY DANGEROUS LOCATION -- SURE, KICK 'EM OUT.
LOOK. THERE ARE PLACES WE'D ALL RATHER BE.
BUT AS FAR AS I'M CONCERNED, SUCKING THEIR DATA BANKS DRY IS AN ETHICAL ACT.
THESE PEOPLE FOUGHT OFF AN INVASION FROM A PARALLEL EARTH, RE-INVADED THAT WORLD AND DESTROYED THEIR RULING POWER IN LESS THAN TWENTY-FOUR HOURS.
THE AUTHORITY MAY AS WELL BE OUR RULING POWER. AND I THINK WE NEED TO KNOW ALL ABOUT THEM IF THAT'S THE CASE.
HOLD IT. GOT A NETWORK SPUR HERE.
THAT'S ALL I NEED TO GET INTO THEIR MAINFRAME. HOPEFULLY WITHOUT LETTING THEM KNOW I'M HERE.

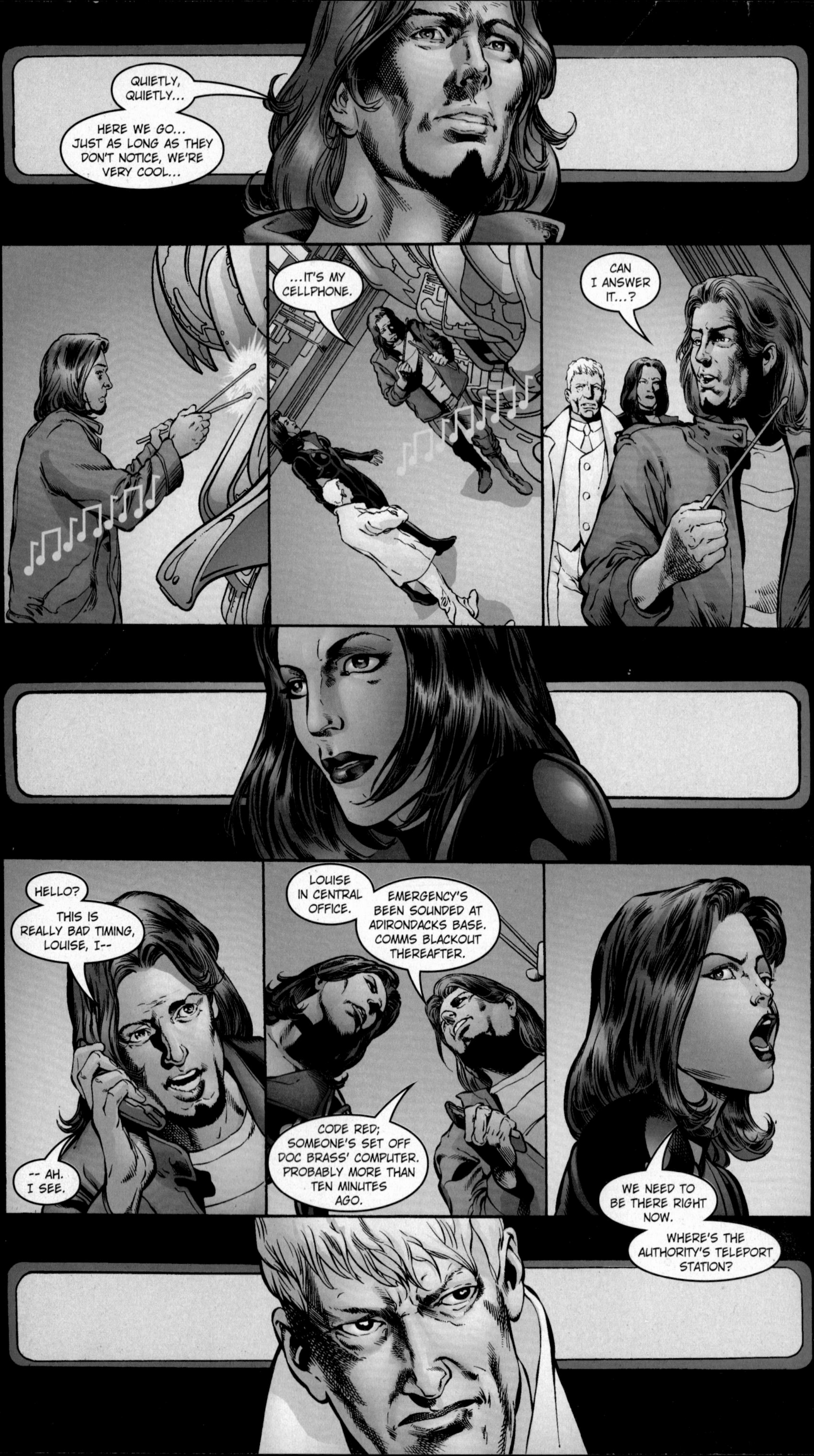
QUIETLY, QUIETLY...
HERE WE GO... JUST AS LONG AS THEY DON'T NOTICE, WE'RE VERY COOL...
...IT'S MY CELLPHONE.
CAN I ANSWER IT...?
HELLO?
THIS IS REALLY BAD TIMING, LOUISE, I--
-- AH. I SEE.
LOUISE IN CENTRAL OFFICE.
EMERGENCY'S BEEN SOUNDED AT ADIRONDACKS BASE. COMMS BLACKOUT THEREAFTER.
CODE RED; SOMEONE'S SET OFF DOC BRASS' COMPUTER. PROBABLY MORE THAN TEN MINUTES AGO.
WE NEED TO BE THERE RIGHT NOW.
WHERE'S THE AUTHORITY'S TELEPORT STATION?

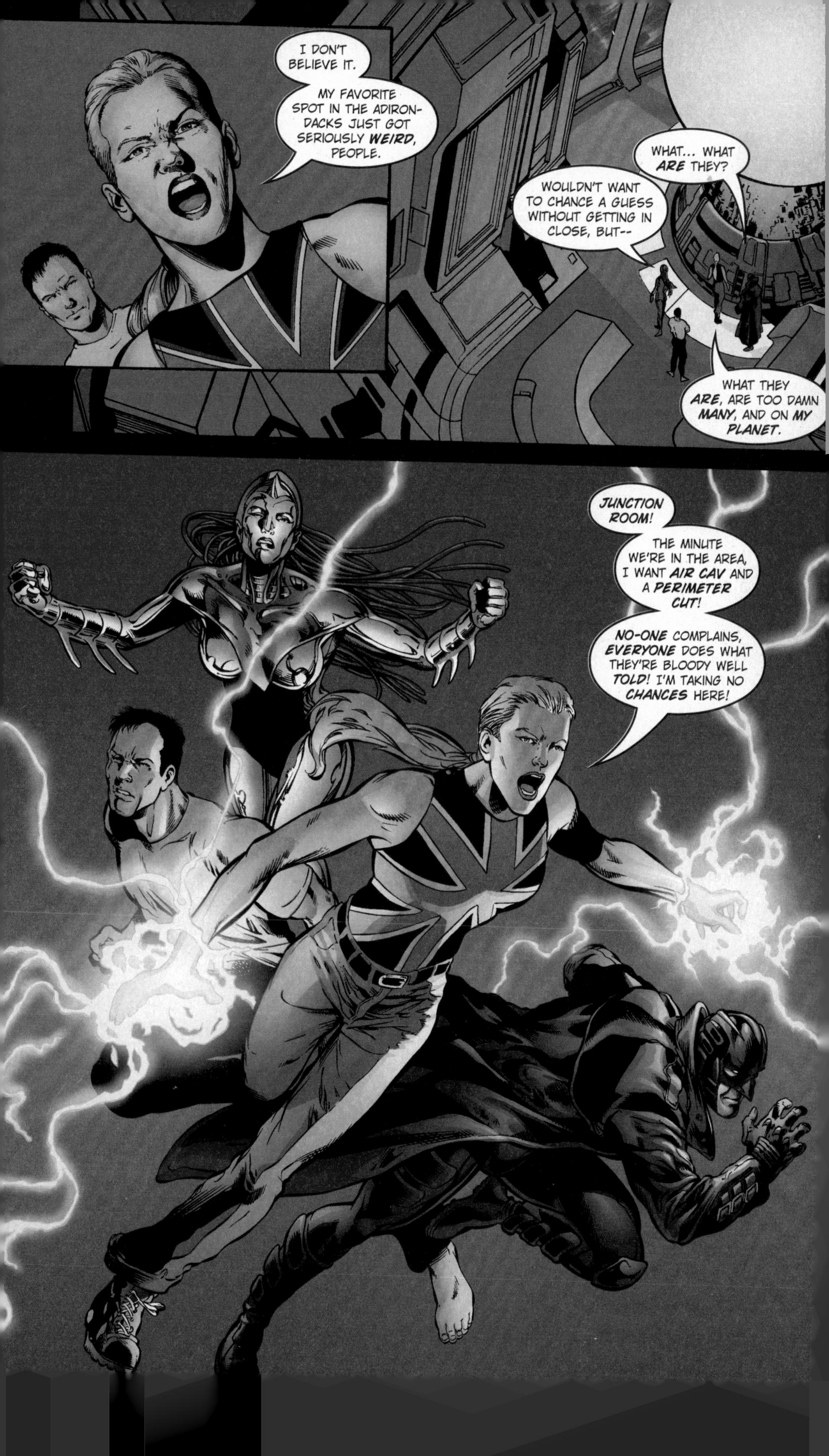
I DON'T BELIEVE IT.
MY FAVORITE SPOT IN THE ADIRONDACKS JUST GOT SERIOUSLY WEIRD, PEOPLE.
WHAT... WHAT ARE THEY?
WOULDN'T WANT TO CHANCE A GUESS WITHOUT GETTING IN CLOSE, BUT--
WHAT THEY ARE, ARE TOO DAMN MANY, AND ON MY PLANET.
JUNCTION ROOM!
THE MINUTE WE'RE IN THE AREA, I WANT AIR CAV AND A PERIMETER CUT!
NO-ONE COMPLAINS, EVERYONE DOES WHAT THEY'RE BLOODY WELL TOLD! I'M TAKING NO CHANCES HERE!

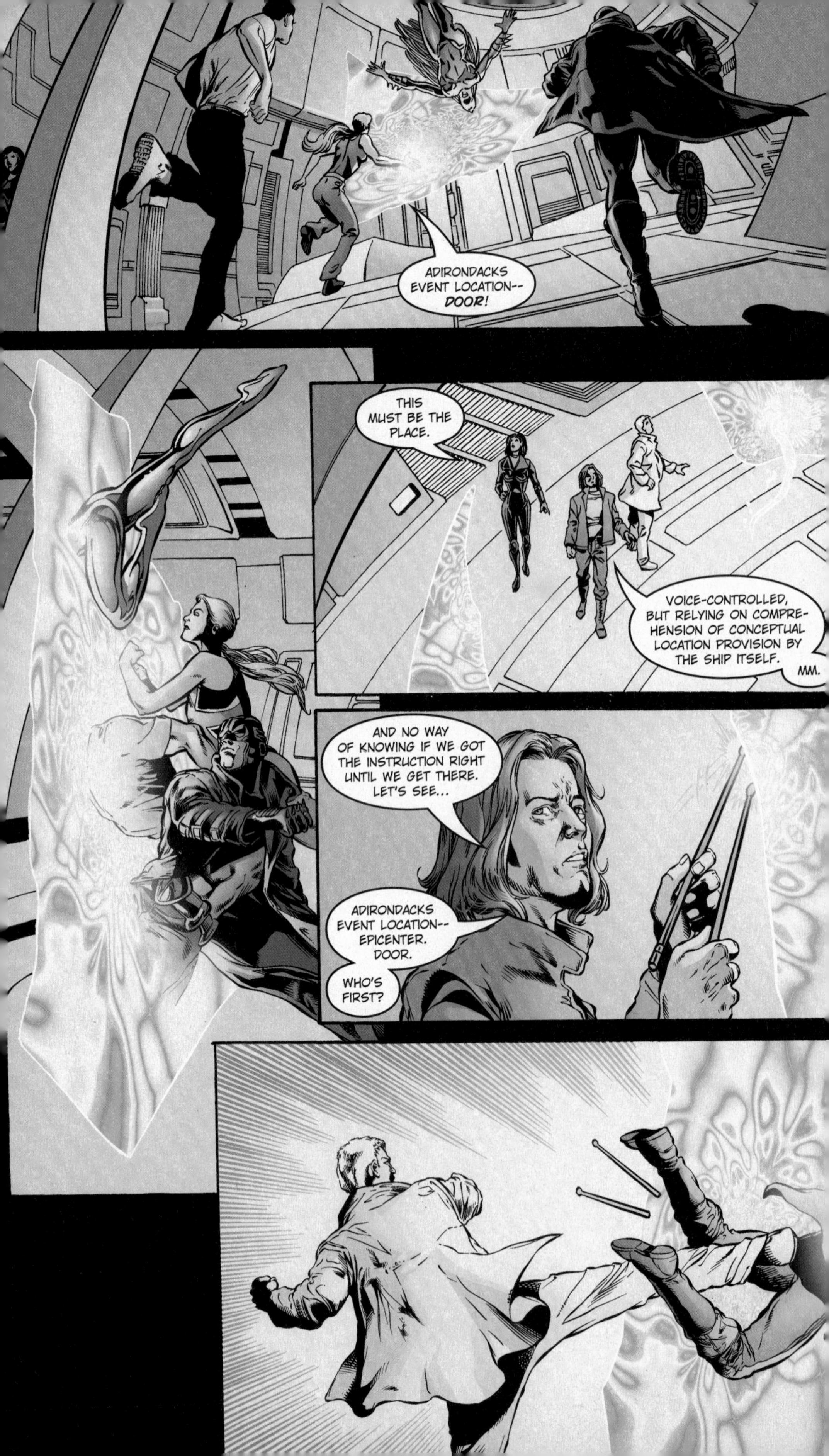
ADIRONDACKS EVENT LOCATION-- DOOR!
THIS MUST BE THE PLACE.
VOICE-CONTROLLED, BUT RELYING ON COMPREHENSION OF CONCEPTUAL LOCATION PROVISION BY THE SHIP ITSELF.
MM.
AND NO WAY OF KNOWING IF WE GOT THE INSTRUCTION RIGHT UNTIL WE GET THERE. LET'S SEE...
ADIRONDACKS EVENT LOCATION-- EPICENTER. DOOR.
WHO'S FIRST?

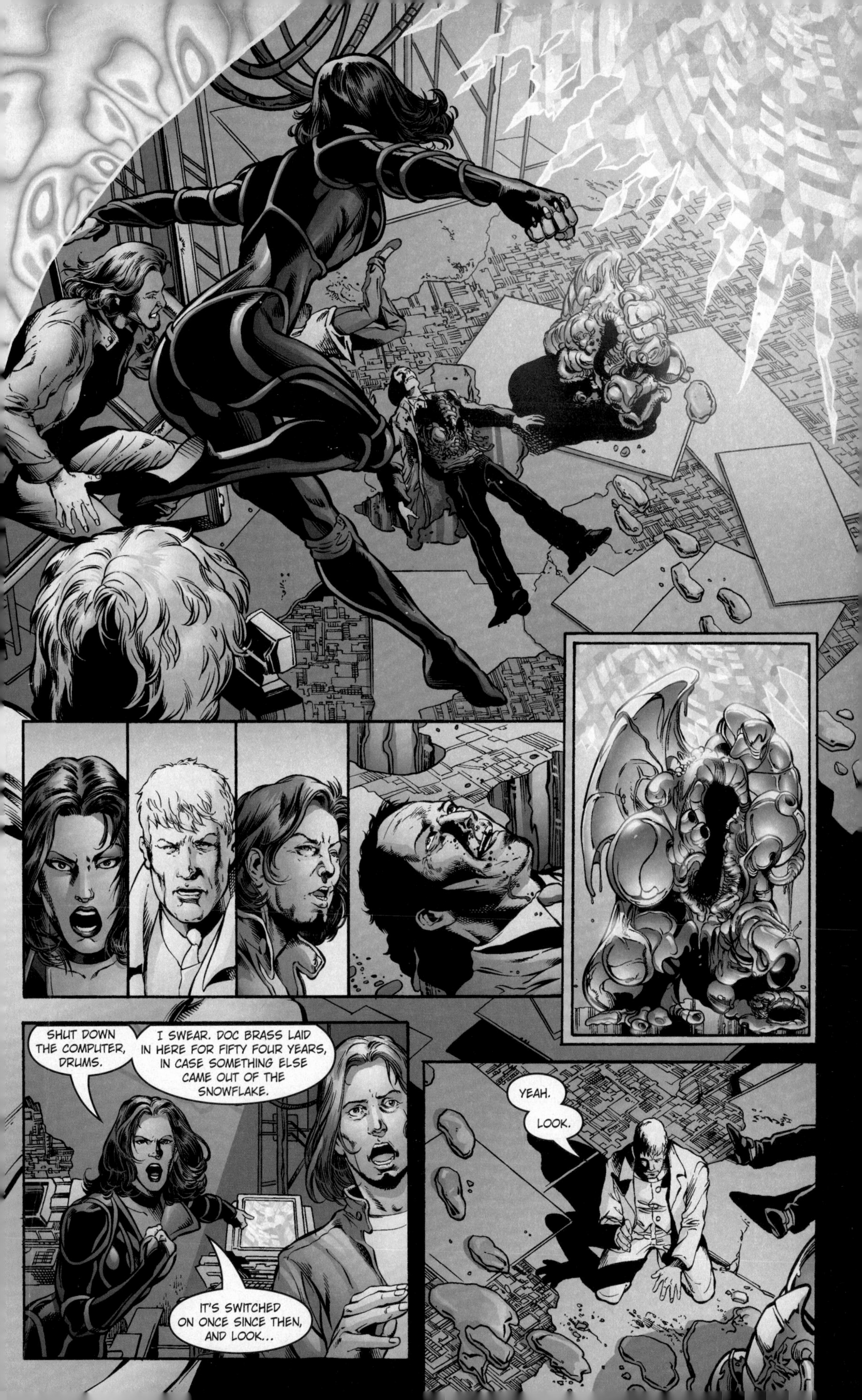
SHUT DOWN THE COMPUTER, DRUMS.
I SWEAR. DOC BRASS LAID IN HERE FOR FIFTY FOUR YEARS, IN CASE SOMETHING ELSE CAME OUT OF THE SNOWFLAKE.
IT'S SWITCHED ON ONCE SINCE THEN, AND LOOK...
YEAH.
LOOK.

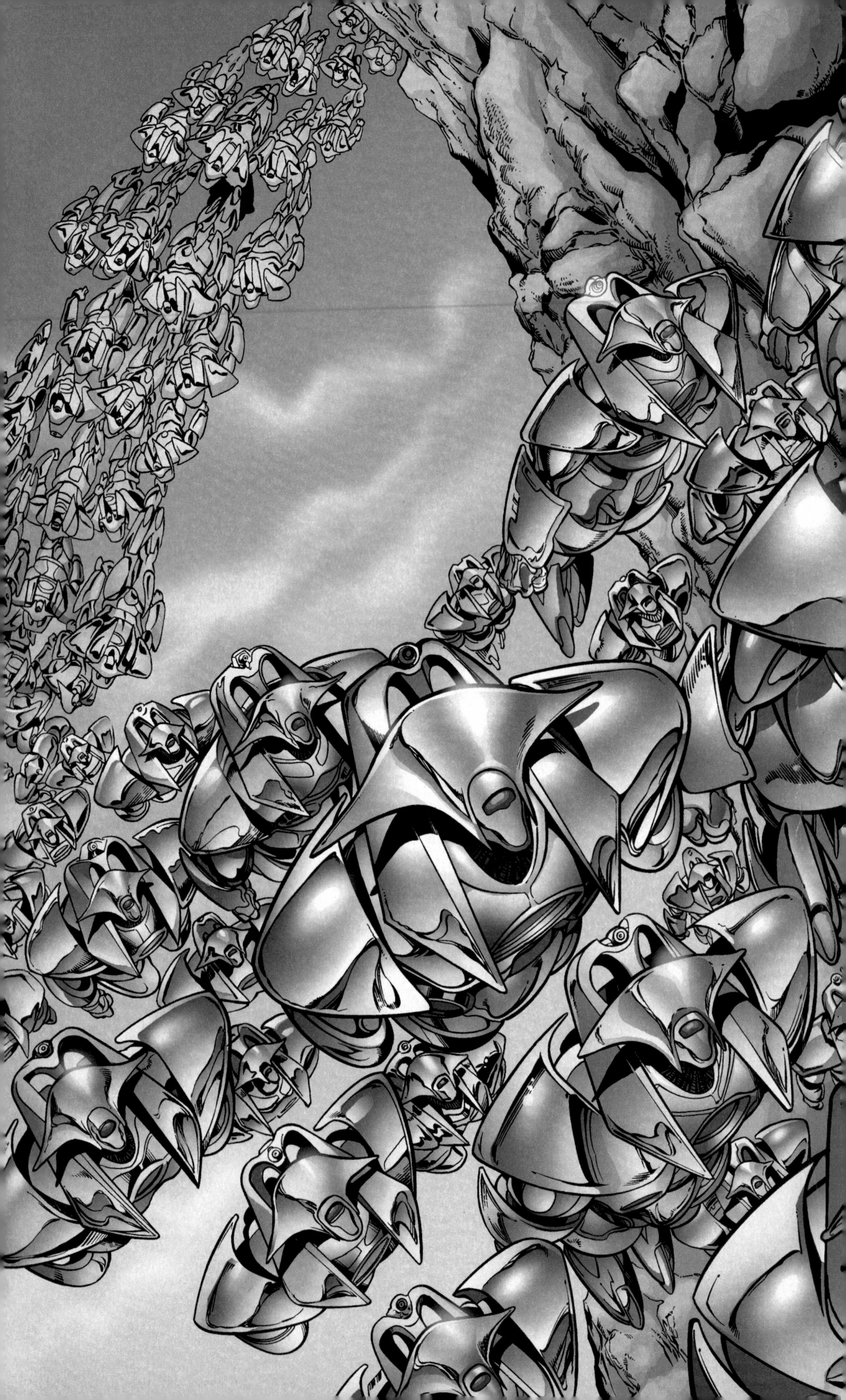

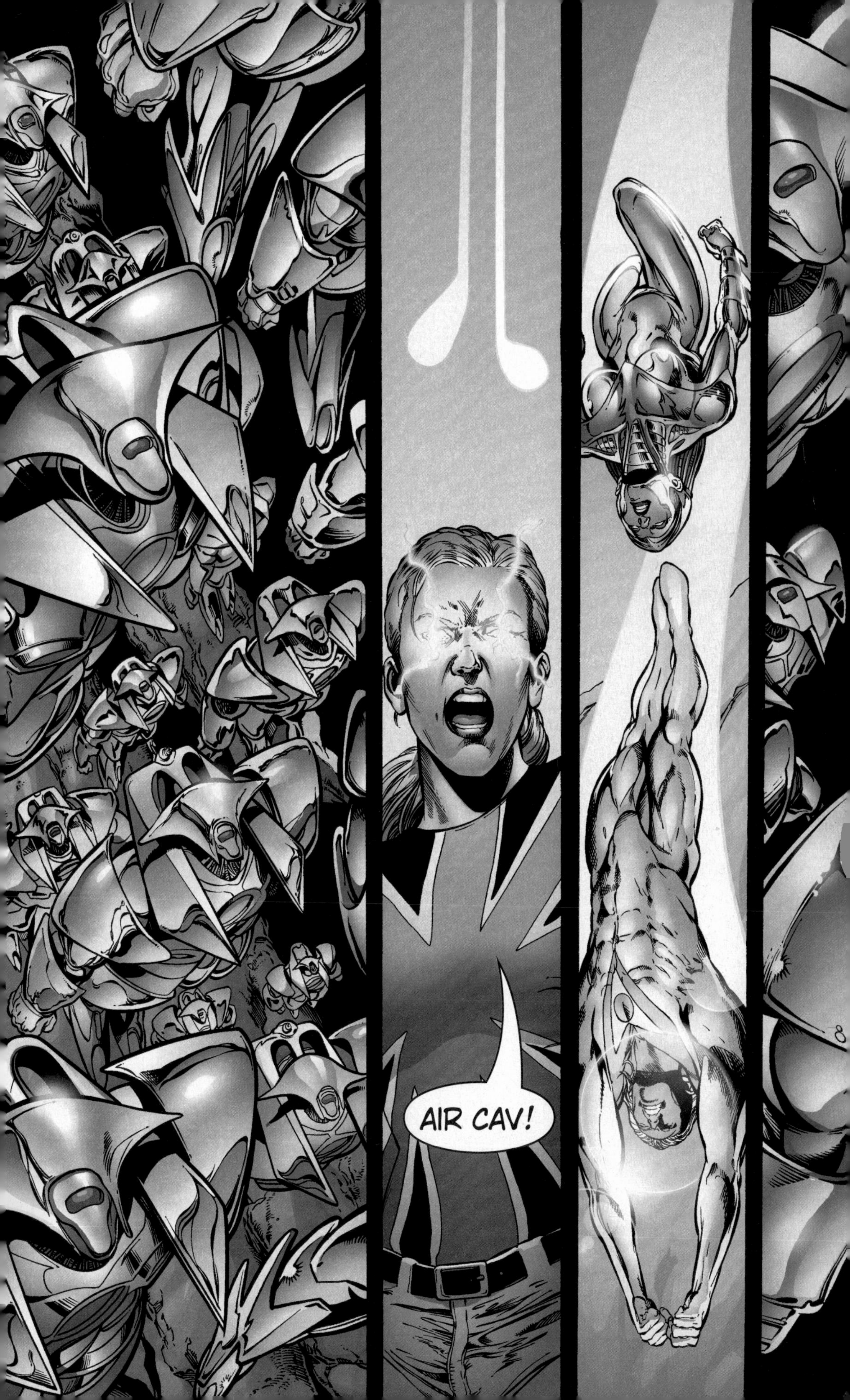
AIR CAV!

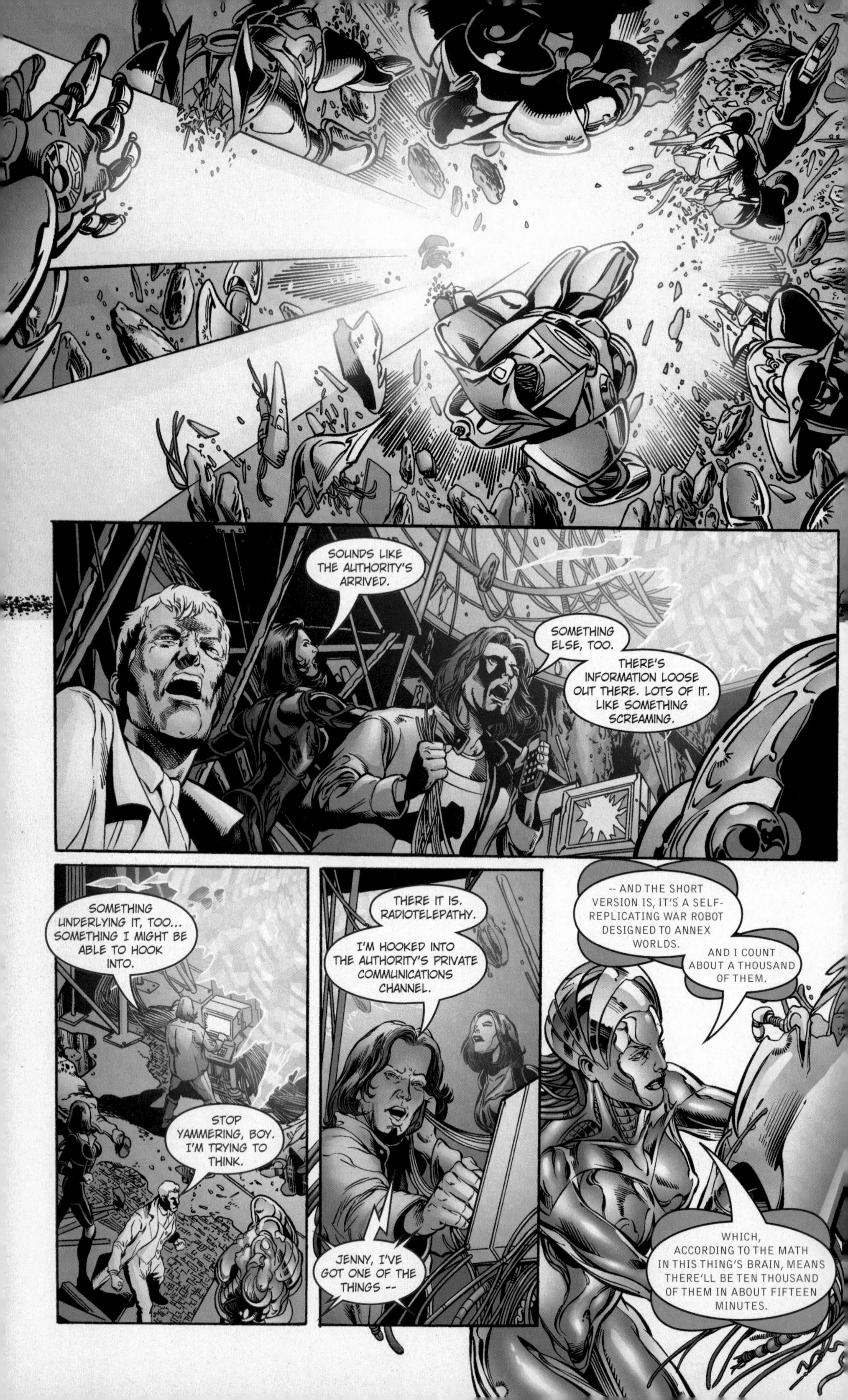
SOUNDS LIKE THE AUTHORITY'S ARRIVED.
SOMETHING ELSE, TOO.
THERE'S INFORMATION LOOSE OUT THERE. LOTS OF IT. LIKE SOMETHING SCREAMING.
SOMETHING UNDERLYING IT, TOO... SOMETHING I MIGHT BE ABLE TO HOOK INTO.
STOP YAMMERING, BOY. I'M TRYING TO THINK.
THERE IT IS. RADIOTELEPATHY.
I'M HOOKED INTO THE AUTHORITY'S PRIVATE COMMUNICATIONS CHANNEL.
JENNY, I'VE GOT ONE OF THE THINGS --
-- AND THE SHORT VERSION IS, IT'S A SELF-REPLICATING WAR ROBOT DESIGNED TO ANNEX WORLDS.
AND I COUNT ABOUT A THOUSAND OF THEM.
WHICH, ACCORDING TO THE MATH IN THIS THING'S BRAIN, MEANS THERE'LL BE TEN THOUSAND OF THEM IN ABOUT FIFTEEN MINUTES.

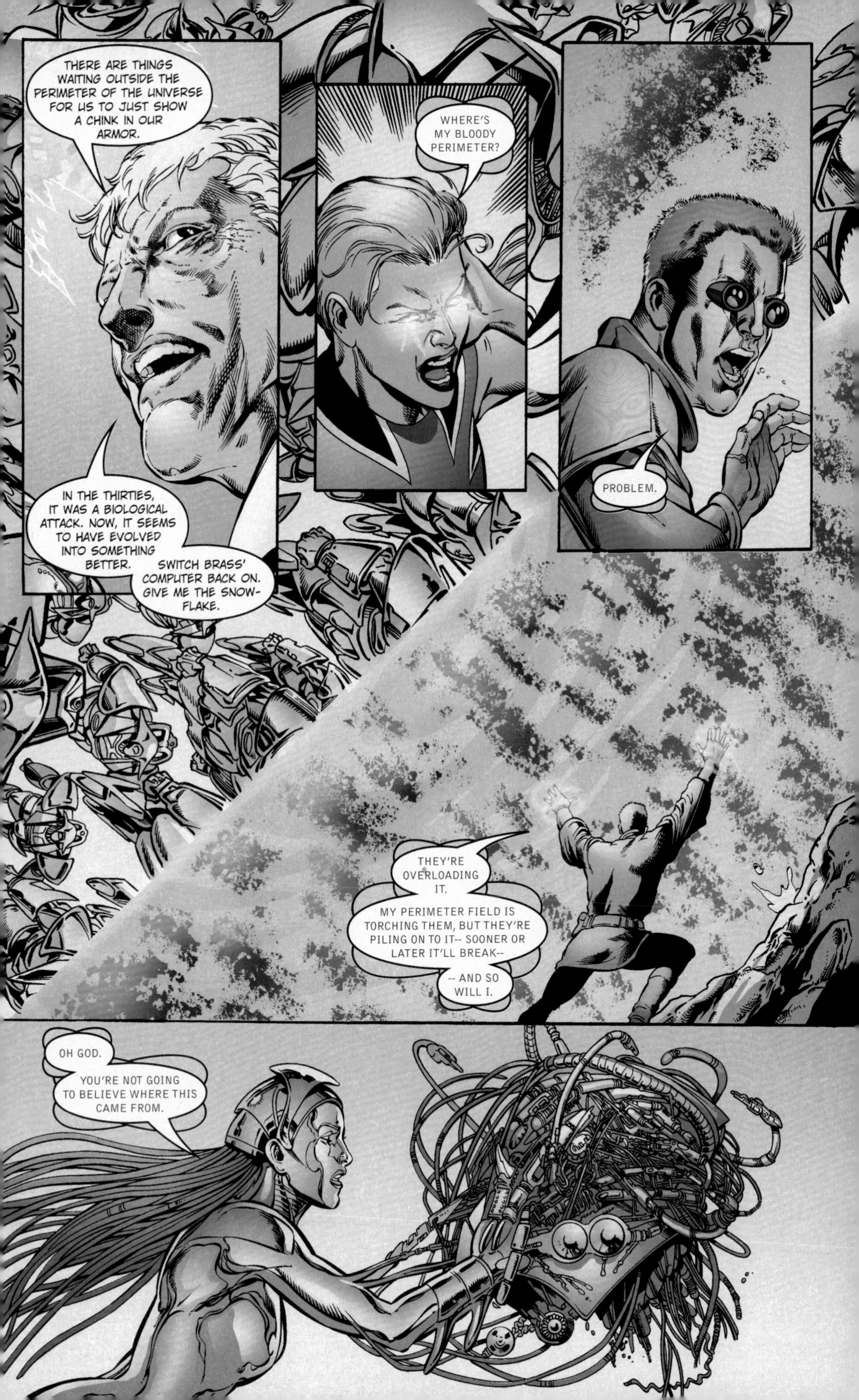
THERE ARE THINGS WAITING OUTSIDE THE PERIMETER OF THE UNIVERSE FOR US TO JUST SHOW A CHINK IN OUR ARMOR.
WHERE'S MY BLOODY PERIMETER?
PROBLEM.
IN THE THIRTIES, IT WAS A BIOLOGICAL ATTACK. NOW, IT SEEMS TO HAVE EVOLVED INTO SOMETHING BETTER.
SWITCH BRASS' COMPUTER BACK ON. GIVE ME THE SNOW-FLAKE.
THEY'RE OVERLOADING IT.
MY PERIMETER FIELD IS TORCHING THEM, BUT THEY'RE PILING ON TO IT-- SOONER OR LATER IT'LL BREAK--
-- AND SO WILL I.
OH GOD.
YOU'RE NOT GOING TO BELIEVE WHERE THIS CAME FROM.

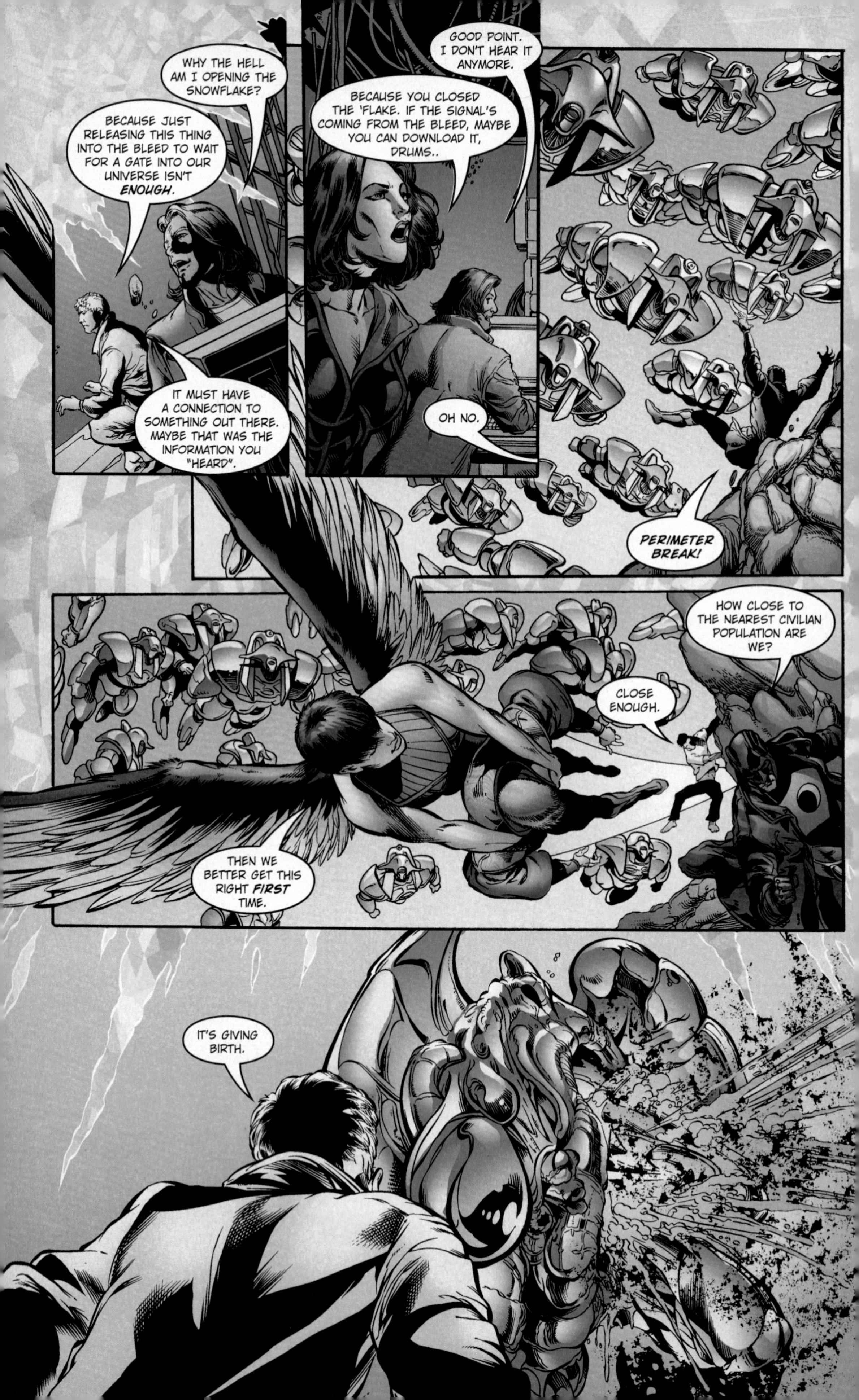
WHY THE HELL AM I OPENING THE SNOWFLAKE?
BECAUSE JUST RELEASING THIS THING INTO THE BLEED TO WAIT FOR A GATE INTO OUR UNIVERSE ISN'T ENOUGH.
IT MUST HAVE A CONNECTION TO SOMETHING OUT THERE. MAYBE THAT WAS THE INFORMATION YOU "HEARD".
GOOD POINT. I DON'T HEAR IT ANYMORE.
BECAUSE YOU CLOSED THE 'FLAKE. IF THE SIGNAL'S COMING FROM THE BLEED, MAYBE YOU CAN DOWNLOAD IT, DRUMS..
OH NO.
PERIMETER BREAK!
HOW CLOSE TO THE NEAREST CIVILIAN POPULATION ARE WE?
CLOSE ENOUGH.
THEN WE BETTER GET THIS RIGHT FIRST TIME.
IT'S GIVING BIRTH.

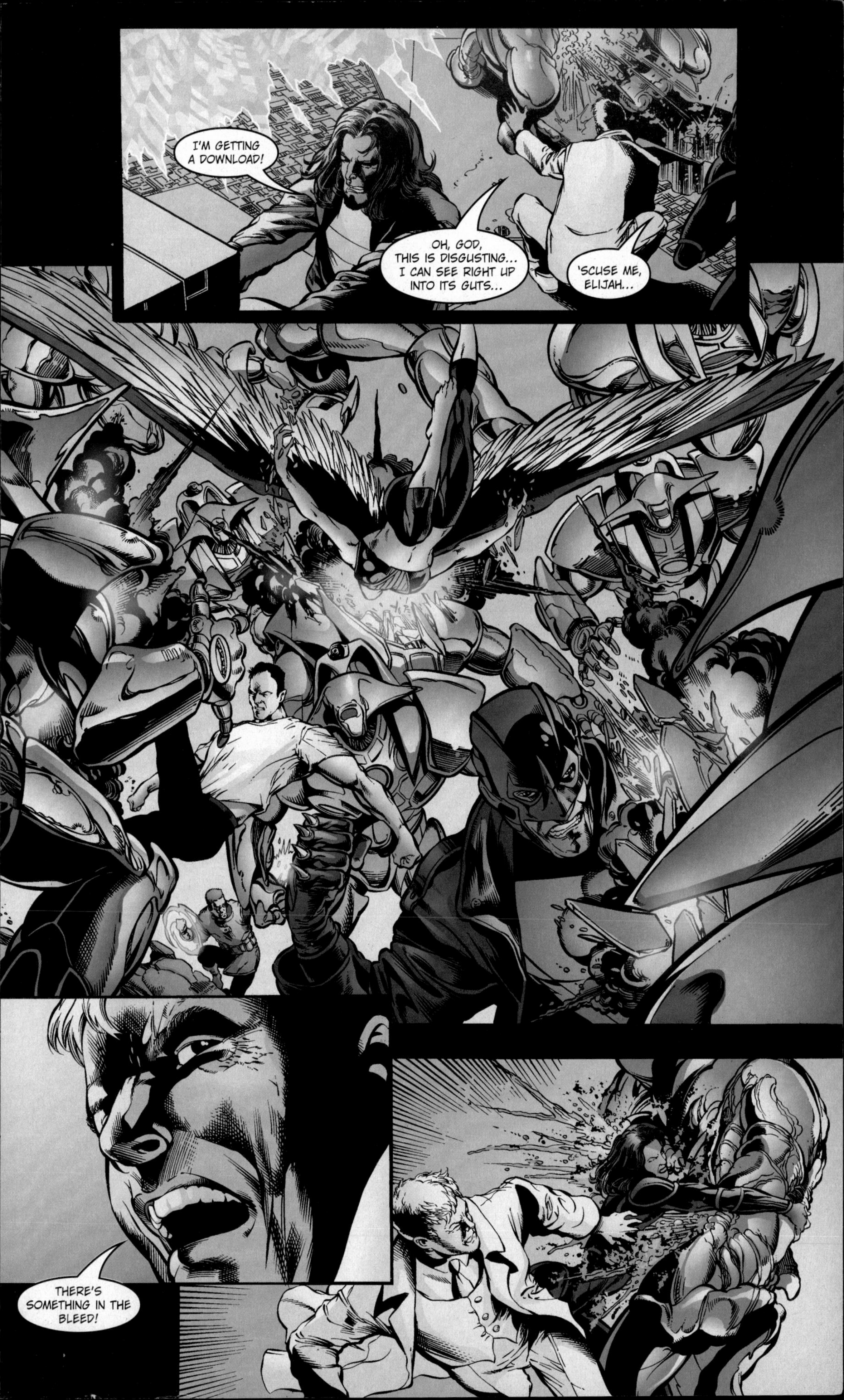
I'M GETTING A DOWNLOAD!
OH, GOD, THIS IS DISGUSTING... I CAN SEE RIGHT UP INTO ITS GUTS...
'SCUSE ME, ELIJAH...
THERE'S SOMETHING IN THE BLEED!

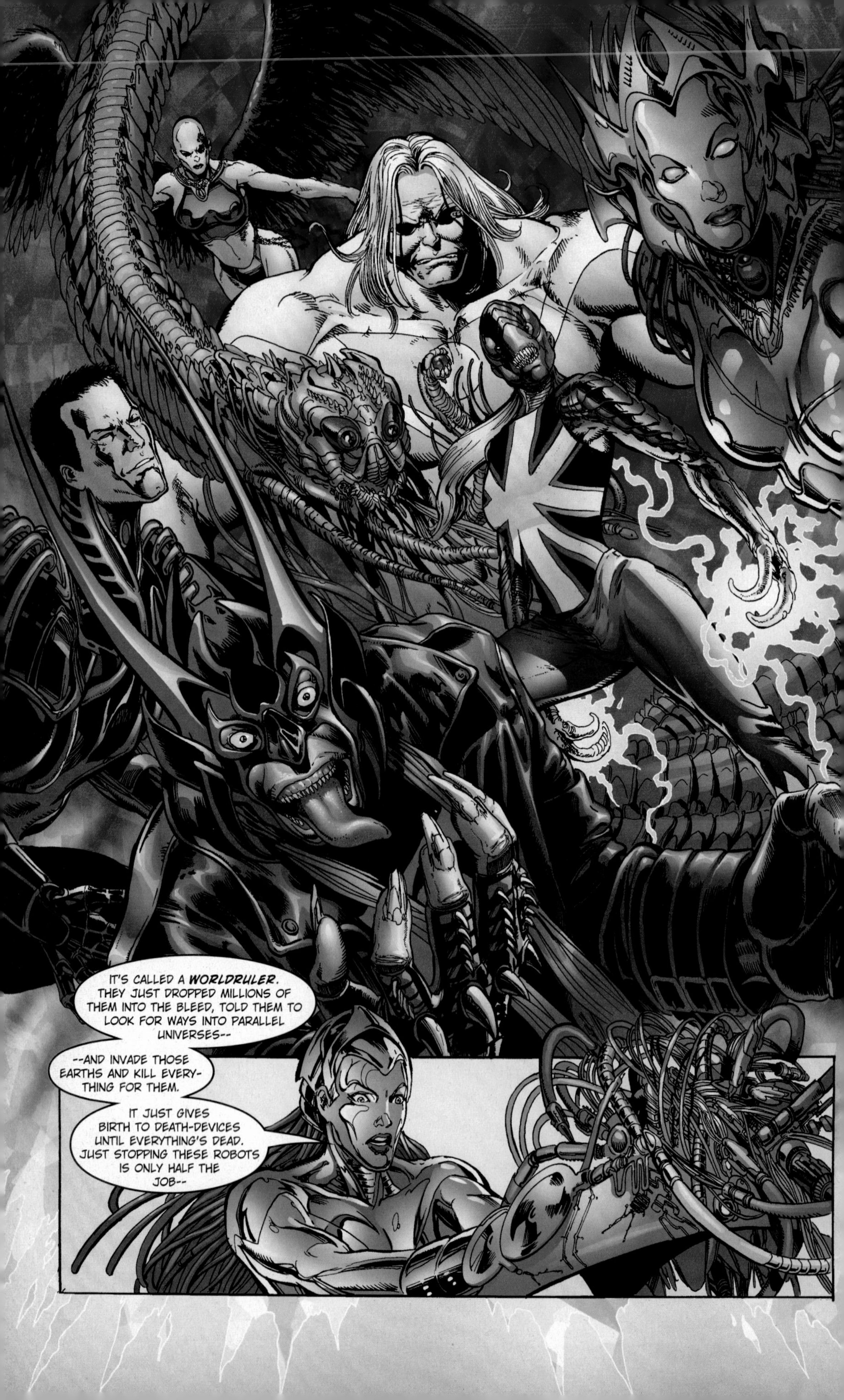
IT'S CALLED A WORLDRULER. THEY JUST DROPPED MILLIONS OF THEM INTO THE BLEED, TOLD THEM TO LOOK FOR WAYS INTO PARALLEL UNIVERSES--
--AND INVADE THOSE EARTHS AND KILL EVERYTHING FOR THEM.
IT JUST GIVES BIRTH TO DEATH-DEVICES UNTIL EVERYTHING'S DEAD. JUST STOPPING THESE ROBOTS IS ONLY HALF THE JOB--

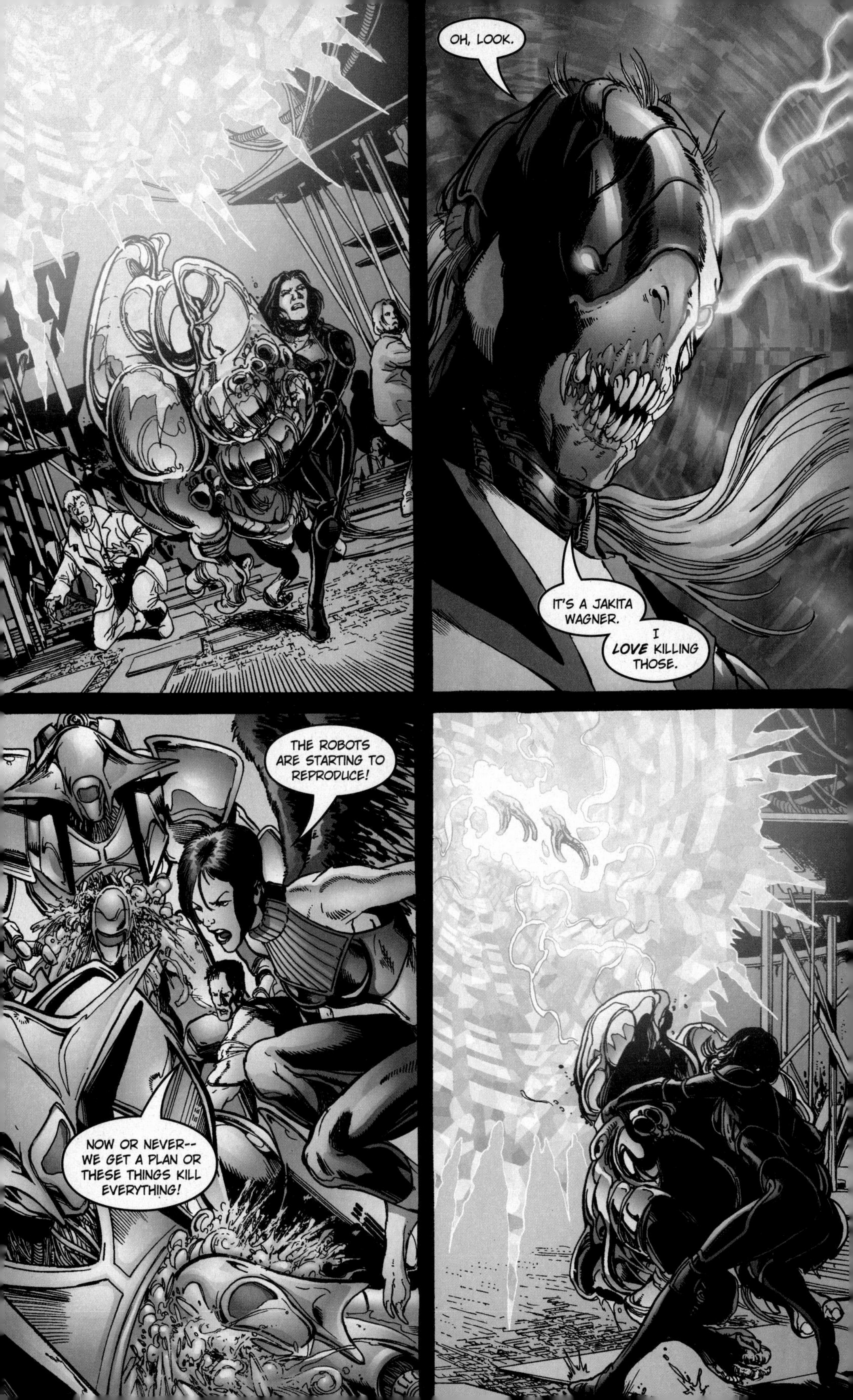
OH, LOOK.
IT'S A JAKITA WAGNER.
I *LOVE* KILLING THOSE.
THE ROBOTS ARE STARTING TO REPRODUCE!
NOW OR NEVER-- WE GET A PLAN OR THESE THINGS KILL EVERYTHING!

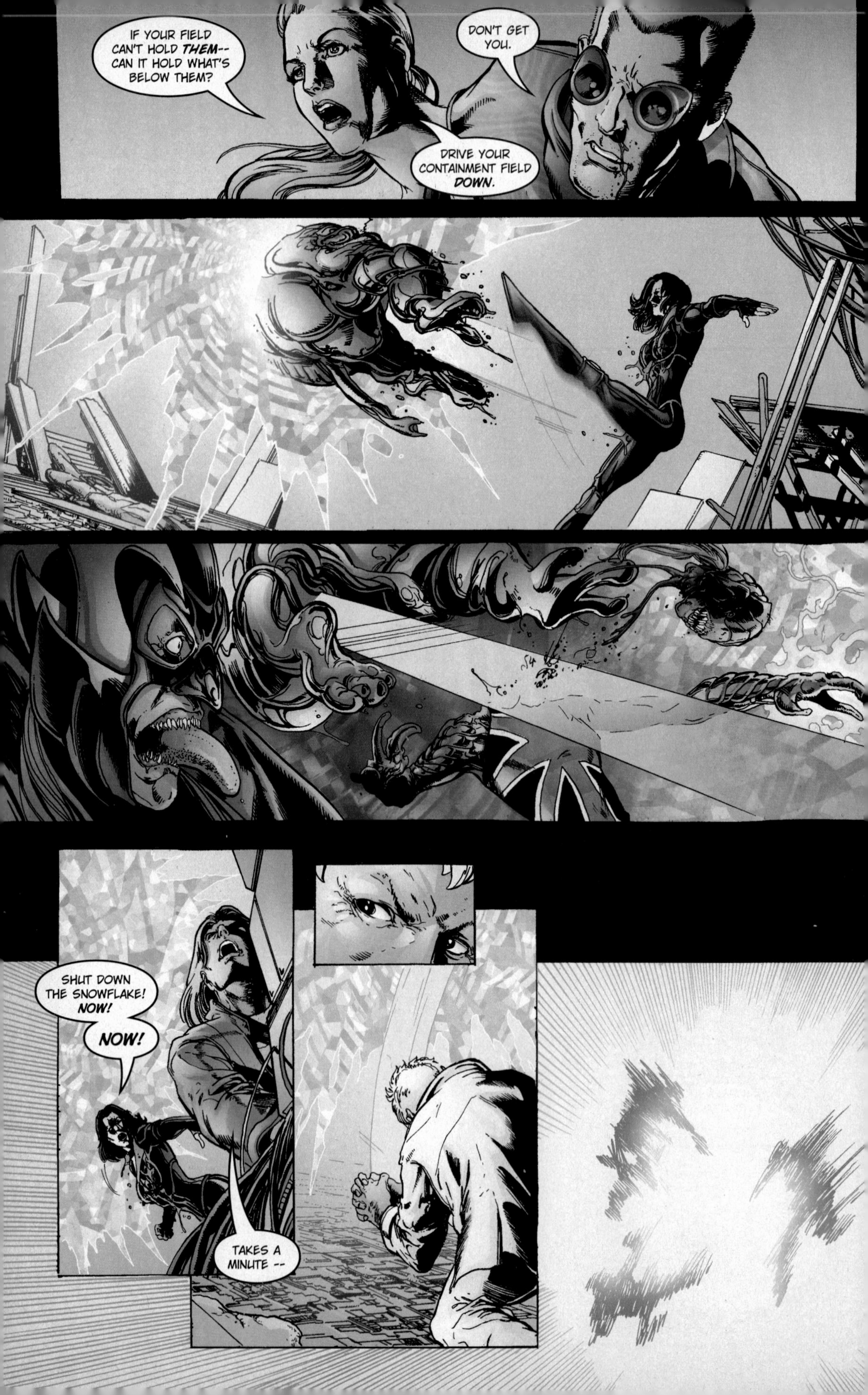
IF YOUR FIELD CAN'T HOLD **THEM**-- CAN IT HOLD WHAT'S BELOW THEM?
DON'T GET YOU.
DRIVE YOUR CONTAINMENT FIELD **DOWN.**
SHUT DOWN THE SNOWFLAKE! **NOW!**
NOW!
TAKES A MINUTE --

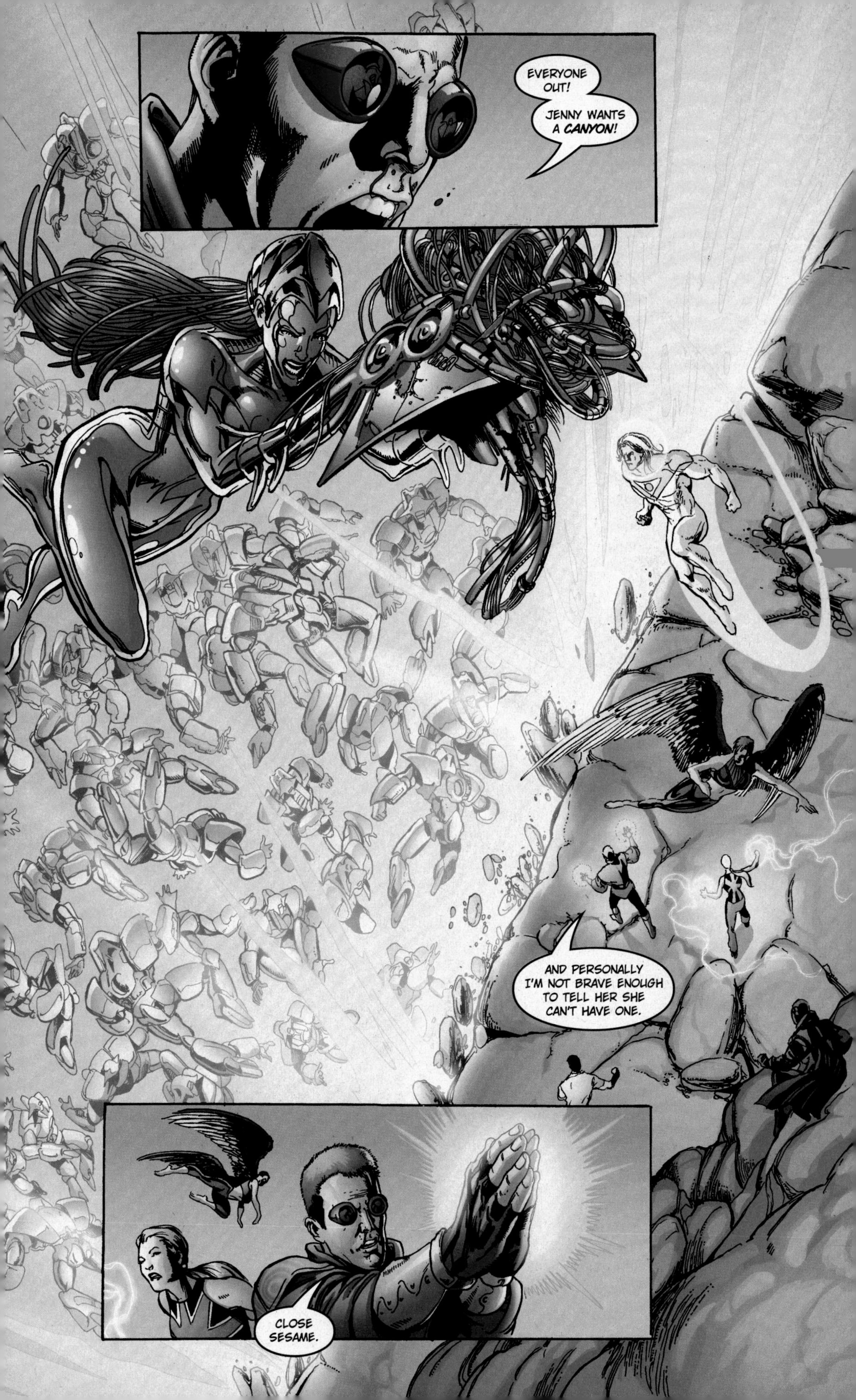
EVERYONE OUT!
JENNY WANTS A CANYON!
AND PERSONALLY I'M NOT BRAVE ENOUGH TO TELL HER SHE CAN'T HAVE ONE.
CLOSE SESAME.

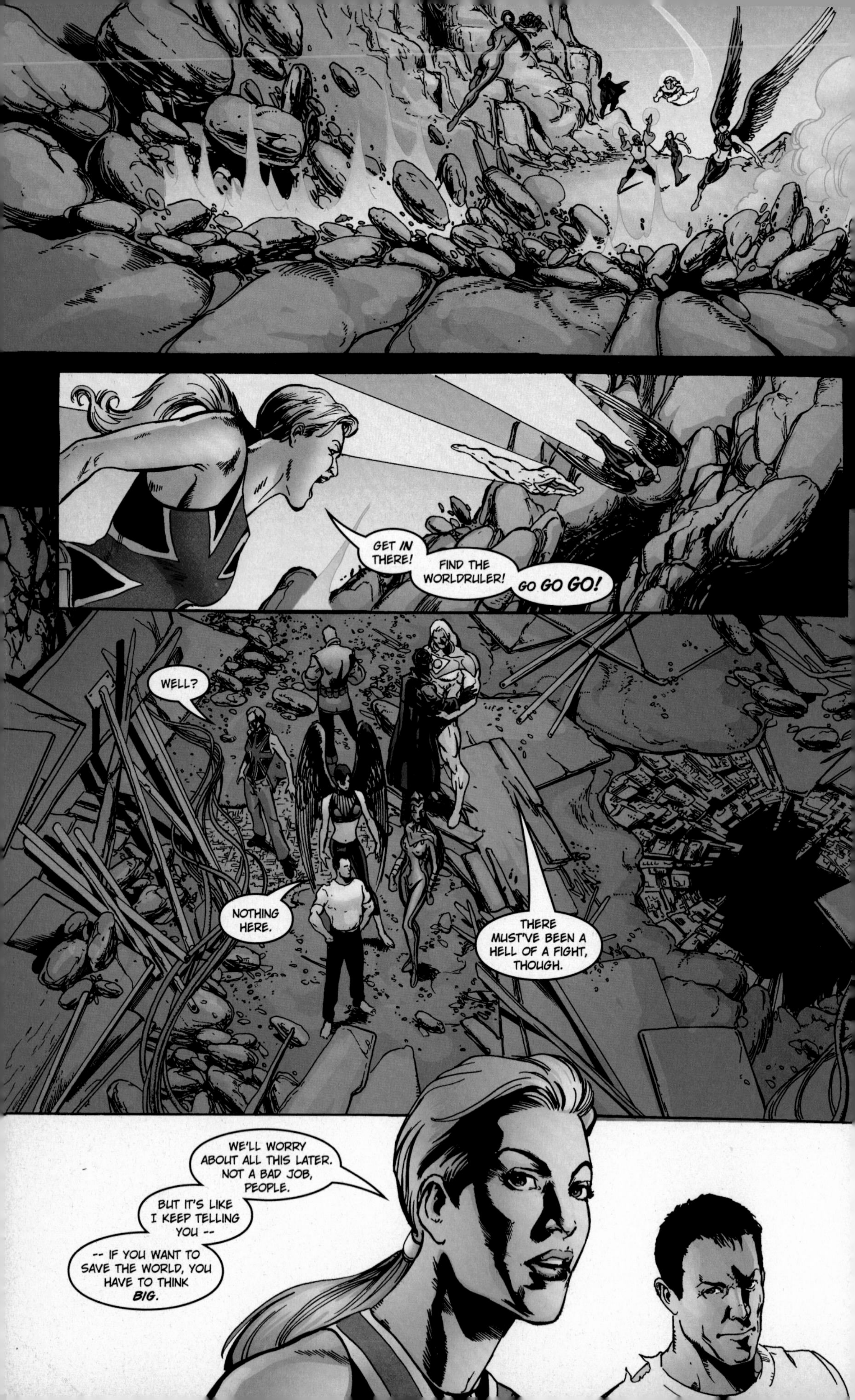
GET *IN* THERE!
FIND THE WORLDRULER!
GO GO *GO!*
WELL?
NOTHING HERE.
THERE MUST'VE BEEN A HELL OF A FIGHT, THOUGH.
WE'LL WORRY ABOUT ALL THIS LATER. NOT A BAD JOB, PEOPLE.
BUT IT'S LIKE I KEEP TELLING YOU --
-- IF YOU WANT TO SAVE THE WORLD, YOU HAVE TO THINK *BIG*.

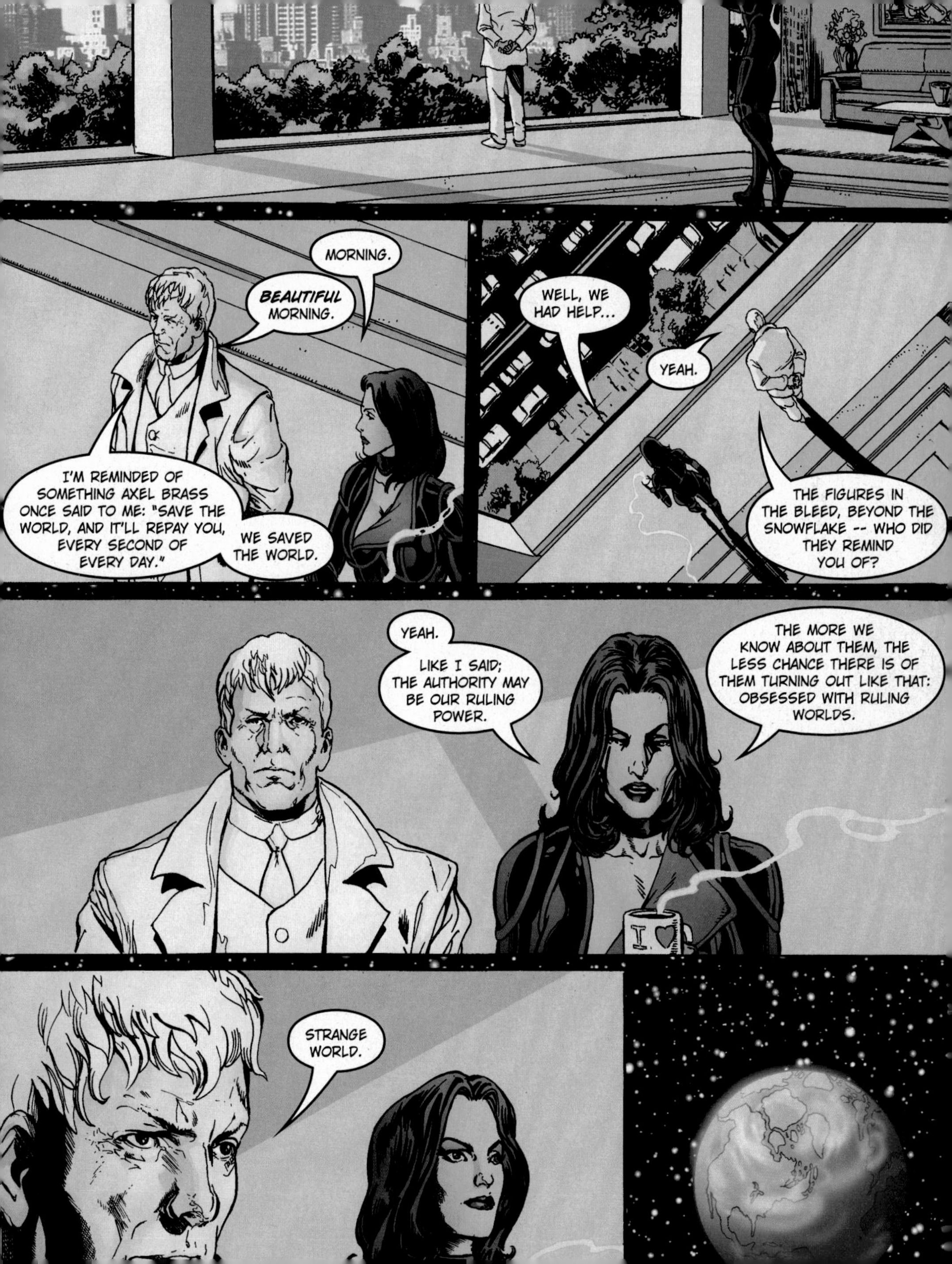
MORNING.
BEAUTIFUL MORNING.
I'M REMINDED OF SOMETHING AXEL BRASS ONCE SAID TO ME: "SAVE THE WORLD, AND IT'LL REPAY YOU, EVERY SECOND OF EVERY DAY."
WE SAVED THE WORLD.
WELL, WE HAD HELP...
YEAH.
THE FIGURES IN THE BLEED, BEYOND THE SNOWFLAKE -- WHO DID THEY REMIND YOU OF?
YEAH.
LIKE I SAID; THE AUTHORITY MAY BE OUR RULING POWER.
THE MORE WE KNOW ABOUT THEM, THE LESS CHANCE THERE IS OF THEM TURNING OUT LIKE THAT: OBSESSED WITH RULING WORLDS.
STRANGE WORLD.

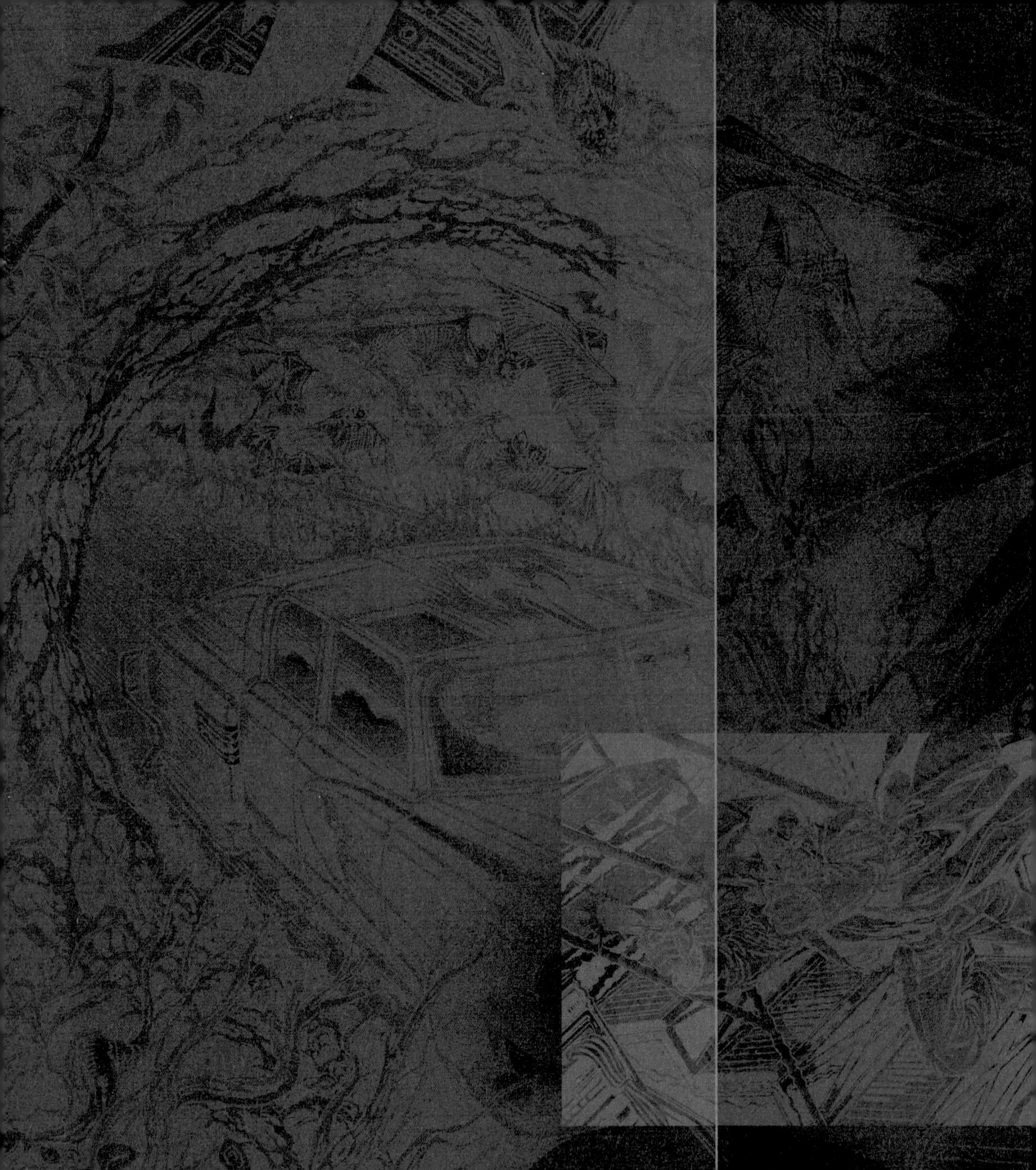

CHAPTER 2

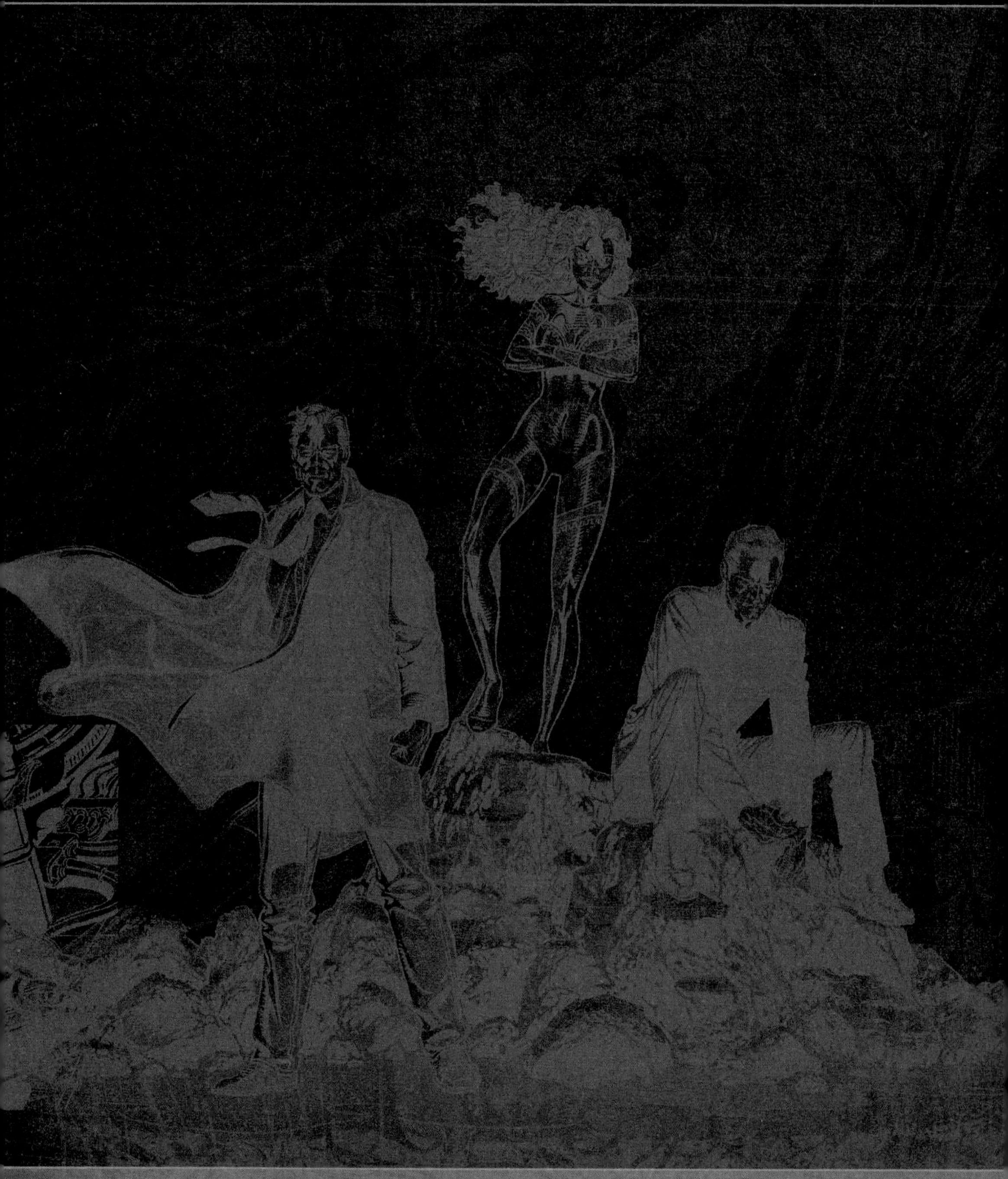

TERRA OCCULTA

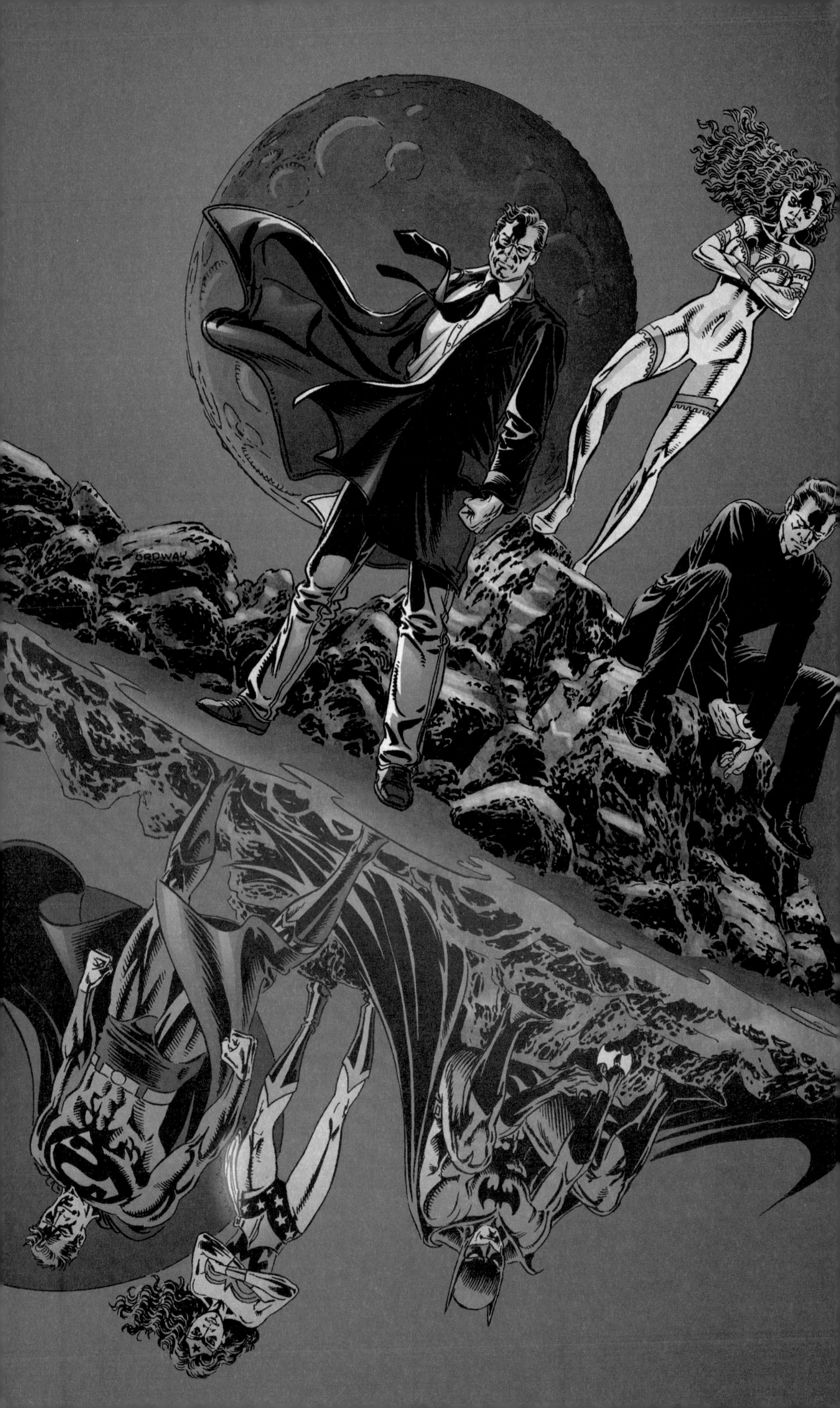
ORDWAY

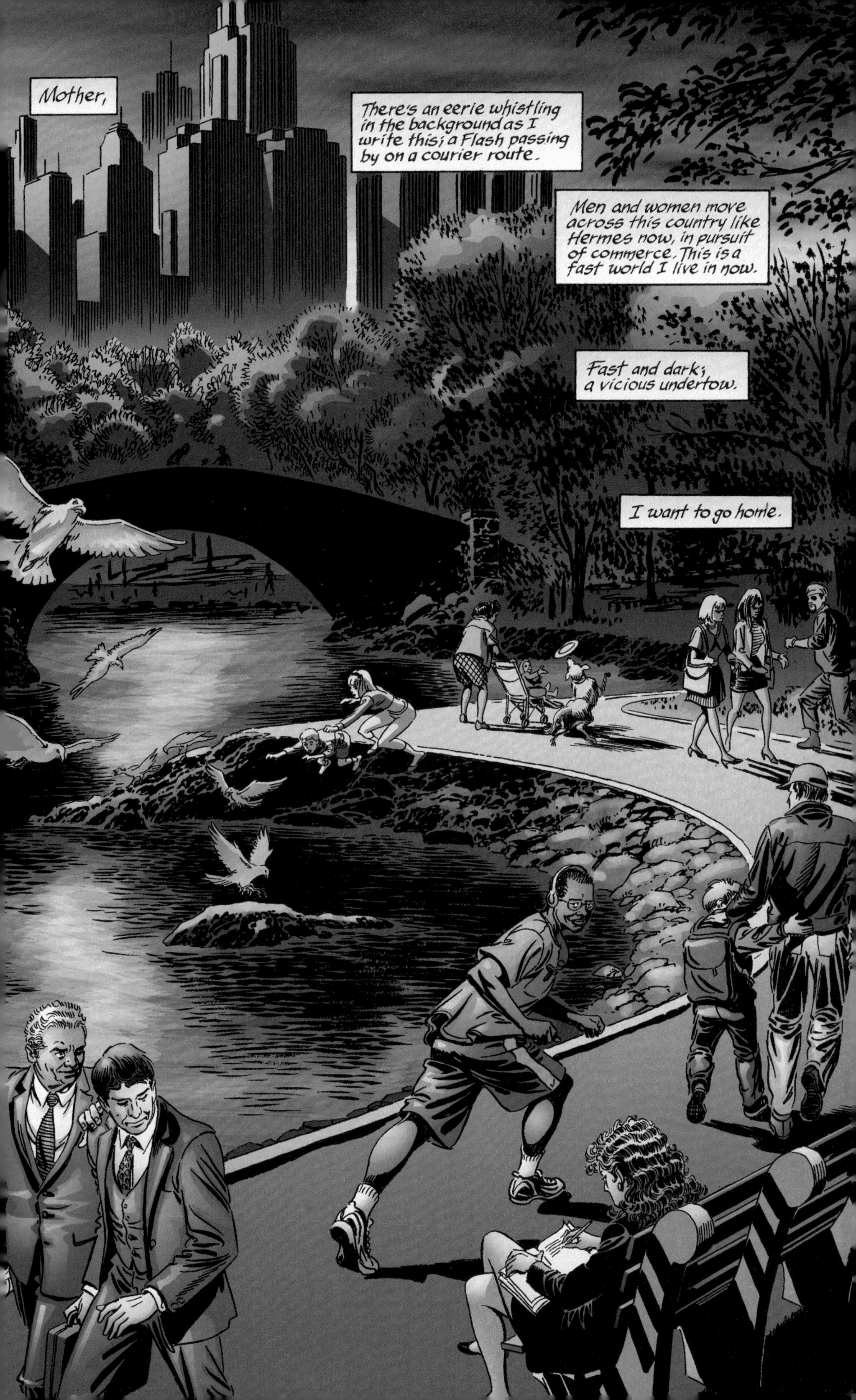
Mother,
There's an eerie whistling in the background as I write this; a Flash passing by on a courier route.
Men and women move across this country like Hermes now, in pursuit of commerce. This is a fast world I live in now.
Fast and dark; a vicious undertow.
I want to go home.

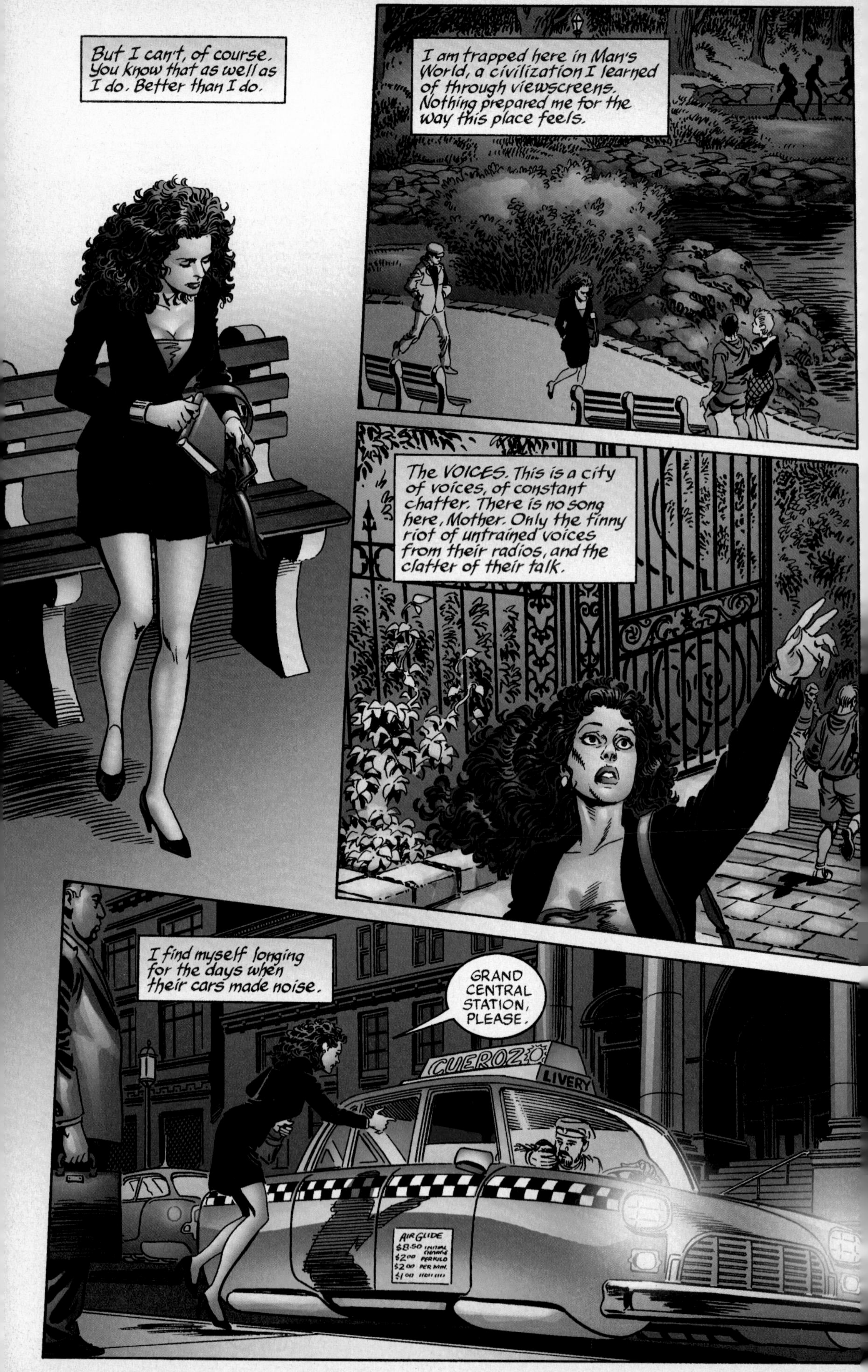
But I can't, of course. You know that as well as I do. Better than I do.
I am trapped here in Man's World, a civilization I learned of through viewscreens. Nothing prepared me for the way this place feels.
The VOICES. This is a city of voices, of constant chatter. There is no song here, Mother. Only the tinny riot of untrained voices from their radios, and the clatter of their talk.
I find myself longing for the days when their cars made noise.
GRAND CENTRAL STATION, PLEASE.
CUEROZ
LIVERY

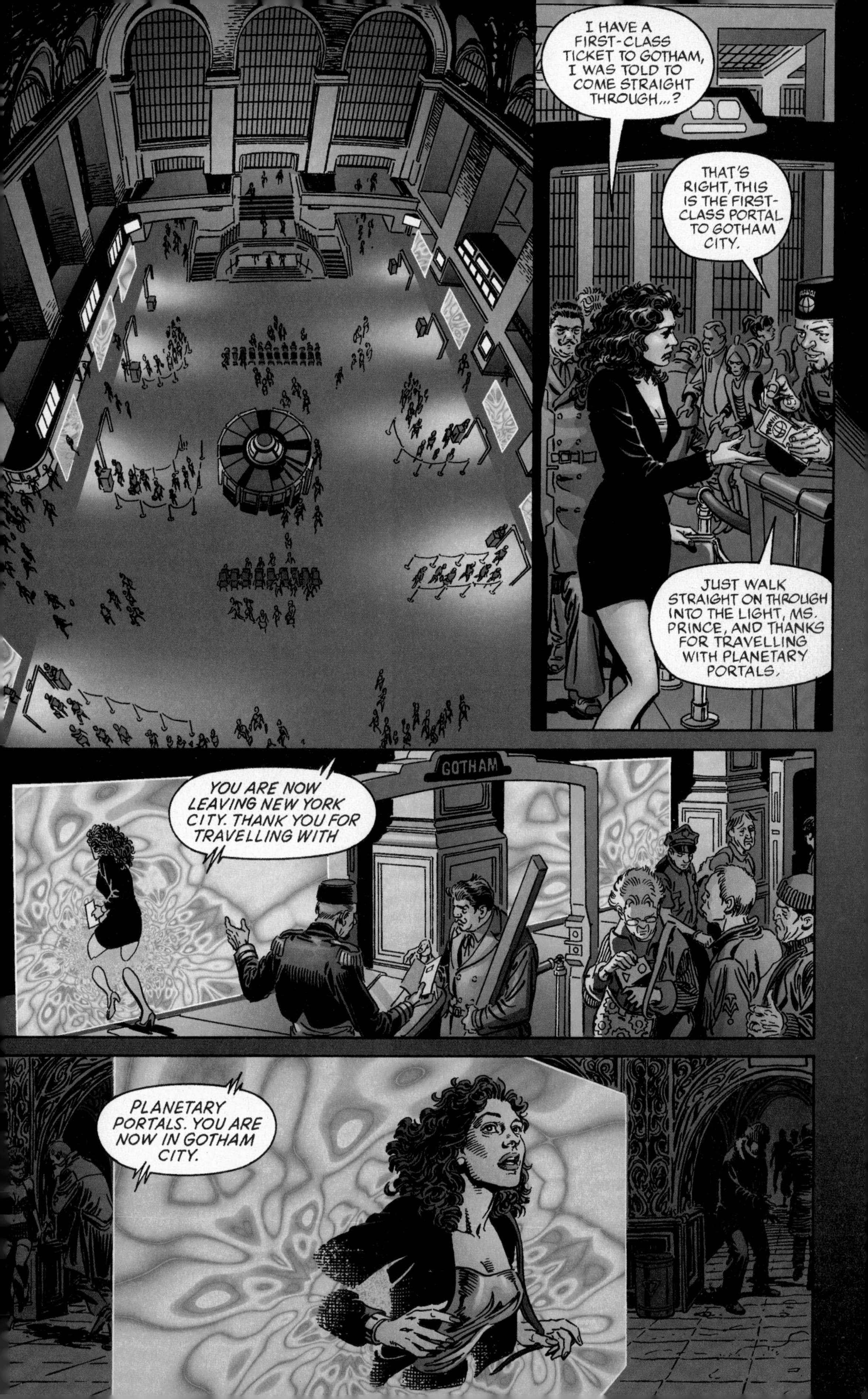
I HAVE A FIRST-CLASS TICKET TO GOTHAM, I WAS TOLD TO COME STRAIGHT THROUGH...?
THAT'S RIGHT, THIS IS THE FIRST-CLASS PORTAL TO GOTHAM CITY.
JUST WALK STRAIGHT ON THROUGH INTO THE LIGHT, MS. PRINCE, AND THANKS FOR TRAVELLING WITH PLANETARY PORTALS.
GOTHAM
YOU ARE NOW LEAVING NEW YORK CITY. THANK YOU FOR TRAVELLING WITH
PLANETARY PORTALS. YOU ARE NOW IN GOTHAM CITY.

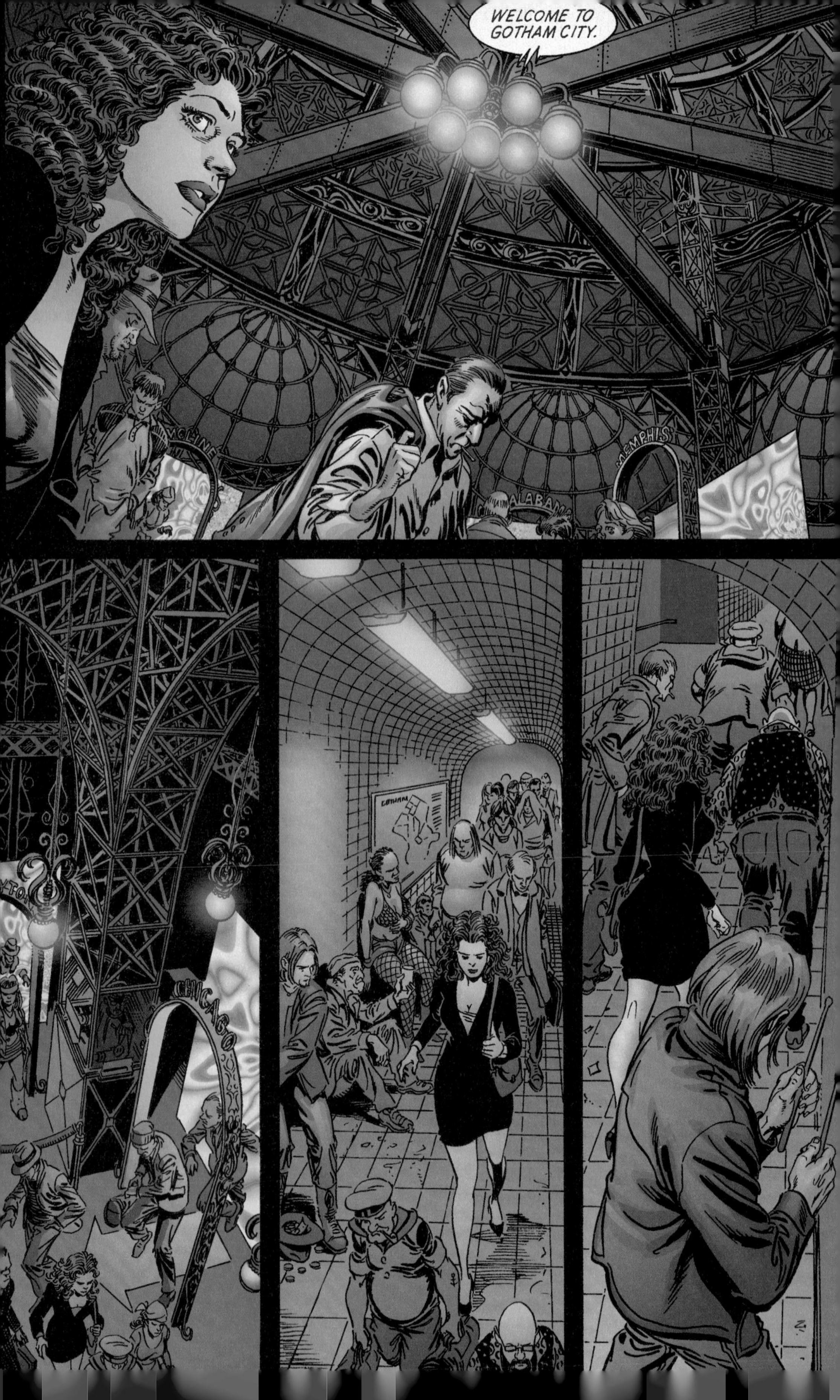
WELCOME TO GOTHAM CITY.
MEMPHIS
CHICAGO
GOTHAM

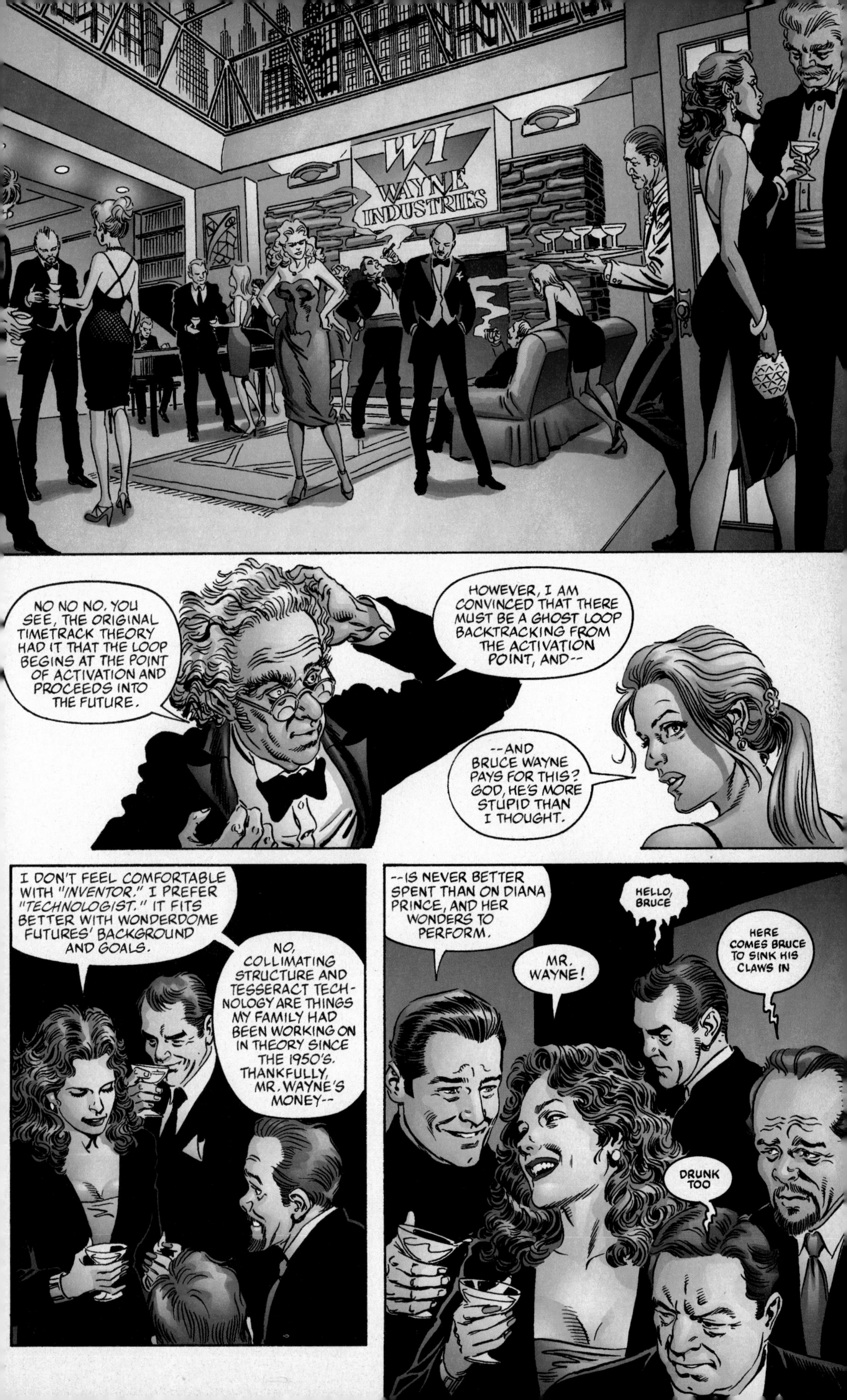
WI
WAYNE INDUSTRIES
NO NO NO. YOU SEE, THE ORIGINAL TIMETRACK THEORY HAD IT THAT THE LOOP BEGINS AT THE POINT OF ACTIVATION AND PROCEEDS INTO THE FUTURE.
HOWEVER, I AM CONVINCED THAT THERE MUST BE A GHOST LOOP BACKTRACKING FROM THE ACTIVATION POINT, AND--
--AND BRUCE WAYNE PAYS FOR THIS? GOD, HE'S MORE STUPID THAN I THOUGHT.
I DON'T FEEL COMFORTABLE WITH "INVENTOR." I PREFER "TECHNOLOGIST." IT FITS BETTER WITH WONDERDOME FUTURES' BACKGROUND AND GOALS.
NO, COLLIMATING STRUCTURE AND TESSERACT TECHNOLOGY ARE THINGS MY FAMILY HAD BEEN WORKING ON IN THEORY SINCE THE 1950'S. THANKFULLY, MR. WAYNE'S MONEY--
--IS NEVER BETTER SPENT THAN ON DIANA PRINCE, AND HER WONDERS TO PERFORM.
HELLO, BRUCE
MR. WAYNE!
HERE COMES BRUCE TO SINK HIS CLAWS IN
DRUNK TOO

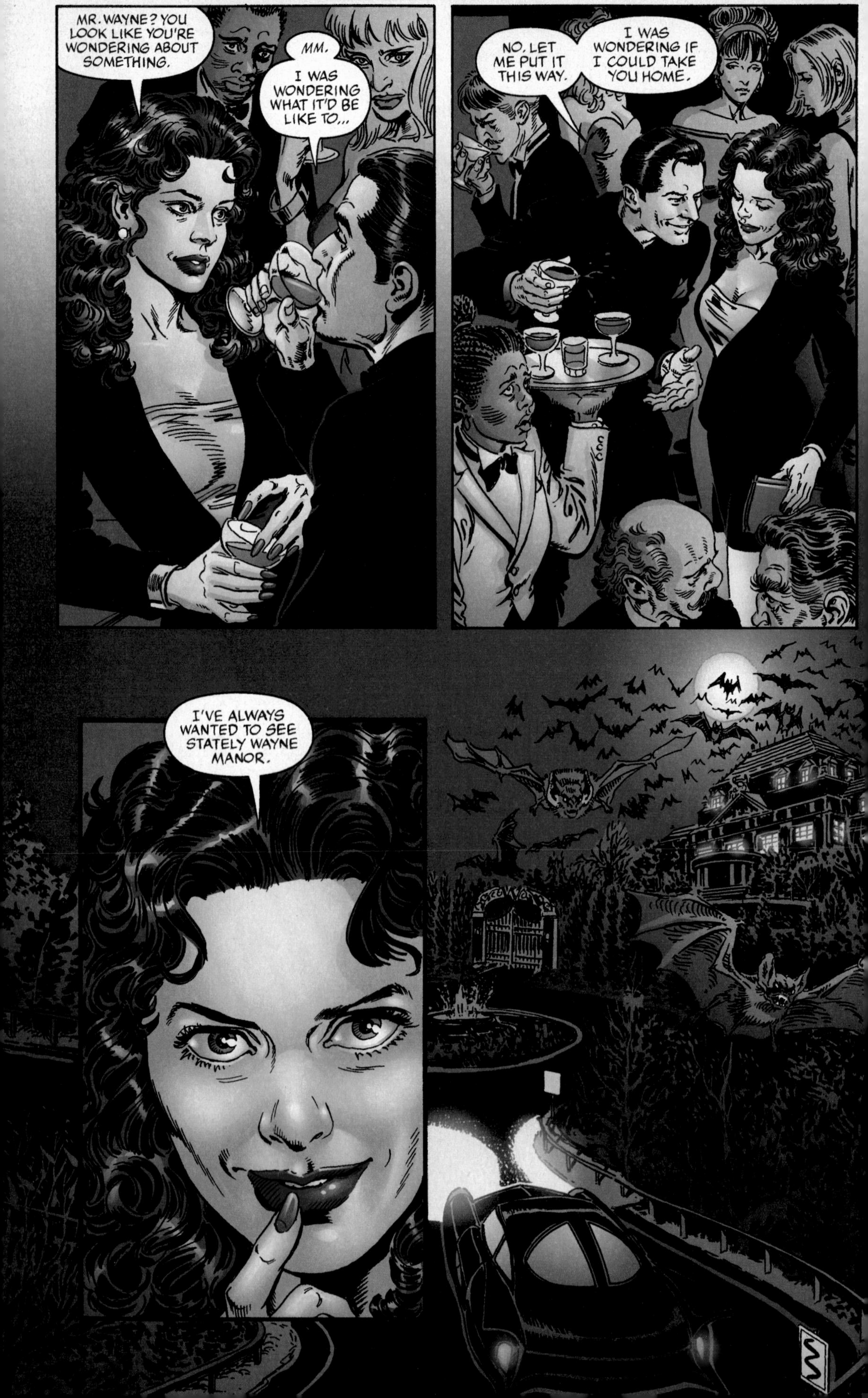
MR. WAYNE? YOU LOOK LIKE YOU'RE WONDERING ABOUT SOMETHING.
MM.
I WAS WONDERING WHAT IT'D BE LIKE TO...
NO. LET ME PUT IT THIS WAY.
I WAS WONDERING IF I COULD TAKE YOU HOME.
I'VE ALWAYS WANTED TO SEE STATELY WAYNE MANOR.

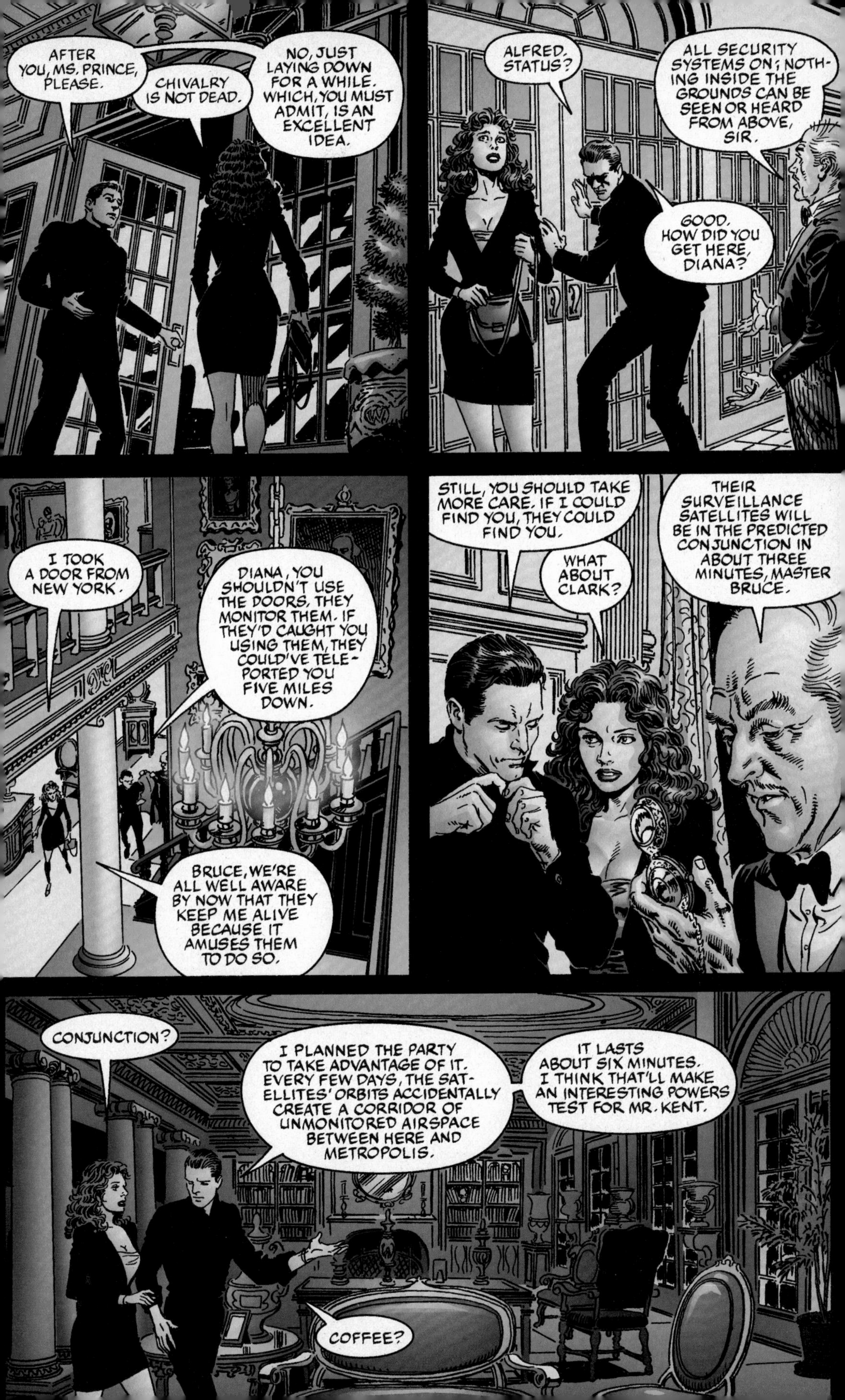
AFTER YOU, MS. PRINCE, PLEASE.
CHIVALRY IS NOT DEAD.
NO, JUST LAYING DOWN FOR A WHILE. WHICH, YOU MUST ADMIT, IS AN EXCELLENT IDEA.
ALFRED. STATUS?
ALL SECURITY SYSTEMS ON; NOTHING INSIDE THE GROUNDS CAN BE SEEN OR HEARD FROM ABOVE, SIR.
GOOD. HOW DID YOU GET HERE, DIANA?
I TOOK A DOOR FROM NEW YORK.
DIANA, YOU SHOULDN'T USE THE DOORS, THEY MONITOR THEM. IF THEY'D CAUGHT YOU USING THEM, THEY COULD'VE TELEPORTED YOU FIVE MILES DOWN.
BRUCE, WE'RE ALL WELL AWARE BY NOW THAT THEY KEEP ME ALIVE BECAUSE IT AMUSES THEM TO DO SO.
STILL, YOU SHOULD TAKE MORE CARE. IF I COULD FIND YOU, THEY COULD FIND YOU.
WHAT ABOUT CLARK?
THEIR SURVEILLANCE SATELLITES WILL BE IN THE PREDICTED CONJUNCTION IN ABOUT THREE MINUTES, MASTER BRUCE.
CONJUNCTION?
I PLANNED THE PARTY TO TAKE ADVANTAGE OF IT. EVERY FEW DAYS, THE SATELLITES' ORBITS ACCIDENTALLY CREATE A CORRIDOR OF UNMONITORED AIRSPACE BETWEEN HERE AND METROPOLIS.
IT LASTS ABOUT SIX MINUTES. I THINK THAT'LL MAKE AN INTERESTING POWERS TEST FOR MR. KENT.
COFFEE?

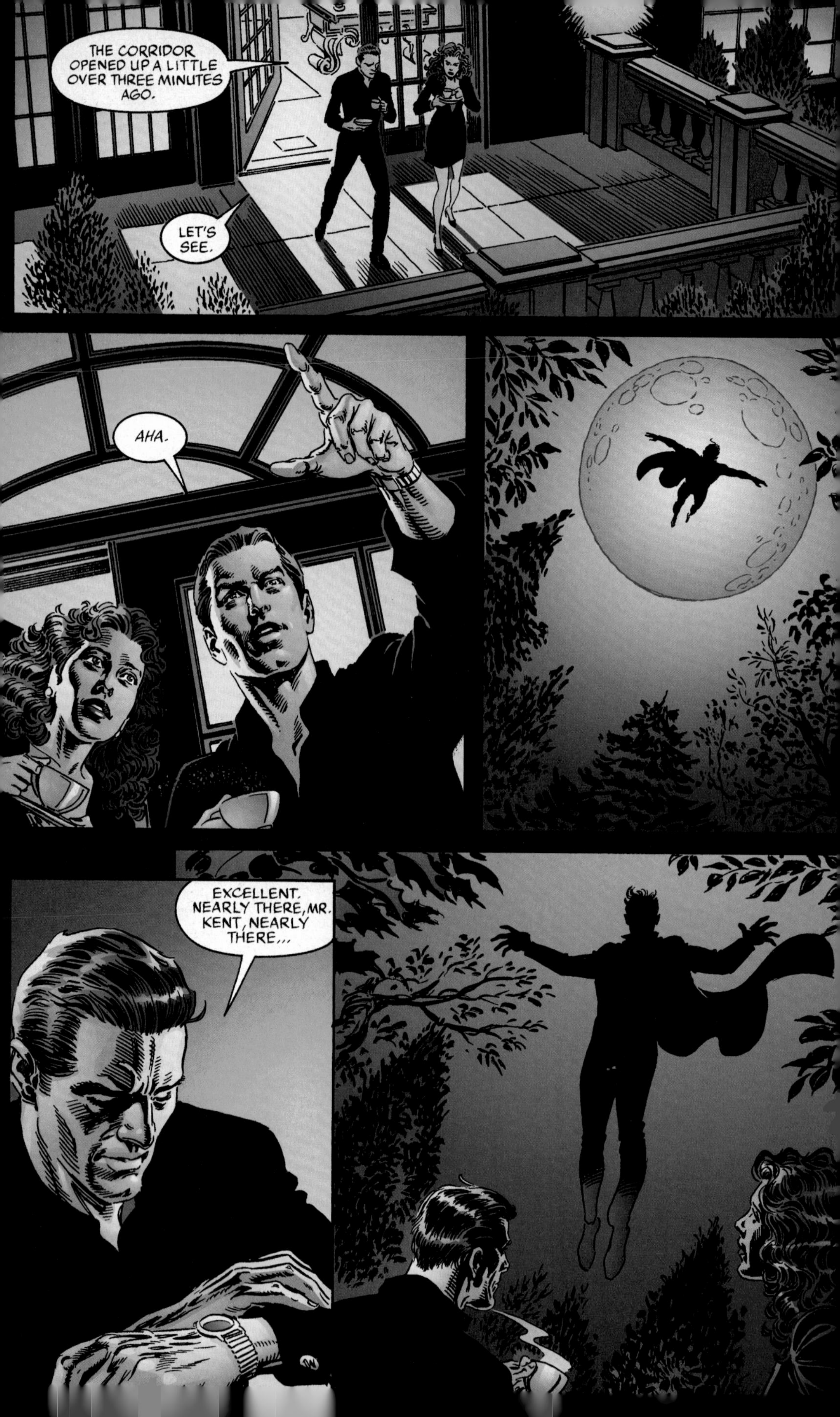
THE CORRIDOR OPENED UP A LITTLE OVER THREE MINUTES AGO.
LET'S SEE.
AHA.
EXCELLENT. NEARLY THERE, MR. KENT, NEARLY THERE...

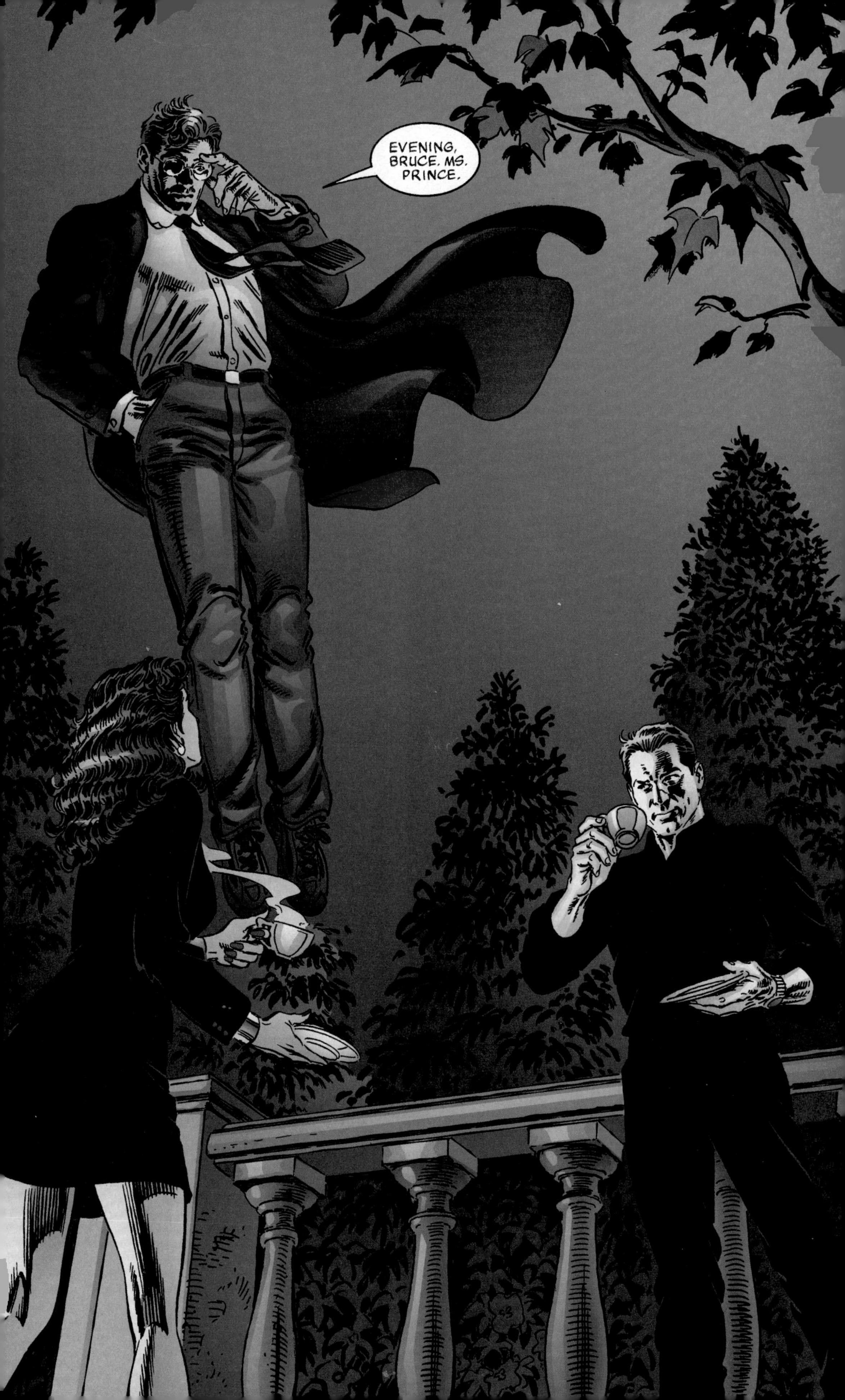
EVENING, BRUCE. MS. PRINCE.

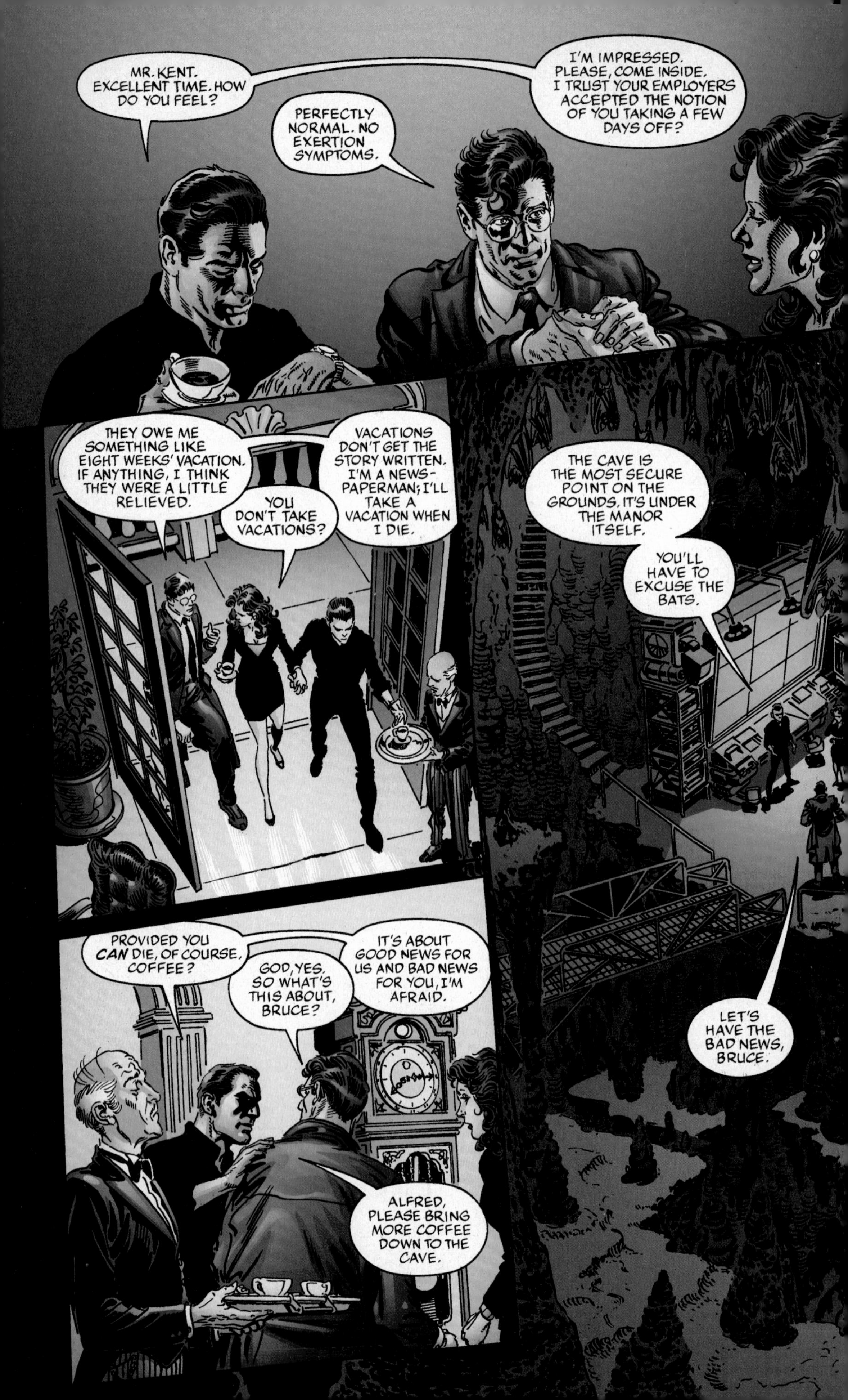
MR. KENT. EXCELLENT TIME. HOW DO YOU FEEL?
PERFECTLY NORMAL. NO EXERTION SYMPTOMS.
I'M IMPRESSED. PLEASE, COME INSIDE. I TRUST YOUR EMPLOYERS ACCEPTED THE NOTION OF YOU TAKING A FEW DAYS OFF?
THEY OWE ME SOMETHING LIKE EIGHT WEEKS' VACATION. IF ANYTHING, I THINK THEY WERE A LITTLE RELIEVED.
YOU DON'T TAKE VACATIONS?
VACATIONS DON'T GET THE STORY WRITTEN. I'M A NEWS-PAPERMAN; I'LL TAKE A VACATION WHEN I DIE.
PROVIDED YOU CAN DIE, OF COURSE. COFFEE?
GOD, YES. SO WHAT'S THIS ABOUT, BRUCE?
IT'S ABOUT GOOD NEWS FOR US AND BAD NEWS FOR YOU, I'M AFRAID.
ALFRED, PLEASE BRING MORE COFFEE DOWN TO THE CAVE.
THE CAVE IS THE MOST SECURE POINT ON THE GROUNDS. IT'S UNDER THE MANOR ITSELF.
YOU'LL HAVE TO EXCUSE THE BATS.
LET'S HAVE THE BAD NEWS, BRUCE.

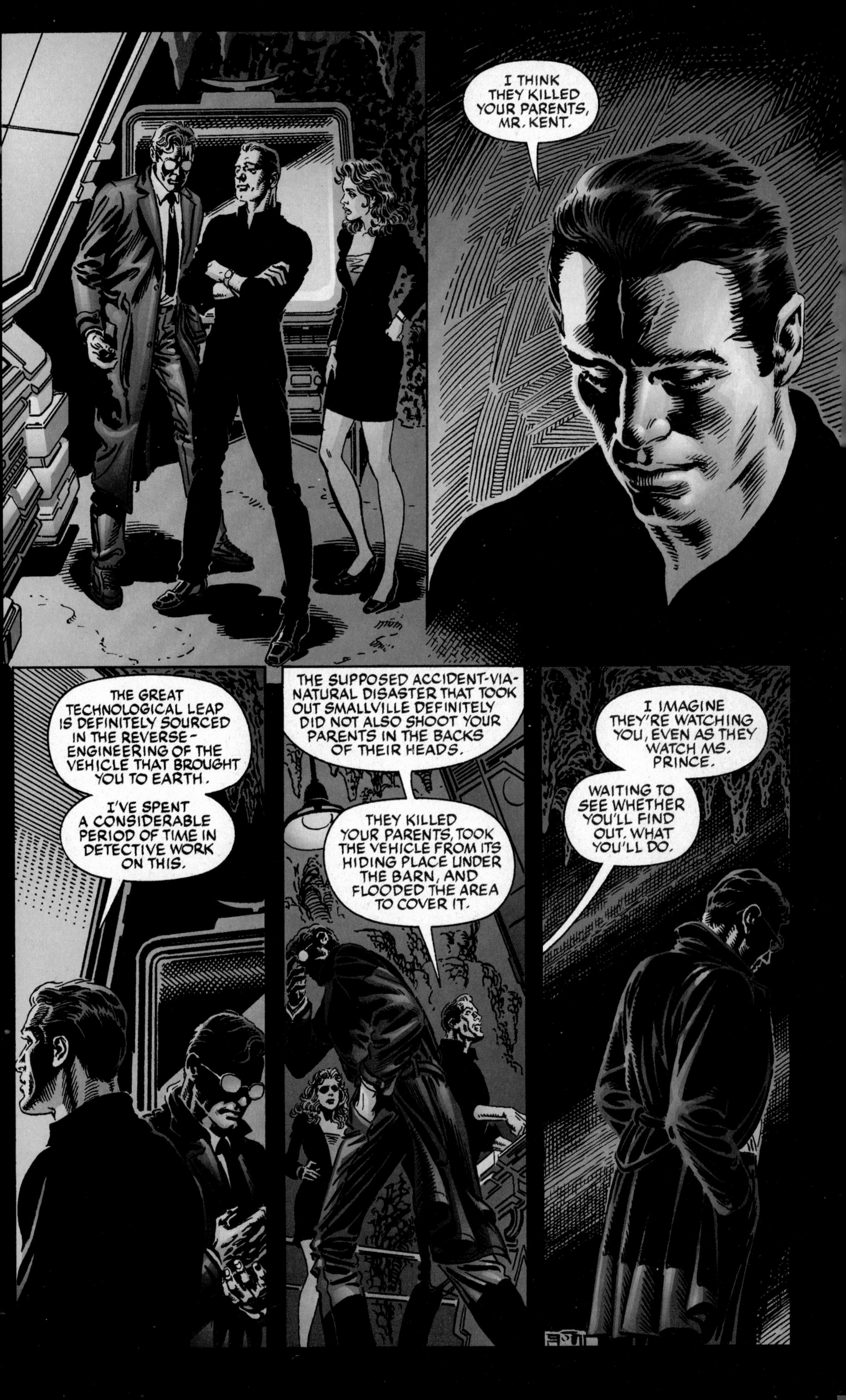
I THINK THEY KILLED YOUR PARENTS, MR. KENT.
THE GREAT TECHNOLOGICAL LEAP IS DEFINITELY SOURCED IN THE REVERSE-ENGINEERING OF THE VEHICLE THAT BROUGHT YOU TO EARTH.
I'VE SPENT A CONSIDERABLE PERIOD OF TIME IN DETECTIVE WORK ON THIS.
THE SUPPOSED ACCIDENT-VIA-NATURAL DISASTER THAT TOOK OUT SMALLVILLE DEFINITELY DID NOT ALSO SHOOT YOUR PARENTS IN THE BACKS OF THEIR HEADS.
THEY KILLED YOUR PARENTS, TOOK THE VEHICLE FROM ITS HIDING PLACE UNDER THE BARN, AND FLOODED THE AREA TO COVER IT.
I IMAGINE THEY'RE WATCHING YOU, EVEN AS THEY WATCH MS. PRINCE.
WAITING TO SEE WHETHER YOU'LL FIND OUT. WHAT YOU'LL DO.

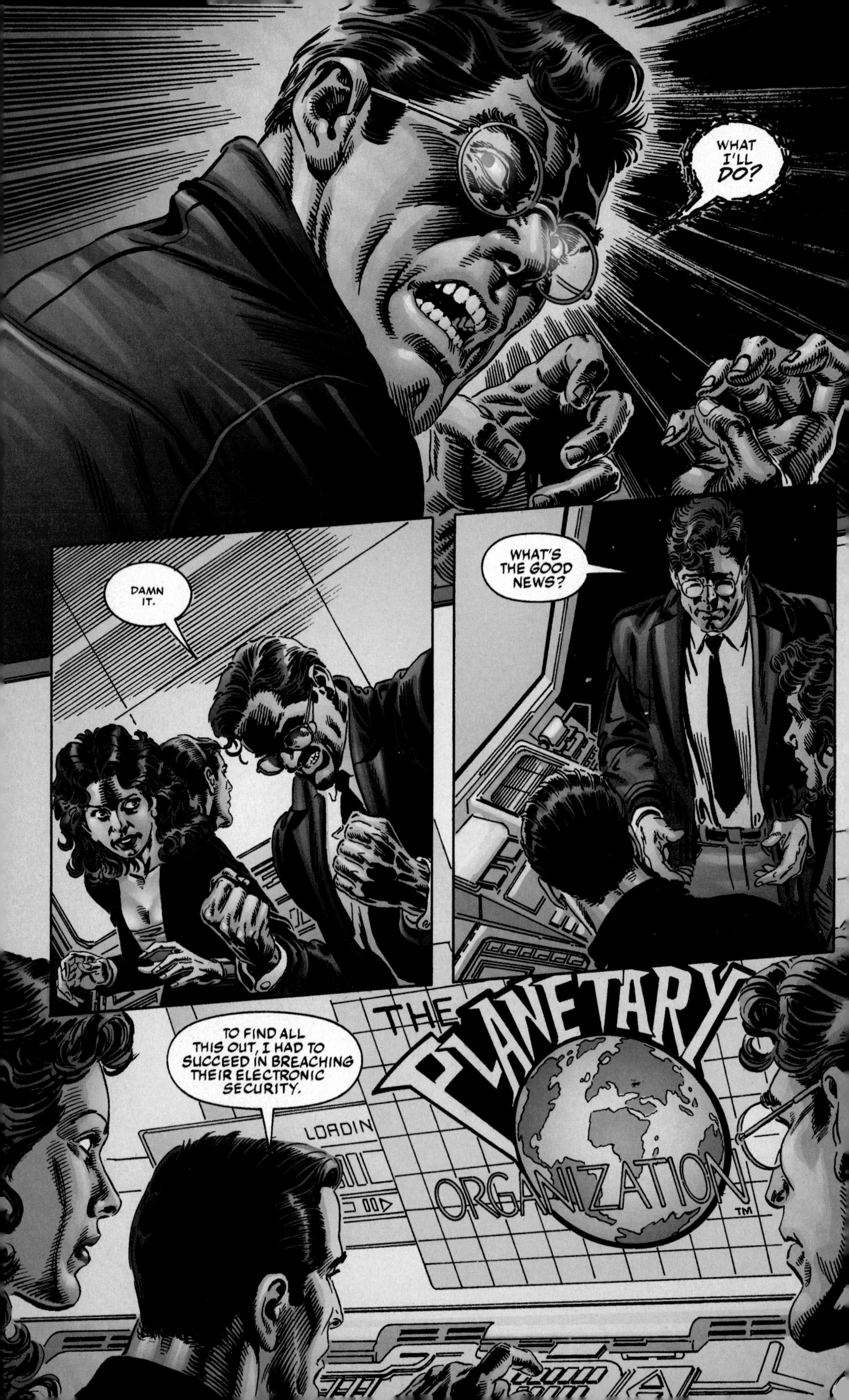
WHAT I'LL DO?
DAMN IT.
WHAT'S THE GOOD NEWS?
TO FIND ALL THIS OUT, I HAD TO SUCCEED IN BREACHING THEIR ELECTRONIC SECURITY.
THE PLANETARY ORGANIZATION™
LOADIN

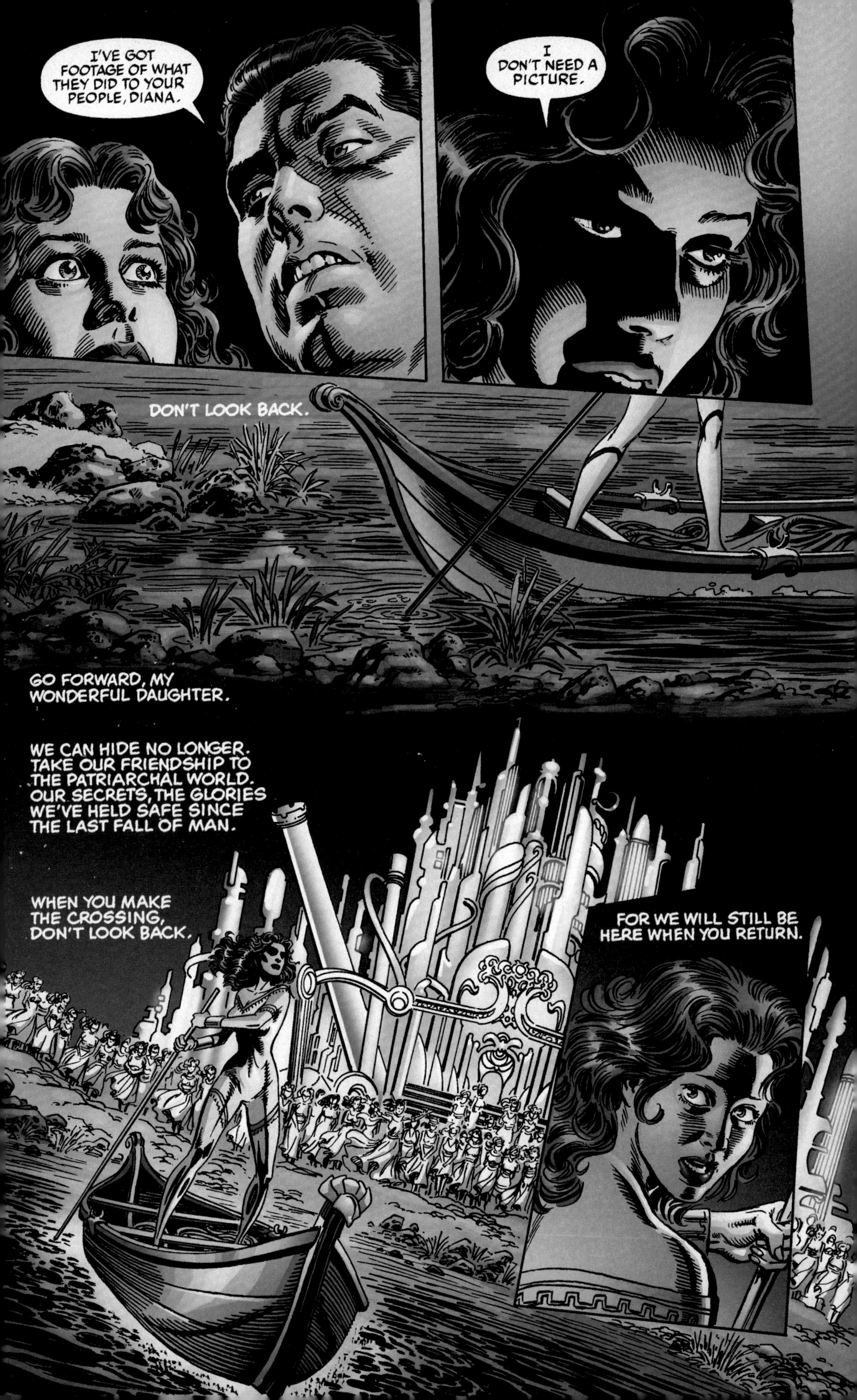
I'VE GOT FOOTAGE OF WHAT THEY DID TO YOUR PEOPLE, DIANA.
I DON'T NEED A PICTURE.
DON'T LOOK BACK.
GO FORWARD, MY WONDERFUL DAUGHTER.
WE CAN HIDE NO LONGER. TAKE OUR FRIENDSHIP TO THE PATRIARCHAL WORLD. OUR SECRETS, THE GLORIES WE'VE HELD SAFE SINCE THE LAST FALL OF MAN.
WHEN YOU MAKE THE CROSSING, DON'T LOOK BACK.
FOR WE WILL STILL BE HERE WHEN YOU RETURN.

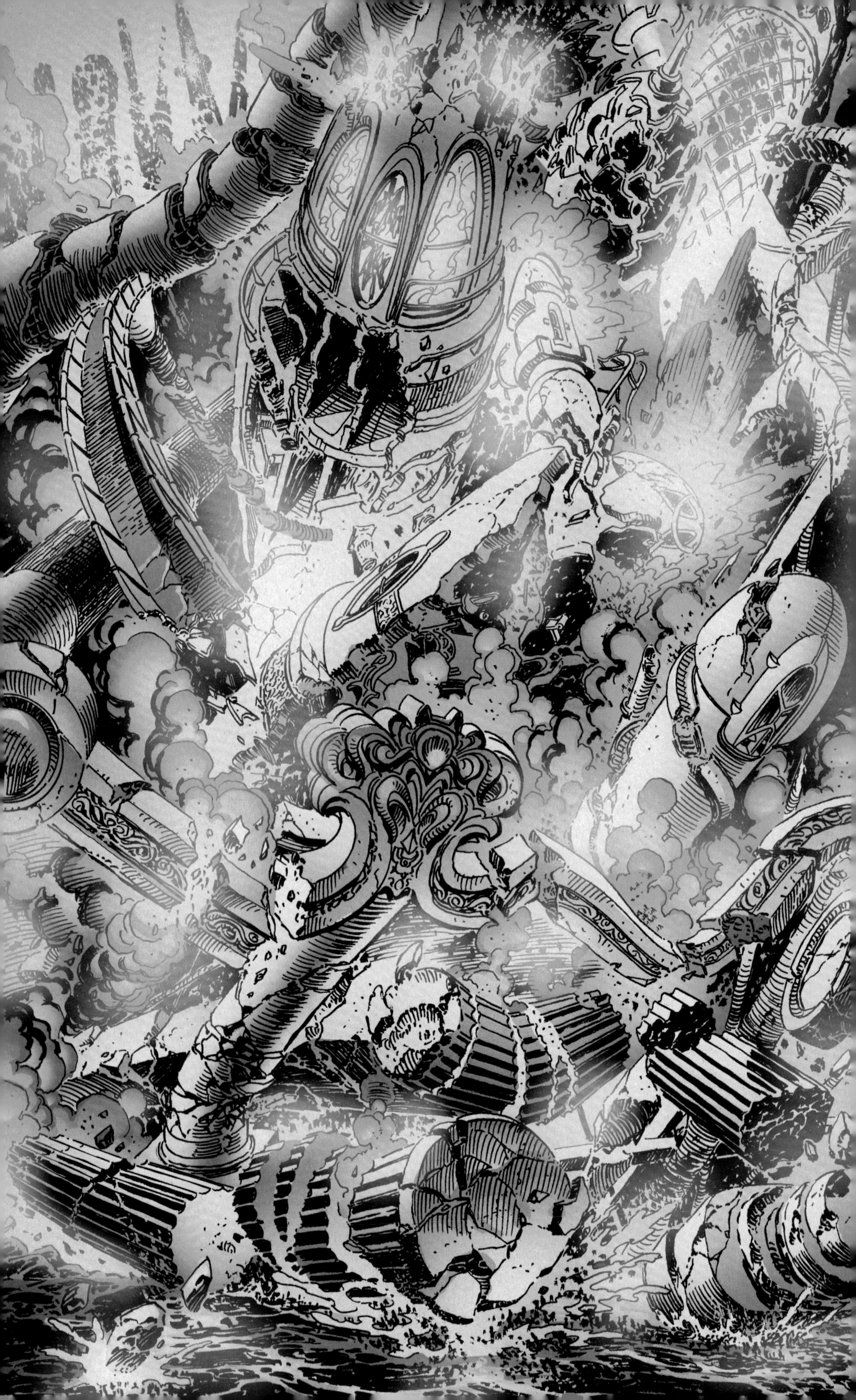

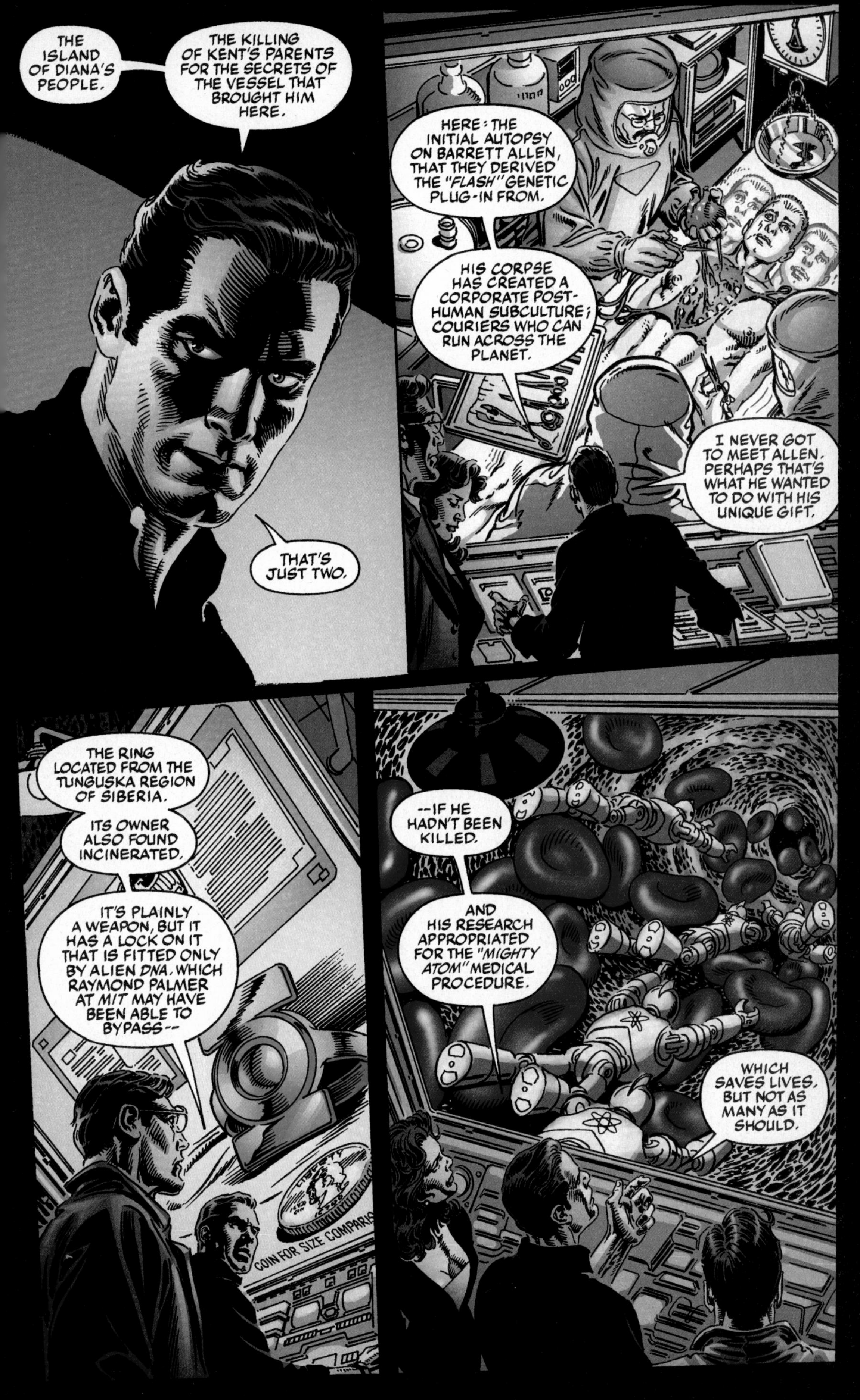
THE ISLAND OF DIANA'S PEOPLE.
THE KILLING OF KENT'S PARENTS FOR THE SECRETS OF THE VESSEL THAT BROUGHT HIM HERE.
THAT'S JUST TWO.
HERE: THE INITIAL AUTOPSY ON BARRETT ALLEN, THAT THEY DERIVED THE "FLASH" GENETIC PLUG-IN FROM.
HIS CORPSE HAS CREATED A CORPORATE POST-HUMAN SUBCULTURE; COURIERS WHO CAN RUN ACROSS THE PLANET.
I NEVER GOT TO MEET ALLEN. PERHAPS THAT'S WHAT HE WANTED TO DO WITH HIS UNIQUE GIFT.
THE RING LOCATED FROM THE TUNGUSKA REGION OF SIBERIA.
ITS OWNER ALSO FOUND INCINERATED.
IT'S PLAINLY A WEAPON, BUT IT HAS A LOCK ON IT THAT IS FITTED ONLY BY ALIEN DNA. WHICH RAYMOND PALMER AT MIT MAY HAVE BEEN ABLE TO BYPASS--
COIN FOR SIZE COMPARIS
--IF HE HADN'T BEEN KILLED.
AND HIS RESEARCH APPROPRIATED FOR THE "MIGHTY ATOM" MEDICAL PROCEDURE.
WHICH SAVES LIVES, BUT NOT AS MANY AS IT SHOULD.

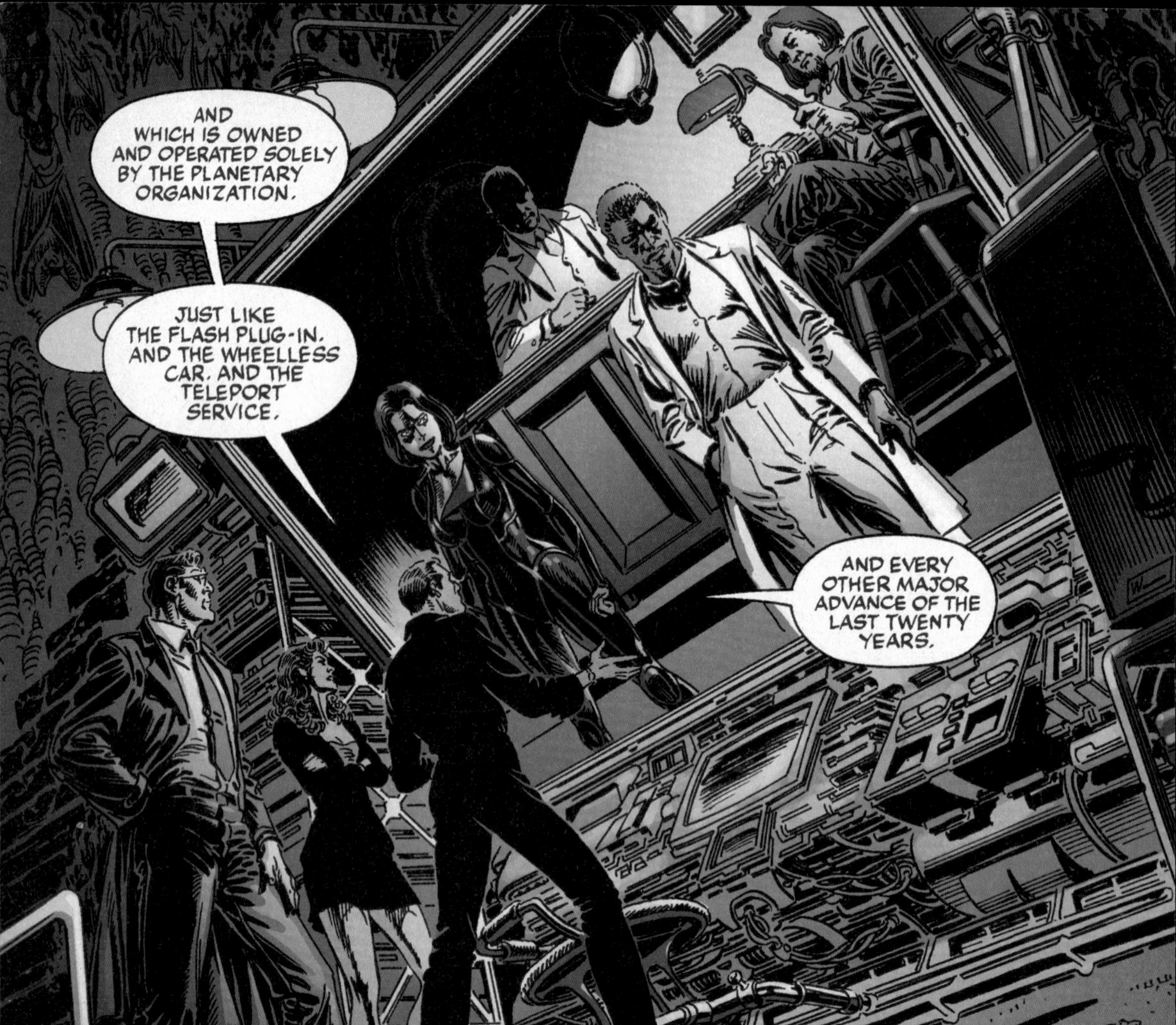
AND WHICH IS OWNED AND OPERATED SOLELY BY THE PLANETARY ORGANIZATION.
JUST LIKE THE FLASH PLUG-IN. AND THE WHEELLESS CAR. AND THE TELEPORT SERVICE.
AND EVERY OTHER MAJOR ADVANCE OF THE LAST TWENTY YEARS.
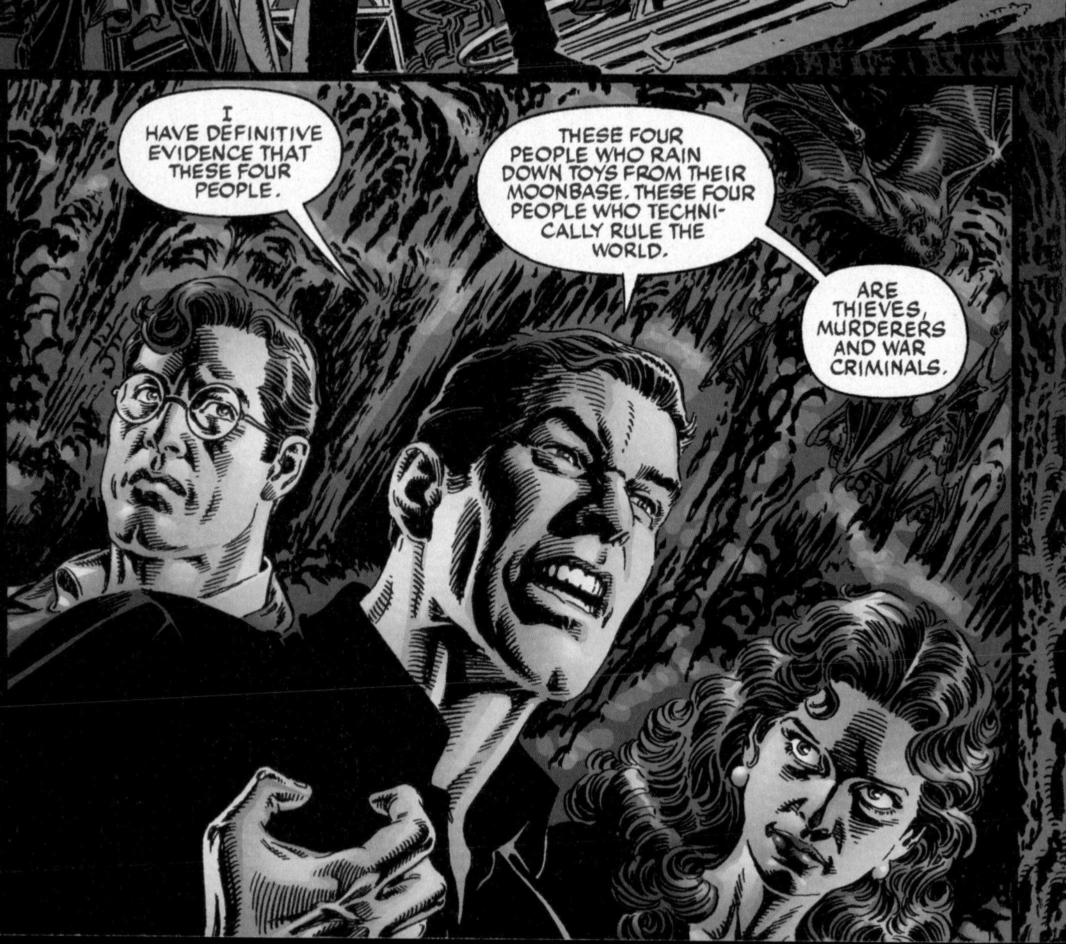
I HAVE DEFINITIVE EVIDENCE THAT THESE FOUR PEOPLE.
THESE FOUR PEOPLE WHO RAIN DOWN TOYS FROM THEIR MOONBASE. THESE FOUR PEOPLE WHO TECHNICALLY RULE THE WORLD.
ARE THIEVES, MURDERERS AND WAR CRIMINALS.

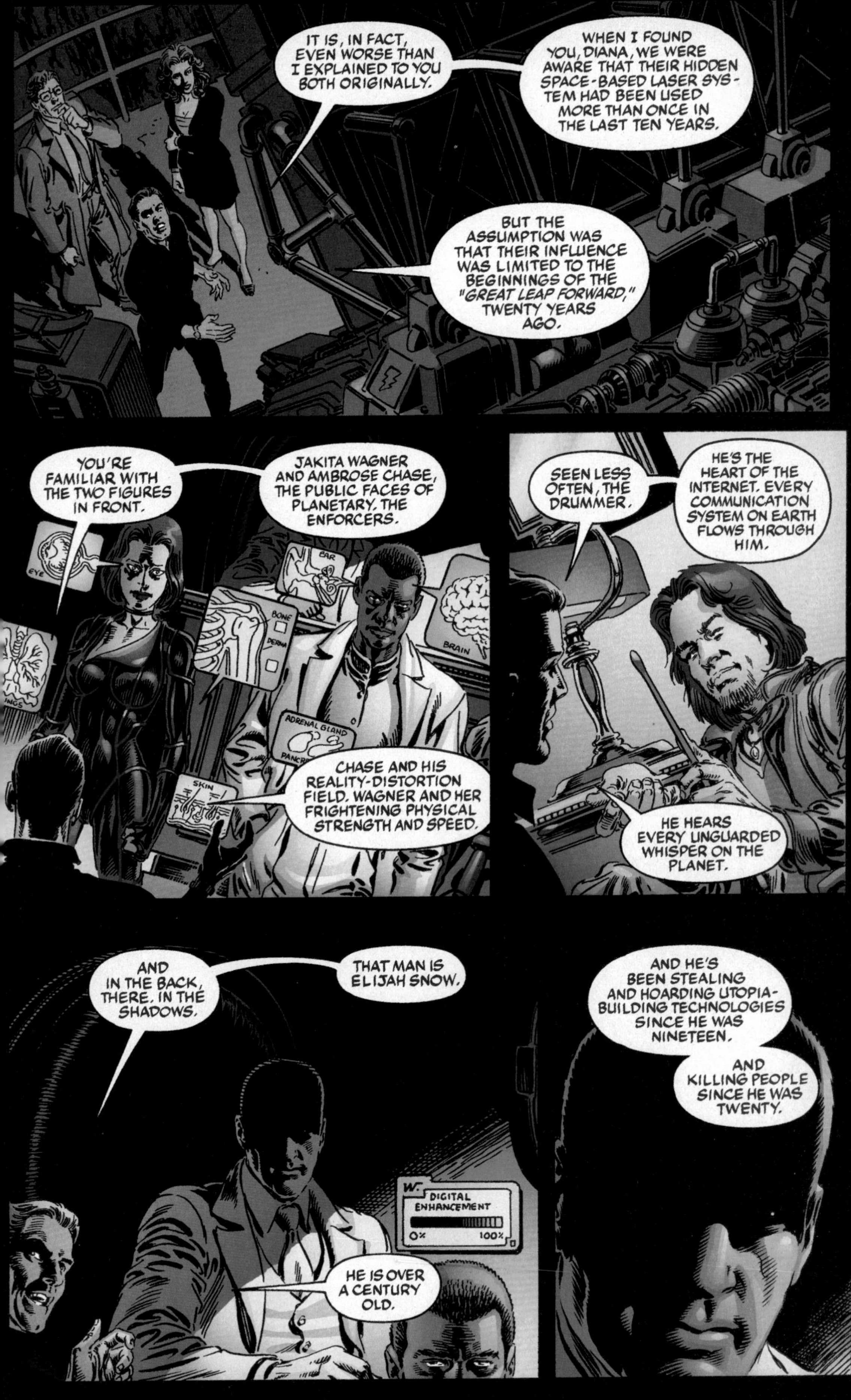
IT IS, IN FACT, EVEN WORSE THAN I EXPLAINED TO YOU BOTH ORIGINALLY.
WHEN I FOUND YOU, DIANA, WE WERE AWARE THAT THEIR HIDDEN SPACE-BASED LASER SYS-TEM HAD BEEN USED MORE THAN ONCE IN THE LAST TEN YEARS.
BUT THE ASSUMPTION WAS THAT THEIR INFLUENCE WAS LIMITED TO THE BEGINNINGS OF THE *"GREAT LEAP FORWARD,"* TWENTY YEARS AGO.
YOU'RE FAMILIAR WITH THE TWO FIGURES IN FRONT.
JAKITA WAGNER AND AMBROSE CHASE, THE PUBLIC FACES OF PLANETARY. THE ENFORCERS.
EYE
EAR
BONE
DERMA
BRAIN
ADRENAL GLAND
SKIN
CHASE AND HIS REALITY-DISTORTION FIELD. WAGNER AND HER FRIGHTENING PHYSICAL STRENGTH AND SPEED.
SEEN LESS OFTEN, THE DRUMMER.
HE'S THE HEART OF THE INTERNET. EVERY COMMUNICATION SYSTEM ON EARTH FLOWS THROUGH HIM.
HE HEARS EVERY UNGUARDED WHISPER ON THE PLANET.
AND IN THE BACK, THERE, IN THE SHADOWS.
THAT MAN IS ELIJAH SNOW.
W.
DIGITAL ENHANCEMENT
0%
100%
HE IS OVER A CENTURY OLD.
AND HE'S BEEN STEALING AND HOARDING UTOPIA-BUILDING TECHNOLOGIES SINCE HE WAS NINETEEN.
AND KILLING PEOPLE SINCE HE WAS TWENTY.

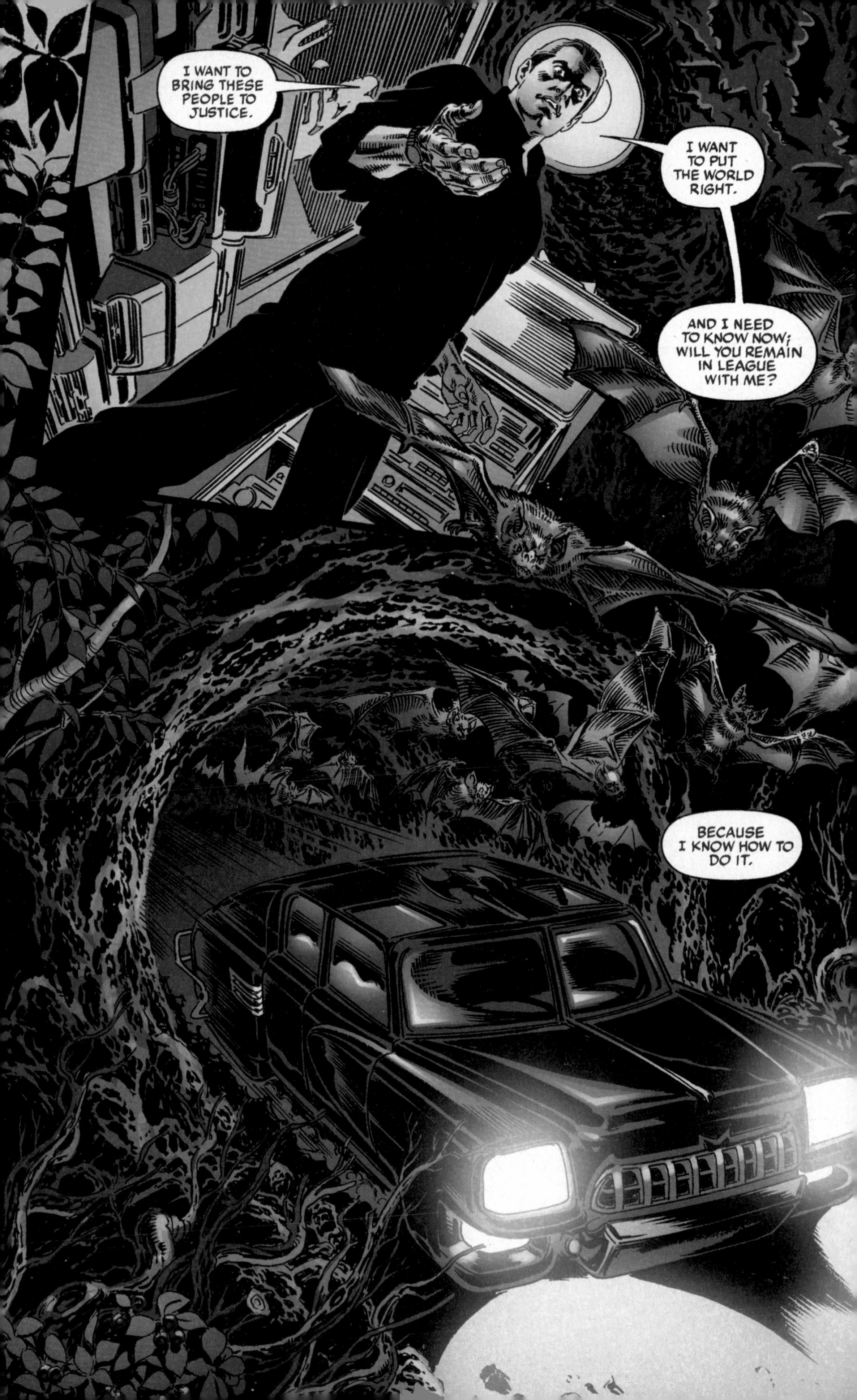
I WANT TO BRING THESE PEOPLE TO JUSTICE.
I WANT TO PUT THE WORLD RIGHT.
AND I NEED TO KNOW NOW; WILL YOU REMAIN IN LEAGUE WITH ME?
BECAUSE I KNOW HOW TO DO IT.

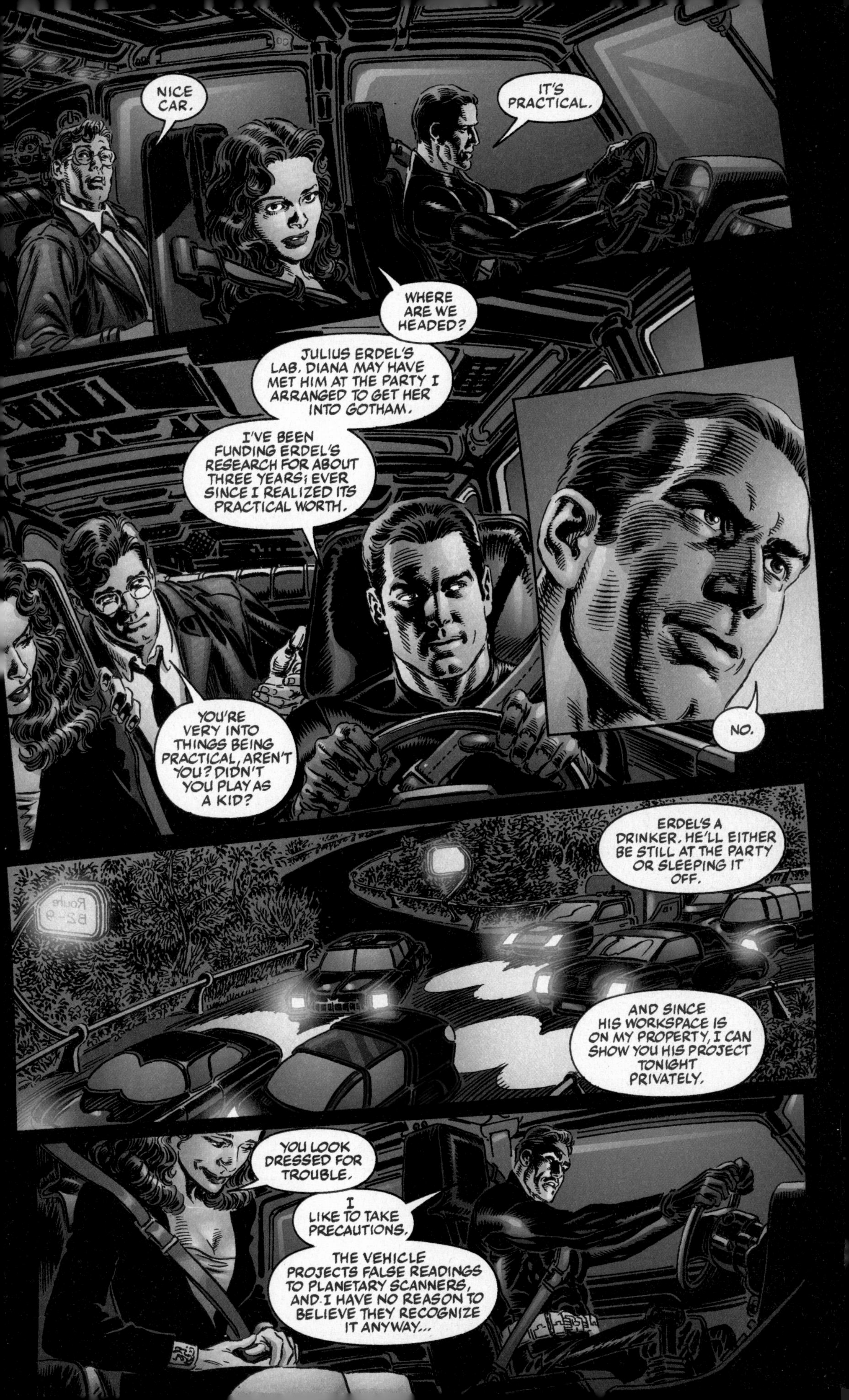
NICE CAR.
IT'S PRACTICAL.
WHERE ARE WE HEADED?
JULIUS ERDEL'S LAB. DIANA MAY HAVE MET HIM AT THE PARTY I ARRANGED TO GET HER INTO GOTHAM.
I'VE BEEN FUNDING ERDEL'S RESEARCH FOR ABOUT THREE YEARS; EVER SINCE I REALIZED ITS PRACTICAL WORTH.
YOU'RE VERY INTO THINGS BEING PRACTICAL, AREN'T YOU? DIDN'T YOU PLAY AS A KID?
NO.
ERDEL'S A DRINKER. HE'LL EITHER BE STILL AT THE PARTY OR SLEEPING IT OFF.
AND SINCE HIS WORKSPACE IS ON MY PROPERTY, I CAN SHOW YOU HIS PROJECT TONIGHT PRIVATELY.
YOU LOOK DRESSED FOR TROUBLE.
I LIKE TO TAKE PRECAUTIONS.
THE VEHICLE PROJECTS FALSE READINGS TO PLANETARY SCANNERS, AND I HAVE NO REASON TO BELIEVE THEY RECOGNIZE IT ANYWAY...

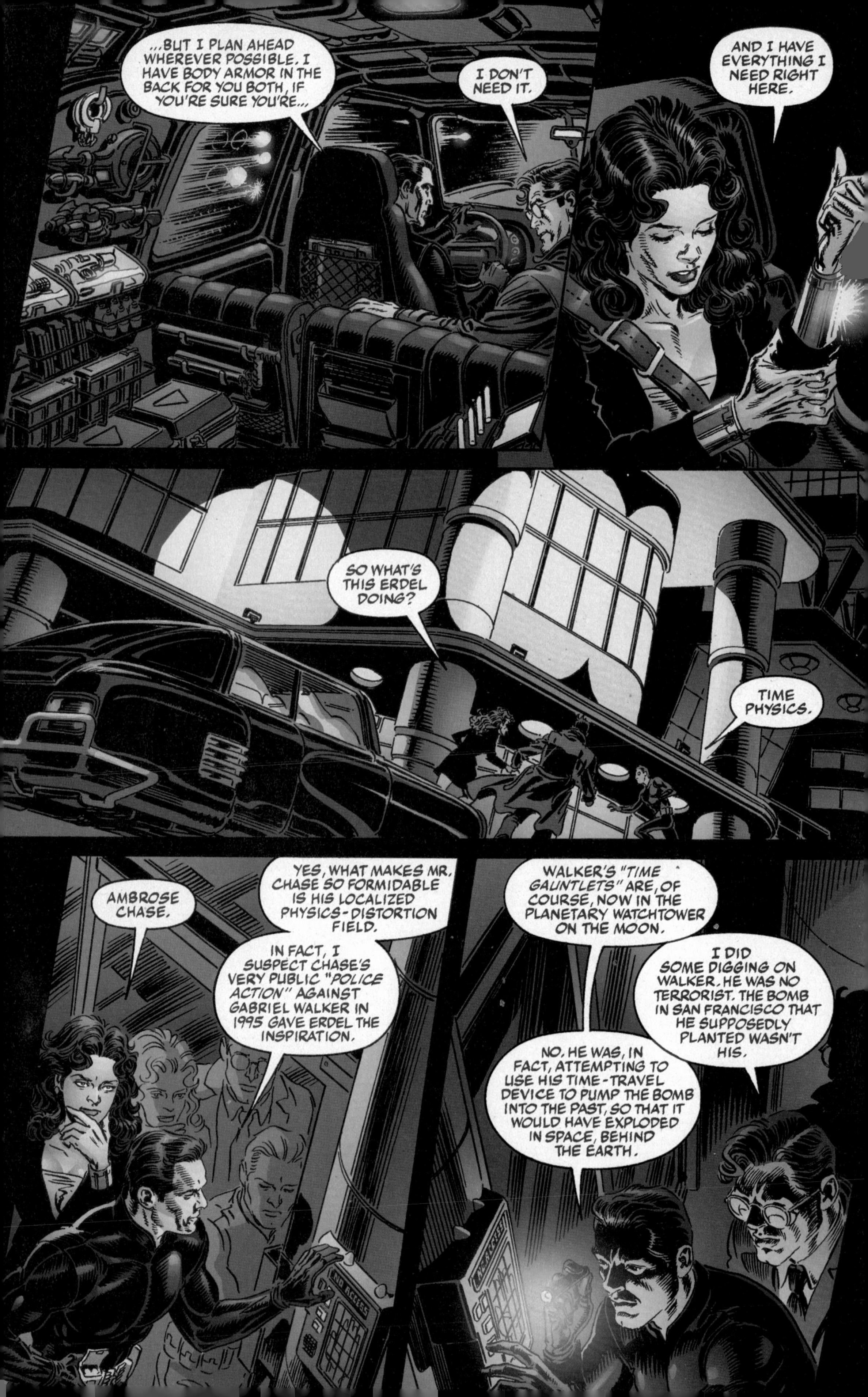
...BUT I PLAN AHEAD WHEREVER POSSIBLE. I HAVE BODY ARMOR IN THE BACK FOR YOU BOTH, IF YOU'RE SURE YOU'RE...
I DON'T NEED IT.
AND I HAVE EVERYTHING I NEED RIGHT HERE.
SO WHAT'S THIS ERDEL DOING?
TIME PHYSICS.
AMBROSE CHASE.
YES, WHAT MAKES MR. CHASE SO FORMIDABLE IS HIS LOCALIZED PHYSICS-DISTORTION FIELD.
IN FACT, I SUSPECT CHASE'S VERY PUBLIC "POLICE ACTION" AGAINST GABRIEL WALKER IN 1995 GAVE ERDEL THE INSPIRATION.
WALKER'S "TIME GAUNTLETS" ARE, OF COURSE, NOW IN THE PLANETARY WATCHTOWER ON THE MOON.
I DID SOME DIGGING ON WALKER. HE WAS NO TERRORIST. THE BOMB IN SAN FRANCISCO THAT HE SUPPOSEDLY PLANTED WASN'T HIS.
NO, HE WAS, IN FACT, ATTEMPTING TO USE HIS TIME-TRAVEL DEVICE TO PUMP THE BOMB INTO THE PAST, SO THAT IT WOULD HAVE EXPLODED IN SPACE, BEHIND THE EARTH.

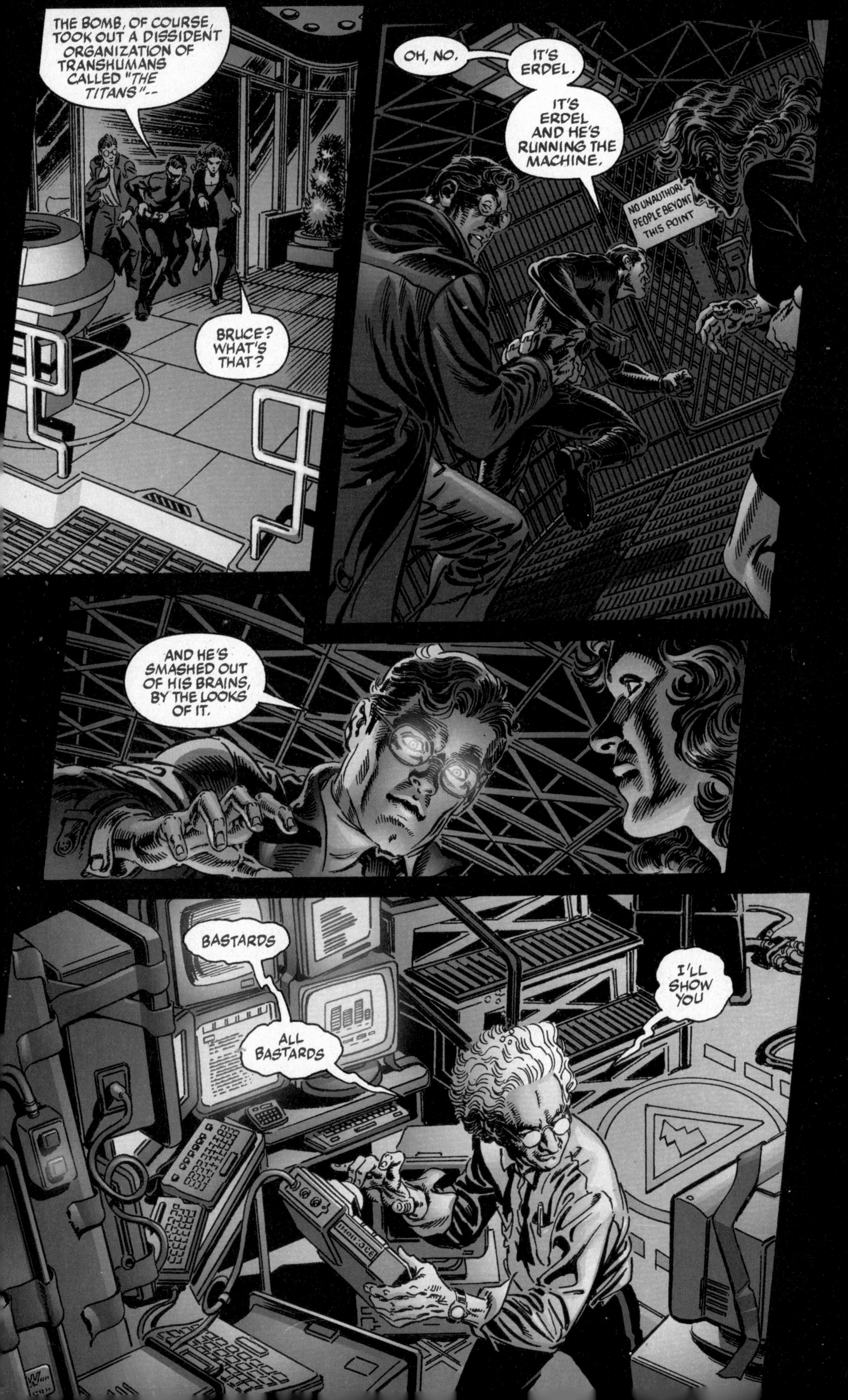

THE BOMB, OF COURSE, TOOK OUT A DISSIDENT ORGANIZATION OF TRANSHUMANS CALLED "THE TITANS"--
BRUCE? WHAT'S THAT?
OH, NO.
IT'S ERDEL.
IT'S ERDEL AND HE'S RUNNING THE MACHINE.
NO UNAUTHORI- PEOPLE BEYOND THIS POINT
AND HE'S SMASHED OUT OF HIS BRAINS, BY THE LOOKS OF IT.
BASTARDS
ALL BASTARDS
I'LL SHOW YOU

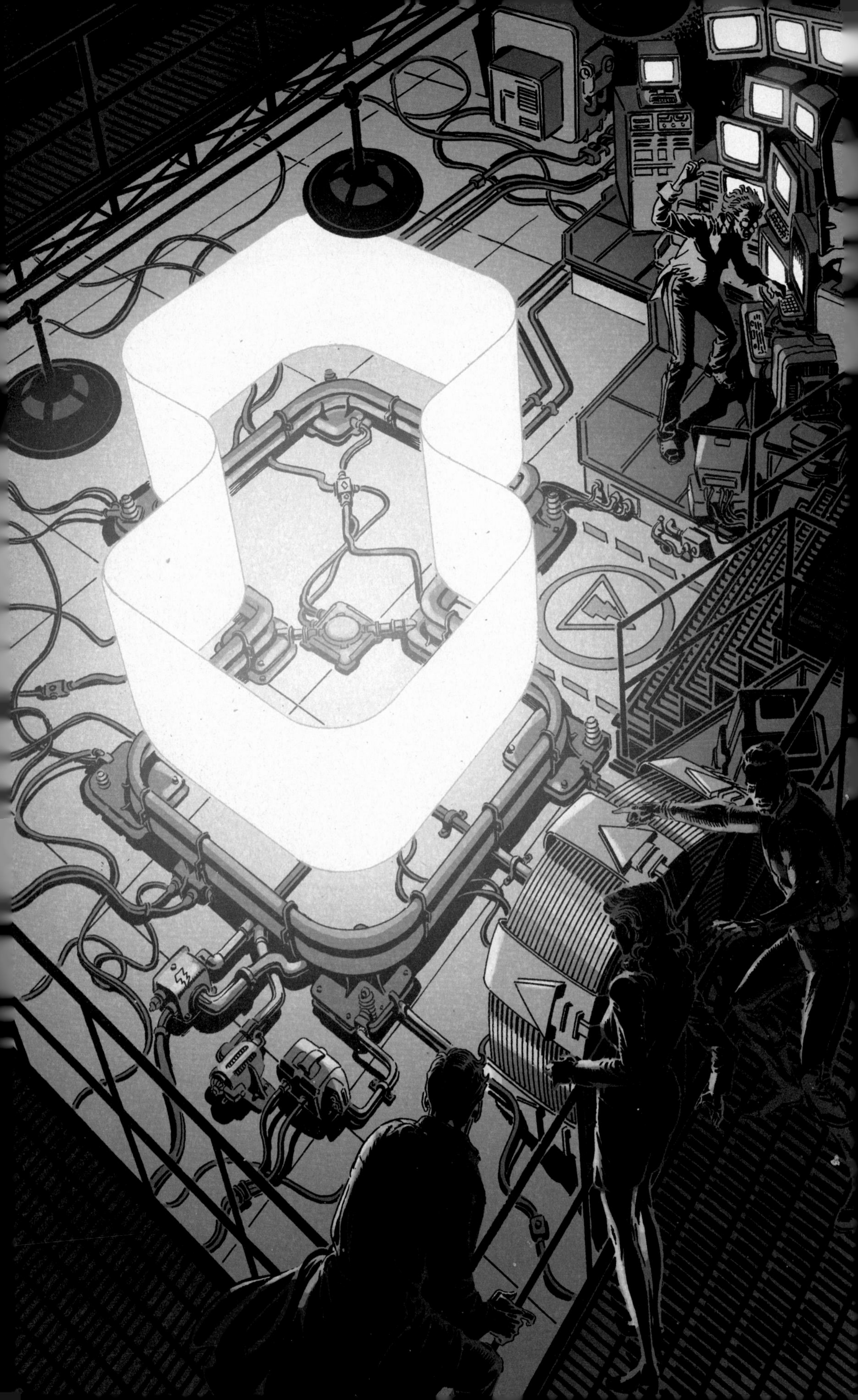

WHAT IS THAT?

IT'S A TIME LOOP.

PHYSICS IS BENT DOUBLE INSIDE THE LOOP.

THE LIGHT CUTS A CHANNEL INTO THE FUTURE AND THEN COMES SCREAMING BACK.

STAND AT THE START POINT OF THE LOOP AND TAKE THREE STEPS FORWARD.

STEP OUT OF THE LOOP AND YOU'RE A YEAR IN THE FUTURE.

STEP BACK IN AND WALK BACK TO THE PRESENT.

I DON'T LIKE THE LOOK OF THE LIGHT.

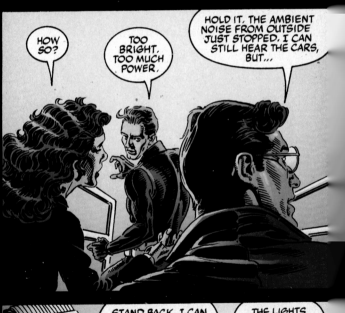

HOW SO?

TOO BRIGHT. TOO MUCH POWER.

HOLD IT. THE AMBIENT NOISE FROM OUTSIDE JUST STOPPED. I CAN STILL HEAR THE CARS, BUT...

STAND BACK. I CAN SEE THROUGH WALLS, BUT THERE'S A SMALL ATTENDANT X-RAY OVERSPLASH.

THE LIGHTS JUST WENT OUT OVER HALF OF GOTHAM.

HE'S ATTACHED THE CITY GRID TO POWER HIS MACHINE.

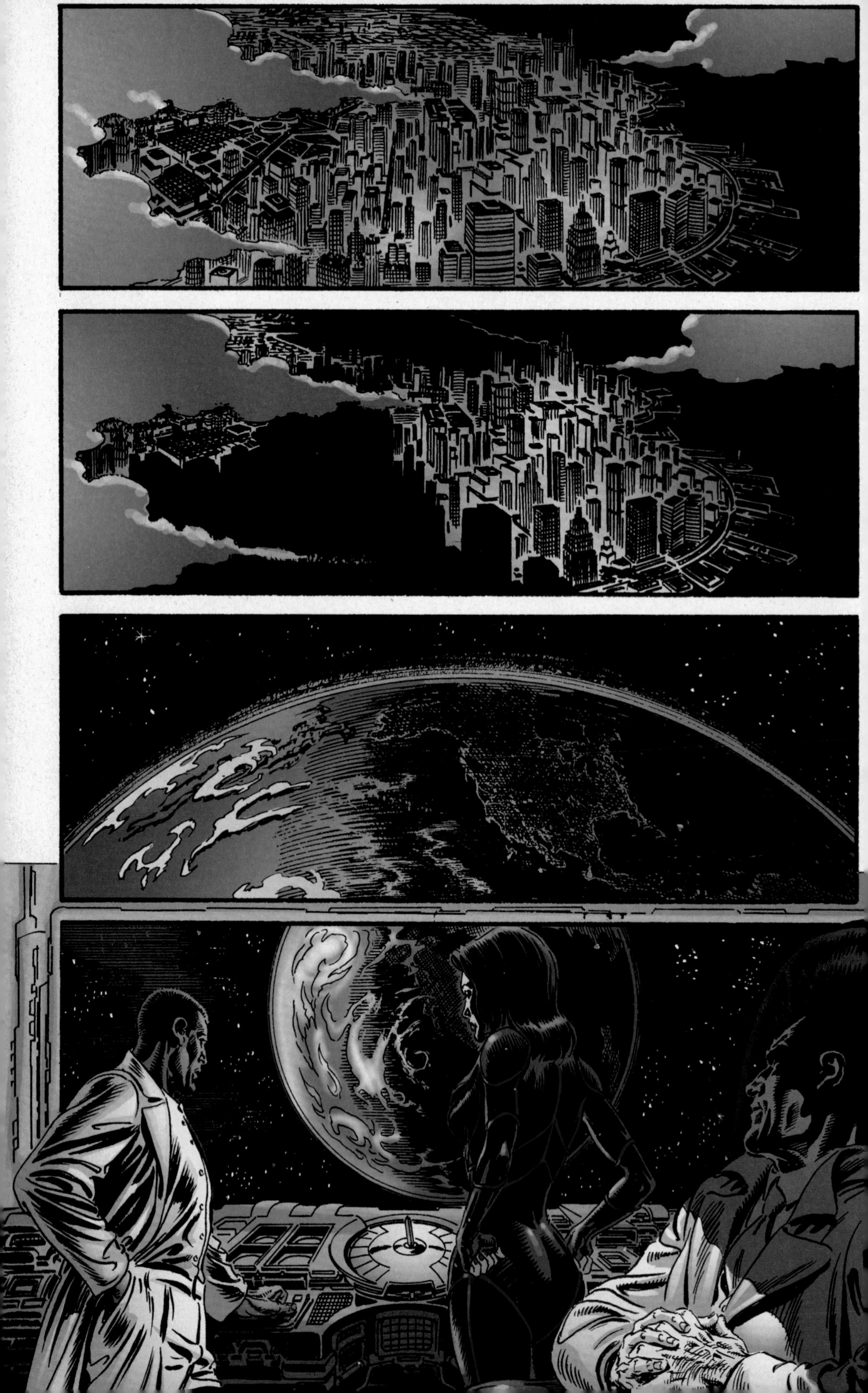

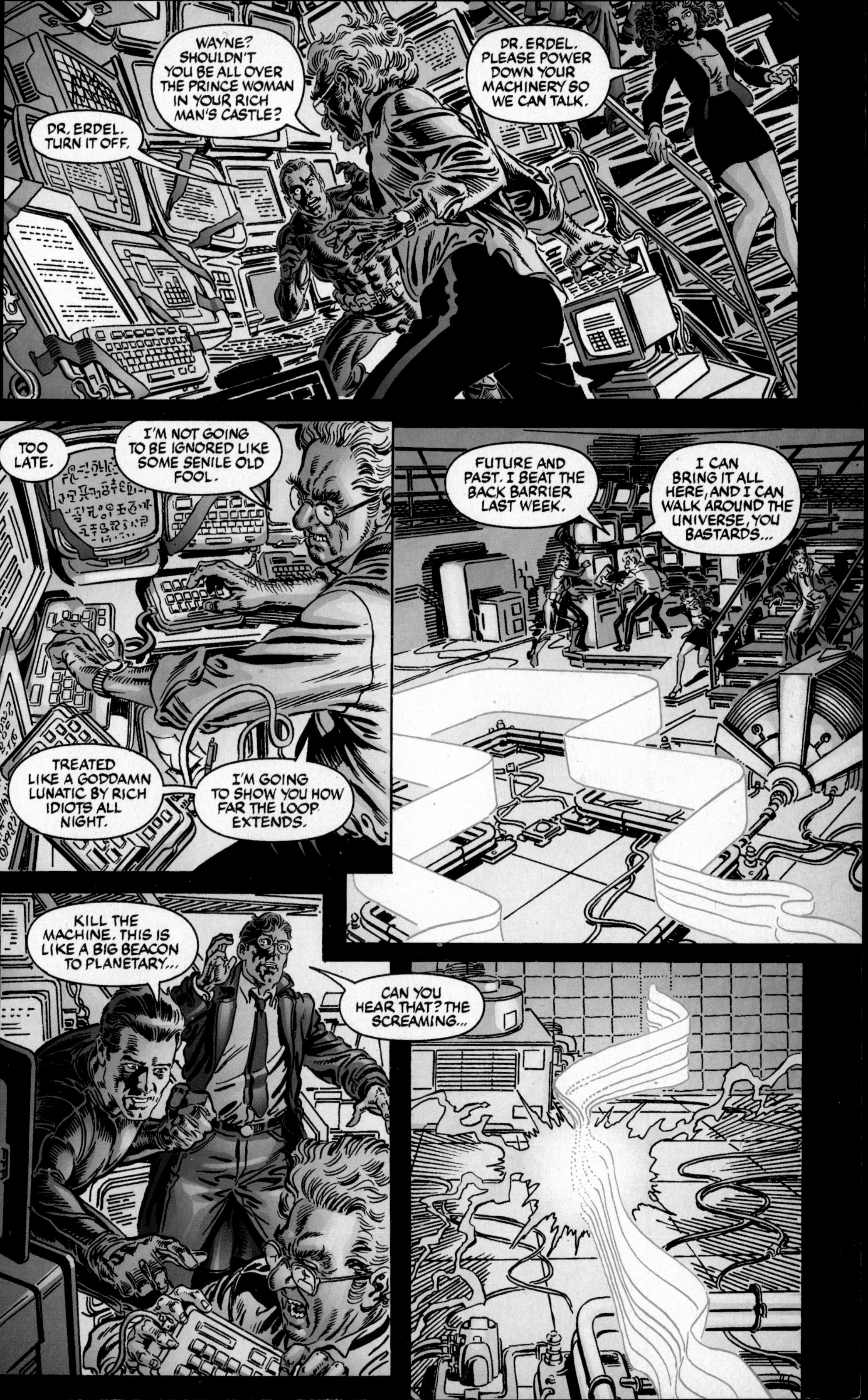
WAYNE? SHOULDN'T YOU BE ALL OVER THE PRINCE WOMAN IN YOUR RICH MAN'S CASTLE?
DR. ERDEL. PLEASE POWER DOWN YOUR MACHINERY SO WE CAN TALK.
DR. ERDEL. TURN IT OFF.
TOO LATE.
I'M NOT GOING TO BE IGNORED LIKE SOME SENILE OLD FOOL.
TREATED LIKE A GODDAMN LUNATIC BY RICH IDIOTS ALL NIGHT.
I'M GOING TO SHOW YOU HOW FAR THE LOOP EXTENDS.
FUTURE AND PAST. I BEAT THE BACK BARRIER LAST WEEK.
I CAN BRING IT ALL HERE, AND I CAN WALK AROUND THE UNIVERSE, YOU BASTARDS...
KILL THE MACHINE. THIS IS LIKE A BIG BEACON TO PLANETARY...
CAN YOU HEAR THAT? THE SCREAMING...

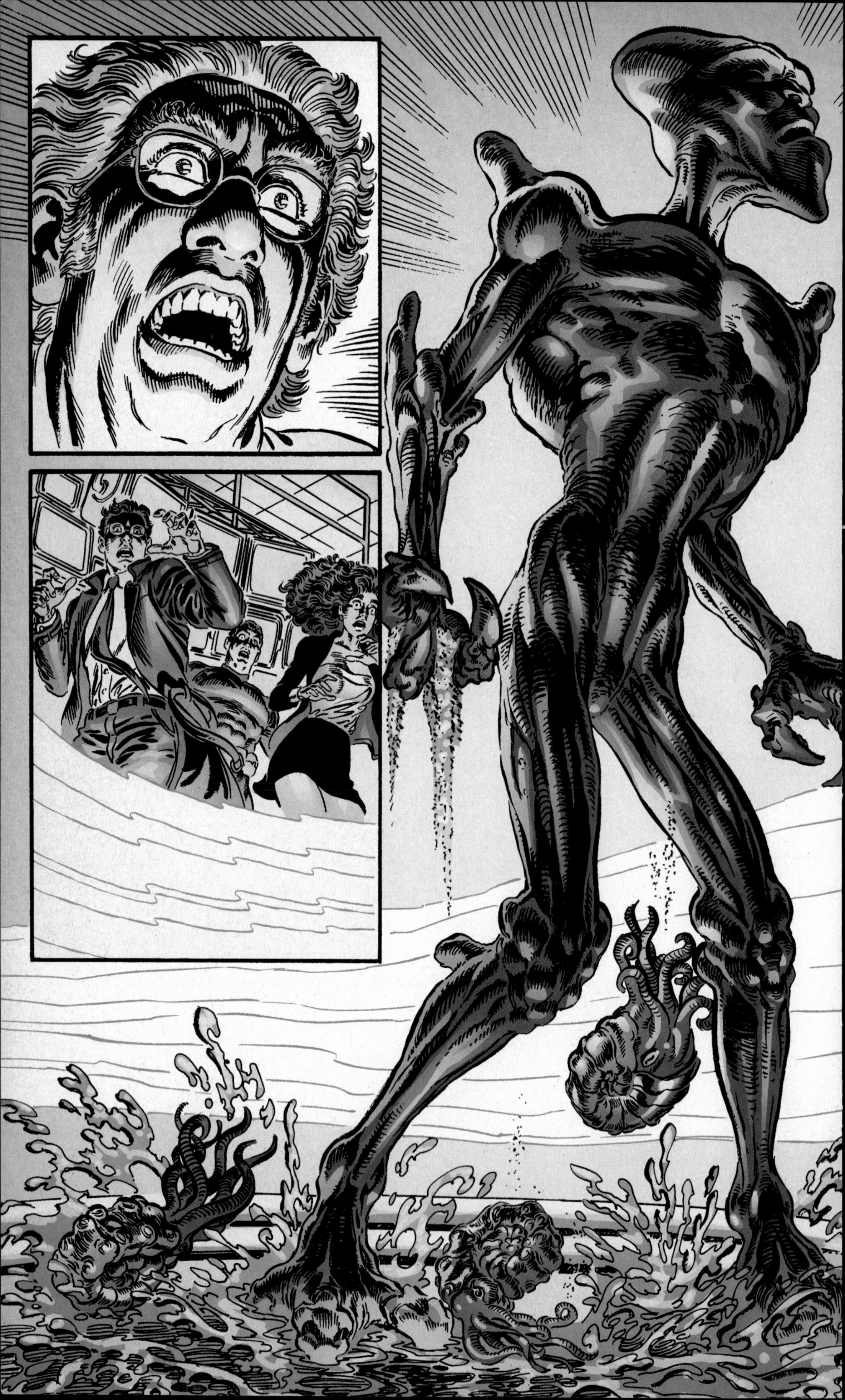

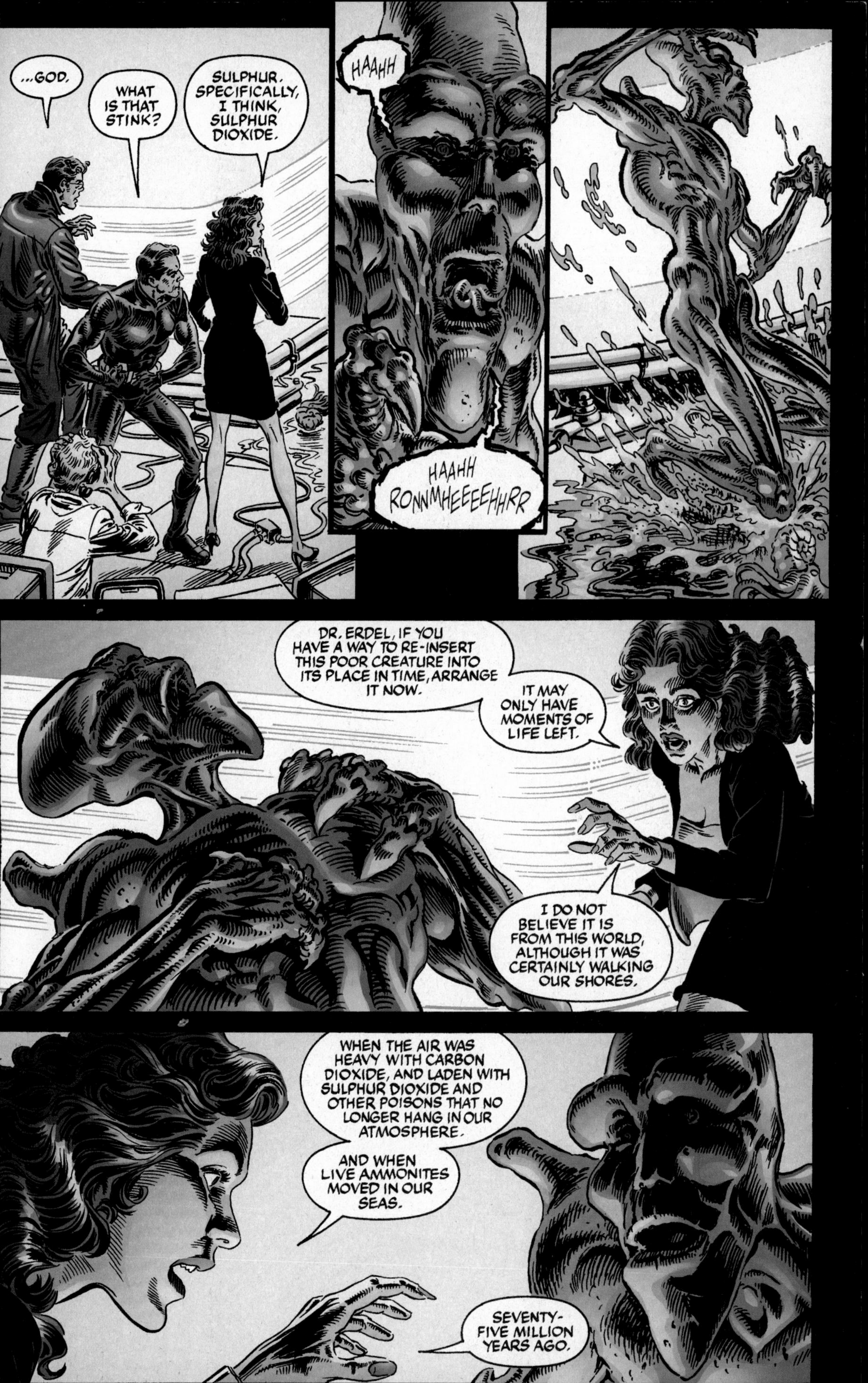
...GOD.
WHAT IS THAT STINK?
SULPHUR. SPECIFICALLY, I THINK, SULPHUR DIOXIDE.
HAAHH
HAAHH RONNMHEEEEHHRR
DR. ERDEL, IF YOU HAVE A WAY TO RE-INSERT THIS POOR CREATURE INTO ITS PLACE IN TIME, ARRANGE IT NOW.
IT MAY ONLY HAVE MOMENTS OF LIFE LEFT.
I DO NOT BELIEVE IT IS FROM THIS WORLD, ALTHOUGH IT WAS CERTAINLY WALKING OUR SHORES.
WHEN THE AIR WAS HEAVY WITH CARBON DIOXIDE, AND LADEN WITH SULPHUR DIOXIDE AND OTHER POISONS THAT NO LONGER HANG IN OUR ATMOSPHERE.
AND WHEN LIVE AMMONITES MOVED IN OUR SEAS.
SEVENTY-FIVE MILLION YEARS AGO.

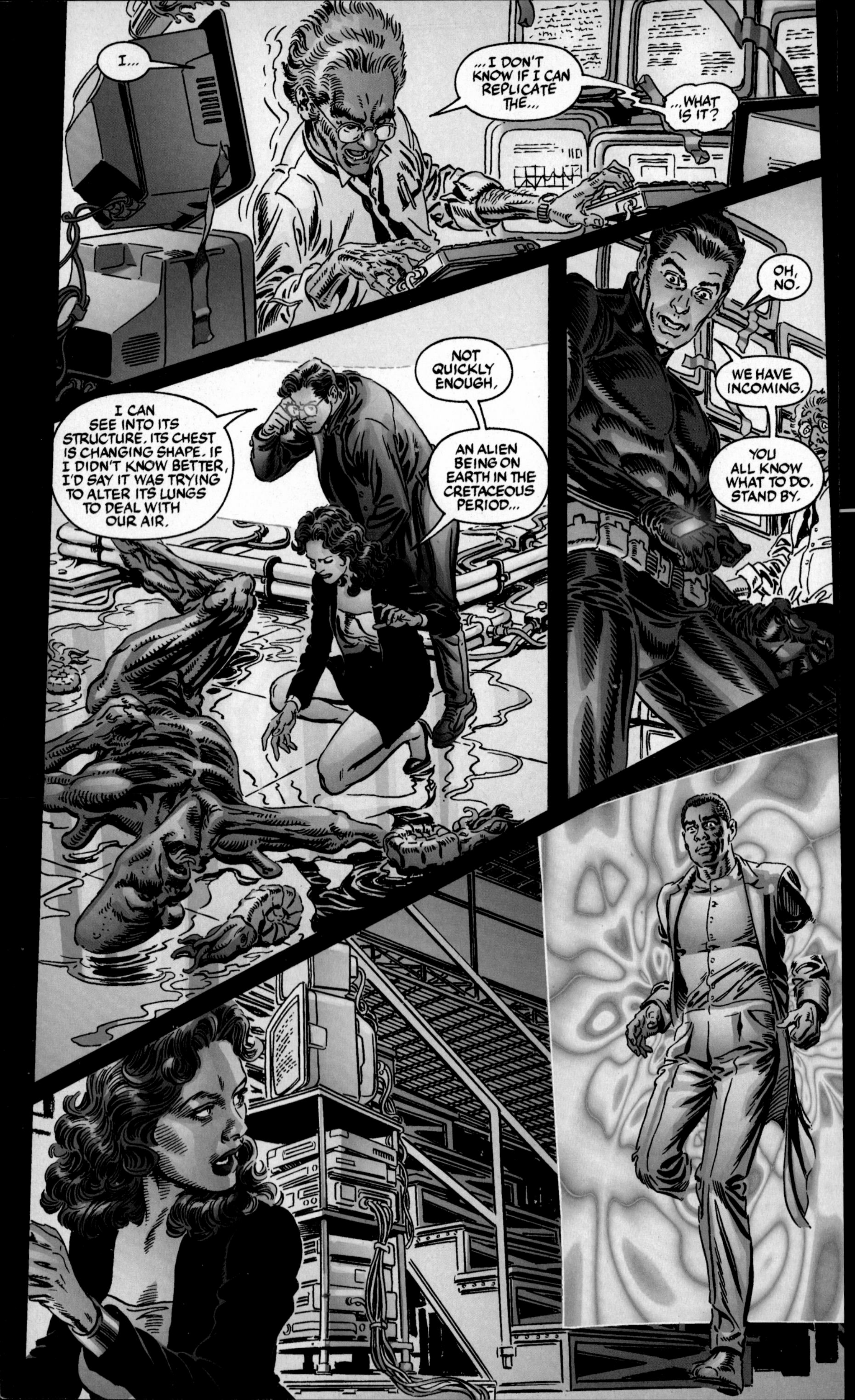
I...
...I DON'T KNOW IF I CAN REPLICATE THE...
...WHAT IS IT?
OH, NO.
WE HAVE INCOMING.
YOU ALL KNOW WHAT TO DO. STAND BY.
I CAN SEE INTO ITS STRUCTURE. ITS CHEST IS CHANGING SHAPE. IF I DIDN'T KNOW BETTER, I'D SAY IT WAS TRYING TO ALTER ITS LUNGS TO DEAL WITH OUR AIR.
NOT QUICKLY ENOUGH.
AN ALIEN BEING ON EARTH IN THE CRETACEOUS PERIOD...

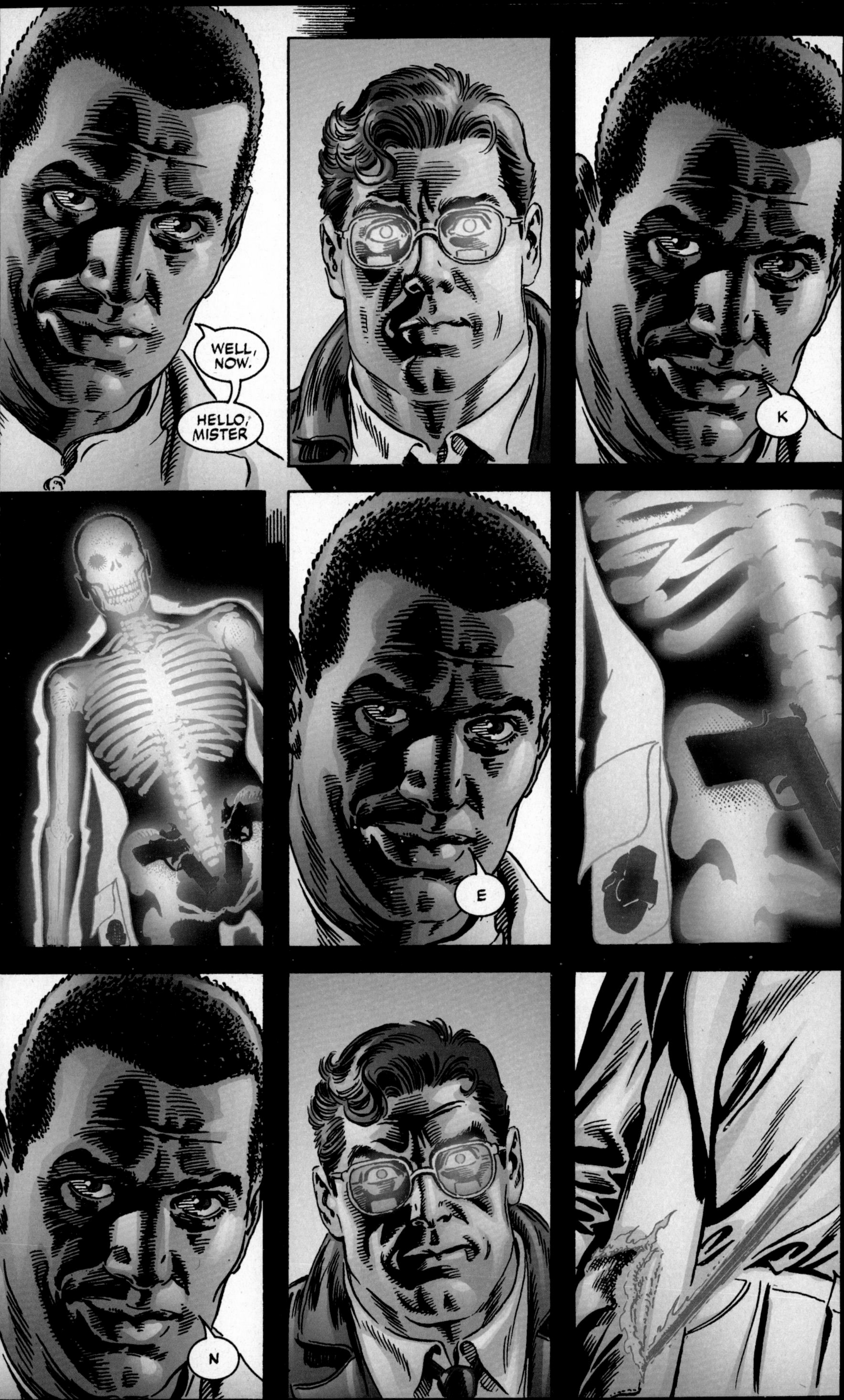

WELL, NOW.
HELLO, MISTER
K
E
N

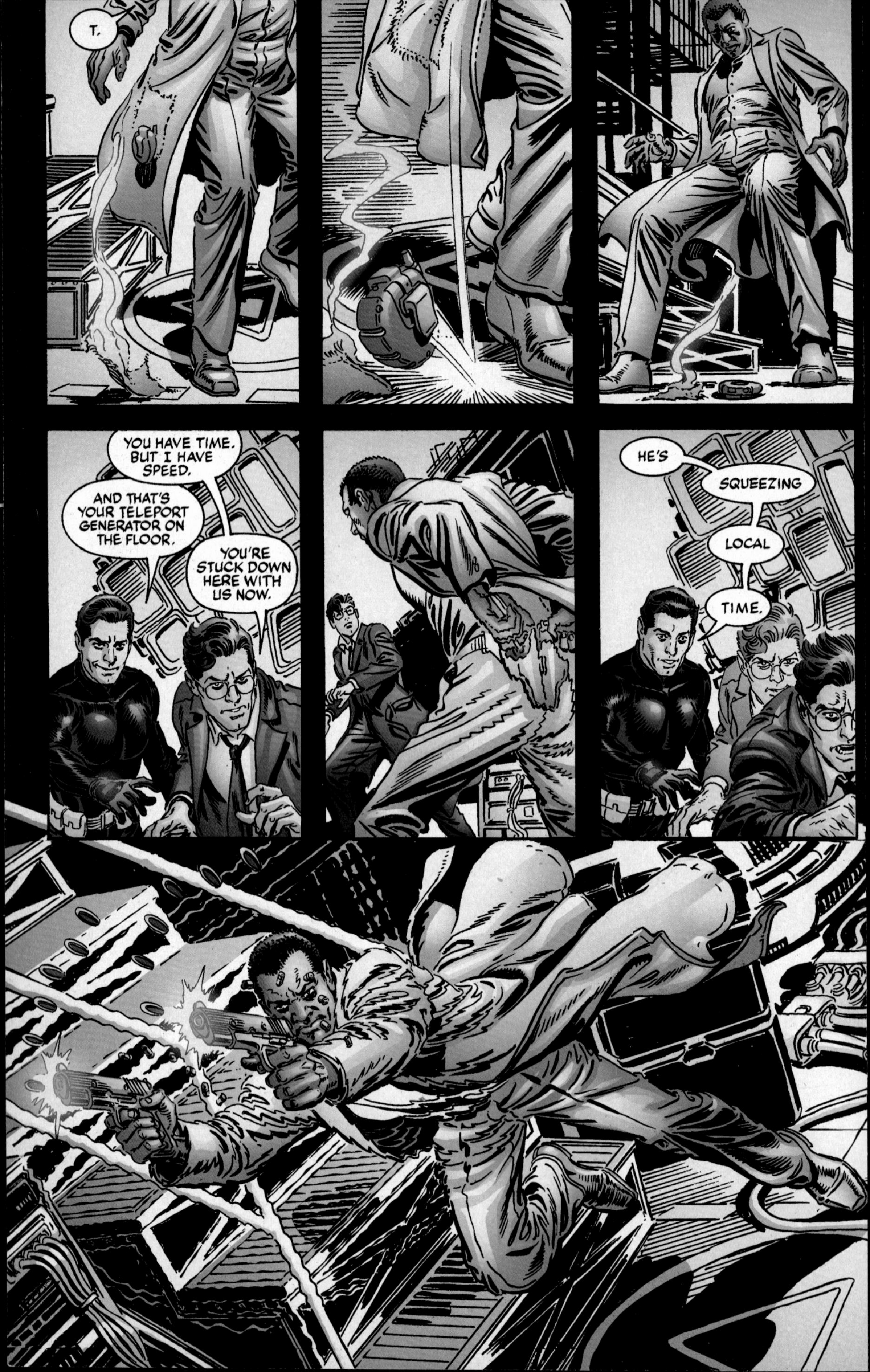
T.
YOU HAVE TIME. BUT I HAVE SPEED.
AND THAT'S YOUR TELEPORT GENERATOR ON THE FLOOR.
YOU'RE STUCK DOWN HERE WITH US NOW.
HE'S
SQUEEZING
LOCAL
TIME.

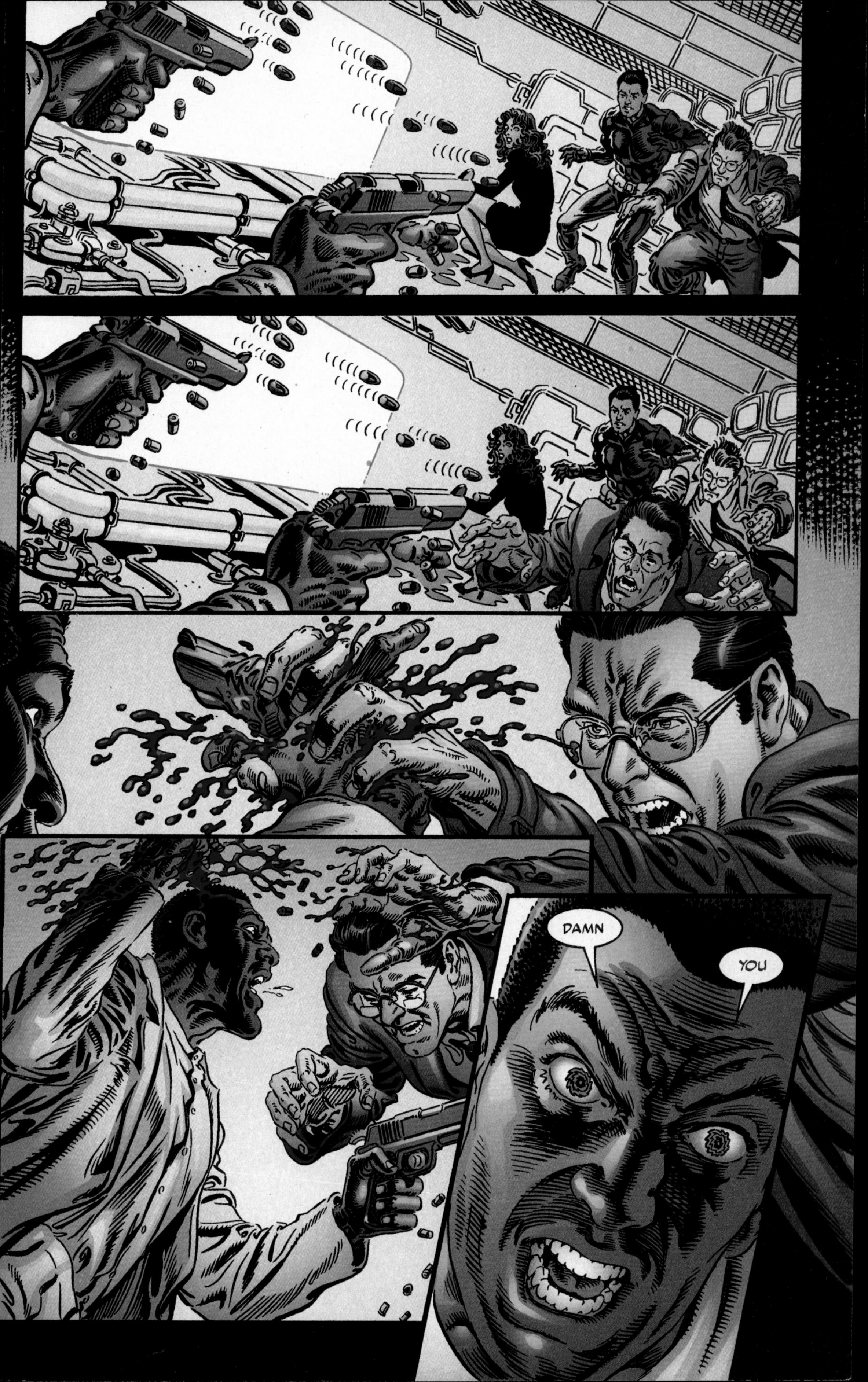
DAMN
YOU

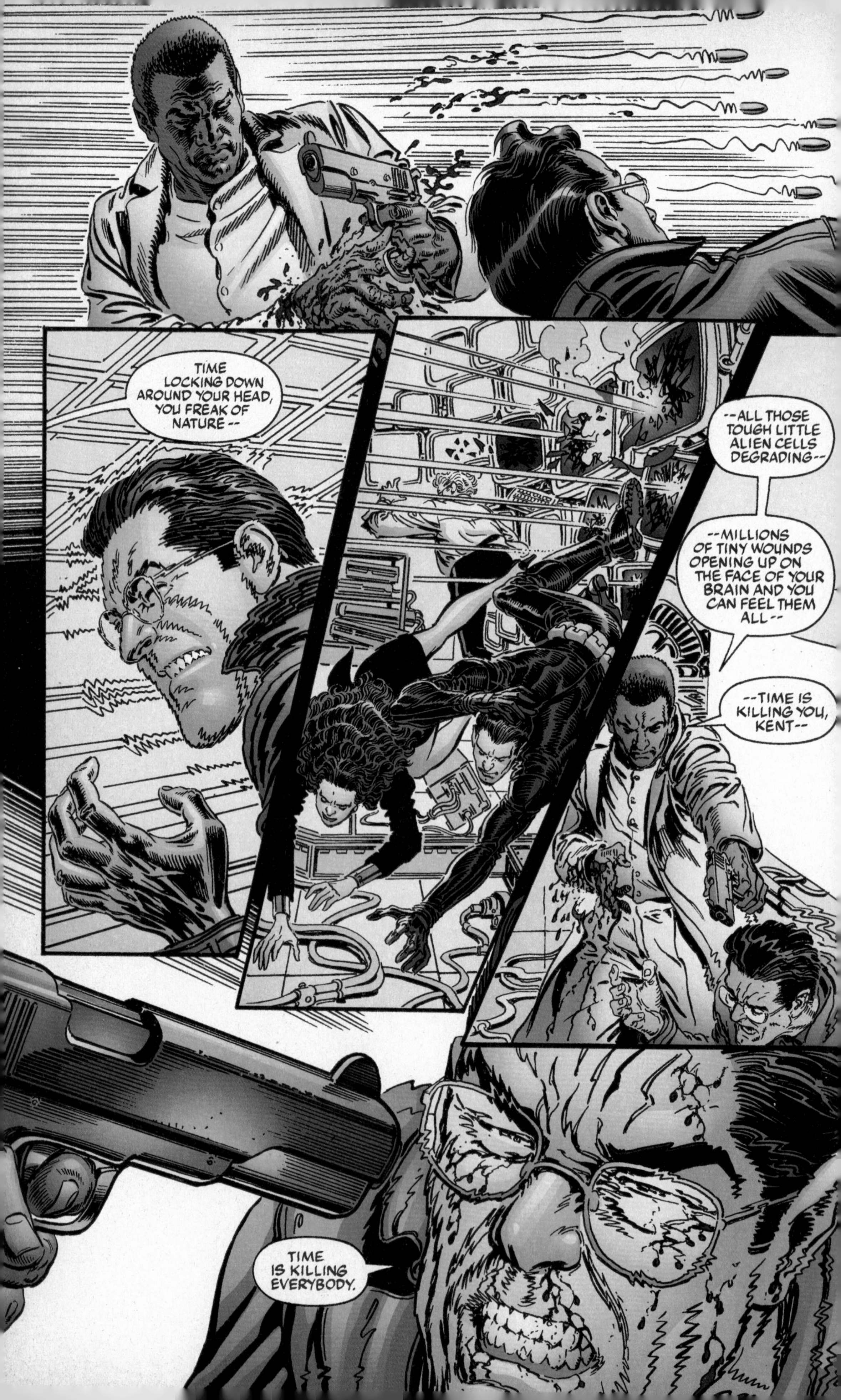
TIME LOCKING DOWN AROUND YOUR HEAD, YOU FREAK OF NATURE--
--ALL THOSE TOUGH LITTLE ALIEN CELLS DEGRADING--
--MILLIONS OF TINY WOUNDS OPENING UP ON THE FACE OF YOUR BRAIN AND YOU CAN FEEL THEM ALL--
--TIME IS KILLING YOU, KENT--
TIME IS KILLING EVERYBODY.

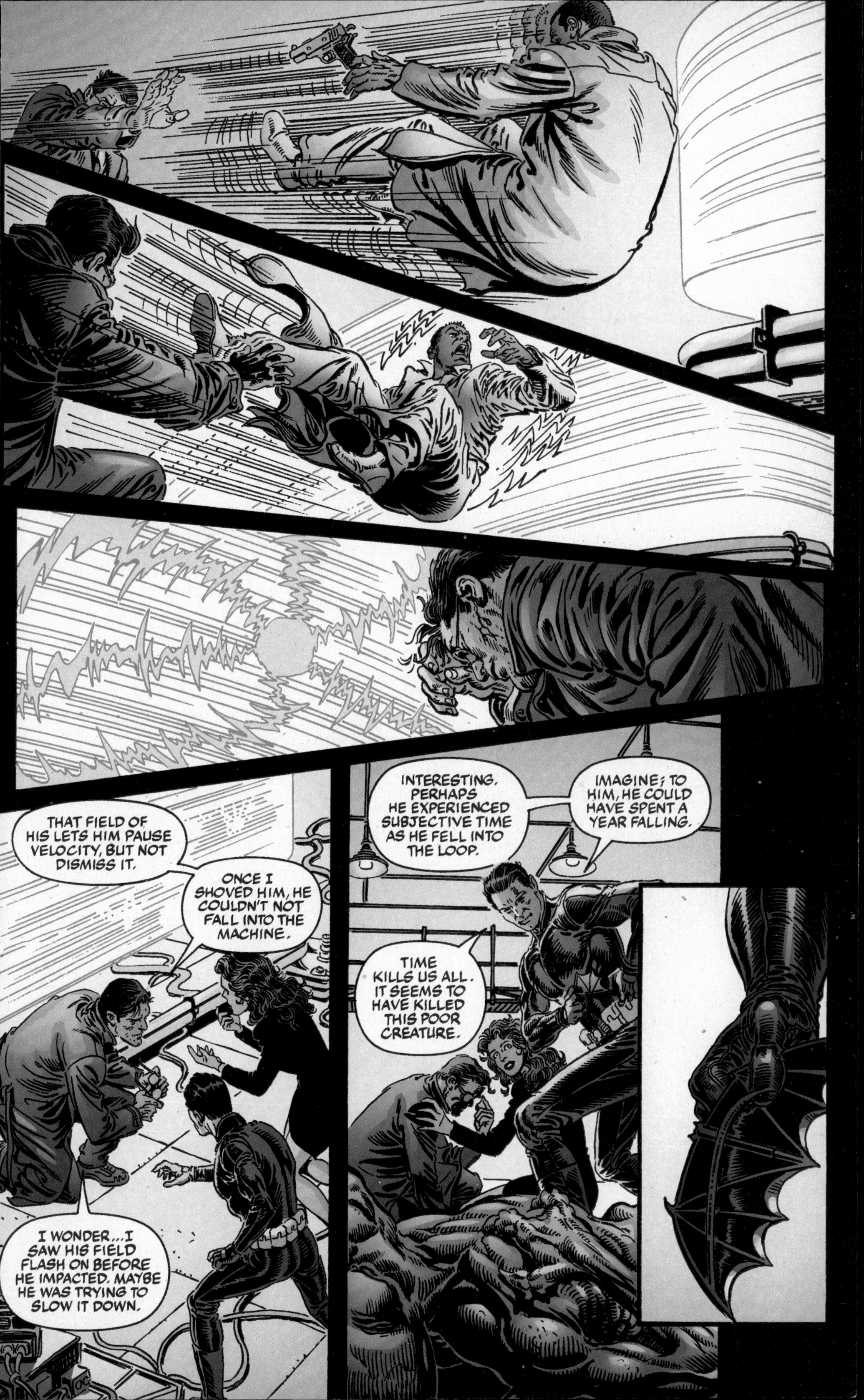

THAT FIELD OF HIS LETS HIM PAUSE VELOCITY, BUT NOT DISMISS IT.
ONCE I SHOVED HIM, HE COULDN'T NOT FALL INTO THE MACHINE.
I WONDER...I SAW HIS FIELD FLASH ON BEFORE HE IMPACTED. MAYBE HE WAS TRYING TO SLOW IT DOWN.
INTERESTING. PERHAPS HE EXPERIENCED SUBJECTIVE TIME AS HE FELL INTO THE LOOP.
IMAGINE; TO HIM, HE COULD HAVE SPENT A YEAR FALLING.
TIME KILLS US ALL. IT SEEMS TO HAVE KILLED THIS POOR CREATURE.

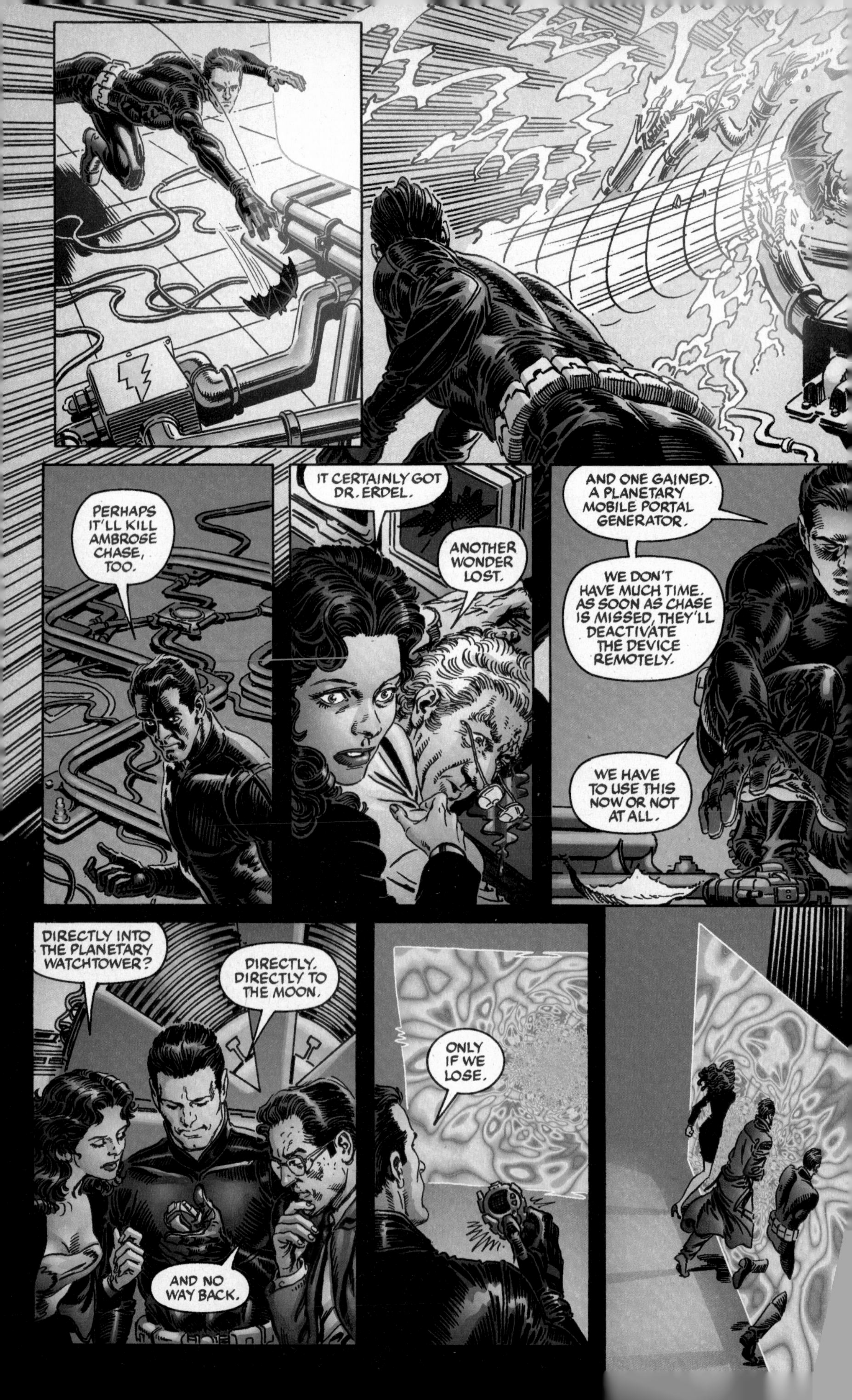
PERHAPS IT'LL KILL AMBROSE CHASE, TOO.
IT CERTAINLY GOT DR. ERDEL.
ANOTHER WONDER LOST.
AND ONE GAINED. A PLANETARY MOBILE PORTAL GENERATOR.
WE DON'T HAVE MUCH TIME. AS SOON AS CHASE IS MISSED, THEY'LL DEACTIVATE THE DEVICE REMOTELY.
WE HAVE TO USE THIS NOW OR NOT AT ALL.
DIRECTLY INTO THE PLANETARY WATCHTOWER?
DIRECTLY. DIRECTLY TO THE MOON.
AND NO WAY BACK.
ONLY IF WE LOSE.

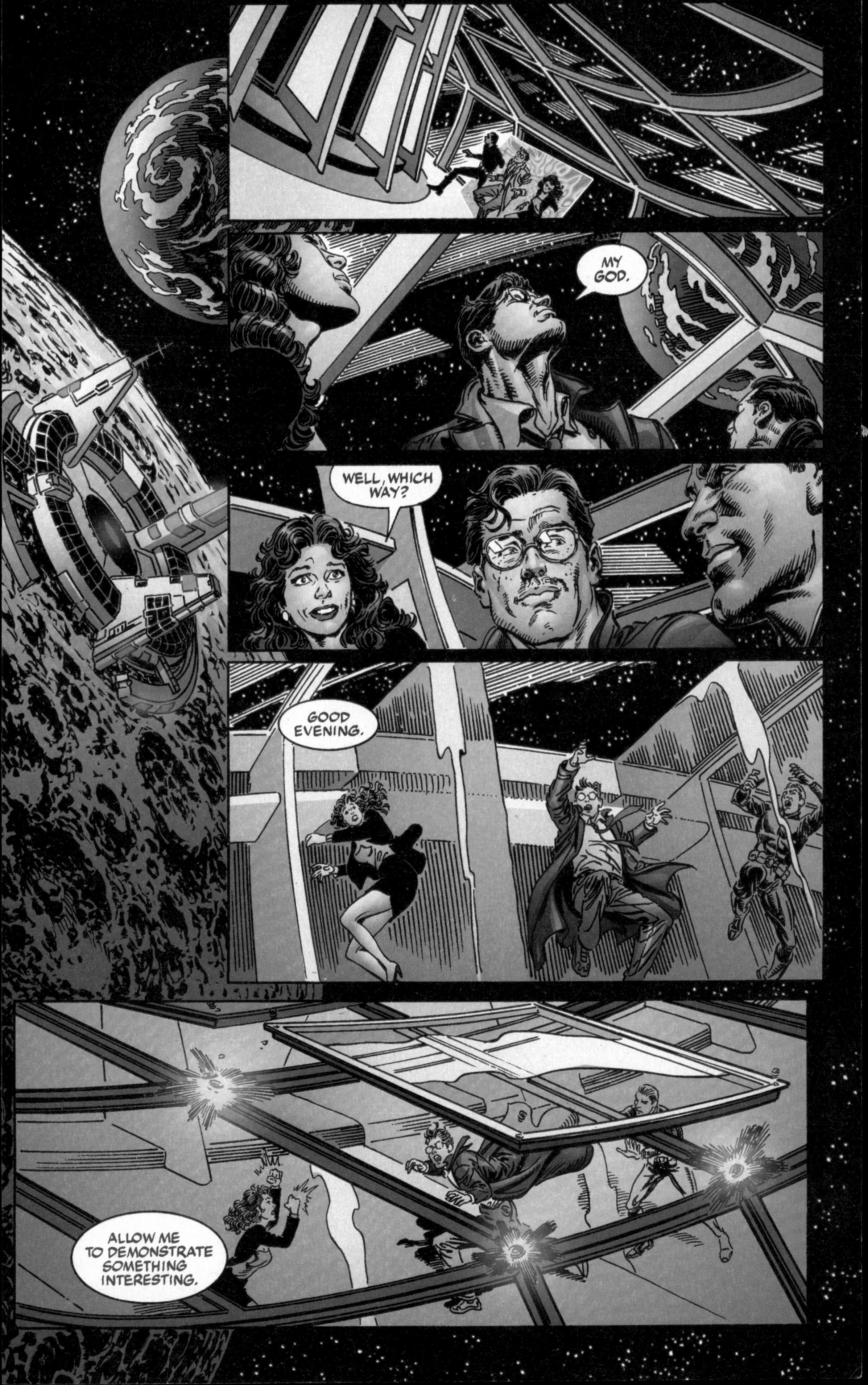
MY GOD.
WELL, WHICH WAY?
GOOD EVENING.
ALLOW ME TO DEMONSTRATE SOMETHING INTERESTING.

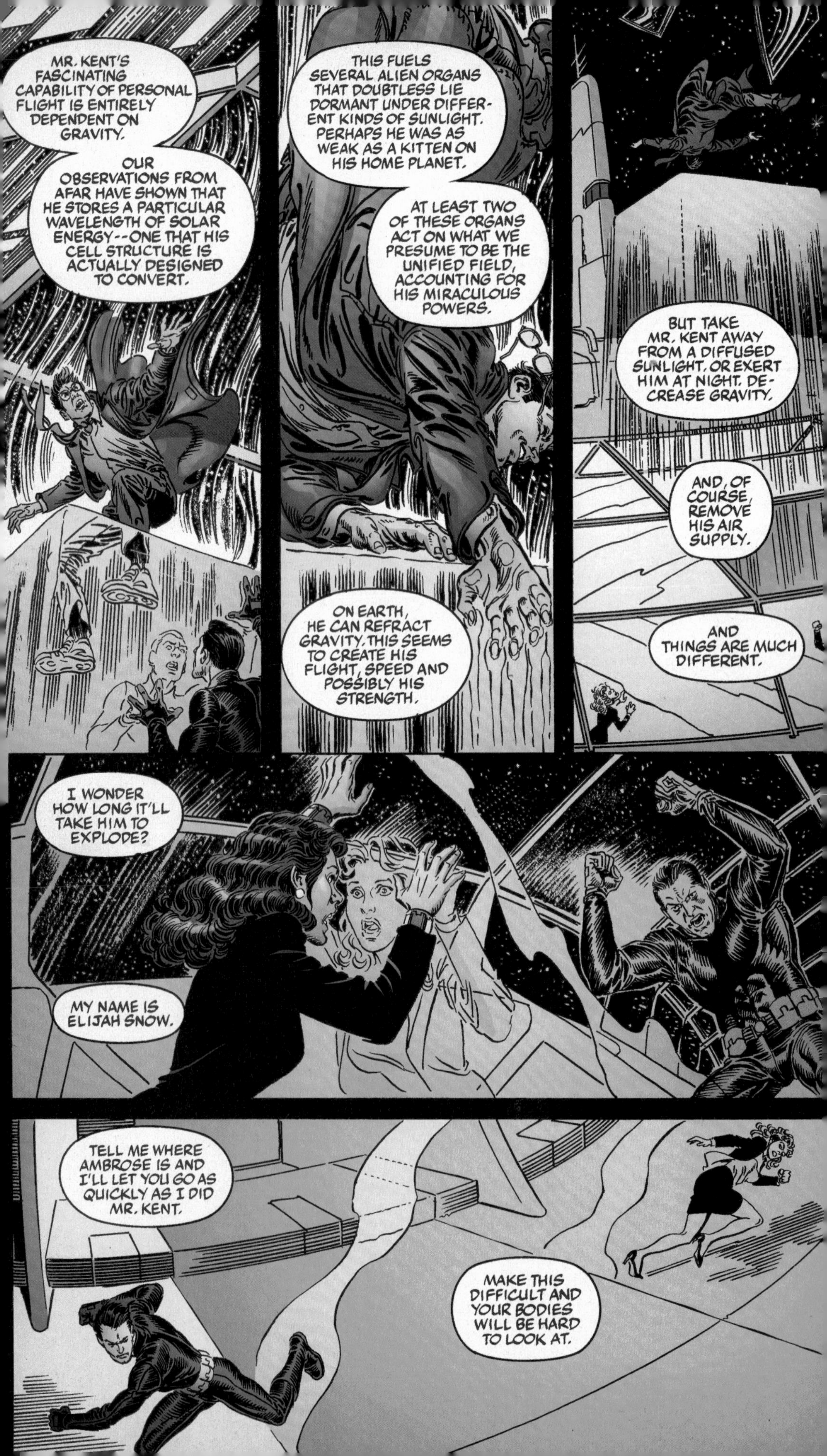
MR. KENT'S FASCINATING CAPABILITY OF PERSONAL FLIGHT IS ENTIRELY DEPENDENT ON GRAVITY.
OUR OBSERVATIONS FROM AFAR HAVE SHOWN THAT HE STORES A PARTICULAR WAVELENGTH OF SOLAR ENERGY--ONE THAT HIS CELL STRUCTURE IS ACTUALLY DESIGNED TO CONVERT.
THIS FUELS SEVERAL ALIEN ORGANS THAT DOUBTLESS LIE DORMANT UNDER DIFFERENT KINDS OF SUNLIGHT. PERHAPS HE WAS AS WEAK AS A KITTEN ON HIS HOME PLANET.
AT LEAST TWO OF THESE ORGANS ACT ON WHAT WE PRESUME TO BE THE UNIFIED FIELD, ACCOUNTING FOR HIS MIRACULOUS POWERS.
ON EARTH, HE CAN REFRACT GRAVITY. THIS SEEMS TO CREATE HIS FLIGHT, SPEED AND POSSIBLY HIS STRENGTH.
BUT TAKE MR. KENT AWAY FROM A DIFFUSED SUNLIGHT, OR EXERT HIM AT NIGHT. DECREASE GRAVITY.
AND, OF COURSE, REMOVE HIS AIR SUPPLY.
AND THINGS ARE MUCH DIFFERENT.
I WONDER HOW LONG IT'LL TAKE HIM TO EXPLODE?
MY NAME IS ELIJAH SNOW.
TELL ME WHERE AMBROSE IS AND I'LL LET YOU GO AS QUICKLY AS I DID MR. KENT.
MAKE THIS DIFFICULT AND YOUR BODIES WILL BE HARD TO LOOK AT.

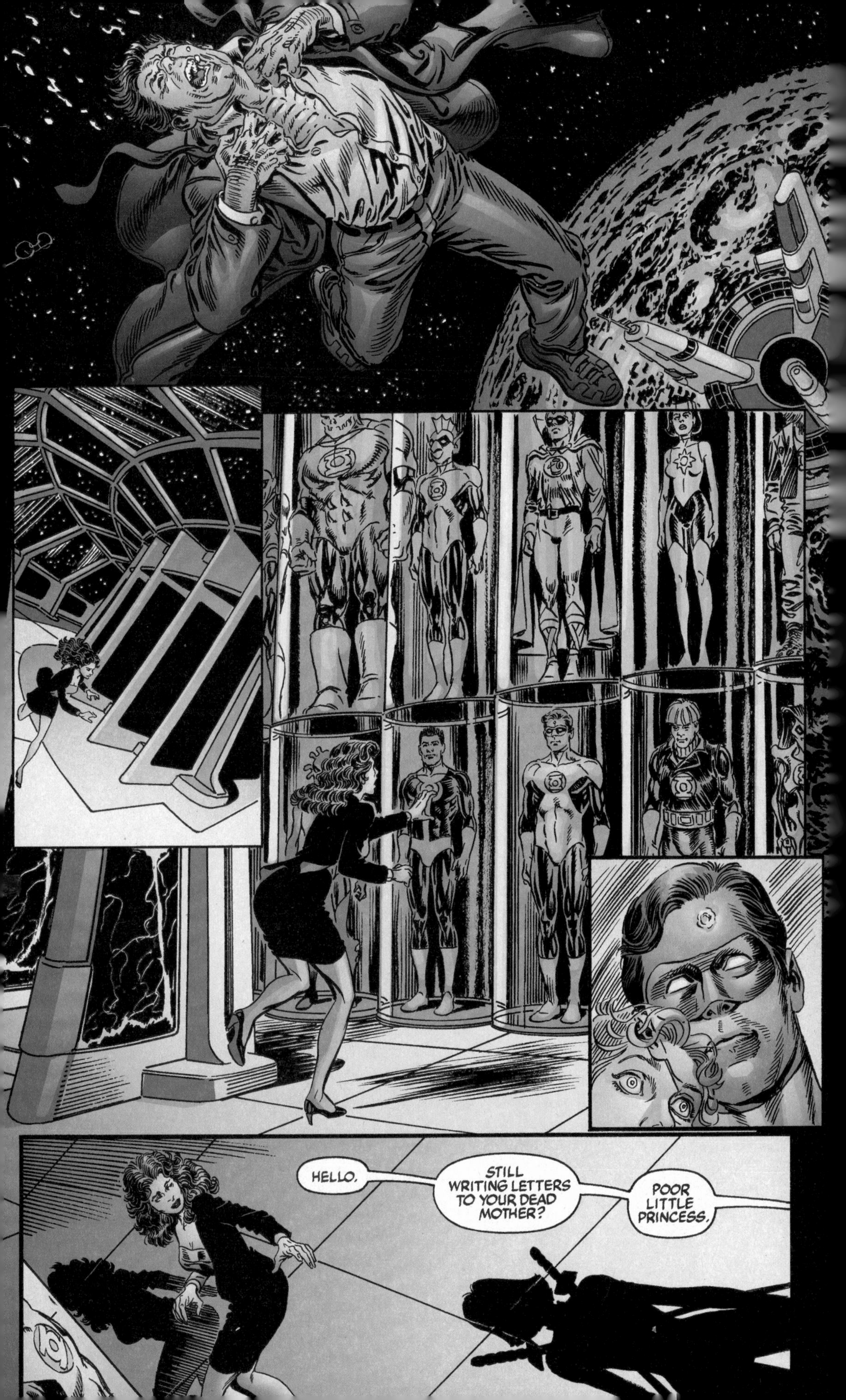
HELLO.
STILL WRITING LETTERS TO YOUR DEAD MOTHER?
POOR LITTLE PRINCESS.

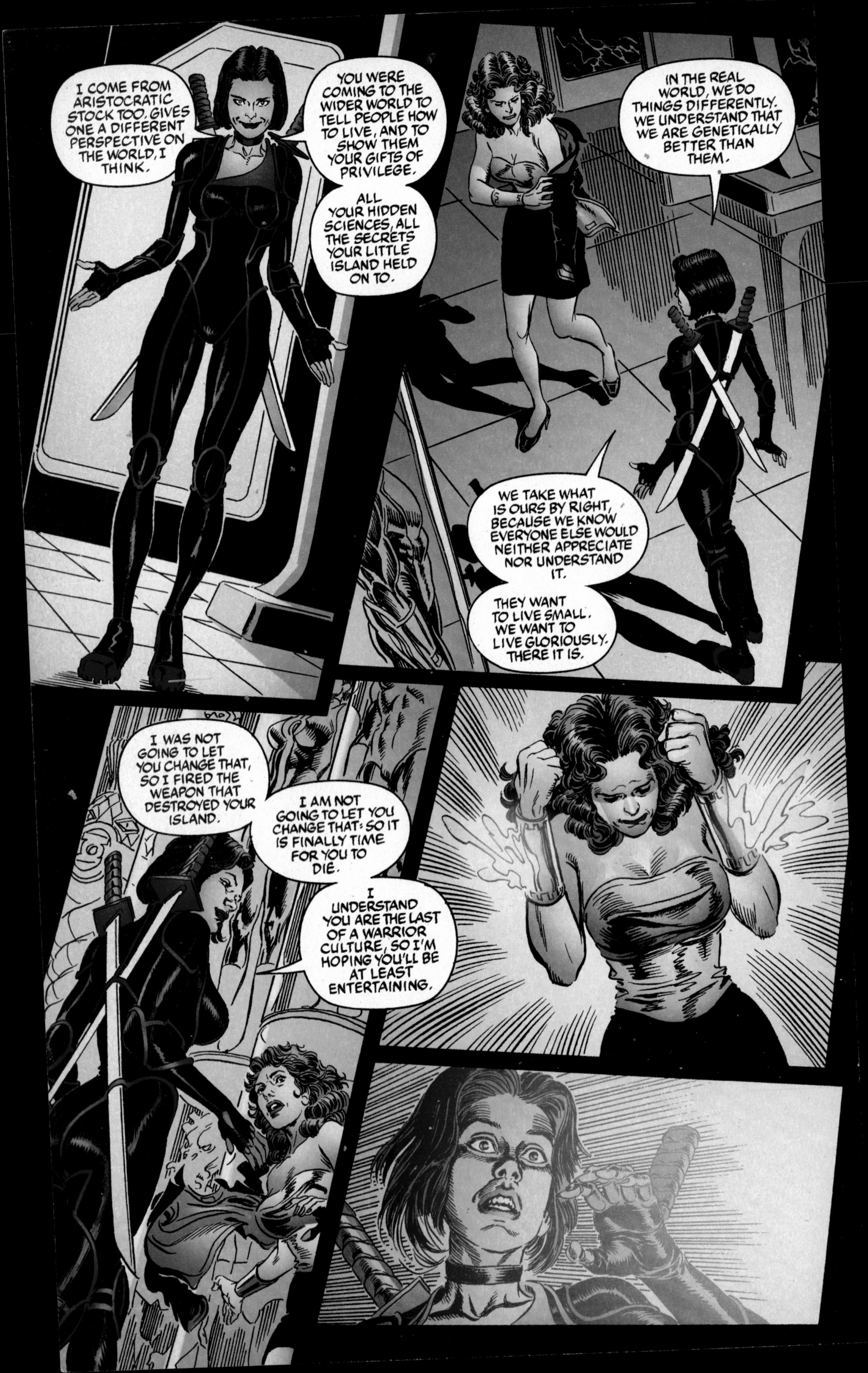
I COME FROM ARISTOCRATIC STOCK TOO. GIVES ONE A DIFFERENT PERSPECTIVE ON THE WORLD, I THINK.
YOU WERE COMING TO THE WIDER WORLD TO TELL PEOPLE HOW TO LIVE, AND TO SHOW THEM YOUR GIFTS OF PRIVILEGE.
ALL YOUR HIDDEN SCIENCES, ALL THE SECRETS YOUR LITTLE ISLAND HELD ON TO.
IN THE REAL WORLD, WE DO THINGS DIFFERENTLY. WE UNDERSTAND THAT WE ARE GENETICALLY BETTER THAN THEM.
WE TAKE WHAT IS OURS BY RIGHT, BECAUSE WE KNOW EVERYONE ELSE WOULD NEITHER APPRECIATE NOR UNDERSTAND IT.
THEY WANT TO LIVE SMALL. WE WANT TO LIVE GLORIOUSLY. THERE IT IS.
I WAS NOT GOING TO LET YOU CHANGE THAT, SO I FIRED THE WEAPON THAT DESTROYED YOUR ISLAND.
I AM NOT GOING TO LET YOU CHANGE THAT: SO IT IS FINALLY TIME FOR YOU TO DIE.
I UNDERSTAND YOU ARE THE LAST OF A WARRIOR CULTURE, SO I'M HOPING YOU'LL BE AT LEAST ENTERTAINING.

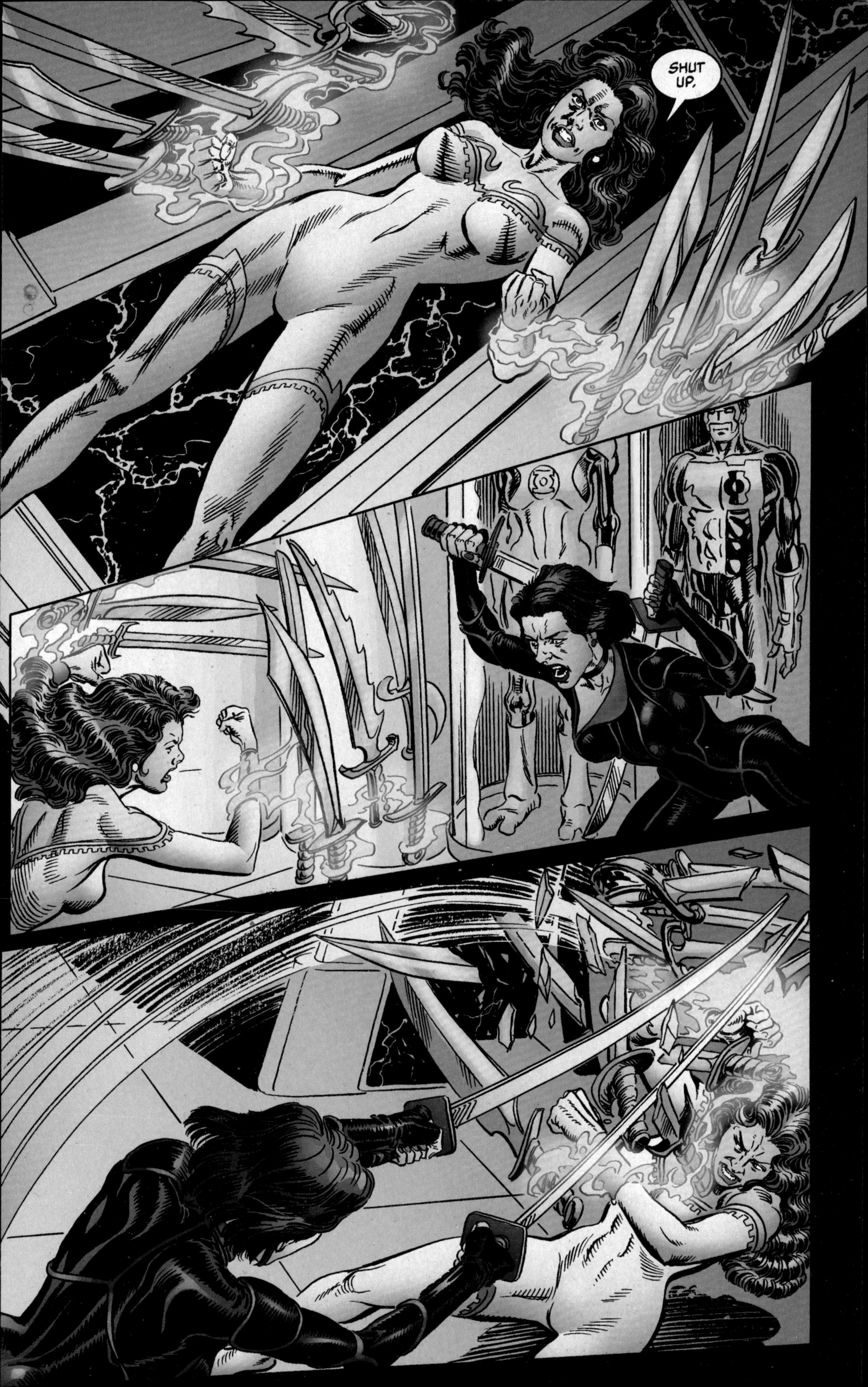
SHUT UP,

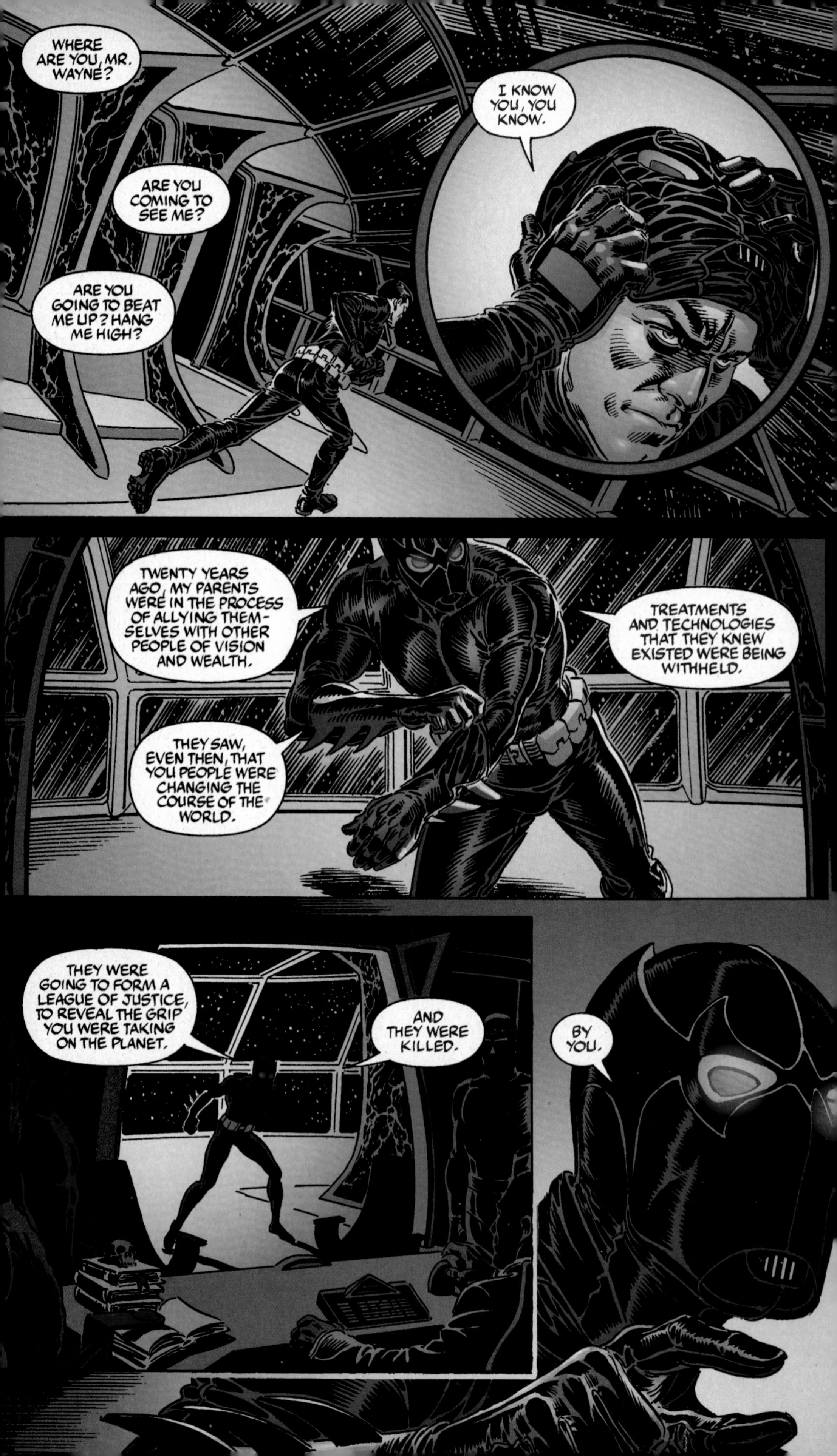
WHERE ARE YOU, MR. WAYNE?
ARE YOU COMING TO SEE ME?
ARE YOU GOING TO BEAT ME UP? HANG ME HIGH?
I KNOW YOU, YOU KNOW.
TWENTY YEARS AGO, MY PARENTS WERE IN THE PROCESS OF ALLYING THEM-SELVES WITH OTHER PEOPLE OF VISION AND WEALTH.
THEY SAW, EVEN THEN, THAT YOU PEOPLE WERE CHANGING THE COURSE OF THE WORLD.
TREATMENTS AND TECHNOLOGIES THAT THEY KNEW EXISTED WERE BEING WITHHELD.
THEY WERE GOING TO FORM A LEAGUE OF JUSTICE, TO REVEAL THE GRIP YOU WERE TAKING ON THE PLANET.
AND THEY WERE KILLED.
BY YOU.

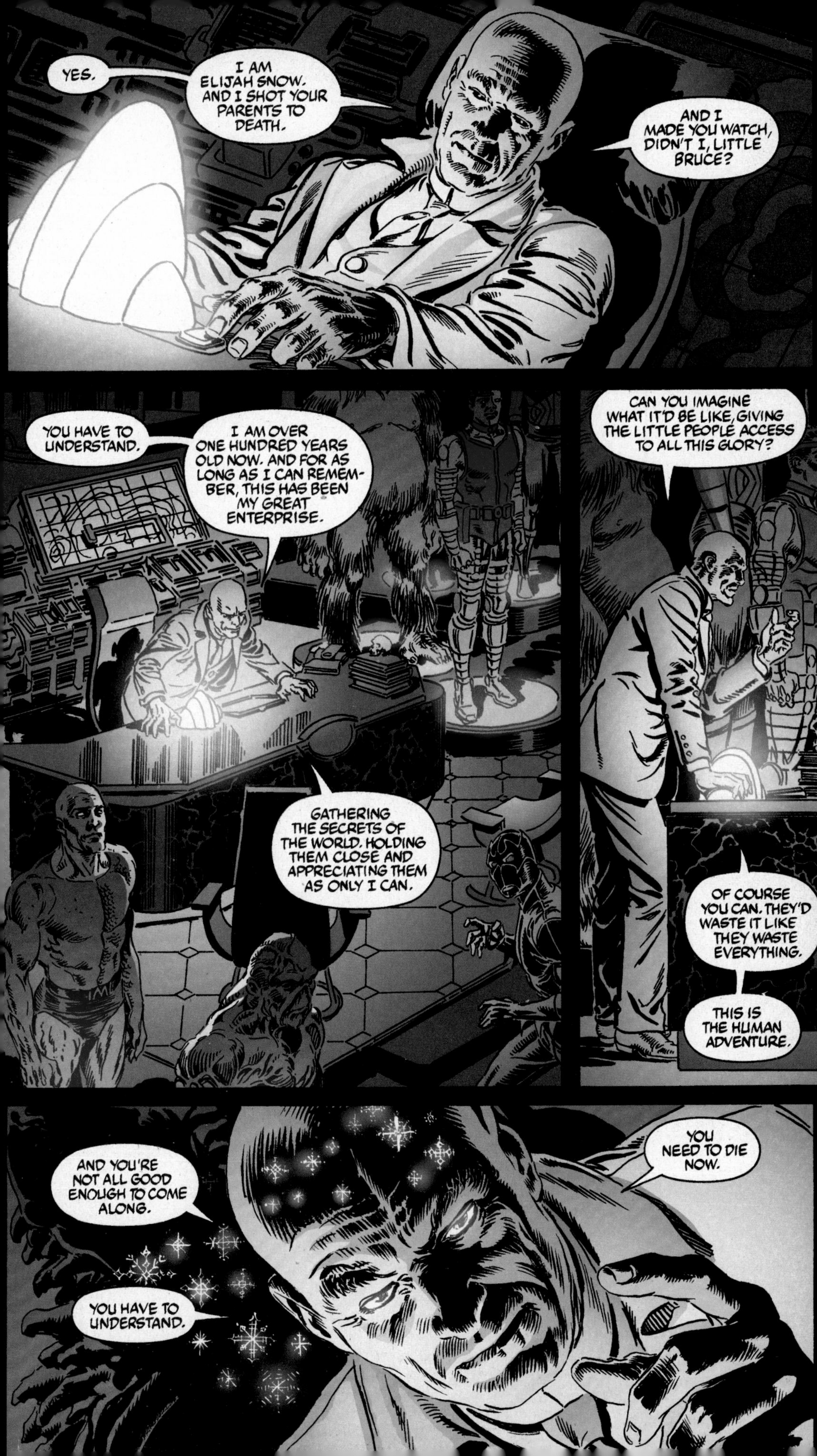
YES.
I AM ELIJAH SNOW. AND I SHOT YOUR PARENTS TO DEATH.
AND I MADE YOU WATCH, DIDN'T I, LITTLE BRUCE?
YOU HAVE TO UNDERSTAND.
I AM OVER ONE HUNDRED YEARS OLD NOW. AND FOR AS LONG AS I CAN REMEMBER, THIS HAS BEEN MY GREAT ENTERPRISE.
GATHERING THE SECRETS OF THE WORLD. HOLDING THEM CLOSE AND APPRECIATING THEM AS ONLY I CAN.
CAN YOU IMAGINE WHAT IT'D BE LIKE, GIVING THE LITTLE PEOPLE ACCESS TO ALL THIS GLORY?
OF COURSE YOU CAN. THEY'D WASTE IT LIKE THEY WASTE EVERYTHING.
THIS IS THE HUMAN ADVENTURE.
AND YOU'RE NOT ALL GOOD ENOUGH TO COME ALONG.
YOU HAVE TO UNDERSTAND.
YOU NEED TO DIE NOW.

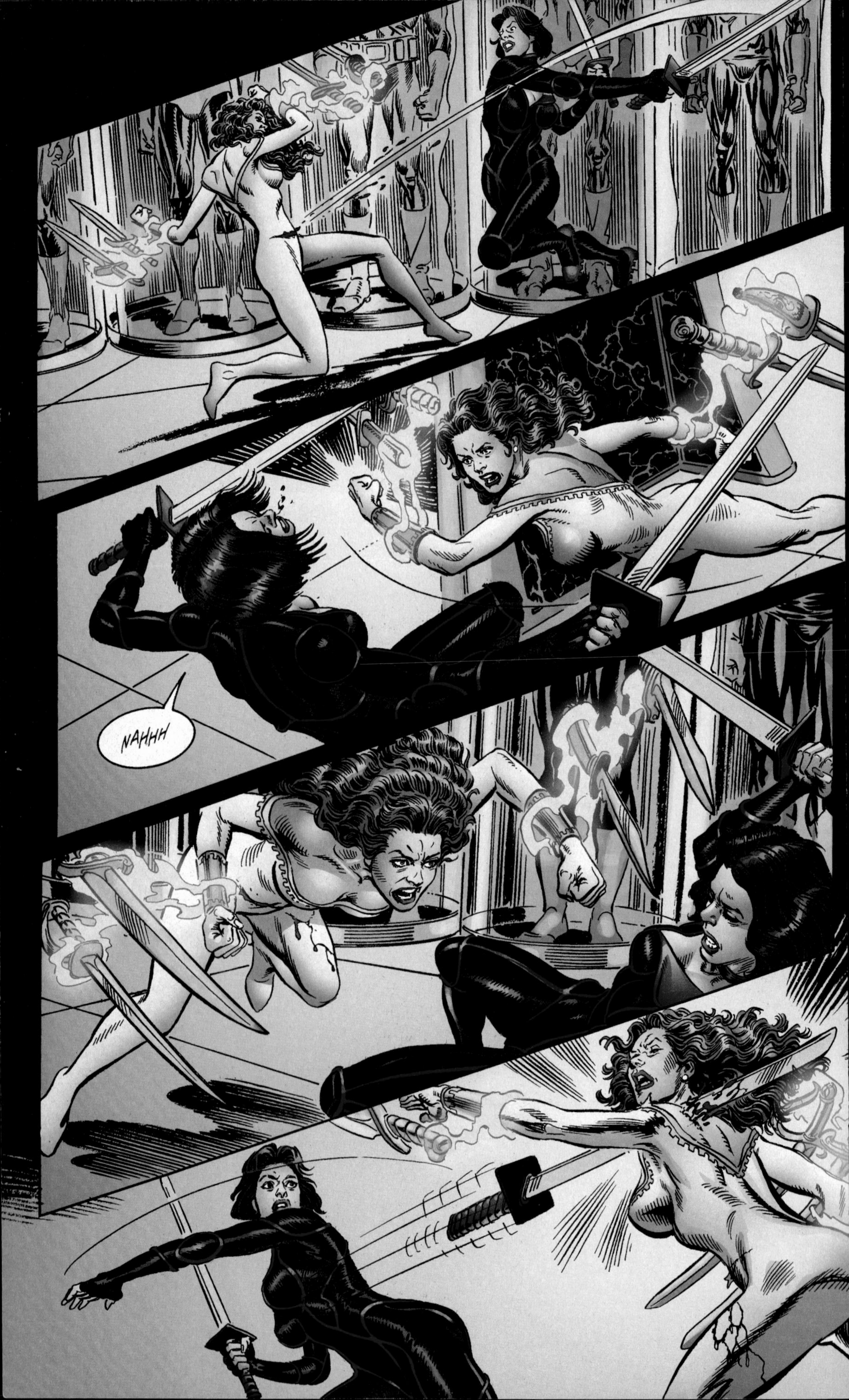
NAHHH

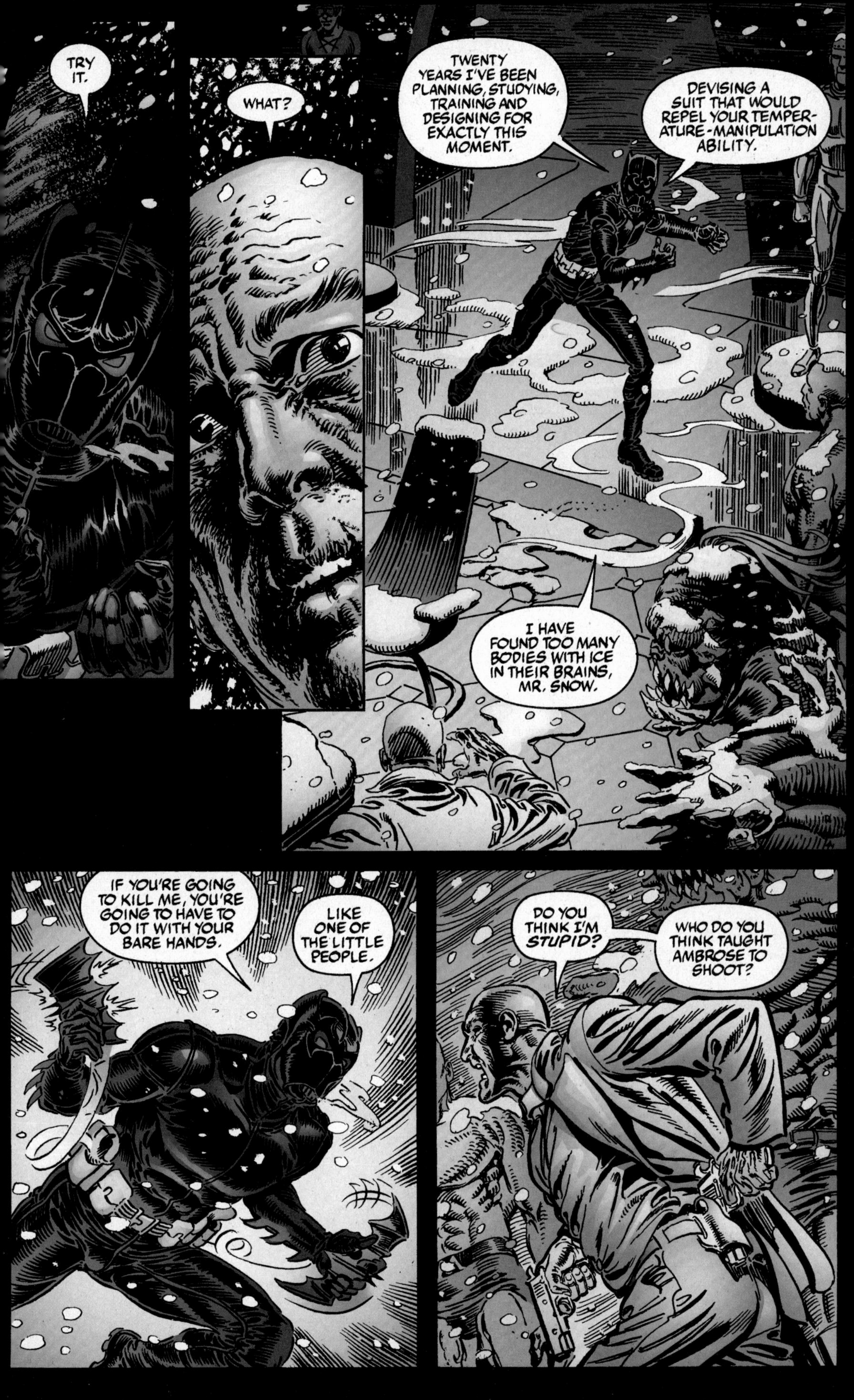
TRY IT.
WHAT?
TWENTY YEARS I'VE BEEN PLANNING, STUDYING, TRAINING AND DESIGNING FOR EXACTLY THIS MOMENT.
DEVISING A SUIT THAT WOULD REPEL YOUR TEMPERATURE-MANIPULATION ABILITY.
I HAVE FOUND TOO MANY BODIES WITH ICE IN THEIR BRAINS, MR. SNOW.
IF YOU'RE GOING TO KILL ME, YOU'RE GOING TO HAVE TO DO IT WITH YOUR BARE HANDS.
LIKE ONE OF THE LITTLE PEOPLE.
DO YOU THINK I'M *STUPID*?
WHO DO YOU THINK TAUGHT AMBROSE TO SHOOT?

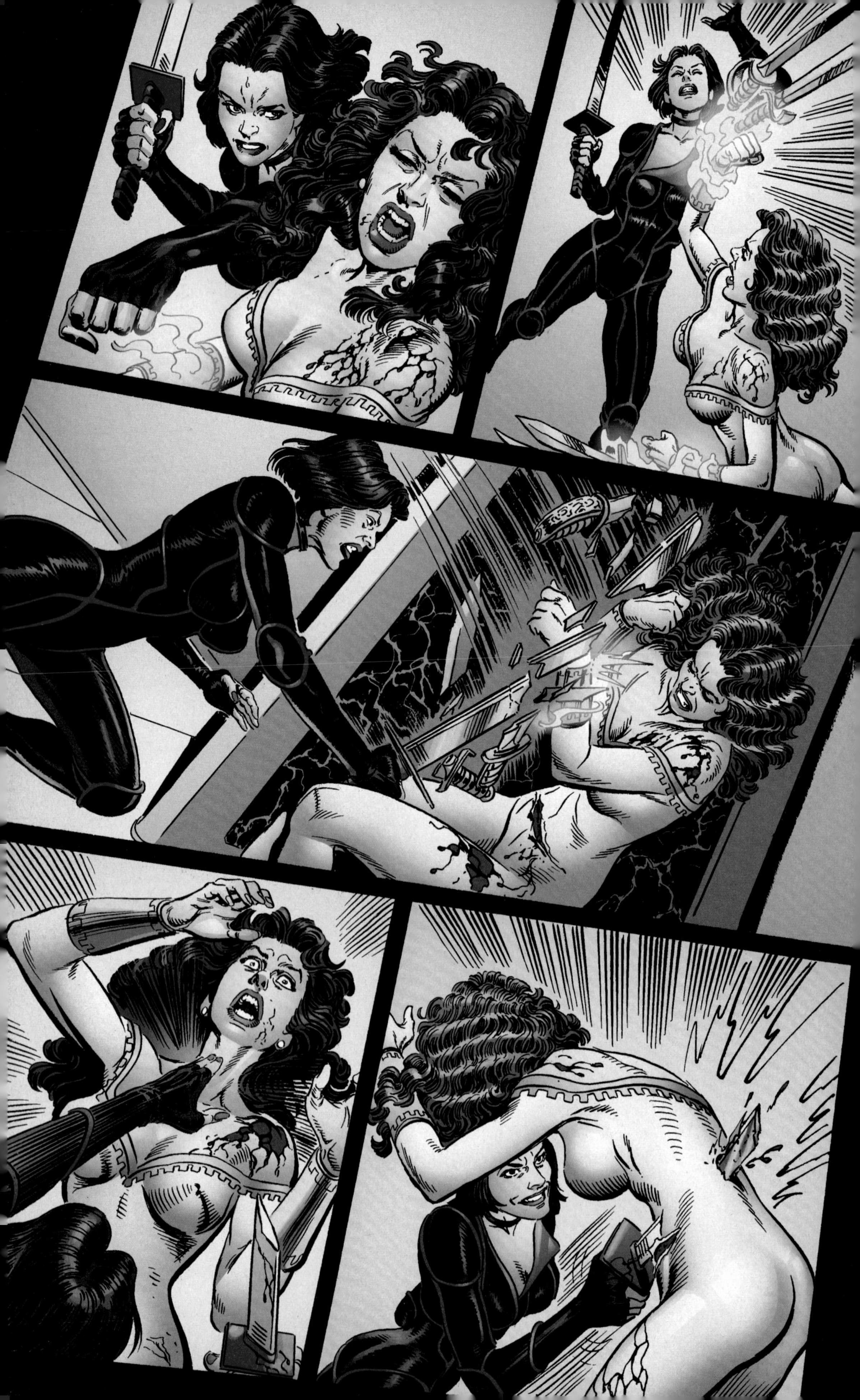

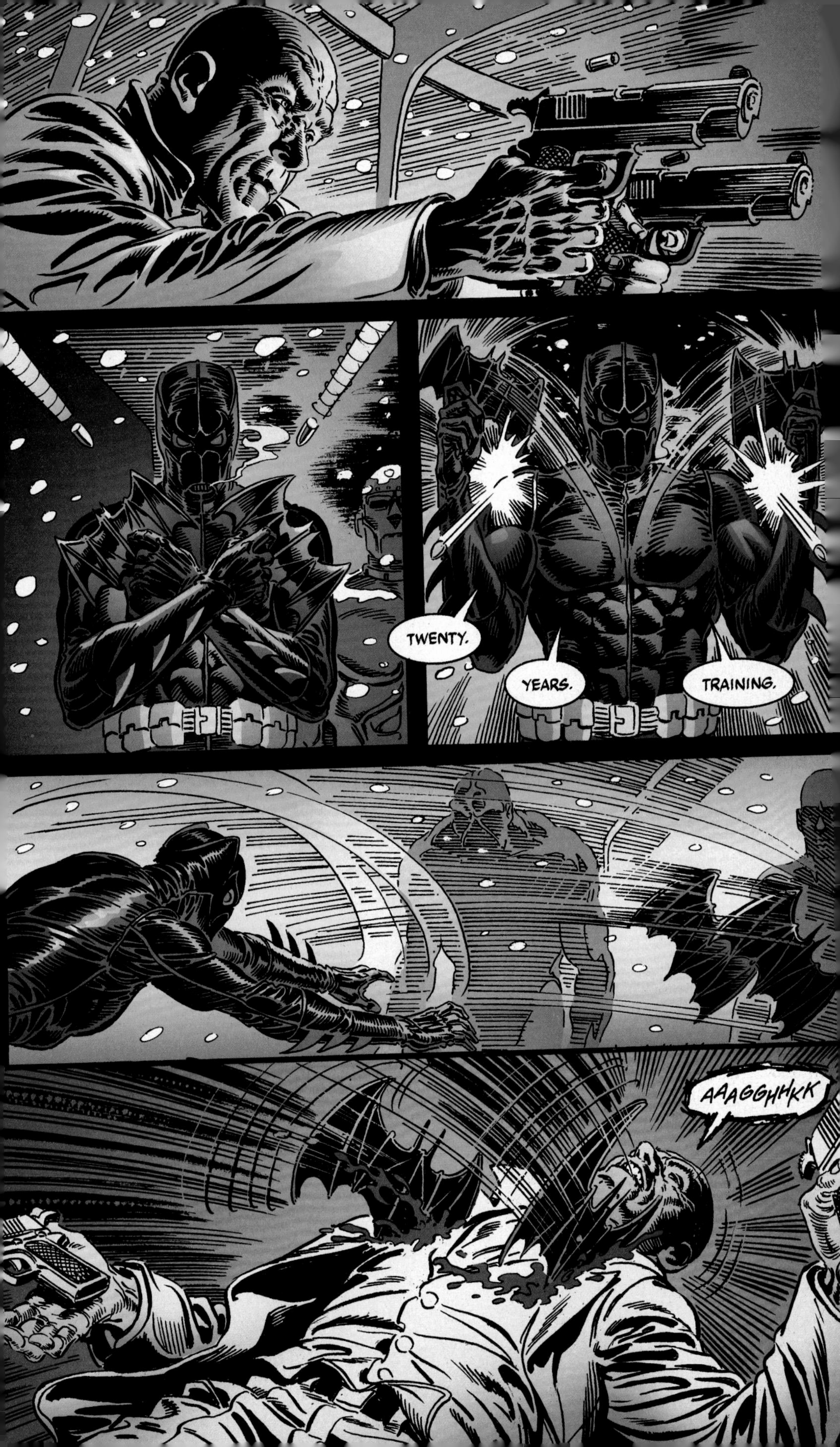
TWENTY.
YEARS.
TRAINING.
AAAGGHHKK

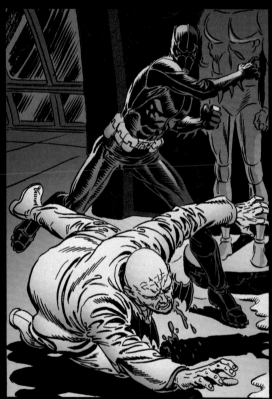

THAT'S IT--
BEAT ME--

--BUT YOU
HAVE TO KILL
ME, YOU LITTLE
BASTARD--
hkk--

--YOU HAVE
TO KILL ME--
hkk
--OR YOU'LL
NEVER EVER
BE SAFE

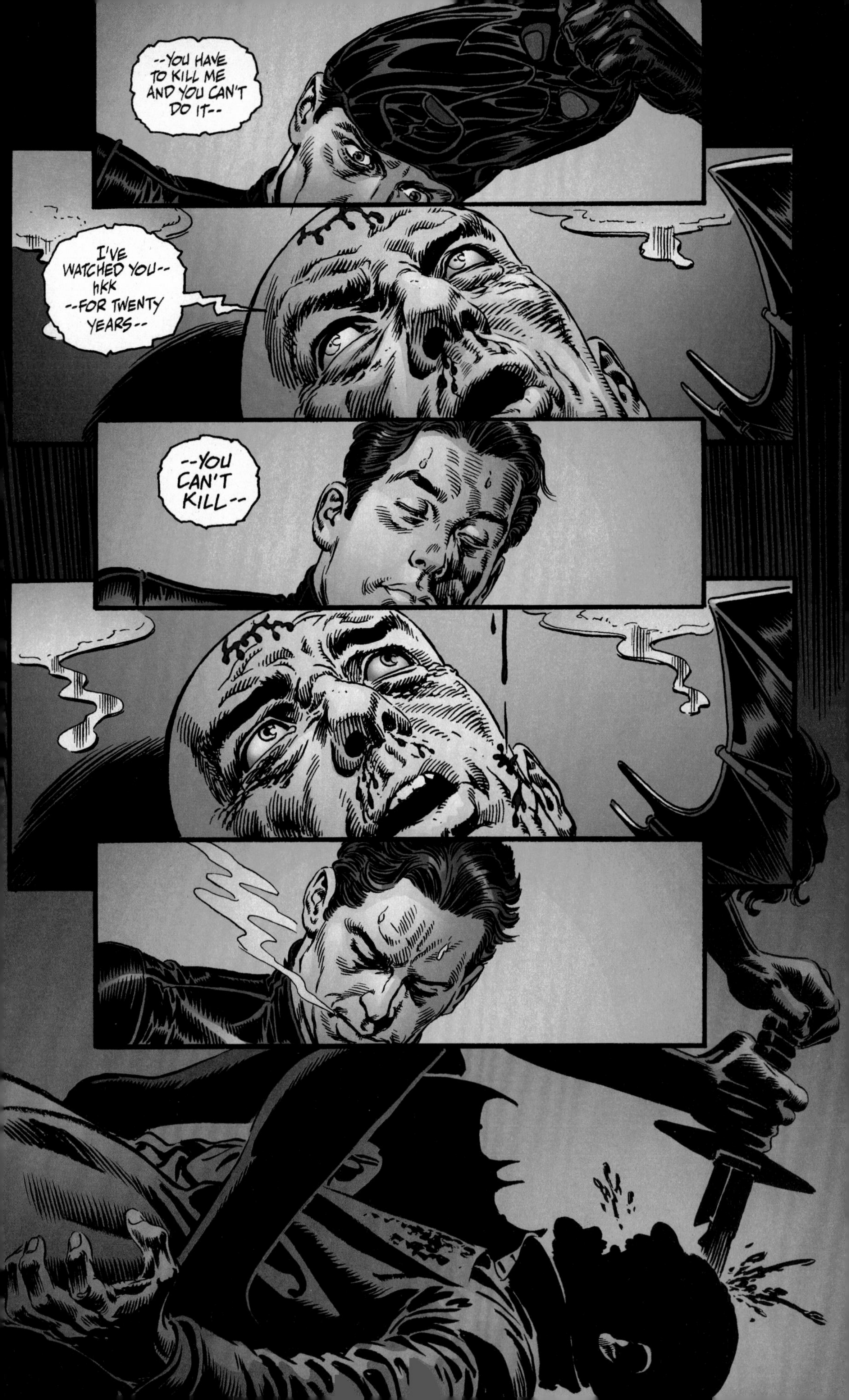

--YOU HAVE TO KILL ME AND YOU CAN'T DO IT--
I'VE WATCHED YOU-- hKK --FOR TWENTY YEARS--
--YOU CAN'T KILL--

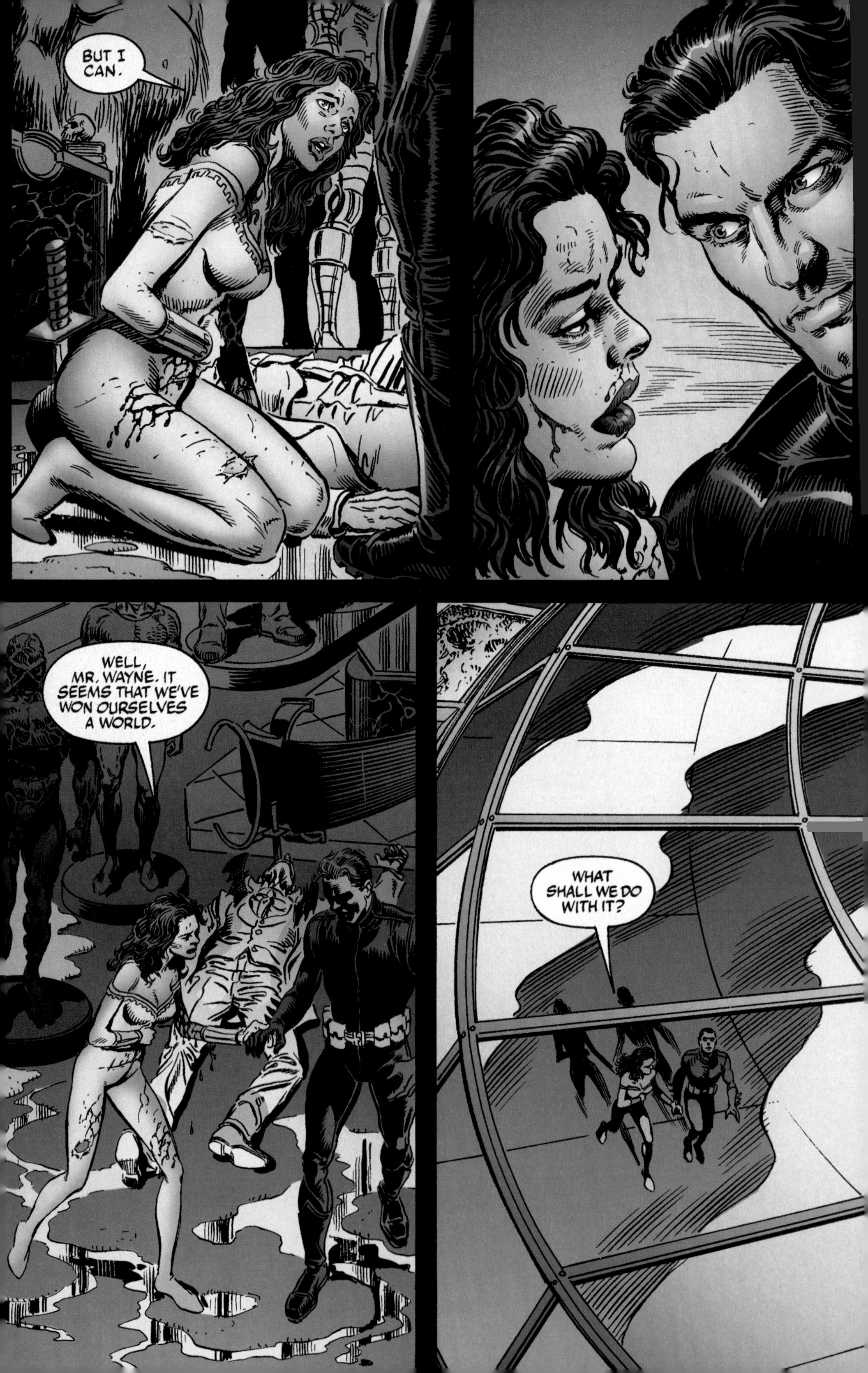
BUT I CAN.
WELL, MR. WAYNE. IT SEEMS THAT WE'VE WON OURSELVES A WORLD.
WHAT SHALL WE DO WITH IT?

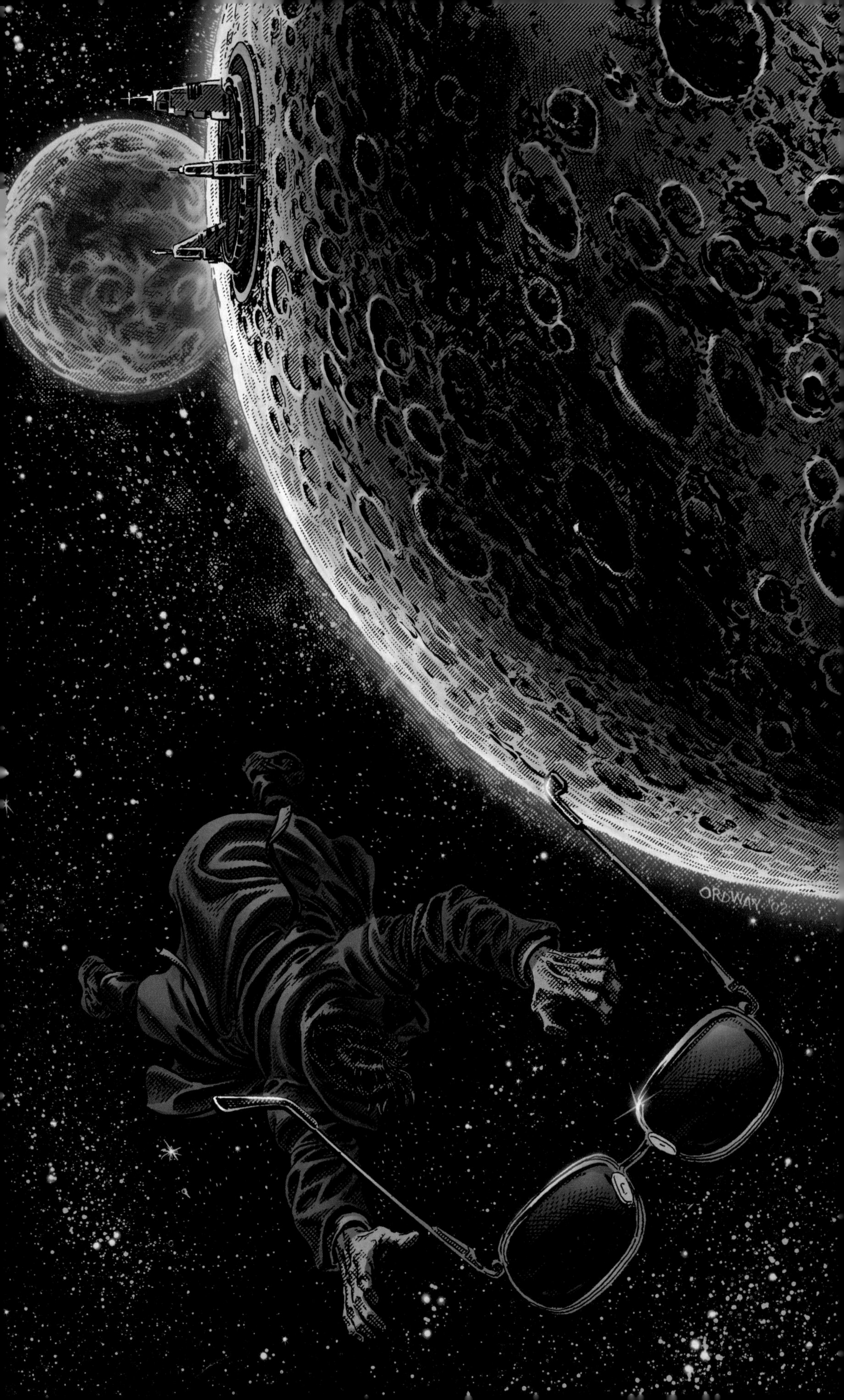
ORDWAY '02

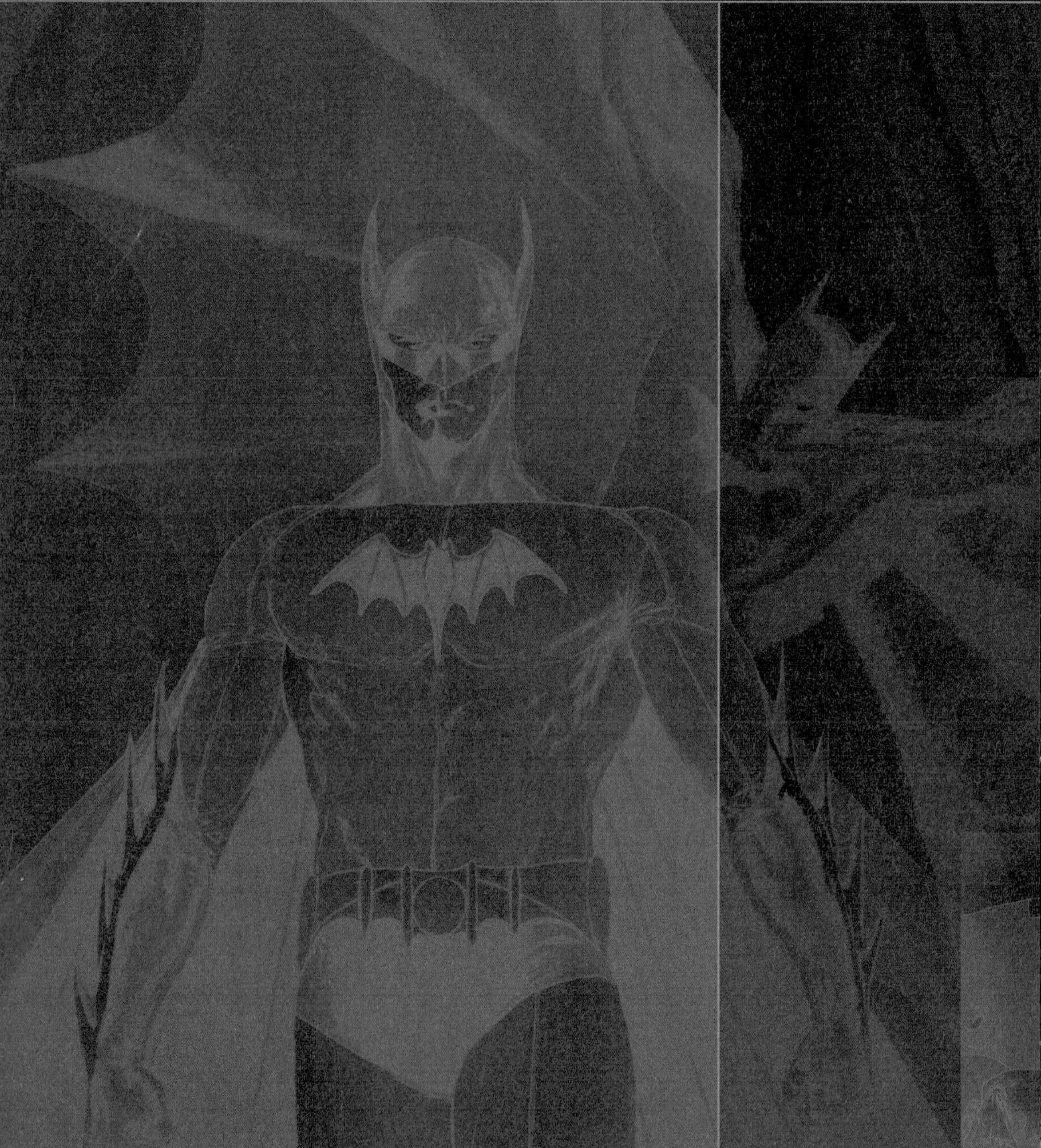

CHAPTER 3

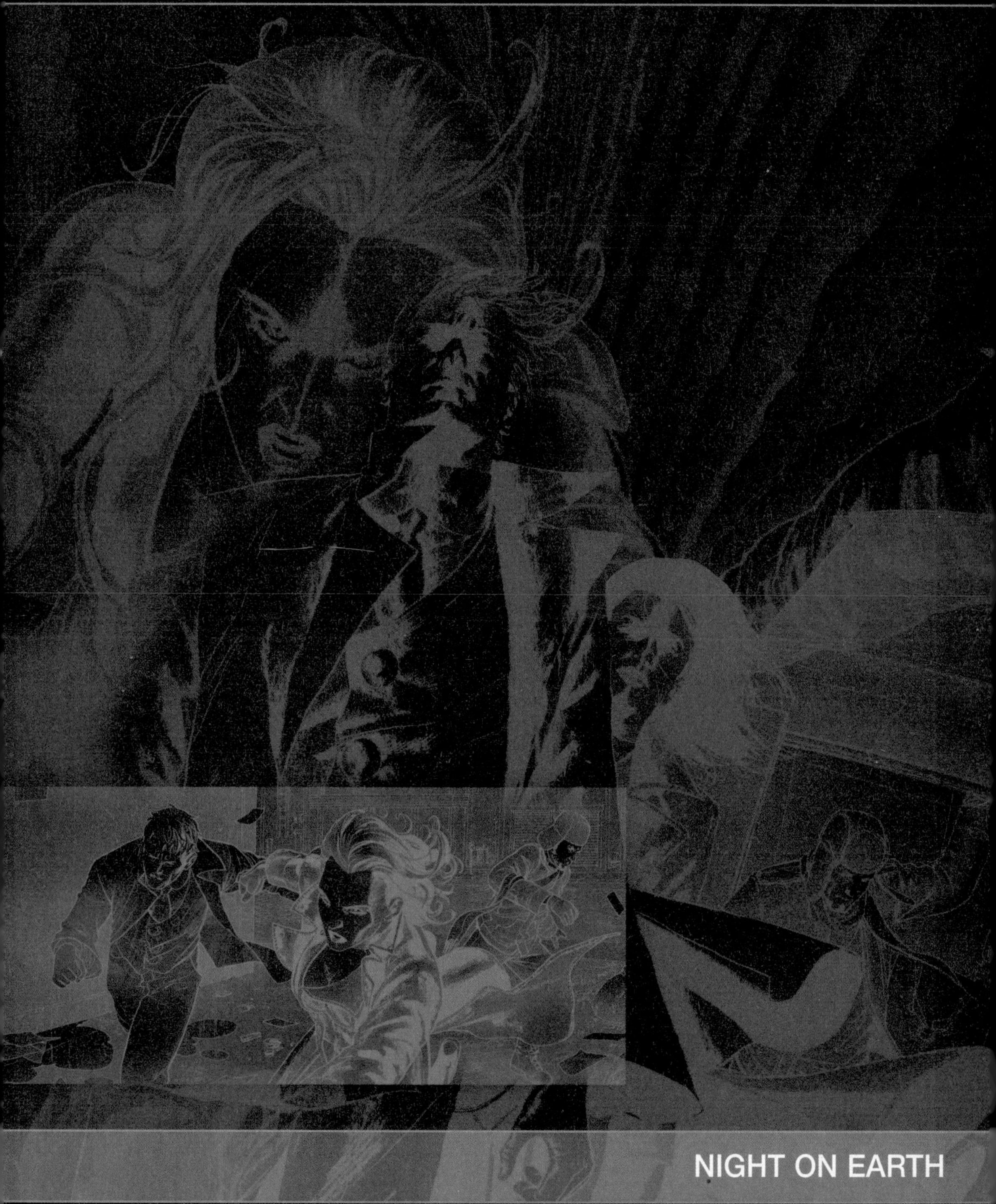

NIGHT ON EARTH

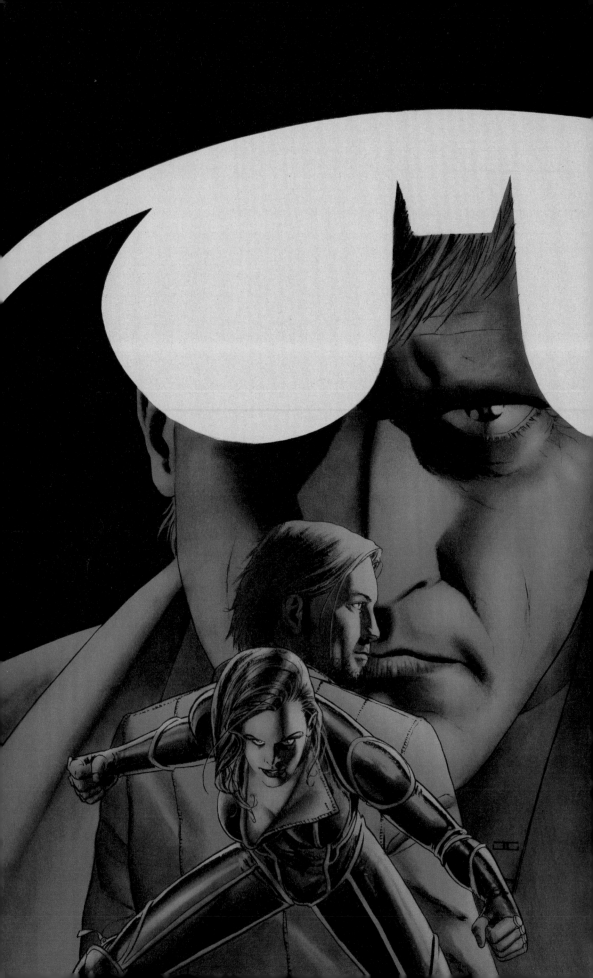

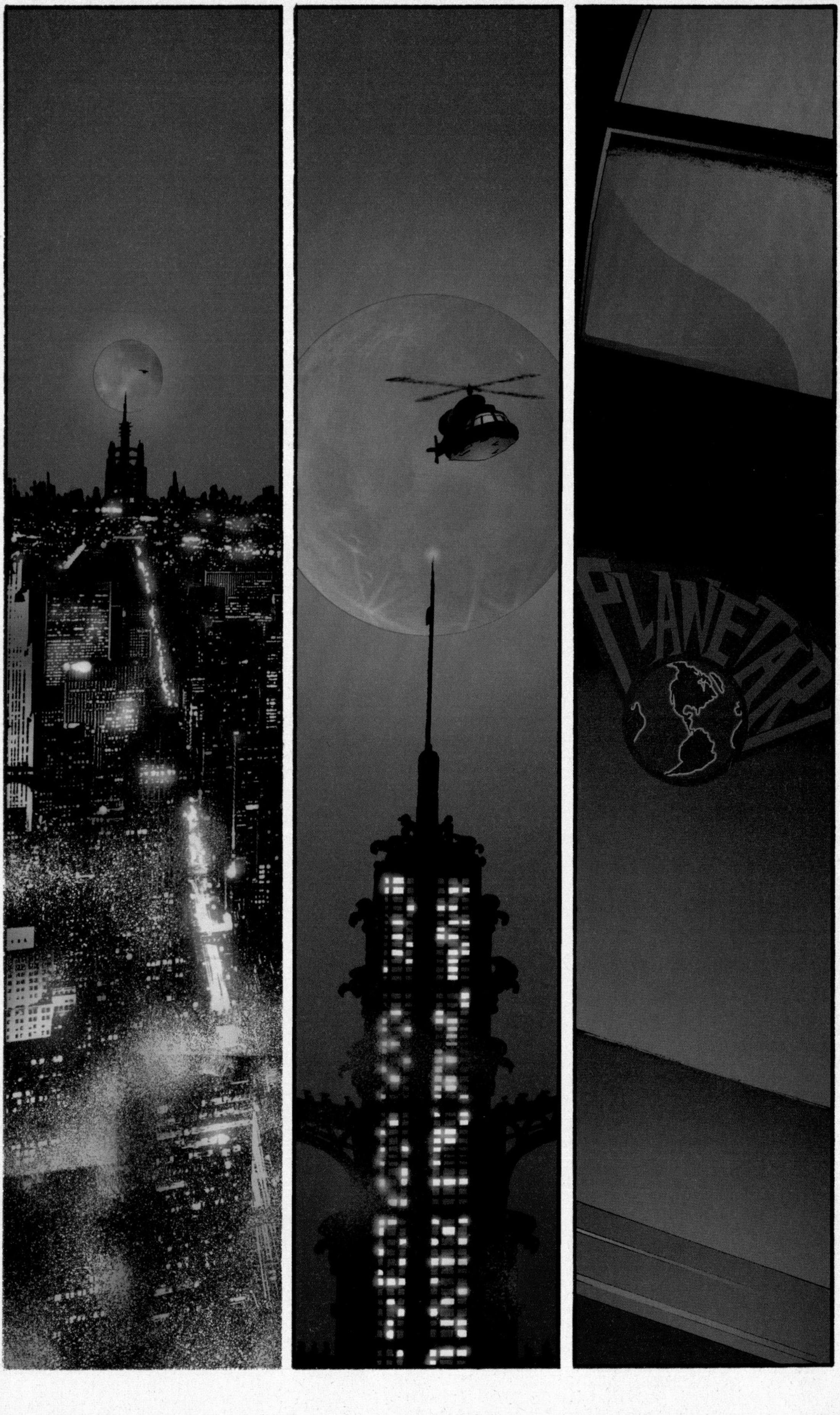
PLANETARY

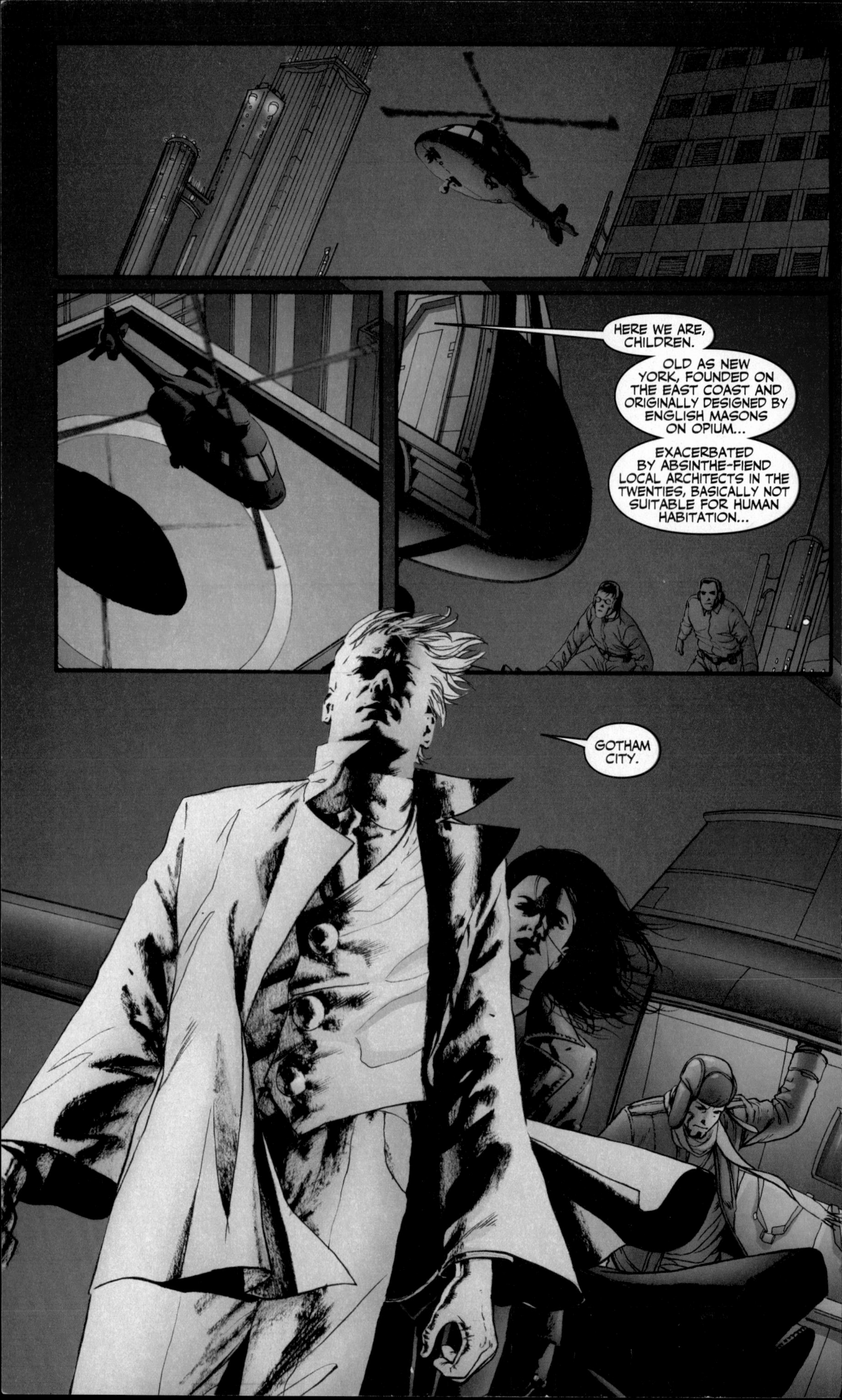
HERE WE ARE, CHILDREN.
OLD AS NEW YORK, FOUNDED ON THE EAST COAST AND ORIGINALLY DESIGNED BY ENGLISH MASONS ON OPIUM...
EXACERBATED BY ABSINTHE-FIEND LOCAL ARCHITECTS IN THE TWENTIES, BASICALLY NOT SUITABLE FOR HUMAN HABITATION...
GOTHAM CITY.

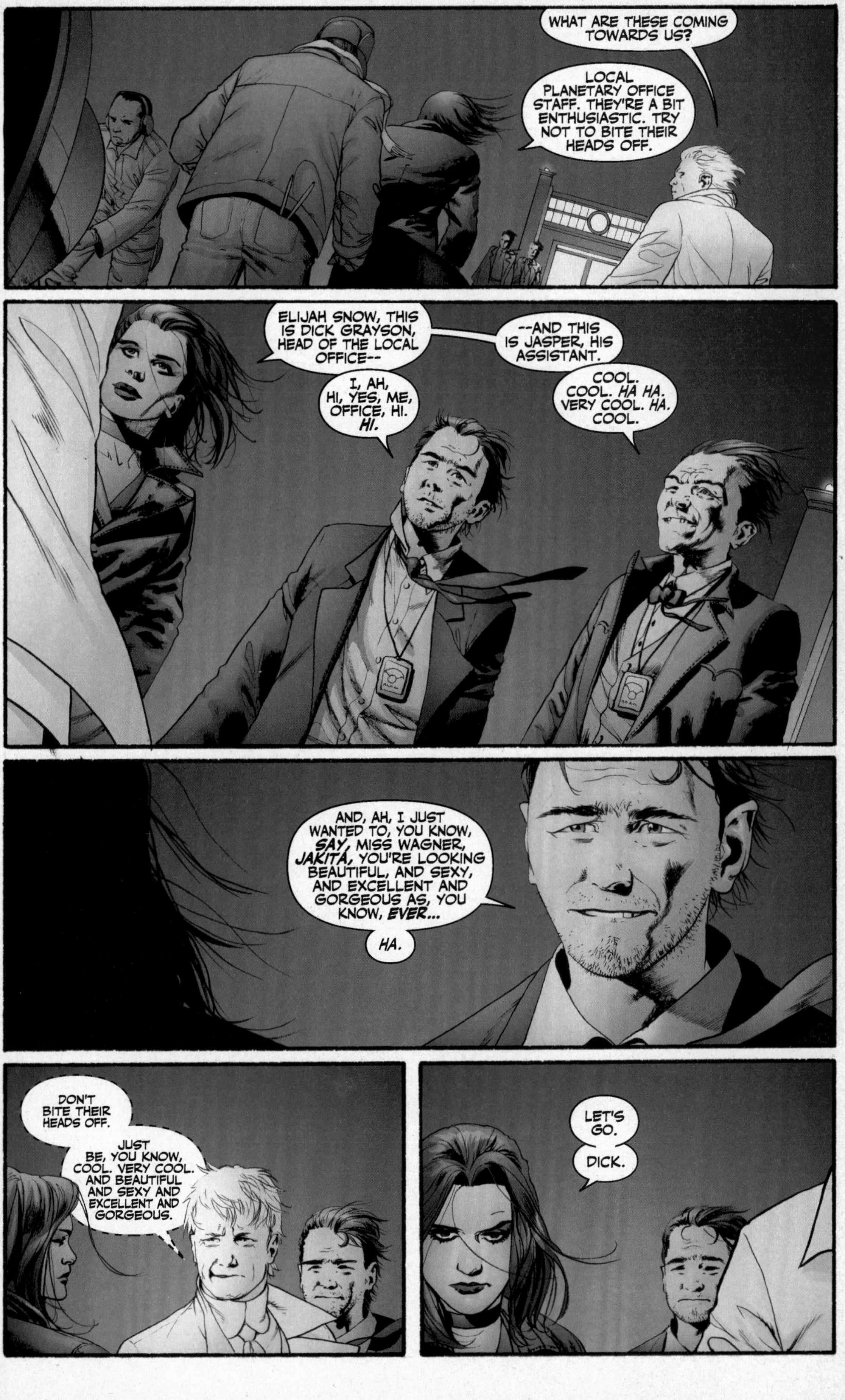
WHAT ARE THESE COMING TOWARDS US?
LOCAL PLANETARY OFFICE STAFF. THEY'RE A BIT ENTHUSIASTIC. TRY NOT TO BITE THEIR HEADS OFF.
ELIJAH SNOW, THIS IS DICK GRAYSON, HEAD OF THE LOCAL OFFICE--
--AND THIS IS JASPER, HIS ASSISTANT.
I, AH, HI, YES, ME, OFFICE, HI. HI.
COOL. COOL. HA HA. VERY COOL. HA. COOL.
AND, AH, I JUST WANTED TO, YOU KNOW, SAY, MISS WAGNER, JAKITA, YOU'RE LOOKING BEAUTIFUL, AND SEXY, AND EXCELLENT AND GORGEOUS AS, YOU KNOW, EVER...
HA.
DON'T BITE THEIR HEADS OFF.
JUST BE, YOU KNOW, COOL. VERY COOL. AND BEAUTIFUL AND SEXY AND EXCELLENT AND GORGEOUS.
LET'S GO.
DICK.

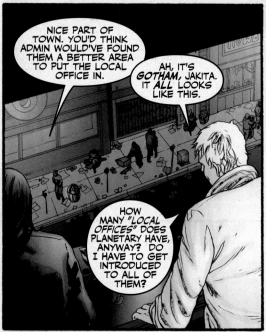

NICE PART OF TOWN. YOU'D THINK ADMIN WOULD'VE FOUND THEM A BETTER AREA TO PUT THE LOCAL OFFICE IN.

AH, IT'S *GOTHAM*, JAKITA. IT *ALL* LOOKS LIKE THIS.

HOW MANY *"LOCAL OFFICES"* DOES PLANETARY HAVE, ANYWAY? DO I HAVE TO GET INTRODUCED TO ALL OF THEM?

WELL, IT'S NOT CALLED PLANETARY BECAUSE WE ONLY HAVE OFFICES IN TWOBLONDES, ARIZONA.

IT'S A BIG JOB WE SET OURSELVES: UNCOVERING THE SECRET HISTORY OF THE WORLD.

SO WE'RE ALL OVER THE PLANET: DIGGING EVERYWHERE AT ONCE.

AH, MISS WAGNER...THE DRUMMER'S DOING SOMETHING TO MY TELEVISION SET AGAIN...

ZIP IT UP, DRUMS.

AND I'VE TOLD YOU BEFORE ABOUT MAKING INNOCENT PEOPLE'S TV SETS PICK UP SHOWS FROM OTHER PLANETS.

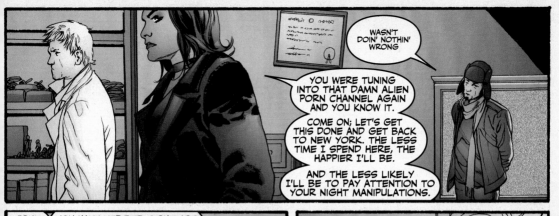

WASN'T DOIN' NOTHIN' WRONG

YOU WERE TUNING INTO THAT DAMN ALIEN PORN CHANNEL AGAIN AND YOU KNOW IT.

COME ON; LET'S GET THIS DONE AND GET BACK TO NEW YORK. THE LESS TIME I SPEND HERE, THE HAPPIER I'LL BE.

AND THE LESS LIKELY I'LL BE TO PAY ATTENTION TO YOUR NIGHT MANIPULATIONS.

JOHN BLACK. YOU HAVE VERIFIED SIGHTINGS OF HIM HERE IN GOTHAM. YOU KNOW WE WANT TO MEET HIM. YOU CALLED CENTRAL OFFICE LIKE GOOD BOYS.

SPEAK.

IT'D HELP THINGS IF WE KNEW WHY YOU WANTED TO TALK TO HIM. HOW URGENT IT IS.

THAT SORT OF THING.

WE'VE ASCERTAINED THAT HIS FATHER WAS ONE OF A HANDFUL OF SURVIVORS OF THE AMERICAN SECRET EXPERIMENTATION CAMP SCIENCE CITY ZERO.

WE'VE REASON TO BELIEVE THAT HIS FATHER'S ENHANCED GENETIC STRUCTURE WILL HAVE GIVEN JOHN SOME KIND OF SUPERHUMAN CAPABILITY.

WE WANT TO KNOW WHAT JOHN'S FATHER TOLD HIM ABOUT CITY ZERO, AND WE'D LIKE TO KNOW WHAT HE CAN DO.

KILL PEOPLE.

HE CAN KILL PEOPLE.

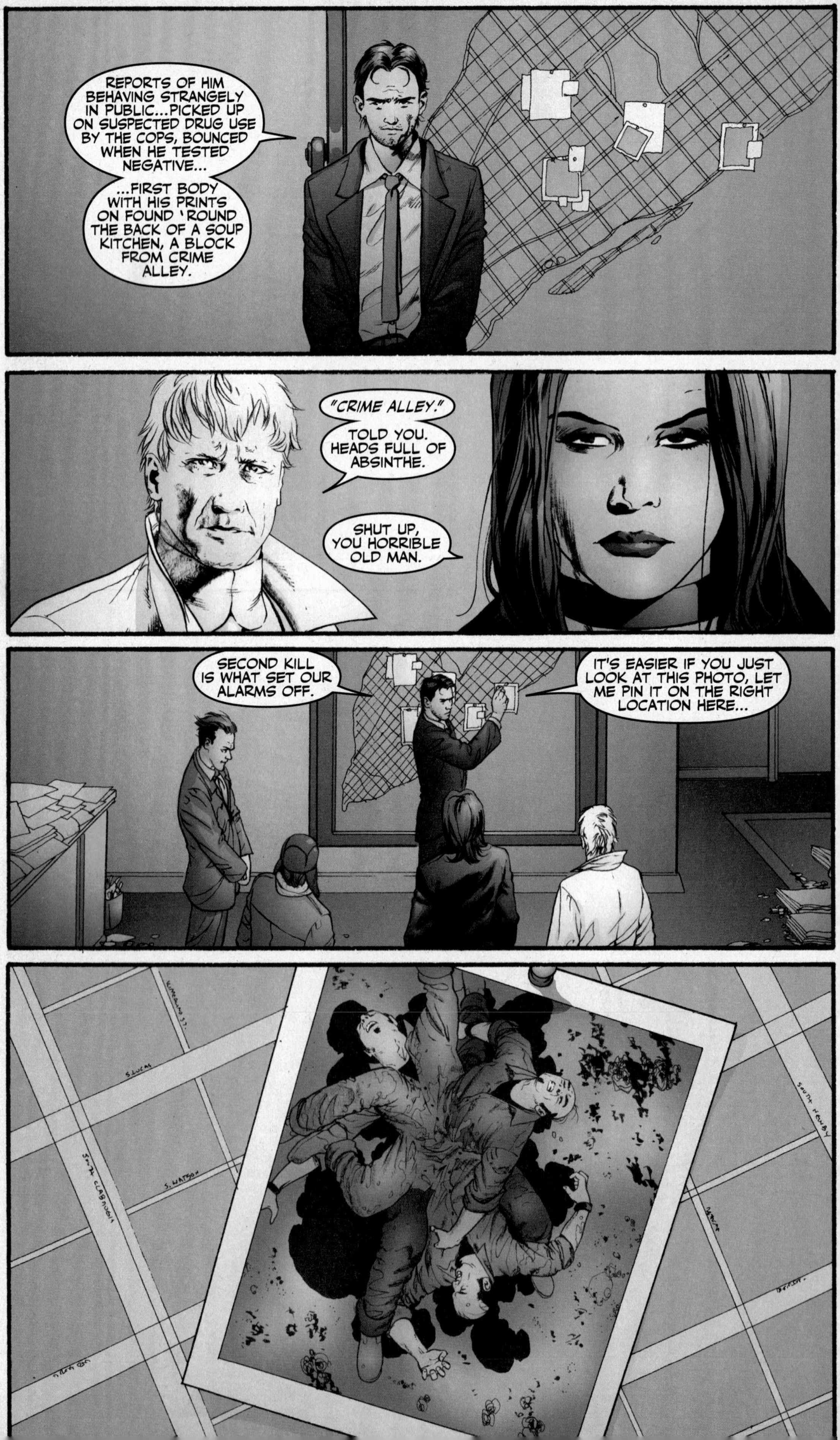
REPORTS OF HIM BEHAVING STRANGELY IN PUBLIC...PICKED UP ON SUSPECTED DRUG USE BY THE COPS, BOUNCED WHEN HE TESTED NEGATIVE...
...FIRST BODY WITH HIS PRINTS ON FOUND 'ROUND THE BACK OF A SOUP KITCHEN, A BLOCK FROM CRIME ALLEY.
"CRIME ALLEY."
TOLD YOU. HEADS FULL OF ABSINTHE.
SHUT UP, YOU HORRIBLE OLD MAN.
SECOND KILL IS WHAT SET OUR ALARMS OFF.
IT'S EASIER IF YOU JUST LOOK AT THIS PHOTO, LET ME PIN IT ON THE RIGHT LOCATION HERE...

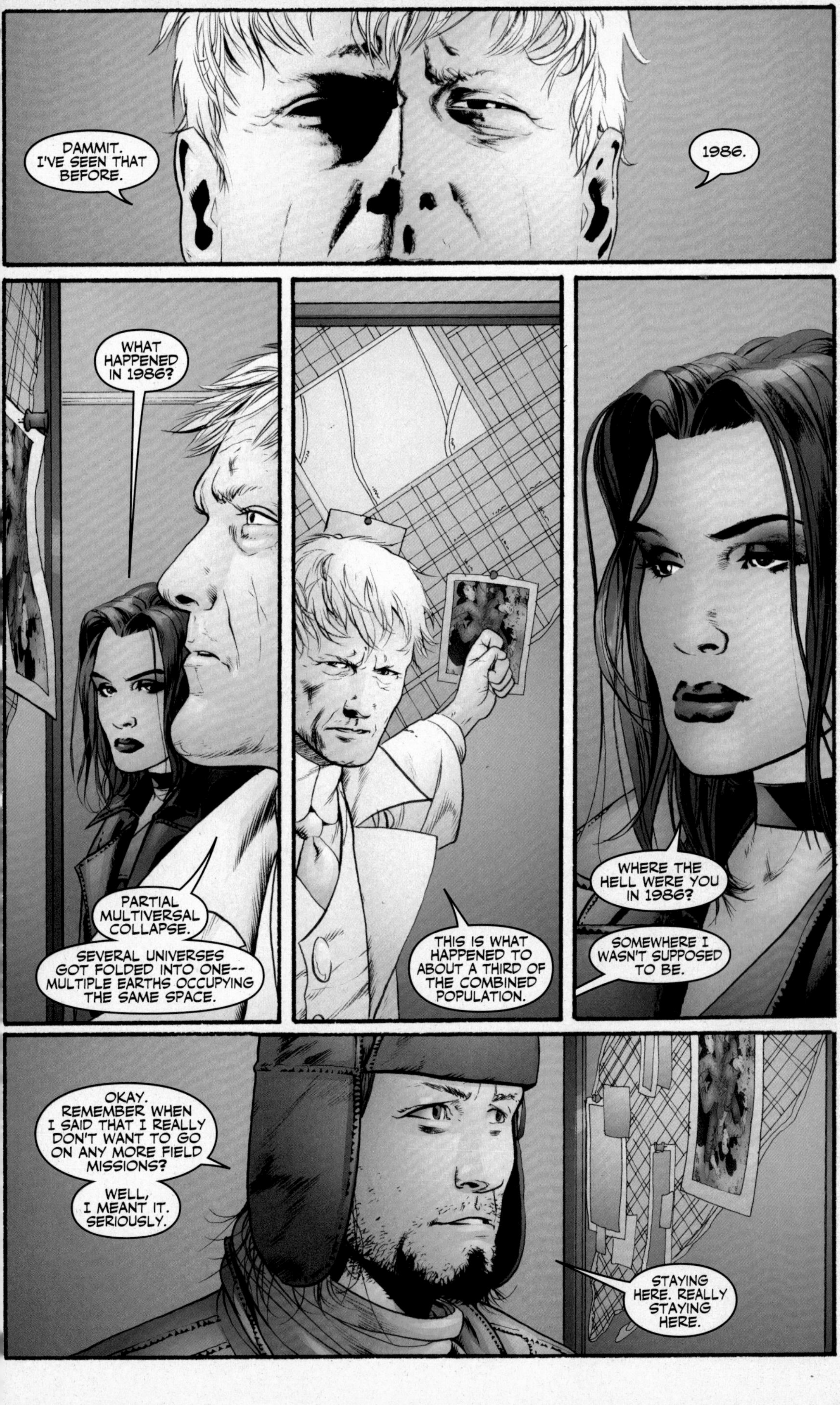
DAMMIT. I'VE SEEN THAT BEFORE.
1986.
WHAT HAPPENED IN 1986?
PARTIAL MULTIVERSAL COLLAPSE.
SEVERAL UNIVERSES GOT FOLDED INTO ONE-- MULTIPLE EARTHS OCCUPYING THE SAME SPACE.
THIS IS WHAT HAPPENED TO ABOUT A THIRD OF THE COMBINED POPULATION.
WHERE THE HELL WERE YOU IN 1986?
SOMEWHERE I WASN'T SUPPOSED TO BE.
OKAY. REMEMBER WHEN I SAID THAT I REALLY DON'T WANT TO GO ON ANY MORE FIELD MISSIONS?
WELL, I MEANT IT. SERIOUSLY.
STAYING HERE. REALLY STAYING HERE.

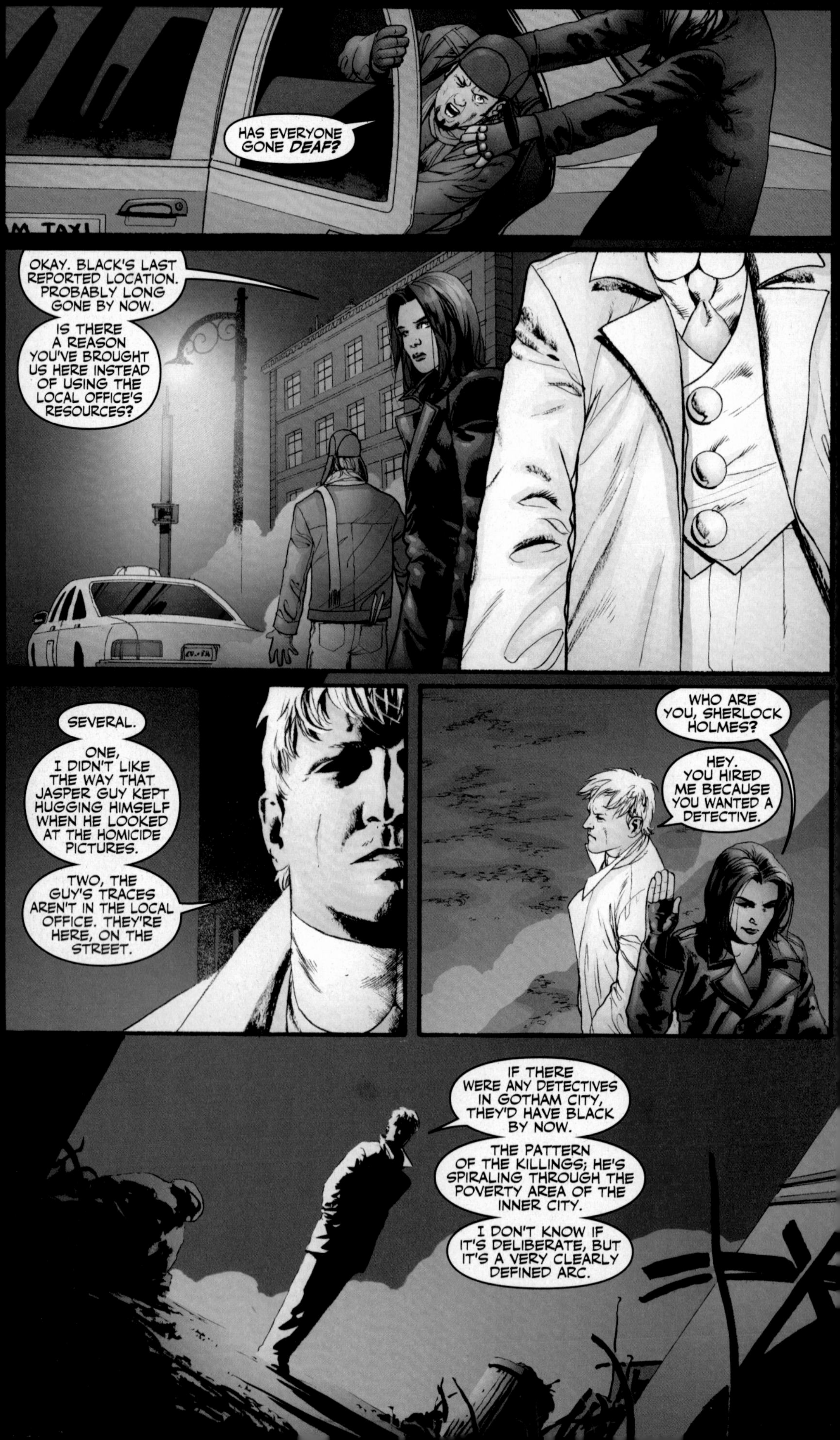
HAS EVERYONE GONE DEAF?
AM TAXI
OKAY. BLACK'S LAST REPORTED LOCATION. PROBABLY LONG GONE BY NOW.
IS THERE A REASON YOU'VE BROUGHT US HERE INSTEAD OF USING THE LOCAL OFFICE'S RESOURCES?
SEVERAL.
ONE, I DIDN'T LIKE THE WAY THAT JASPER GUY KEPT HUGGING HIMSELF WHEN HE LOOKED AT THE HOMICIDE PICTURES.
TWO, THE GUY'S TRACES AREN'T IN THE LOCAL OFFICE. THEY'RE HERE, ON THE STREET.
WHO ARE YOU, SHERLOCK HOLMES?
HEY. YOU HIRED ME BECAUSE YOU WANTED A DETECTIVE.
IF THERE WERE ANY DETECTIVES IN GOTHAM CITY, THEY'D HAVE BLACK BY NOW.
THE PATTERN OF THE KILLINGS; HE'S SPIRALING THROUGH THE POVERTY AREA OF THE INNER CITY.
I DON'T KNOW IF IT'S DELIBERATE, BUT IT'S A VERY CLEARLY DEFINED ARC.

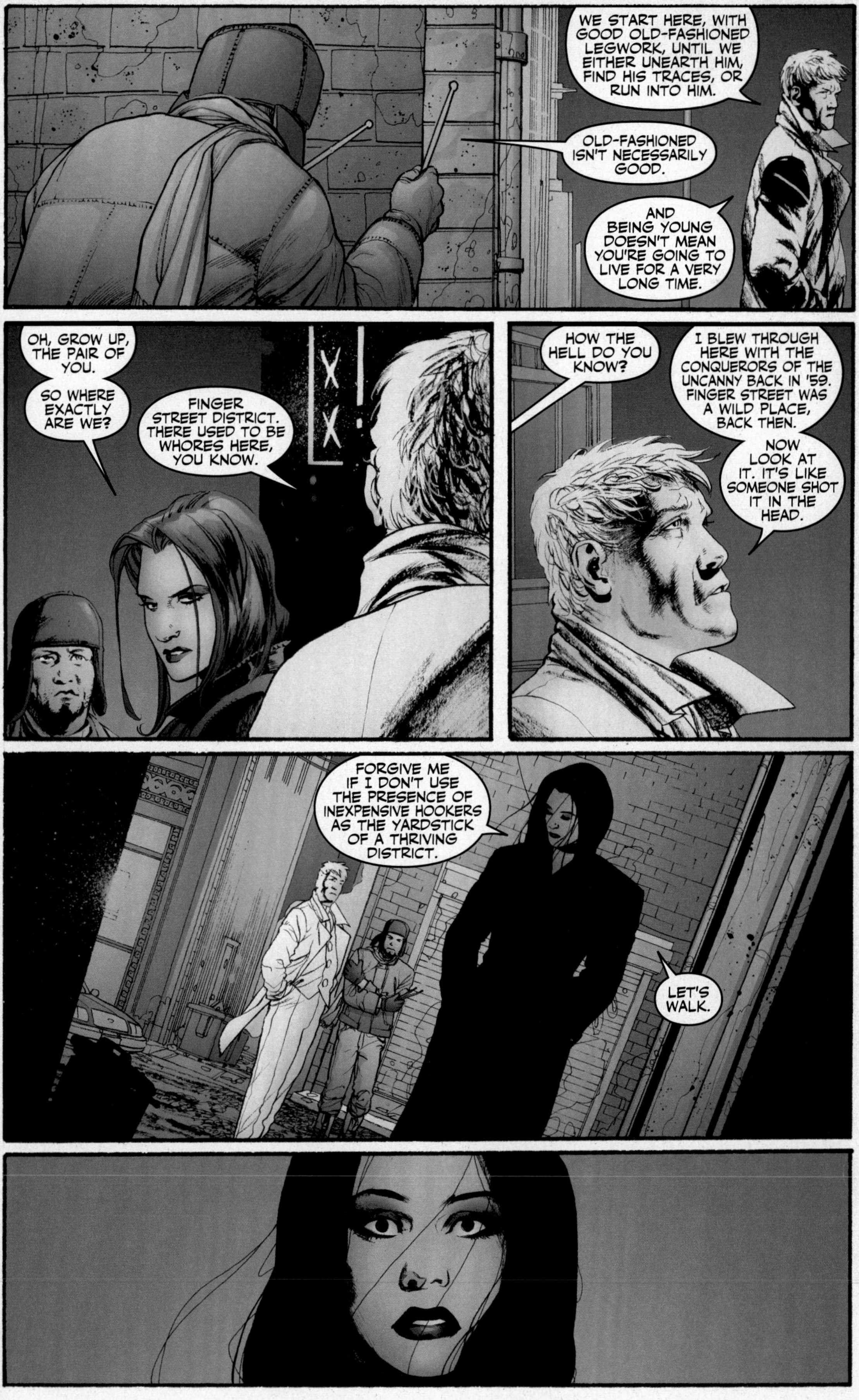
WE START HERE, WITH GOOD OLD-FASHIONED LEGWORK, UNTIL WE EITHER UNEARTH HIM, FIND HIS TRACES, OR RUN INTO HIM.
OLD-FASHIONED ISN'T NECESSARILY GOOD.
AND BEING YOUNG DOESN'T MEAN YOU'RE GOING TO LIVE FOR A VERY LONG TIME.
OH, GROW UP, THE PAIR OF YOU.
SO WHERE EXACTLY ARE WE?
FINGER STREET DISTRICT. THERE USED TO BE WHORES HERE, YOU KNOW.
HOW THE HELL DO YOU KNOW?
I BLEW THROUGH HERE WITH THE CONQUERORS OF THE UNCANNY BACK IN '59. FINGER STREET WAS A WILD PLACE, BACK THEN.
NOW LOOK AT IT. IT'S LIKE SOMEONE SHOT IT IN THE HEAD.
FORGIVE ME IF I DON'T USE THE PRESENCE OF INEXPENSIVE HOOKERS AS THE YARDSTICK OF A THRIVING DISTRICT.
LET'S WALK.

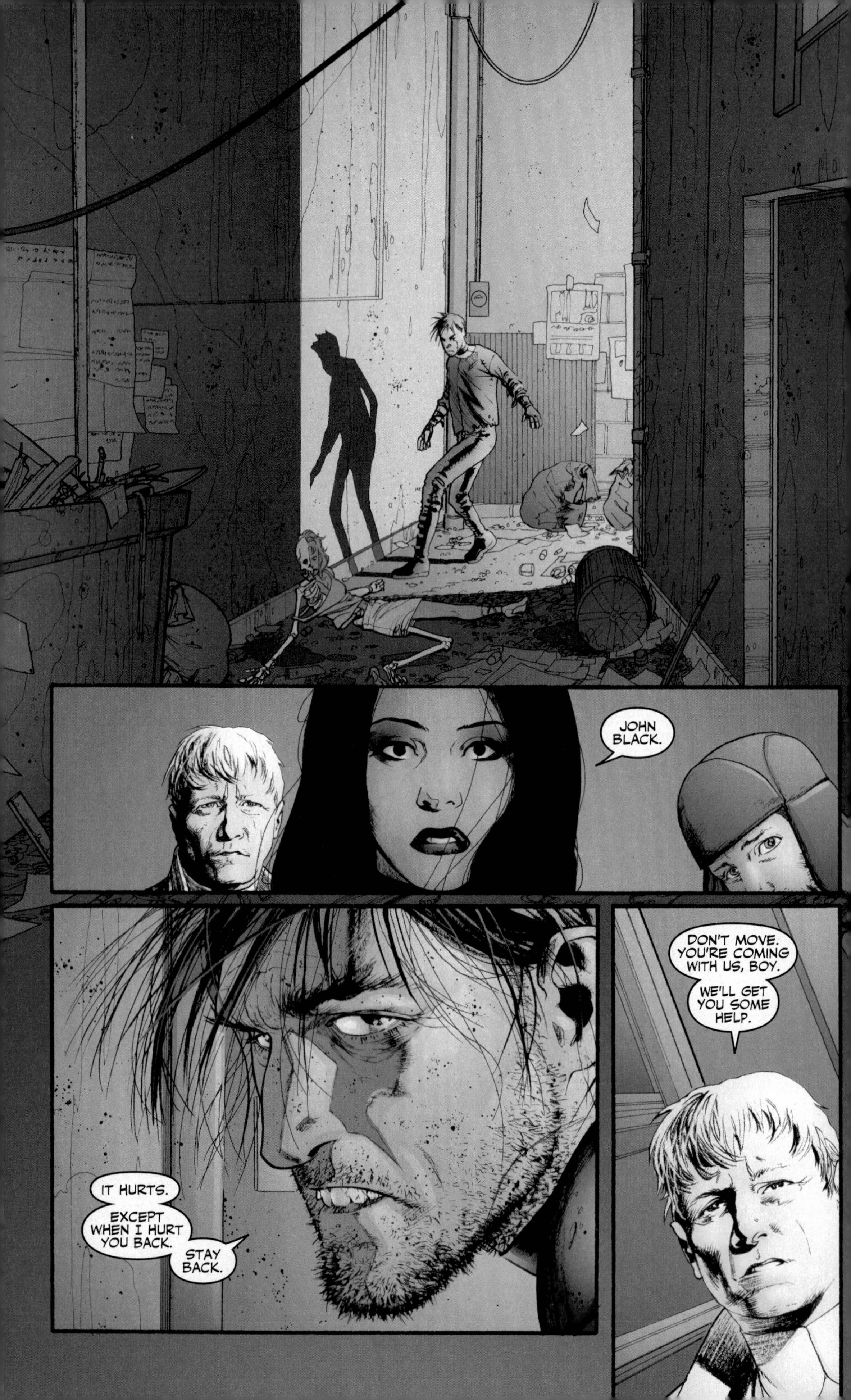
JOHN BLACK.
IT HURTS.
EXCEPT WHEN I HURT YOU BACK.
STAY BACK.
DON'T MOVE. YOU'RE COMING WITH US, BOY.
WE'LL GET YOU SOME HELP.

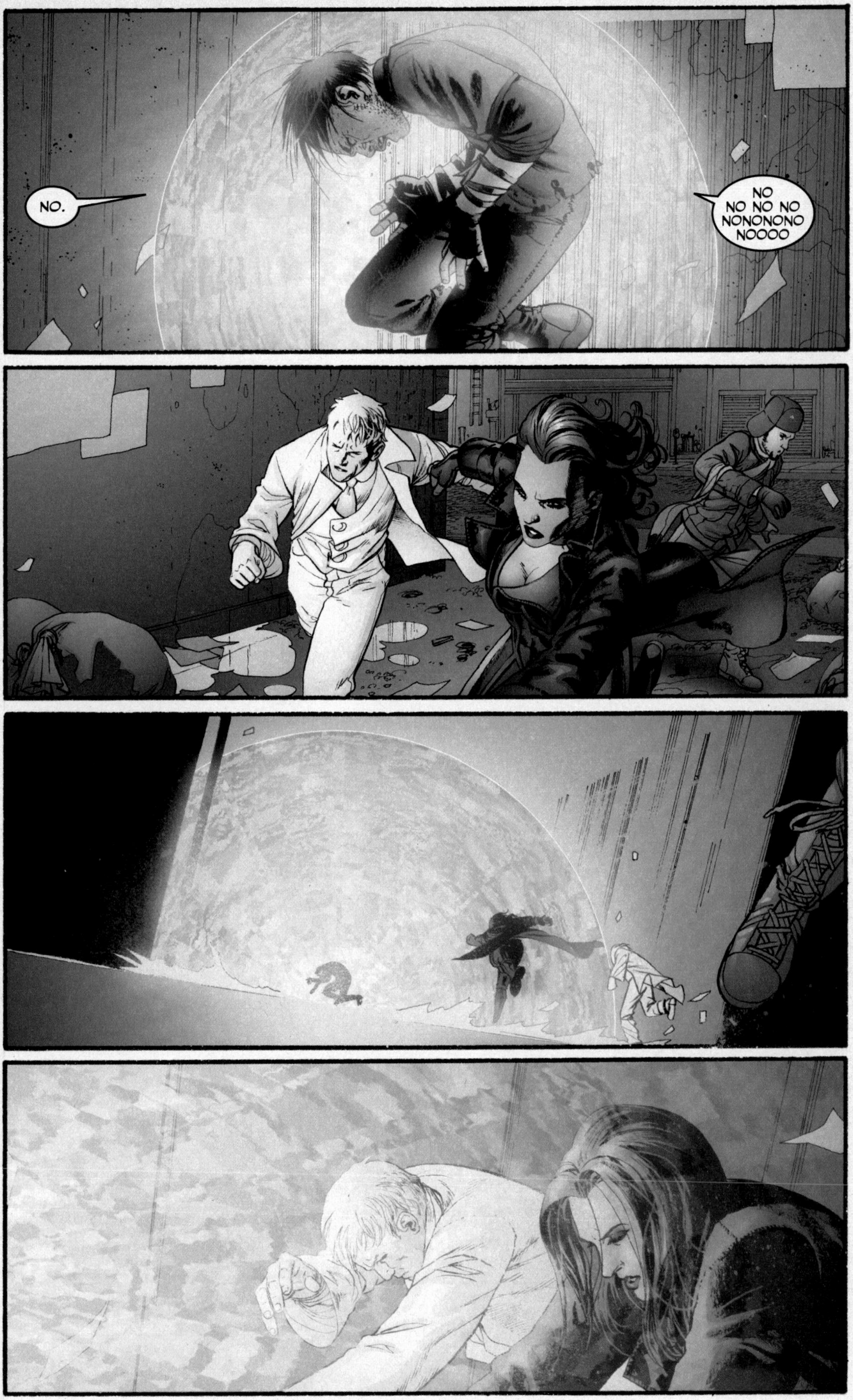
NO.
NO NO NO NO NONONONO NOOOO

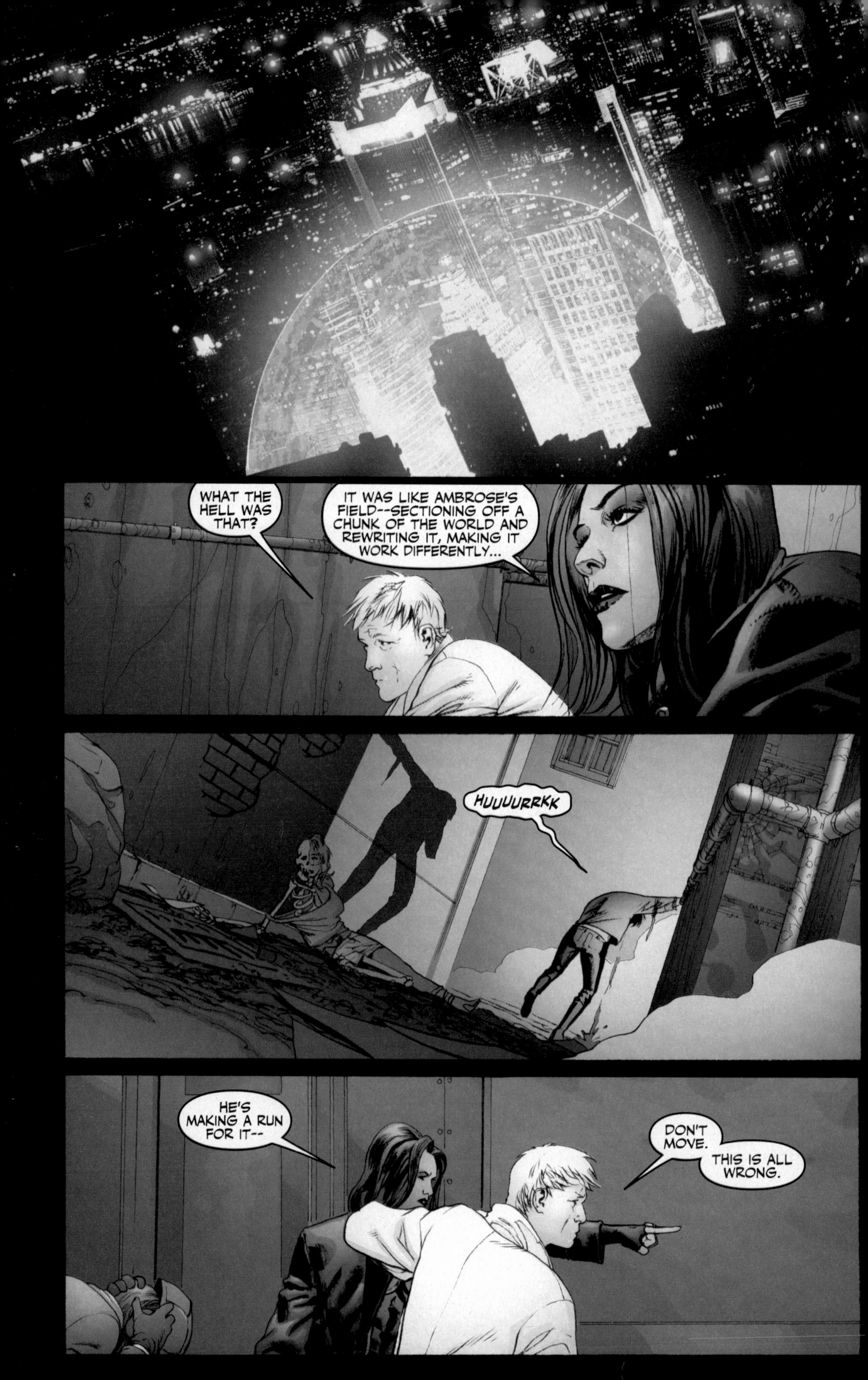
WHAT THE HELL WAS THAT?
IT WAS LIKE AMBROSE'S FIELD--SECTIONING OFF A CHUNK OF THE WORLD AND REWRITING IT, MAKING IT WORK DIFFERENTLY...
HUUUURRKK
HE'S MAKING A RUN FOR IT--
DON'T MOVE.
THIS IS ALL WRONG.

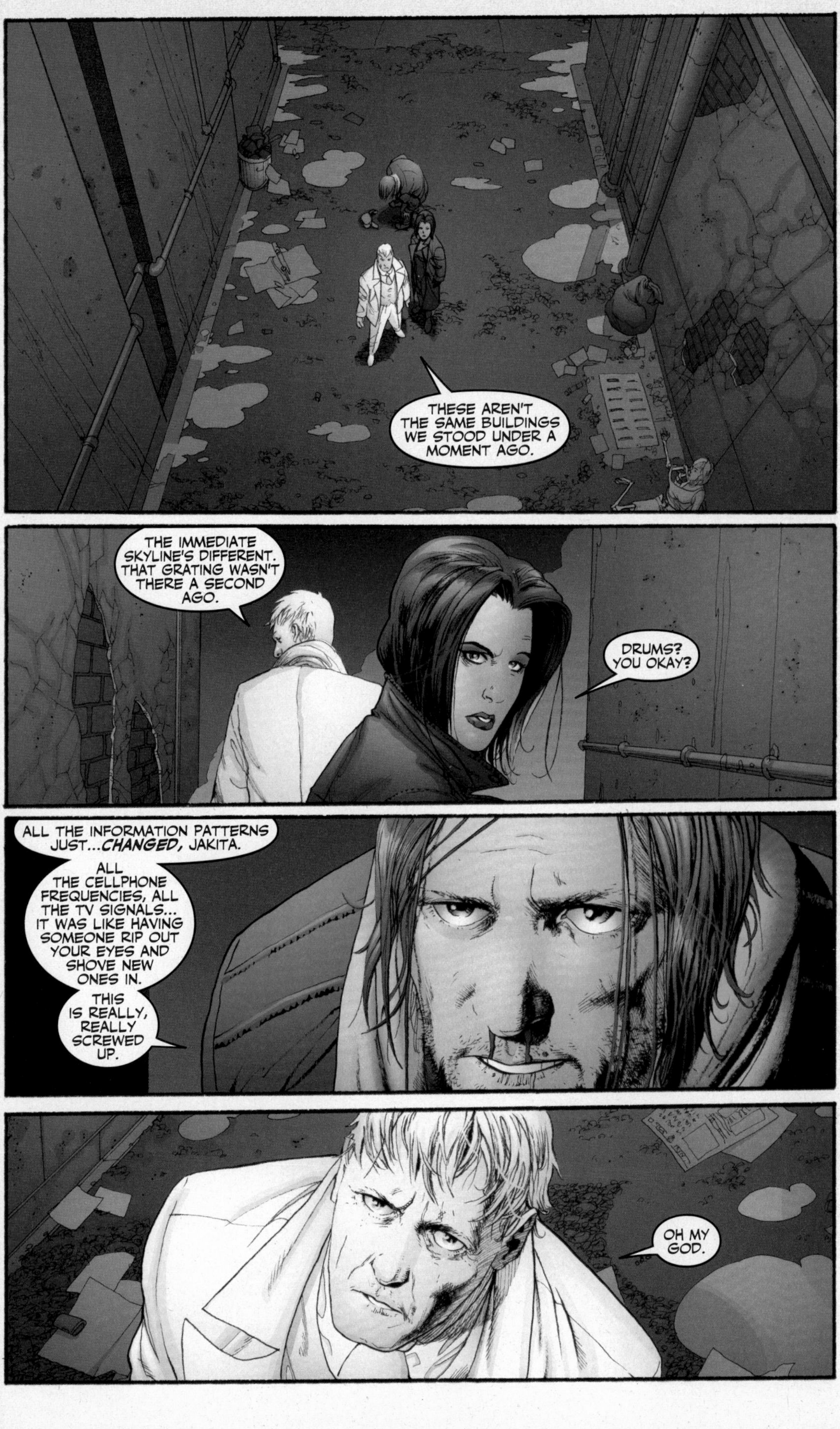
THESE AREN'T THE SAME BUILDINGS WE STOOD UNDER A MOMENT AGO.
THE IMMEDIATE SKYLINE'S DIFFERENT. THAT GRATING WASN'T THERE A SECOND AGO.
DRUMS? YOU OKAY?
ALL THE INFORMATION PATTERNS JUST...*CHANGED,* JAKITA.
ALL THE CELLPHONE FREQUENCIES, ALL THE TV SIGNALS... IT WAS LIKE HAVING SOMEONE RIP OUT YOUR EYES AND SHOVE NEW ONES IN.
THIS IS REALLY, REALLY SCREWED UP.
OH MY GOD.

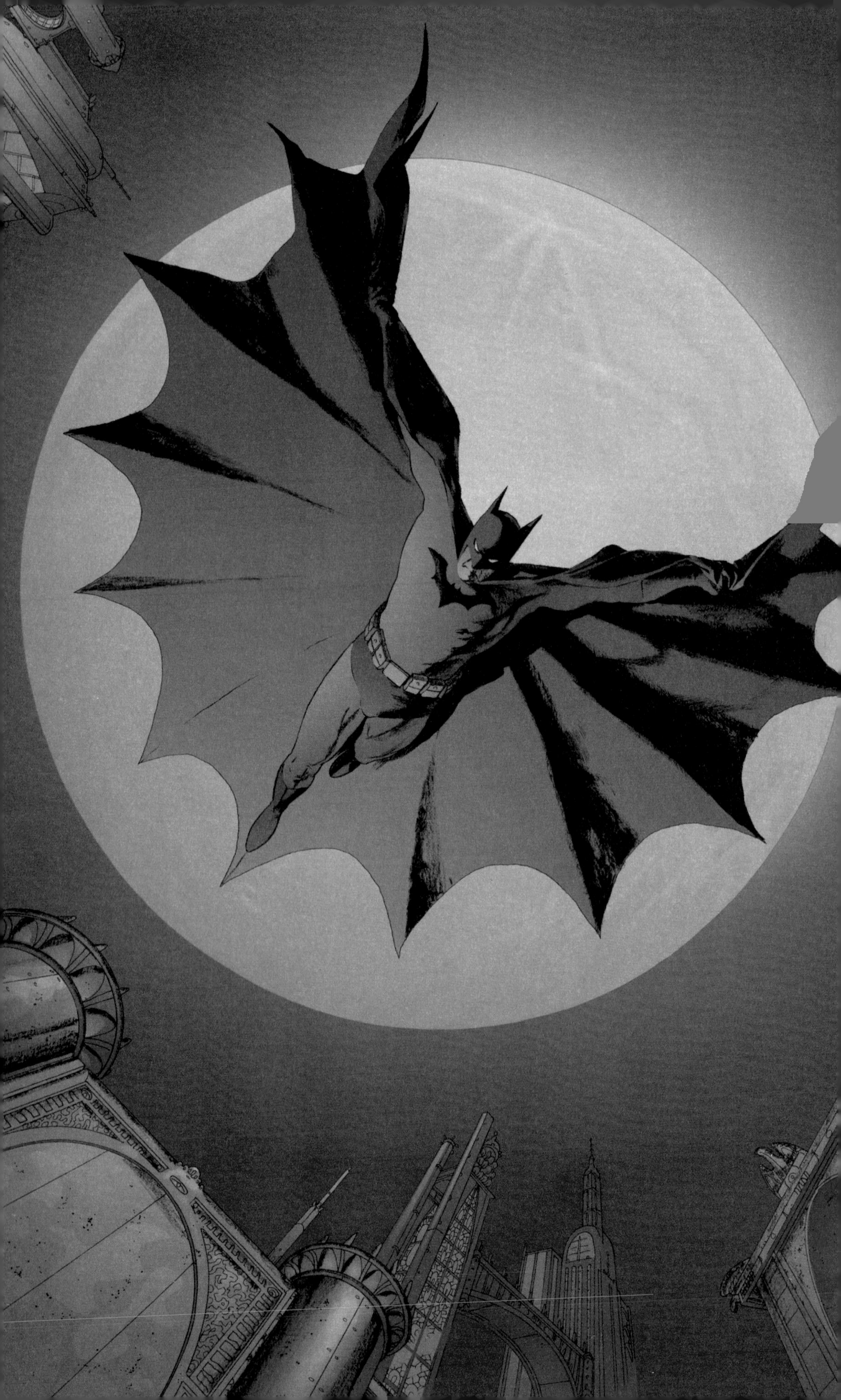

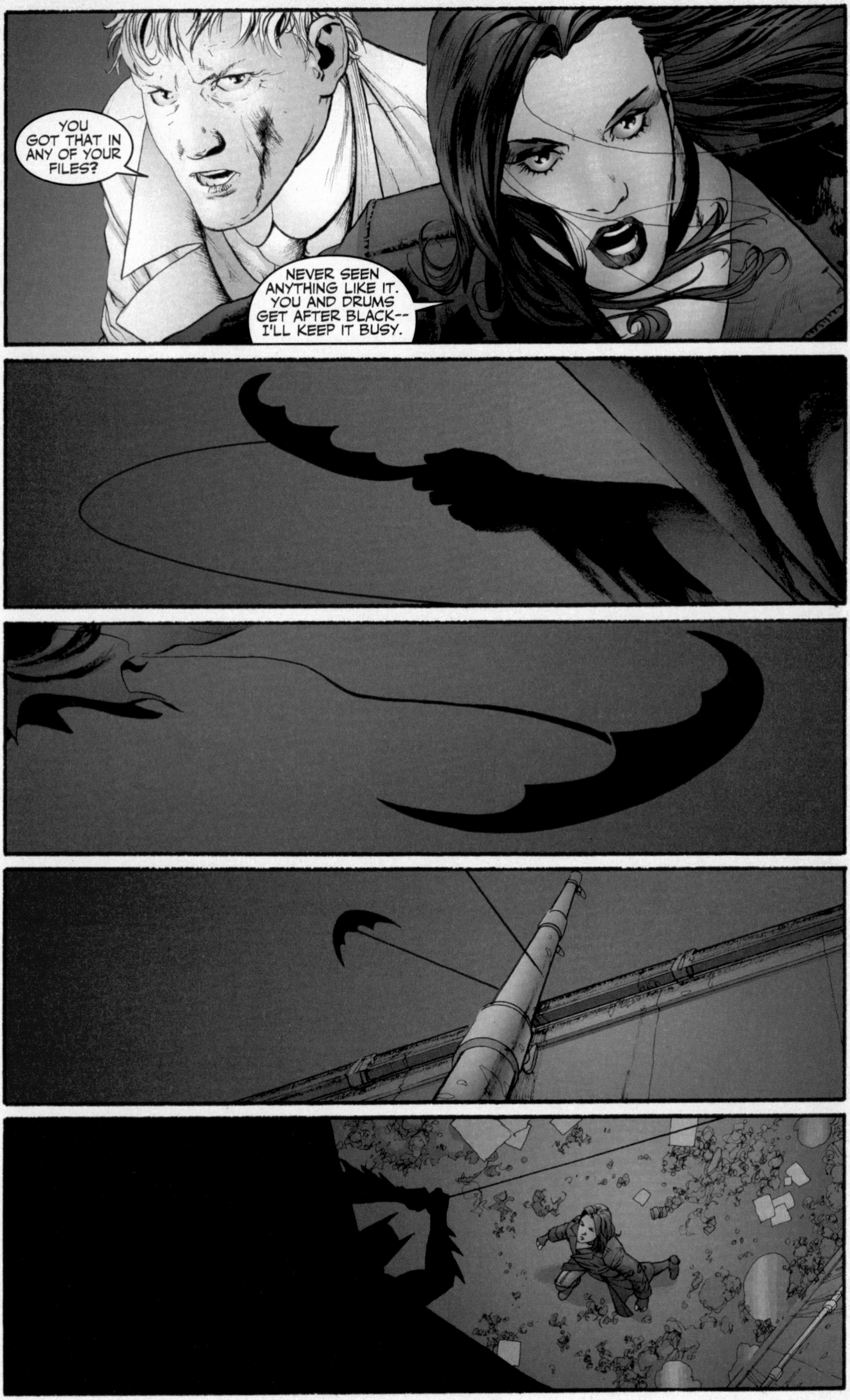
YOU GOT THAT IN ANY OF YOUR FILES?
NEVER SEEN ANYTHING LIKE IT. YOU AND DRUMS GET AFTER BLACK-- I'LL KEEP IT BUSY.

NOT A MURDER METHOD I'VE SEEN.

AND I'VE SEEN MOST OF THEM.

WHAT DO YOU KNOW ABOUT THIS?

NOTHING YOU NEED TO KNOW ABOUT.

MY ASSOCIATES ARE RUNNING DOWN THE MAN RESPONSIBLE. HE HAS AN UNUSUAL MEDICAL CONDITION.

WE'RE TAKING HIM OUT OF THE CITY, AND HE'LL BE DEALT WITH.

HE'LL BE DEALT WITH HERE.

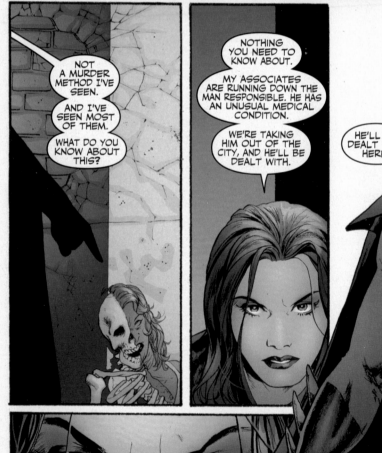

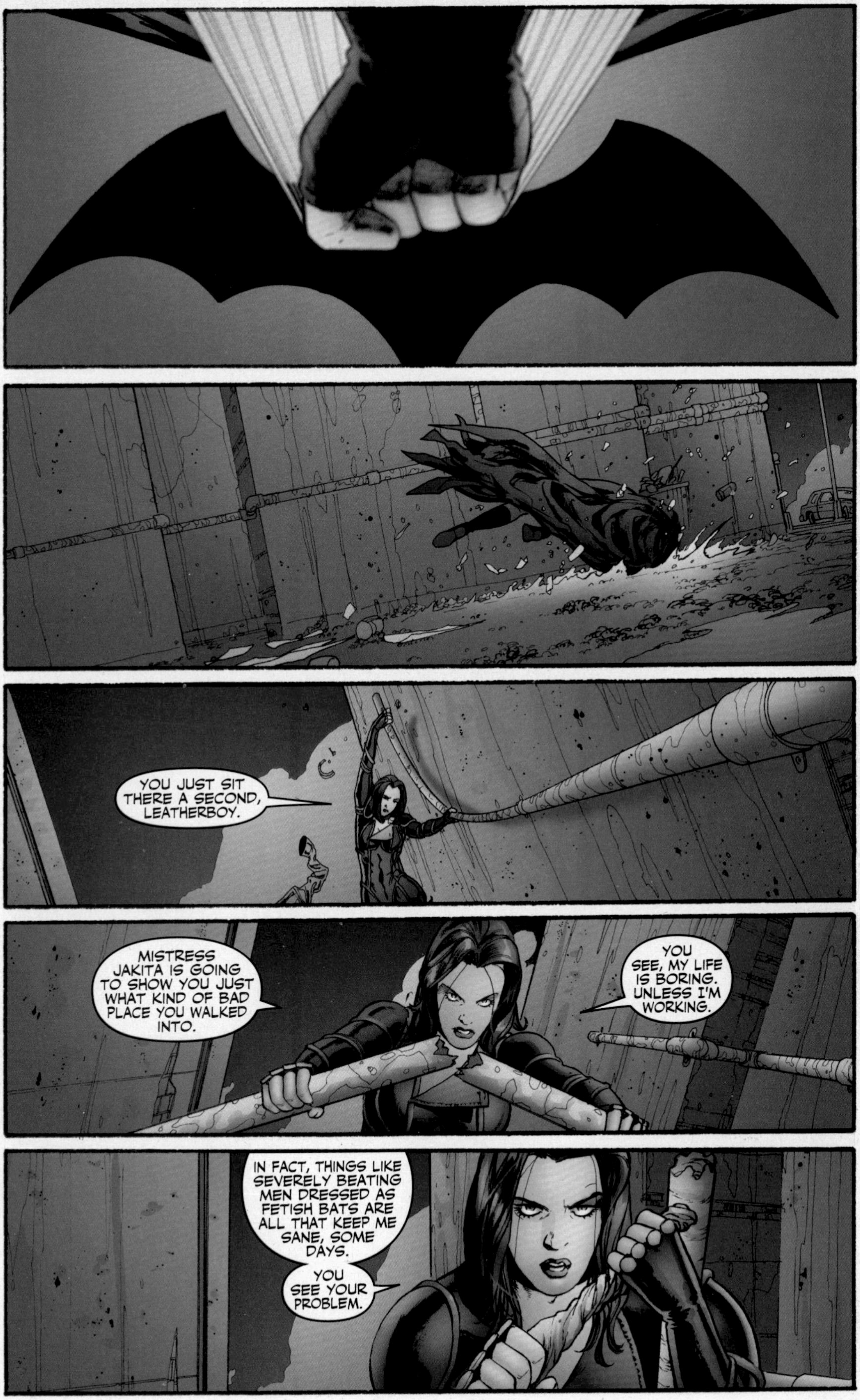
YOU JUST SIT THERE A SECOND, LEATHERBOY.
MISTRESS JAKITA IS GOING TO SHOW YOU JUST WHAT KIND OF BAD PLACE YOU WALKED INTO.
YOU SEE, MY LIFE IS BORING. UNLESS I'M WORKING.
IN FACT, THINGS LIKE SEVERELY BEATING MEN DRESSED AS FETISH BATS ARE ALL THAT KEEP ME SANE, SOME DAYS.
YOU SEE YOUR PROBLEM.

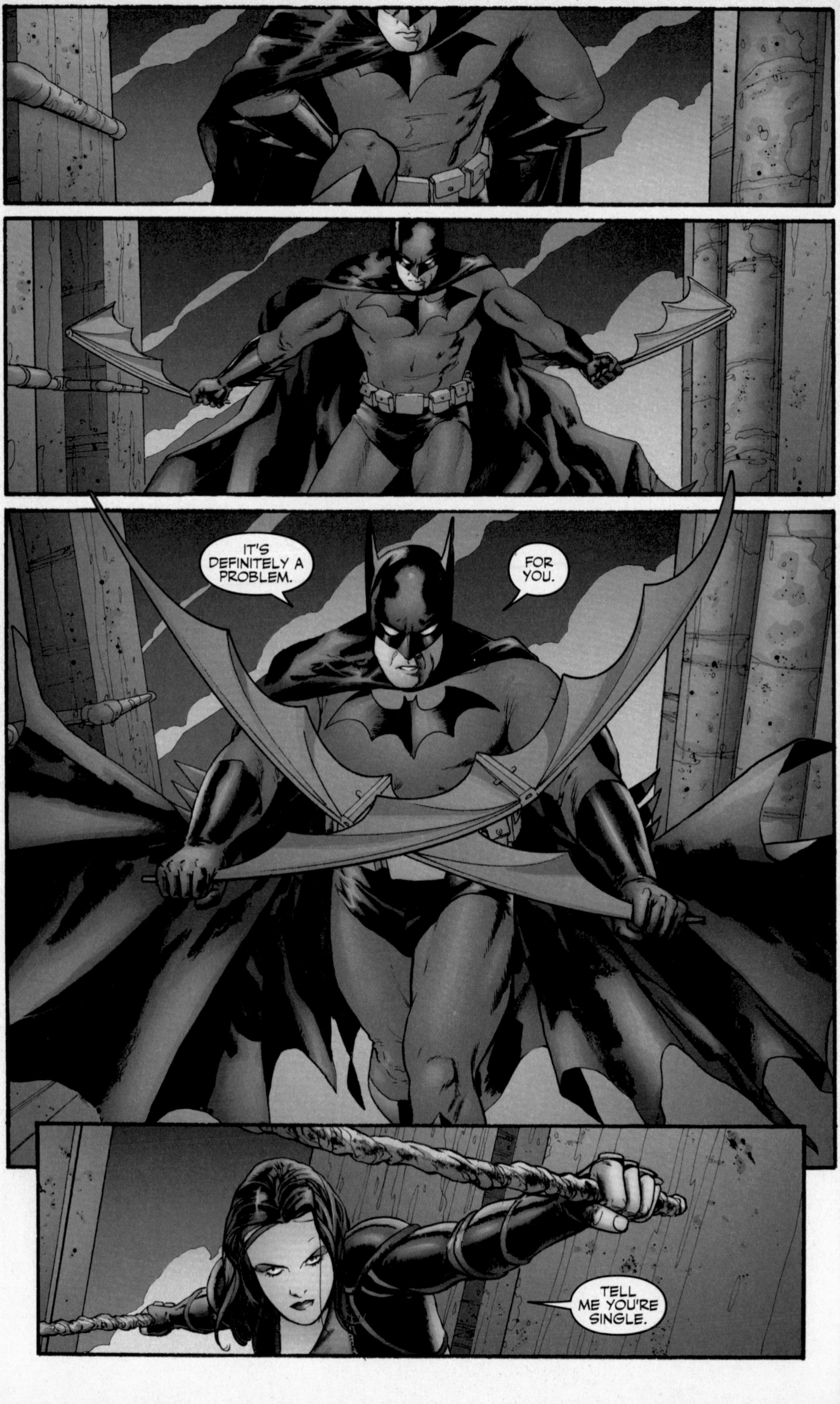
IT'S DEFINITELY A PROBLEM.
FOR YOU.
TELL ME YOU'RE SINGLE.

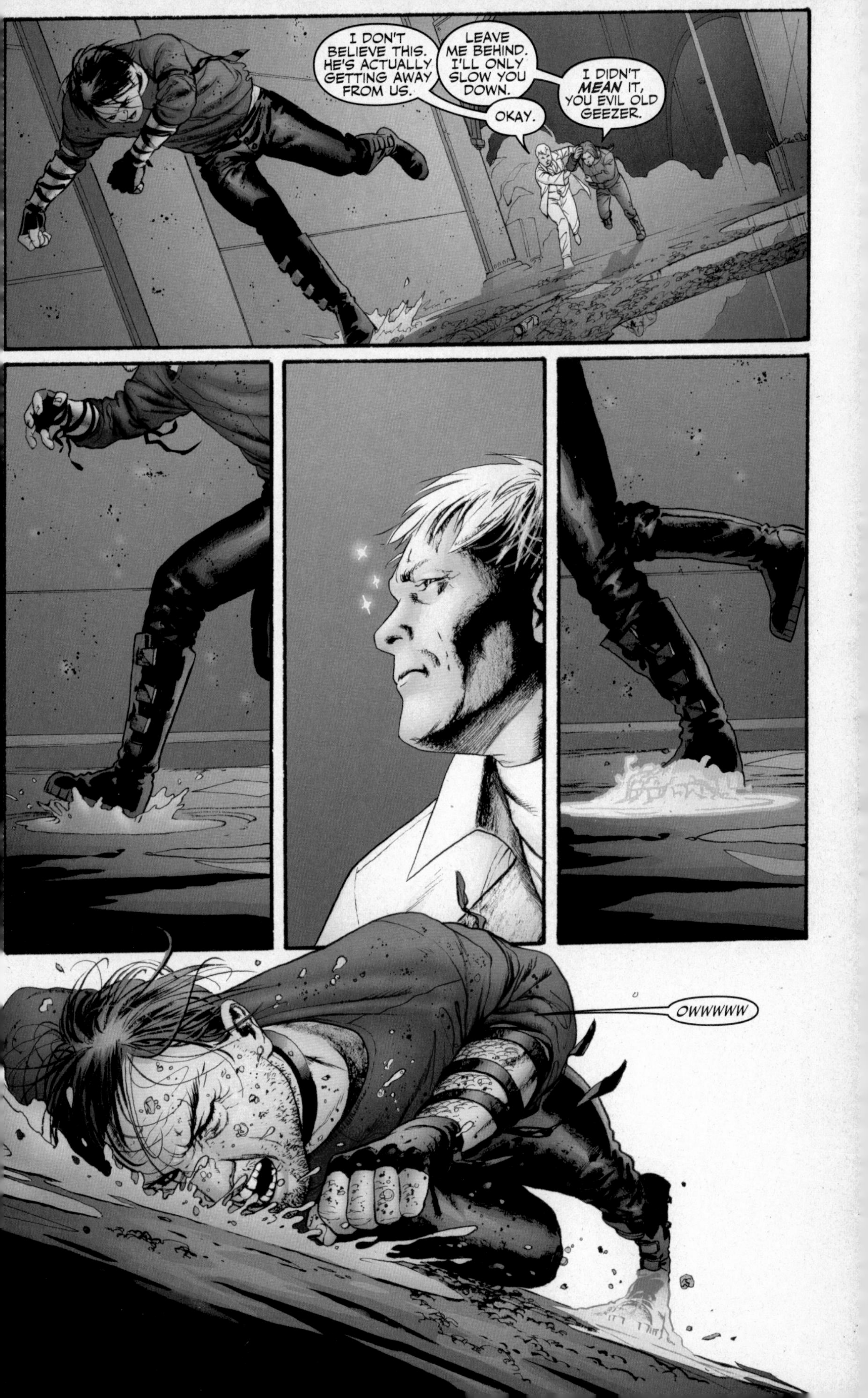
I DON'T BELIEVE THIS. HE'S ACTUALLY GETTING AWAY FROM US.
LEAVE ME BEHIND. I'LL ONLY SLOW YOU DOWN.
OKAY.
I DIDN'T MEAN IT, YOU EVIL OLD GEEZER.
OWWWWW

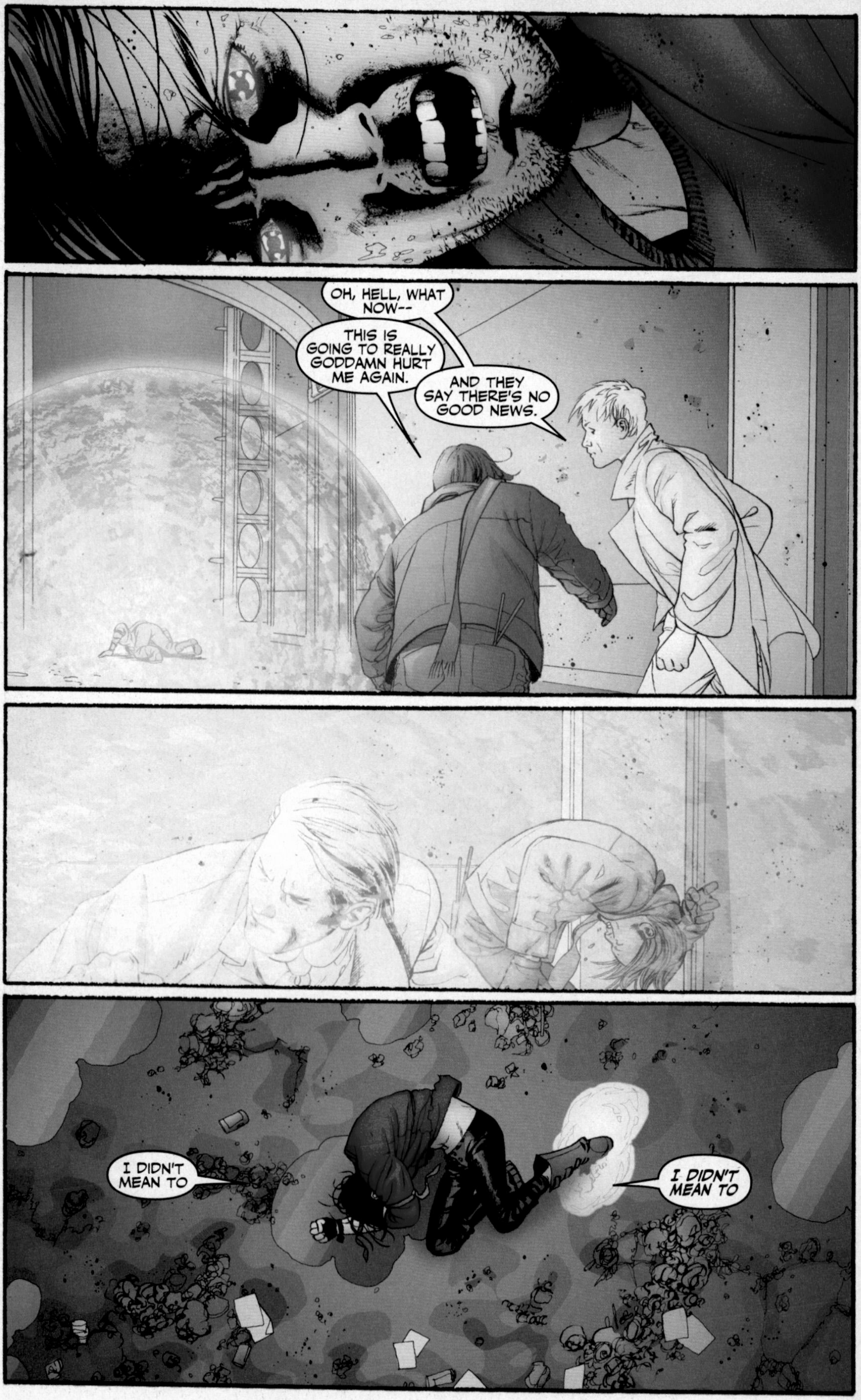
OH, HELL, WHAT NOW--
THIS IS GOING TO REALLY GODDAMN HURT ME AGAIN.
AND THEY SAY THERE'S NO GOOD NEWS.
I DIDN'T MEAN TO
I DIDN'T MEAN TO

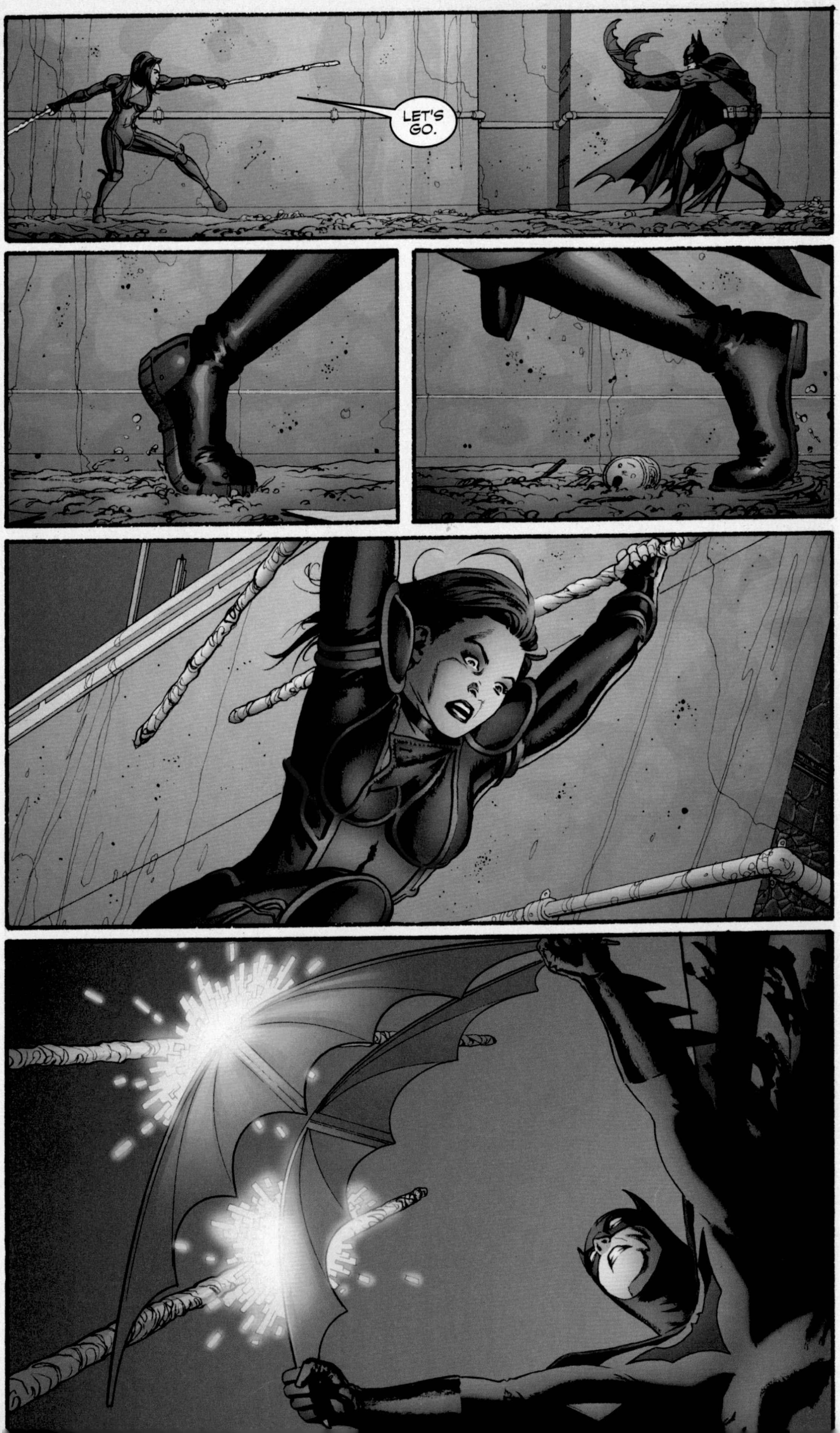
LET'S GO.

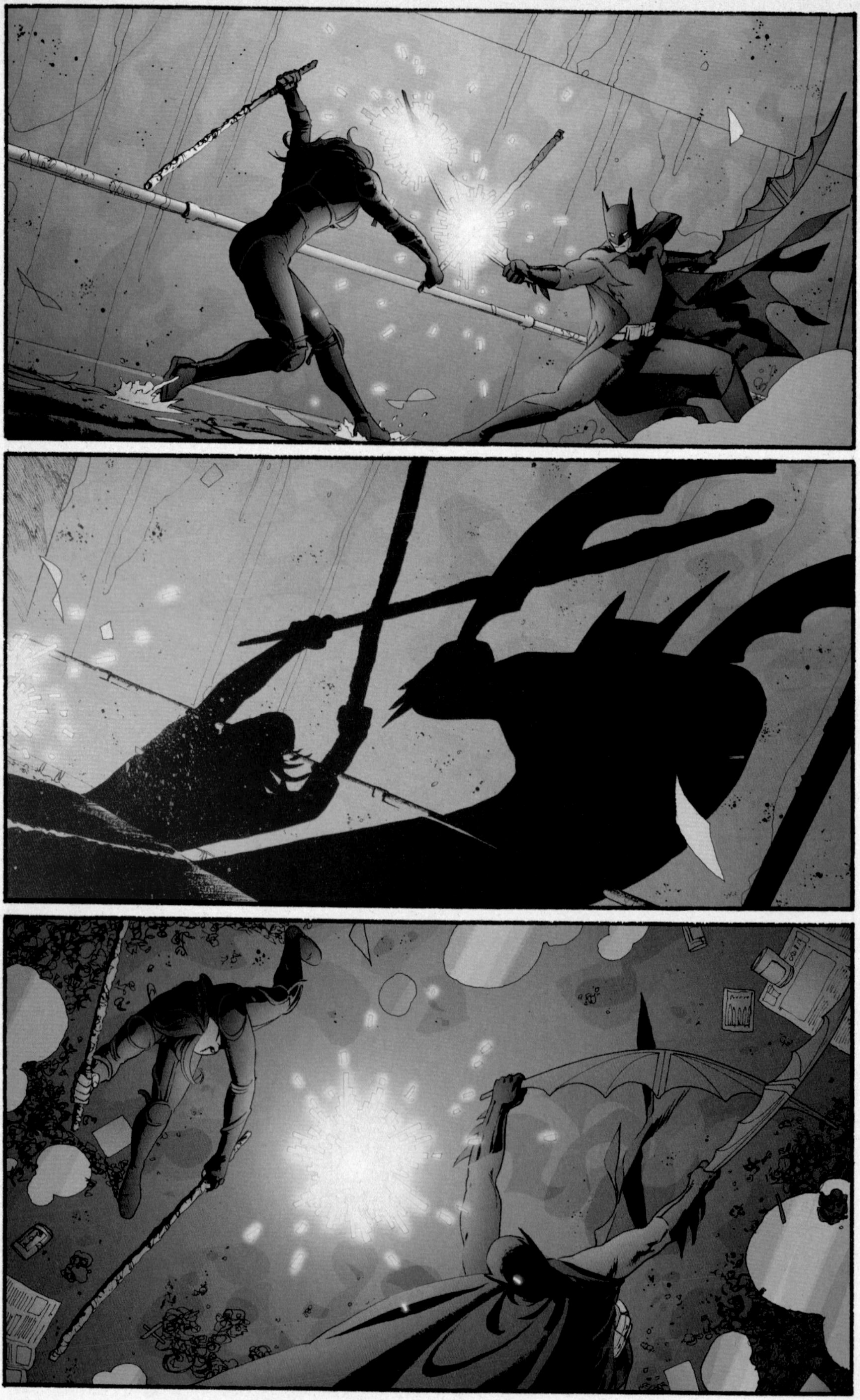

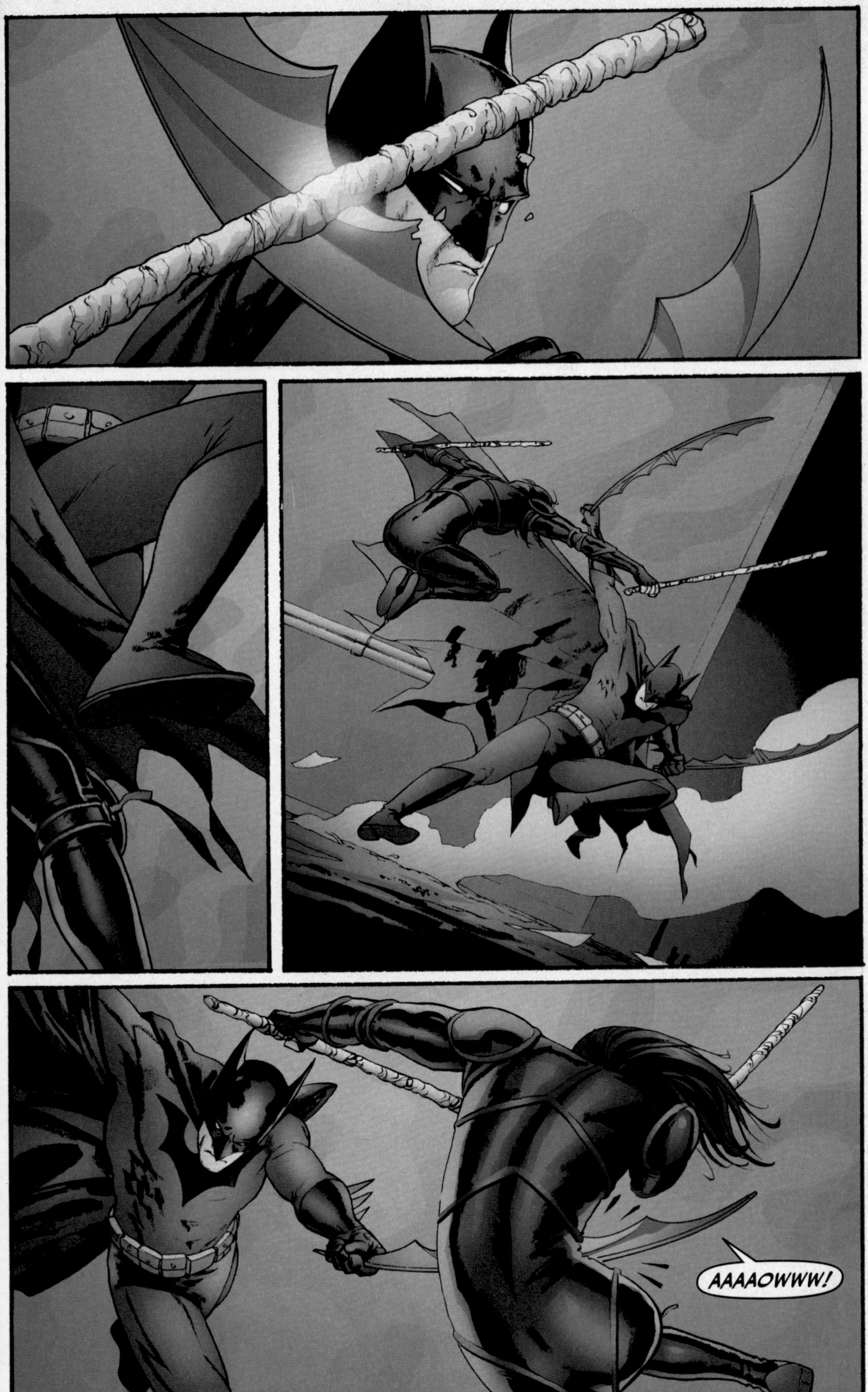
AAAAOWWW!

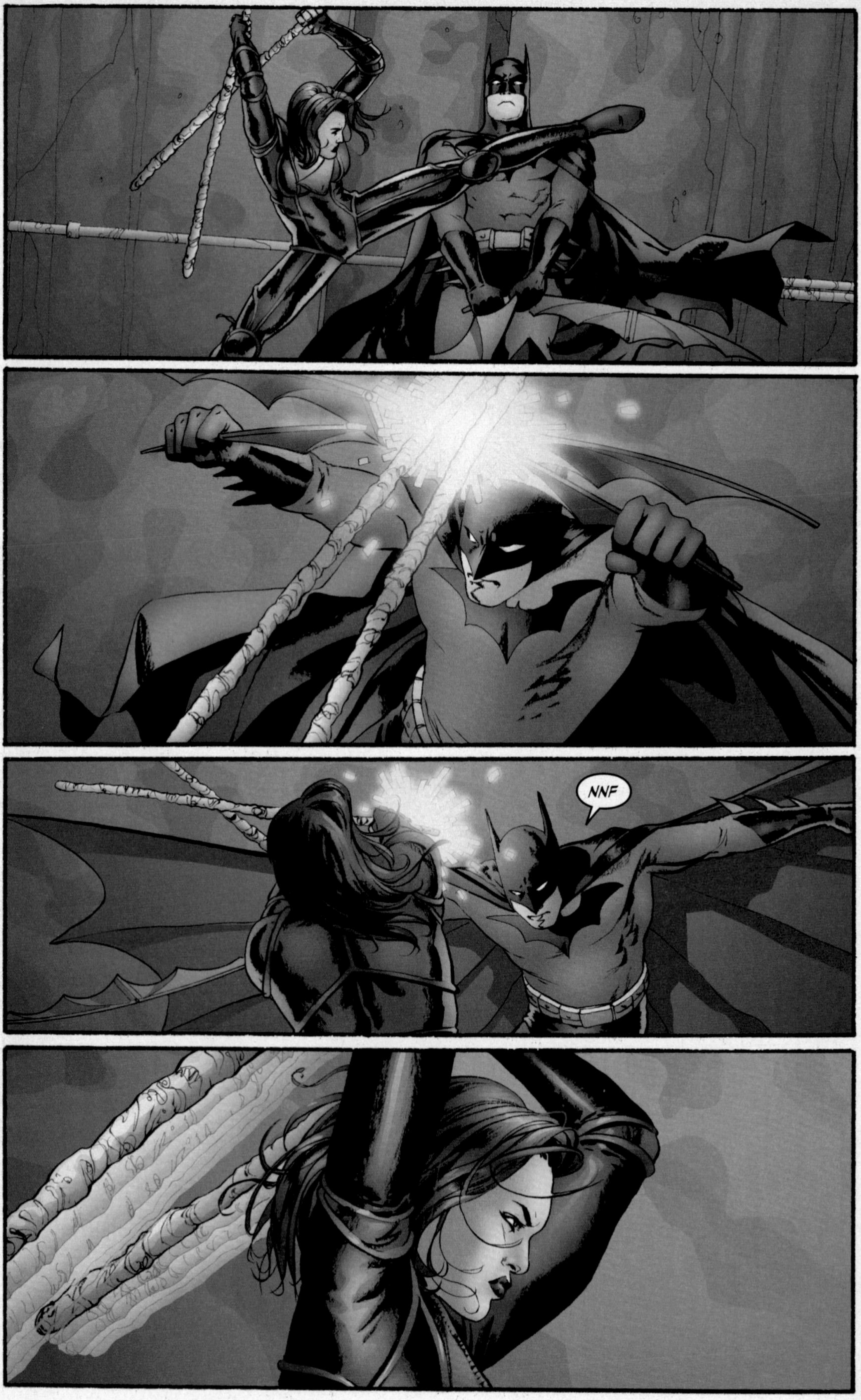
NNF

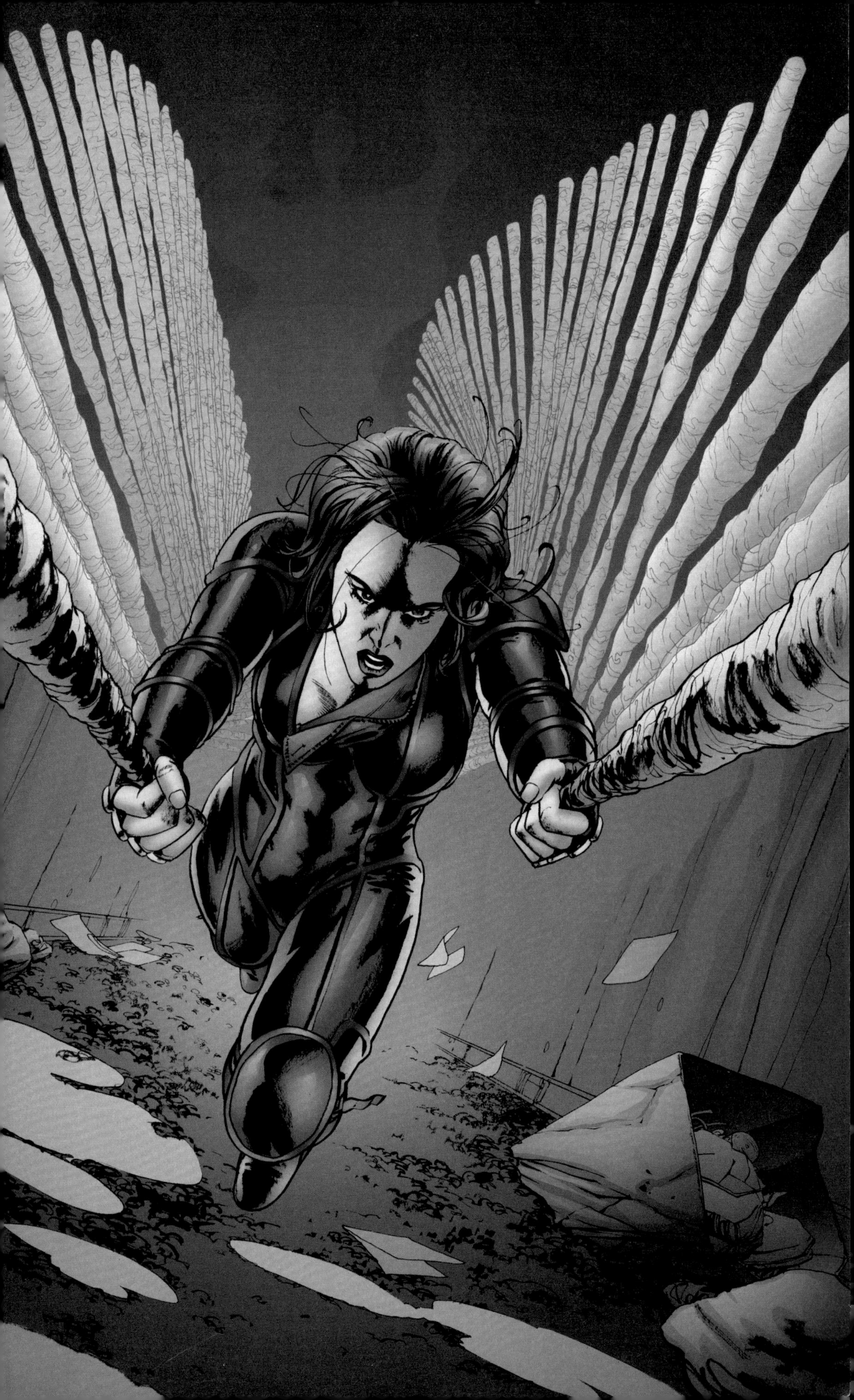

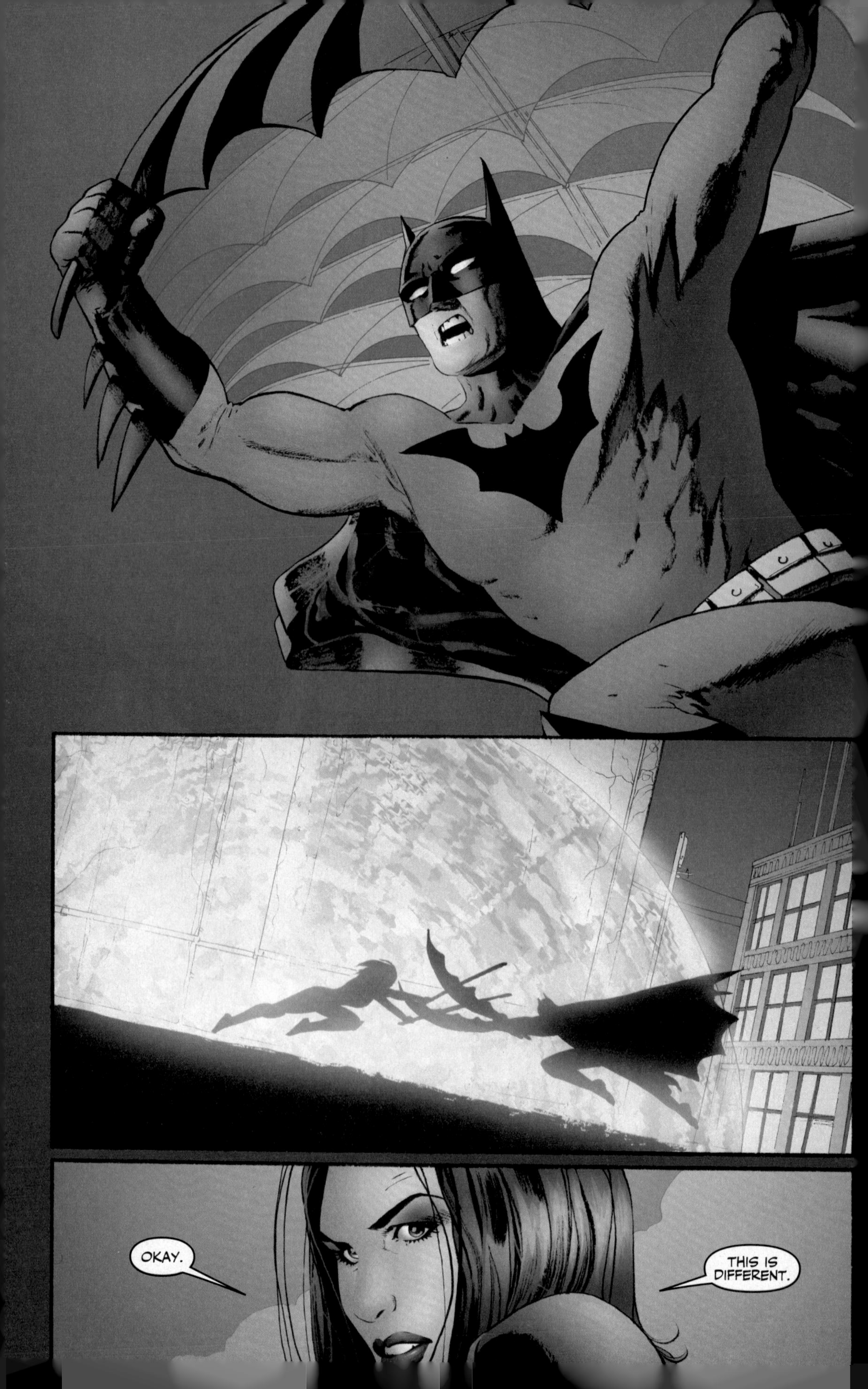
OKAY.
THIS IS DIFFERENT.

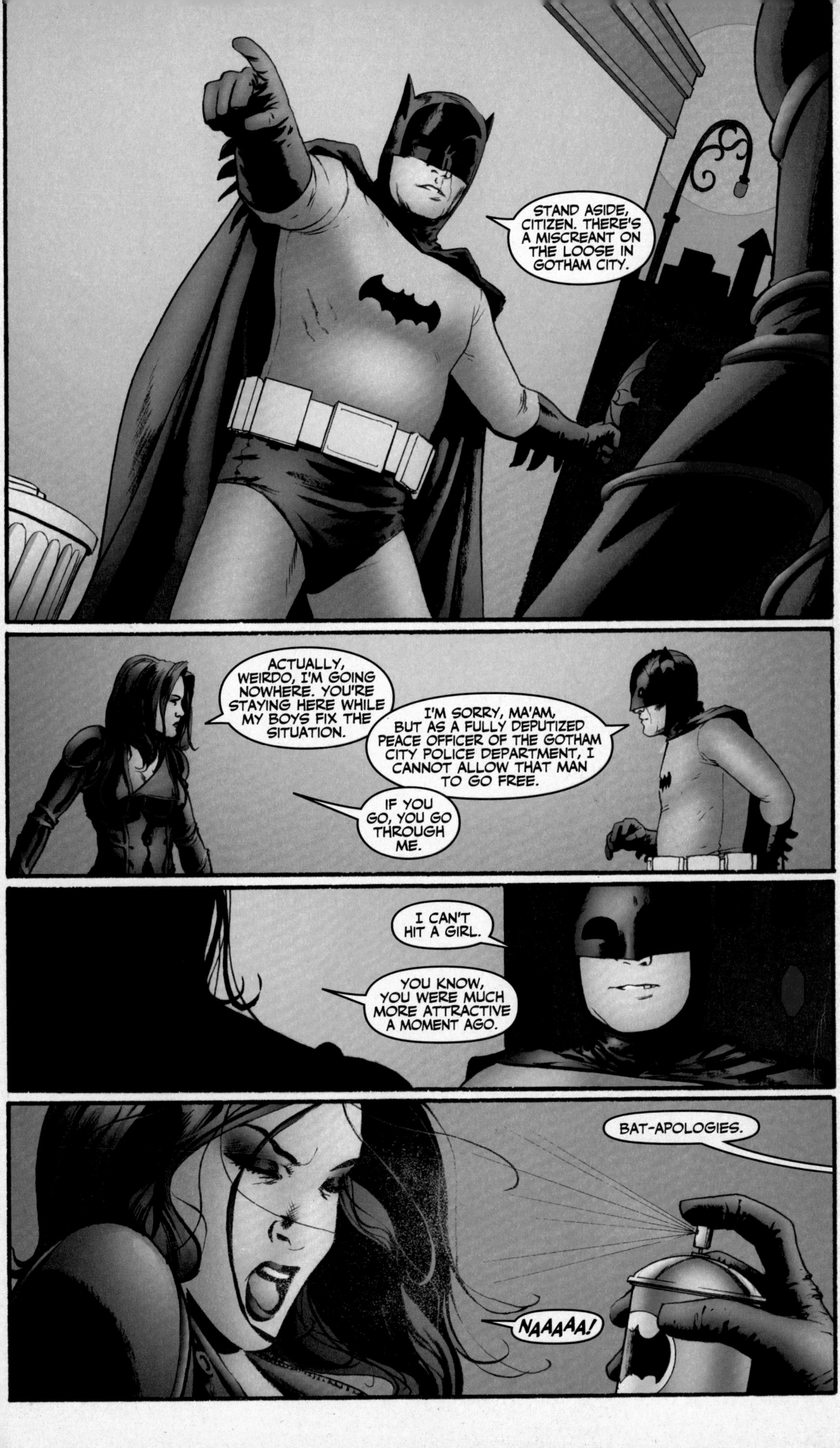
STAND ASIDE, CITIZEN. THERE'S A MISCREANT ON THE LOOSE IN GOTHAM CITY.
ACTUALLY, WEIRDO, I'M GOING NOWHERE. YOU'RE STAYING HERE WHILE MY BOYS FIX THE SITUATION.
I'M SORRY, MA'AM, BUT AS A FULLY DEPUTIZED PEACE OFFICER OF THE GOTHAM CITY POLICE DEPARTMENT, I CANNOT ALLOW THAT MAN TO GO FREE.
IF YOU GO, YOU GO THROUGH ME.
I CAN'T HIT A GIRL.
YOU KNOW, YOU WERE MUCH MORE ATTRACTIVE A MOMENT AGO.
BAT-APOLOGIES.
NAAAAA!

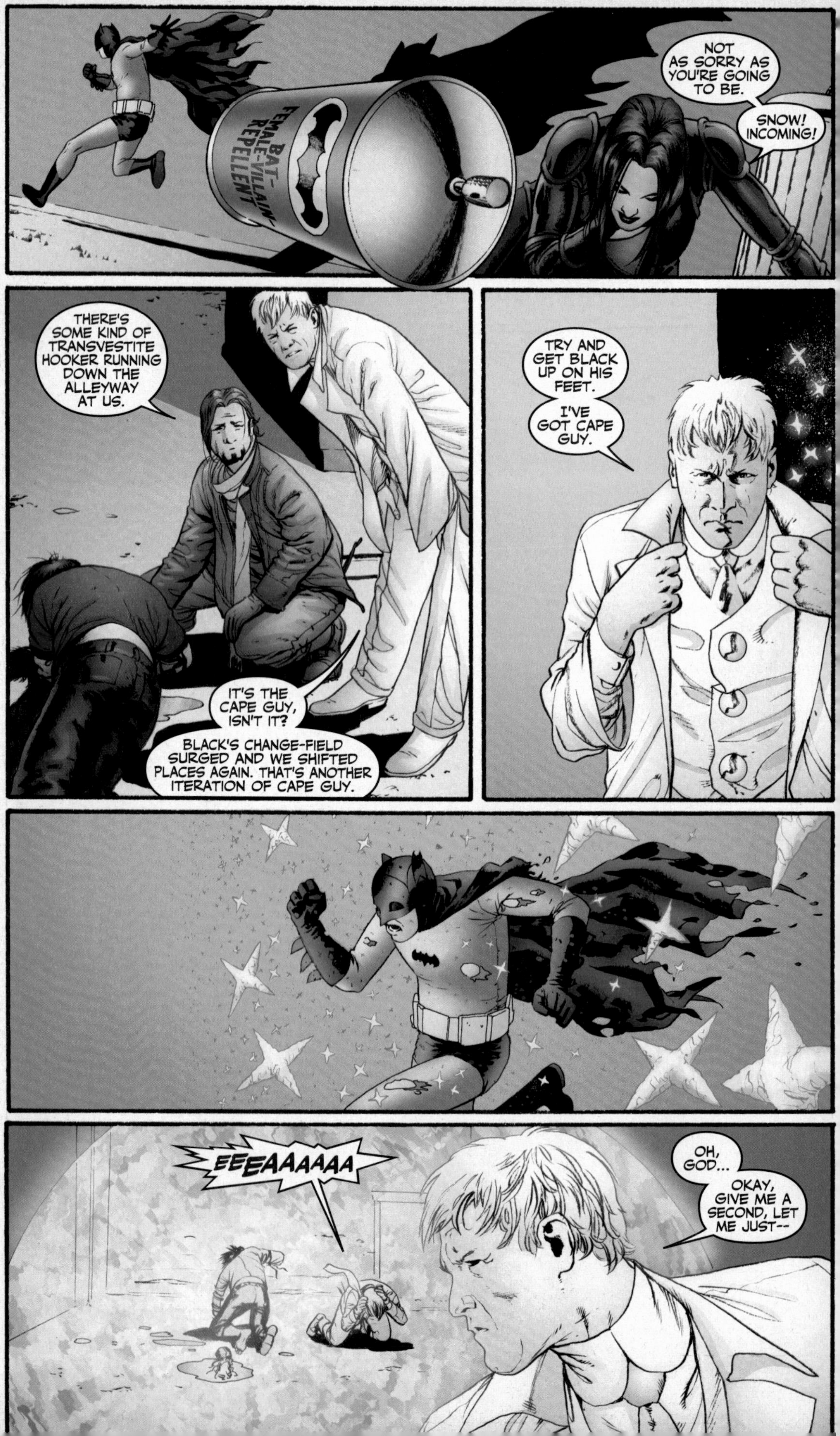
FEMALE-VILLAIN-REPELLENT
BAT-
NOT AS SORRY AS YOU'RE GOING TO BE.
SNOW! INCOMING!
THERE'S SOME KIND OF TRANSVESTITE HOOKER RUNNING DOWN THE ALLEYWAY AT US.
IT'S THE CAPE GUY, ISN'T IT?
BLACK'S CHANGE-FIELD SURGED AND WE SHIFTED PLACES AGAIN. THAT'S ANOTHER ITERATION OF CAPE GUY.
TRY AND GET BLACK UP ON HIS FEET.
I'VE GOT CAPE GUY.
EEEAAAAAA
OH, GOD...
OKAY, GIVE ME A SECOND, LET ME JUST--

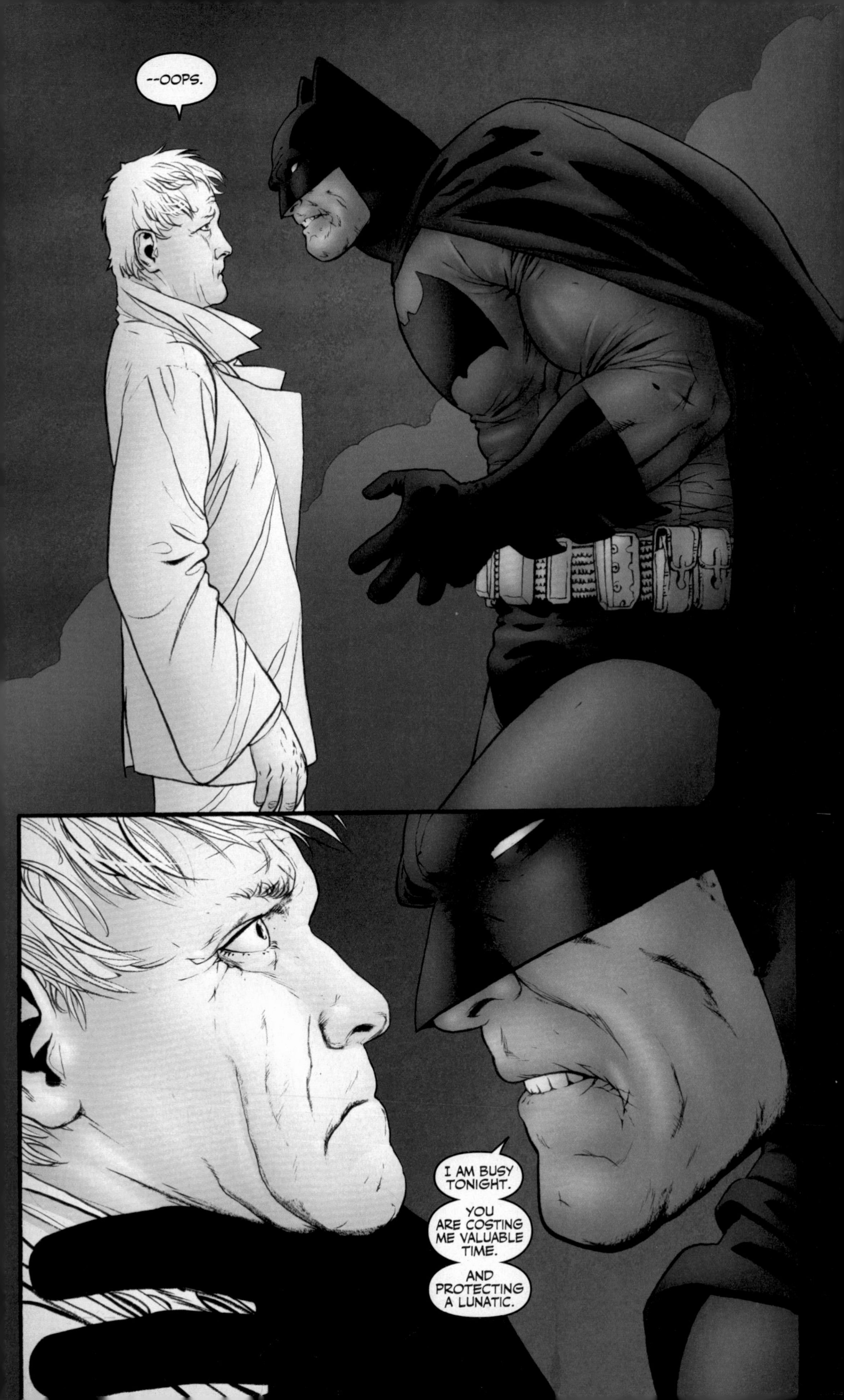
--OOPS.
I AM BUSY TONIGHT.
YOU ARE COSTING ME VALUABLE TIME.
AND PROTECTING A LUNATIC.

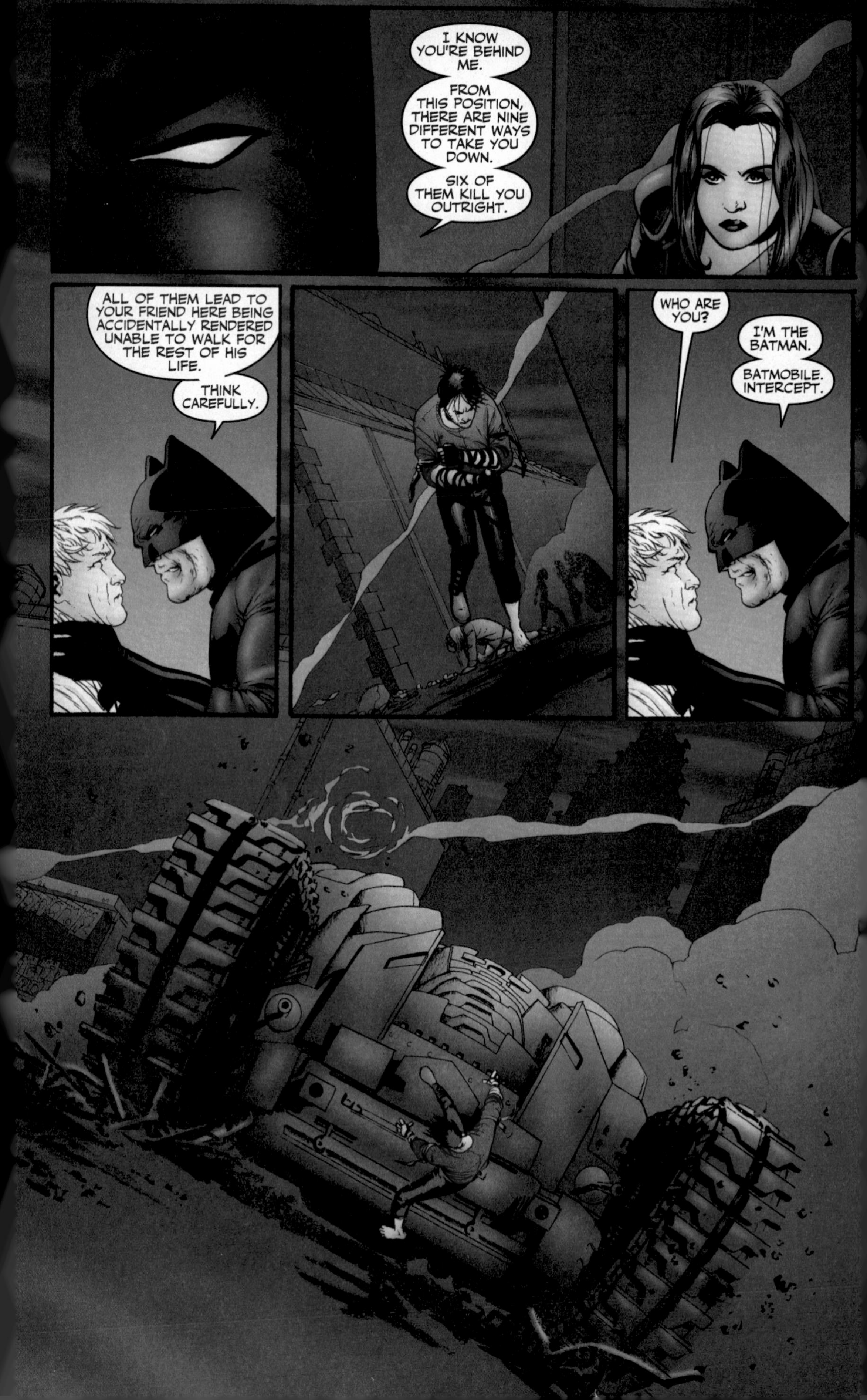
I KNOW YOU'RE BEHIND ME.
FROM THIS POSITION, THERE ARE NINE DIFFERENT WAYS TO TAKE YOU DOWN.
SIX OF THEM KILL YOU OUTRIGHT.
ALL OF THEM LEAD TO YOUR FRIEND HERE BEING ACCIDENTALLY RENDERED UNABLE TO WALK FOR THE REST OF HIS LIFE.
THINK CAREFULLY.
WHO ARE YOU?
I'M THE BATMAN.
BATMOBILE. INTERCEPT.

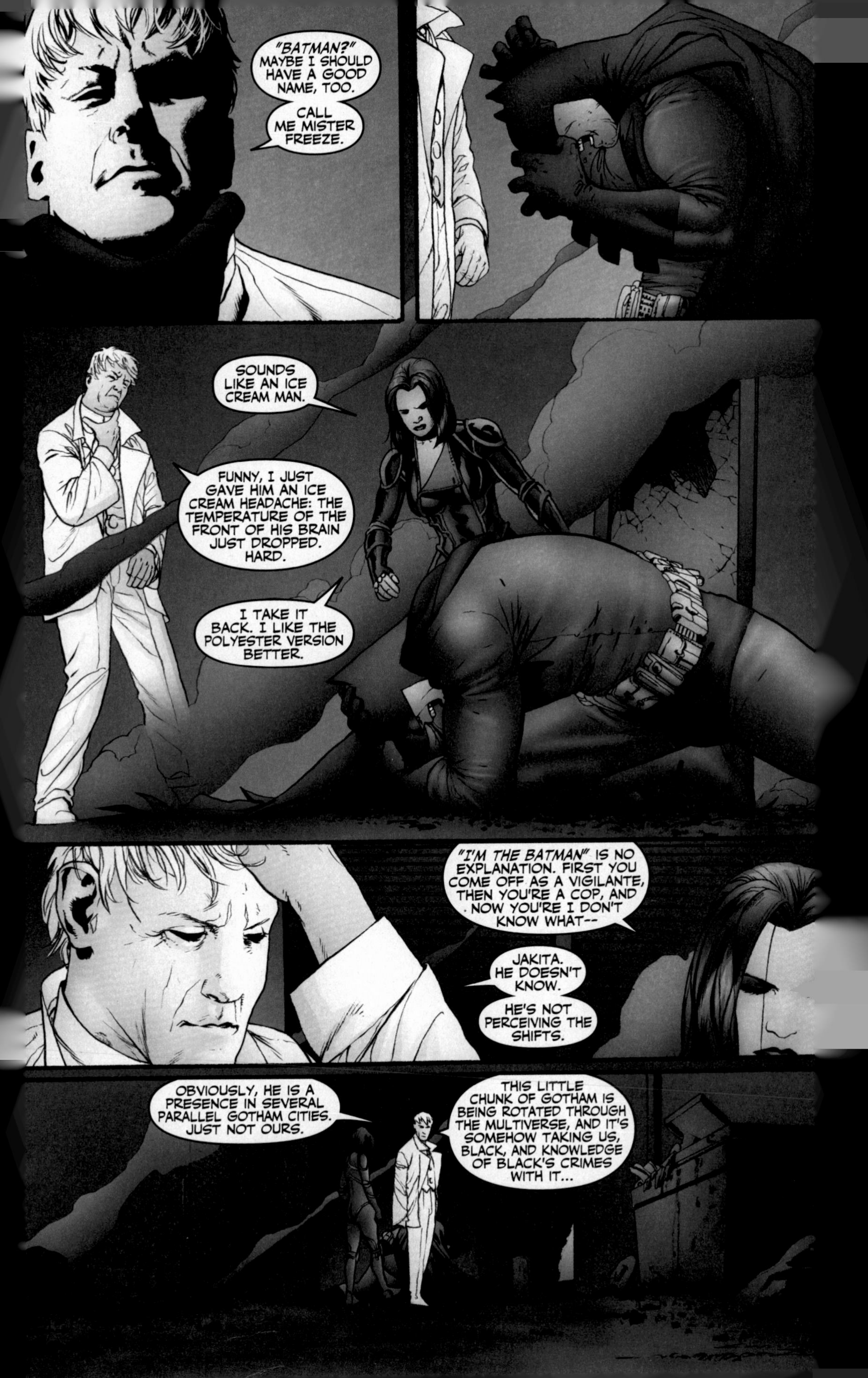
"BATMAN?" MAYBE I SHOULD HAVE A GOOD NAME, TOO.
CALL ME MISTER FREEZE.
SOUNDS LIKE AN ICE CREAM MAN.
FUNNY, I JUST GAVE HIM AN ICE CREAM HEADACHE: THE TEMPERATURE OF THE FRONT OF HIS BRAIN JUST DROPPED. HARD.
I TAKE IT BACK. I LIKE THE POLYESTER VERSION BETTER.
"I'M THE BATMAN" IS NO EXPLANATION. FIRST YOU COME OFF AS A VIGILANTE, THEN YOU'RE A COP, AND NOW YOU'RE I DON'T KNOW WHAT--
JAKITA. HE DOESN'T KNOW.
HE'S NOT PERCEIVING THE SHIFTS.
OBVIOUSLY, HE IS A PRESENCE IN SEVERAL PARALLEL GOTHAM CITIES. JUST NOT OURS.
THIS LITTLE CHUNK OF GOTHAM IS BEING ROTATED THROUGH THE MULTIVERSE, AND IT'S SOMEHOW TAKING US, BLACK, AND KNOWLEDGE OF BLACK'S CRIMES WITH IT...

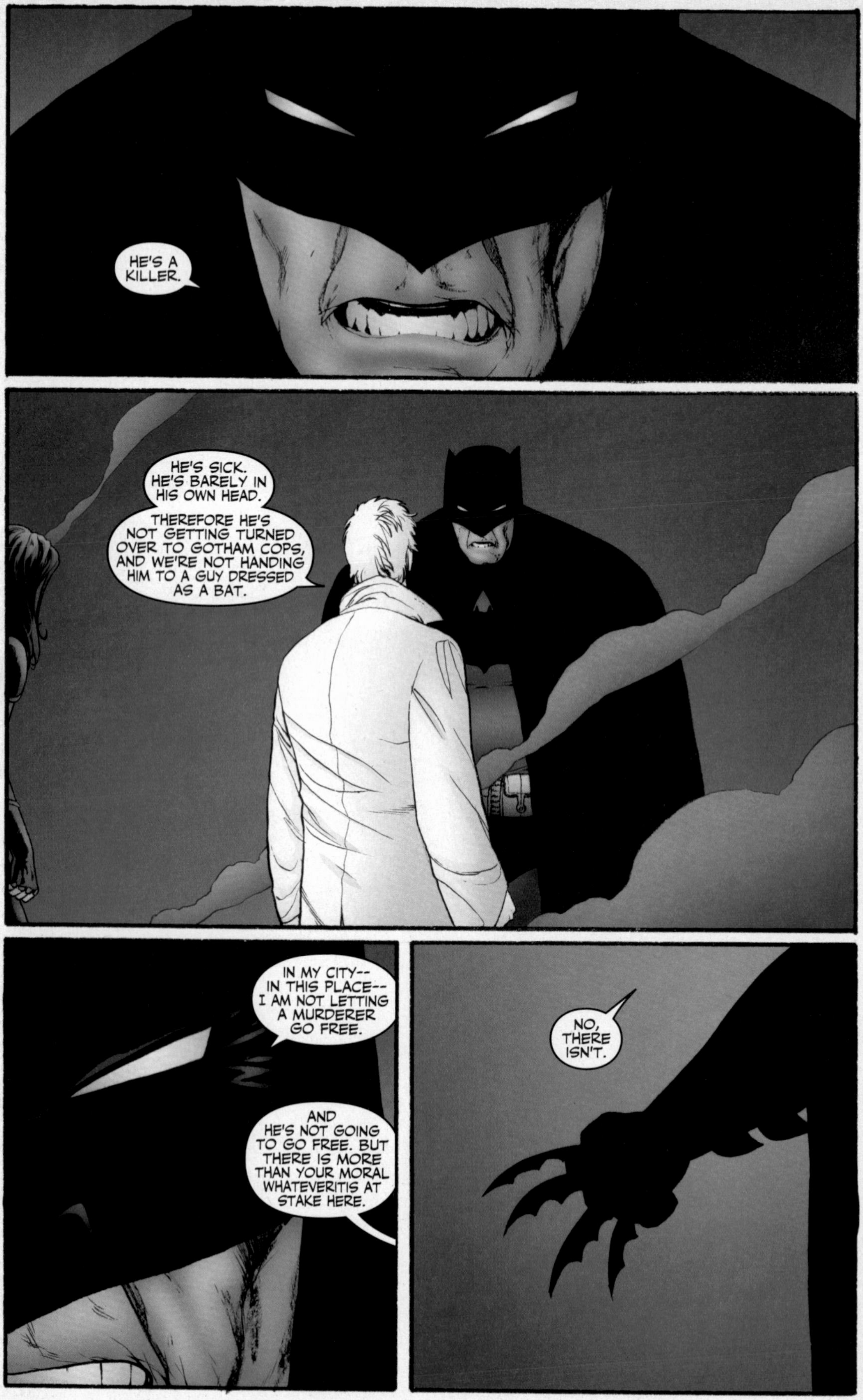
HE'S A KILLER.
HE'S SICK. HE'S BARELY IN HIS OWN HEAD.
THEREFORE HE'S NOT GETTING TURNED OVER TO GOTHAM COPS, AND WE'RE NOT HANDING HIM TO A GUY DRESSED AS A BAT.
IN MY CITY-- IN THIS PLACE-- I AM NOT LETTING A MURDERER GO FREE.
AND HE'S NOT GOING TO GO FREE. BUT THERE IS MORE THAN YOUR MORAL WHATEVERITIS AT STAKE HERE.
NO, THERE ISN'T.

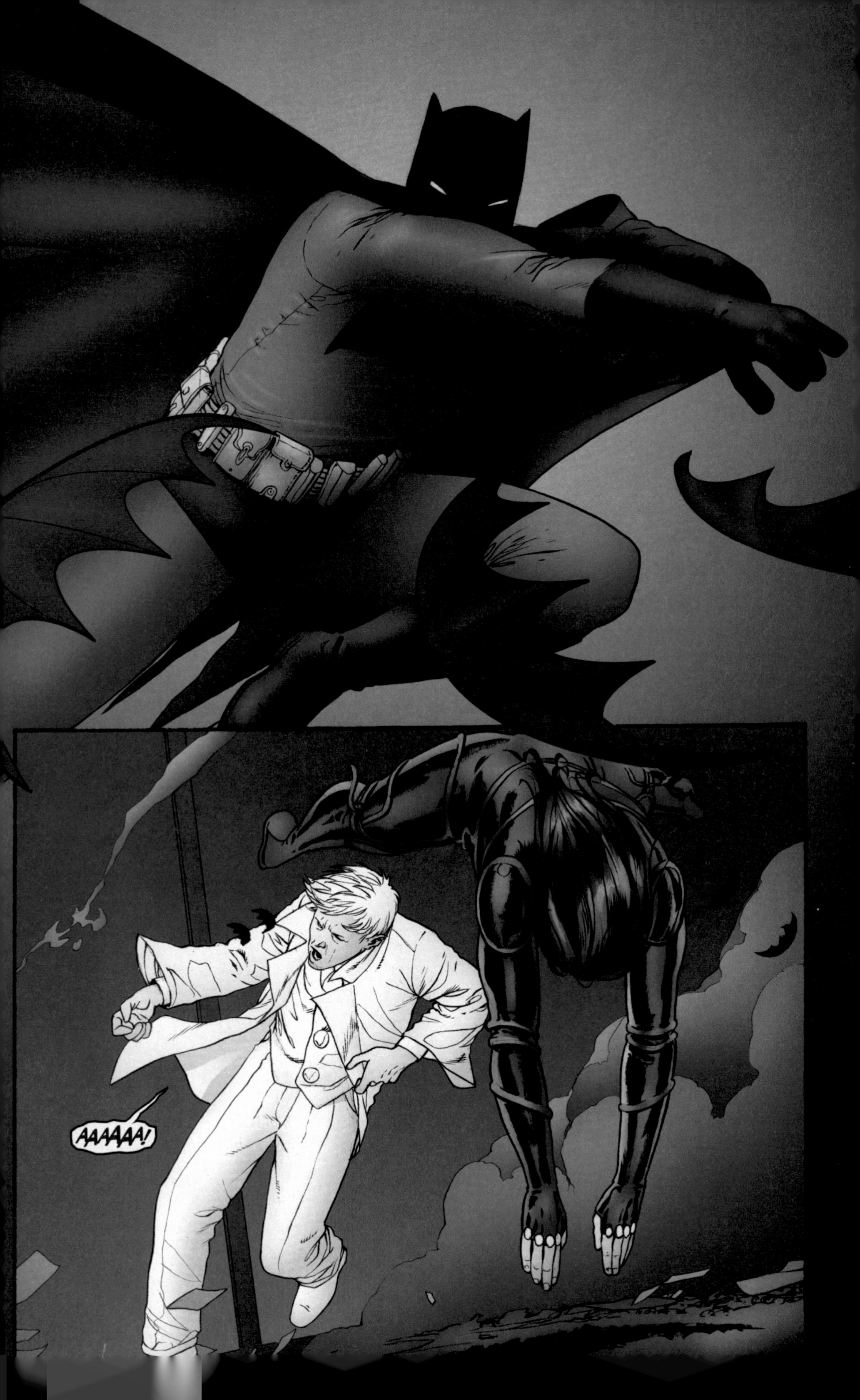
AAAAAA!

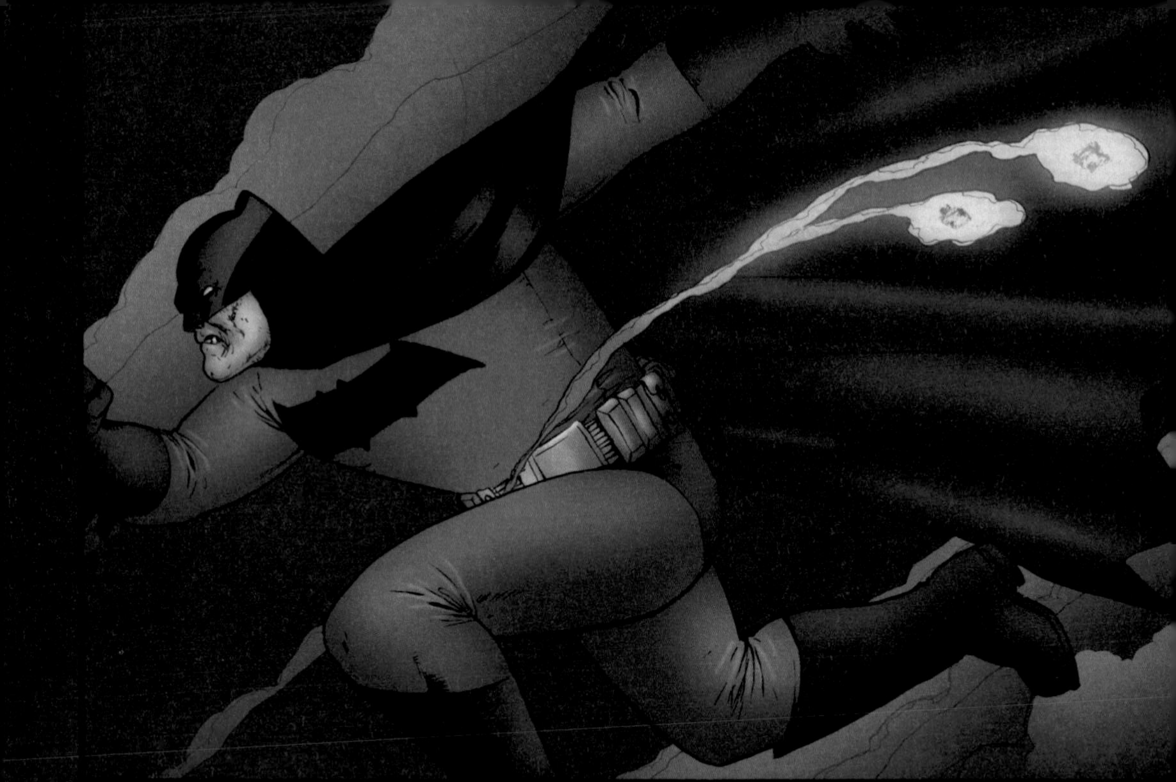
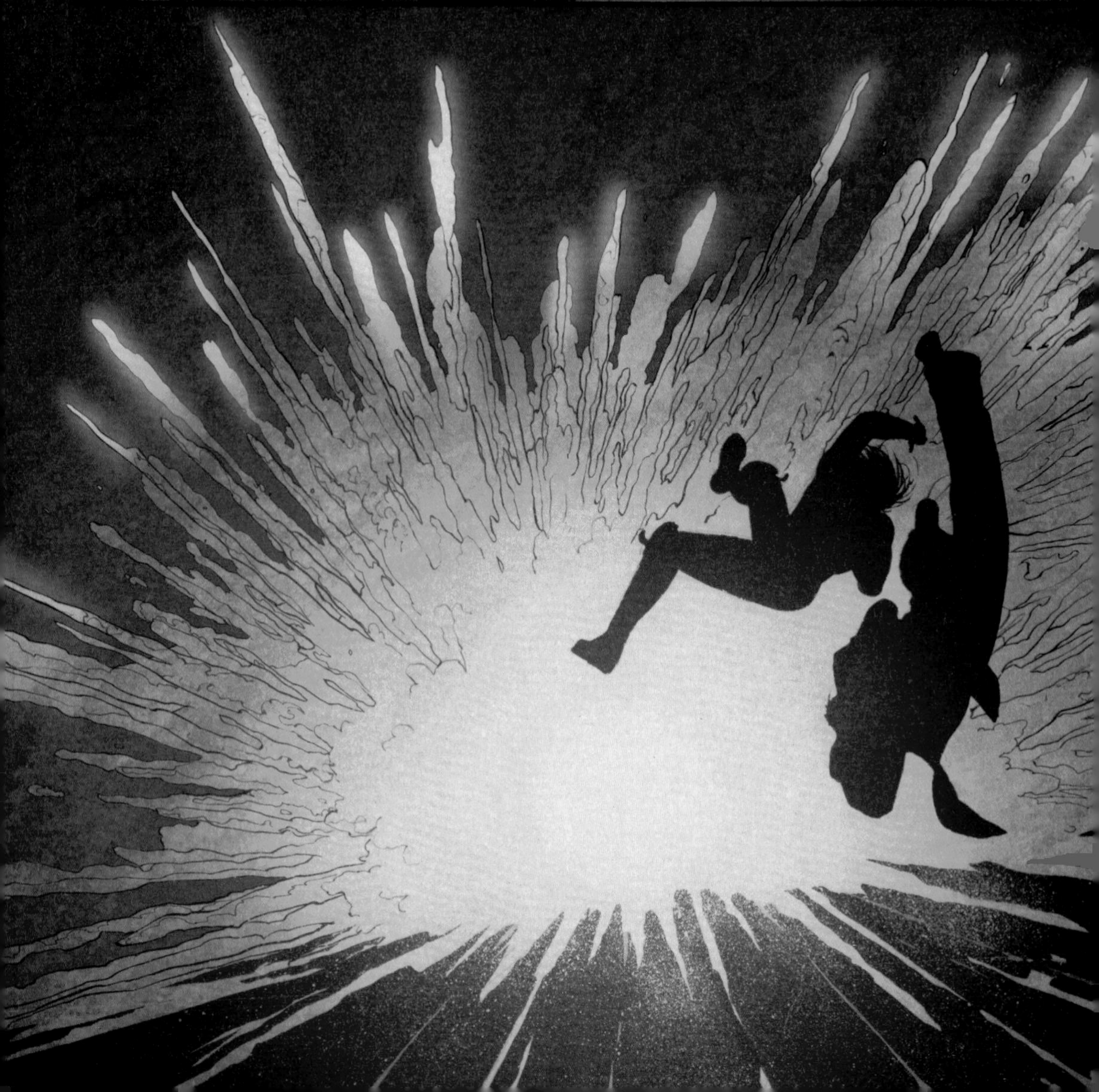

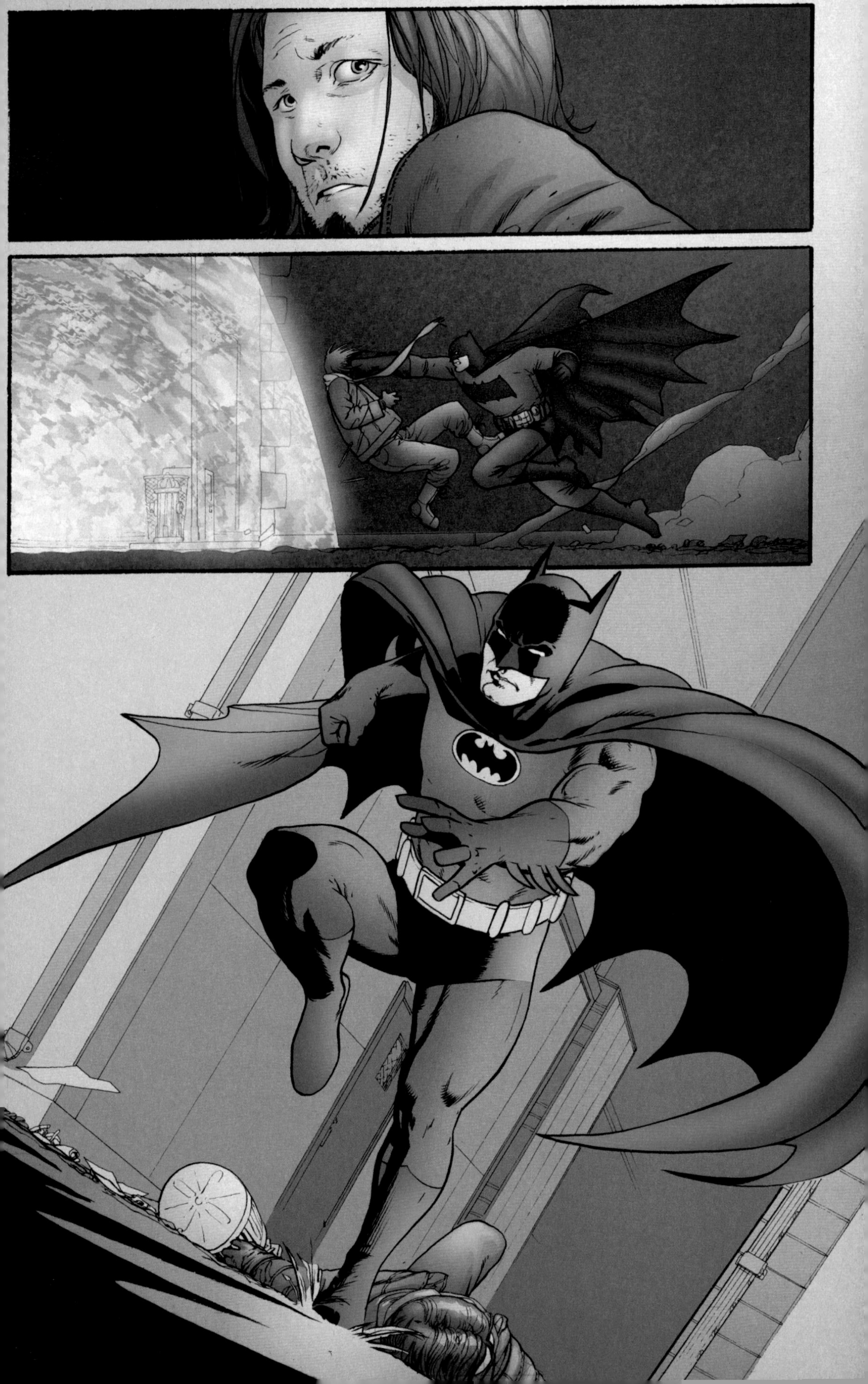

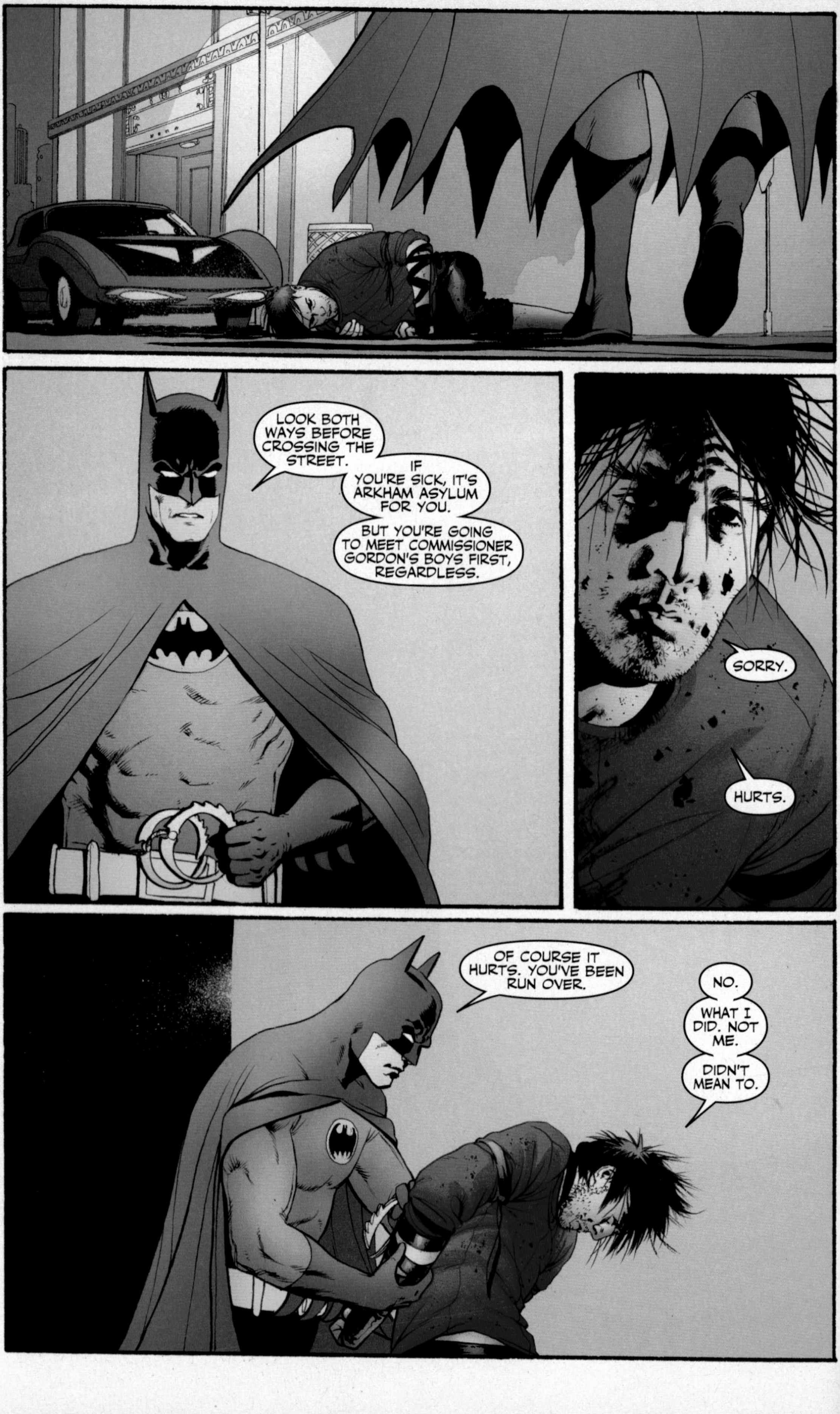
LOOK BOTH WAYS BEFORE CROSSING THE STREET.
IF YOU'RE SICK, IT'S ARKHAM ASYLUM FOR YOU.
BUT YOU'RE GOING TO MEET COMMISSIONER GORDON'S BOYS FIRST, REGARDLESS.
SORRY.
HURTS.
OF COURSE IT HURTS. YOU'VE BEEN RUN OVER.
NO.
WHAT I DID. NOT ME.
DIDN'T MEAN TO.

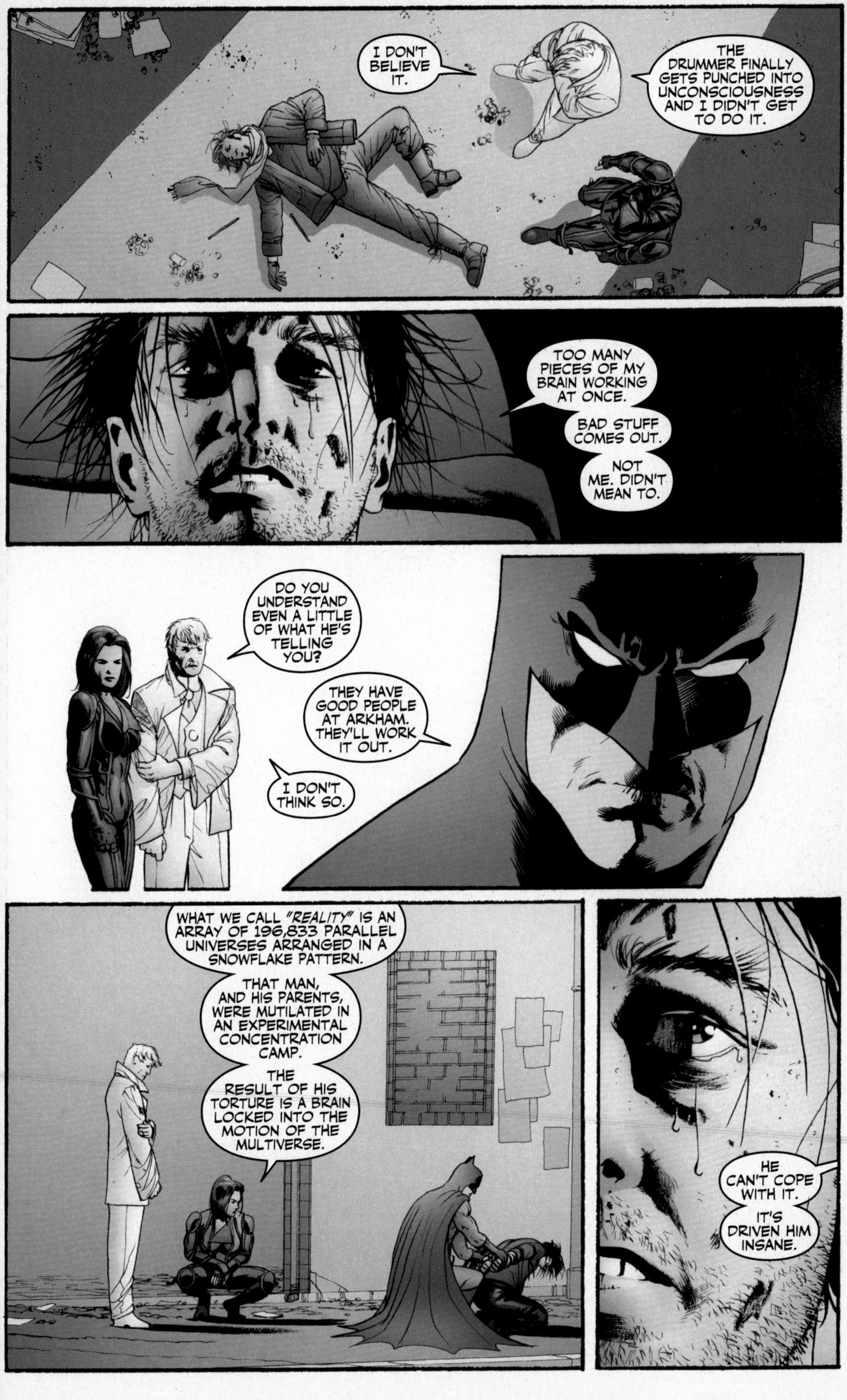
I DON'T BELIEVE IT.
THE DRUMMER FINALLY GETS PUNCHED INTO UNCONSCIOUSNESS AND I DIDN'T GET TO DO IT.
TOO MANY PIECES OF MY BRAIN WORKING AT ONCE.
BAD STUFF COMES OUT.
NOT ME. DIDN'T MEAN TO.
DO YOU UNDERSTAND EVEN A LITTLE OF WHAT HE'S TELLING YOU?
THEY HAVE GOOD PEOPLE AT ARKHAM. THEY'LL WORK IT OUT.
I DON'T THINK SO.
WHAT WE CALL "REALITY" IS AN ARRAY OF 196,833 PARALLEL UNIVERSES ARRANGED IN A SNOWFLAKE PATTERN.
THAT MAN, AND HIS PARENTS, WERE MUTILATED IN AN EXPERIMENTAL CONCENTRATION CAMP.
THE RESULT OF HIS TORTURE IS A BRAIN LOCKED INTO THE MOTION OF THE MULTIVERSE.
HE CAN'T COPE WITH IT.
IT'S DRIVEN HIM INSANE.

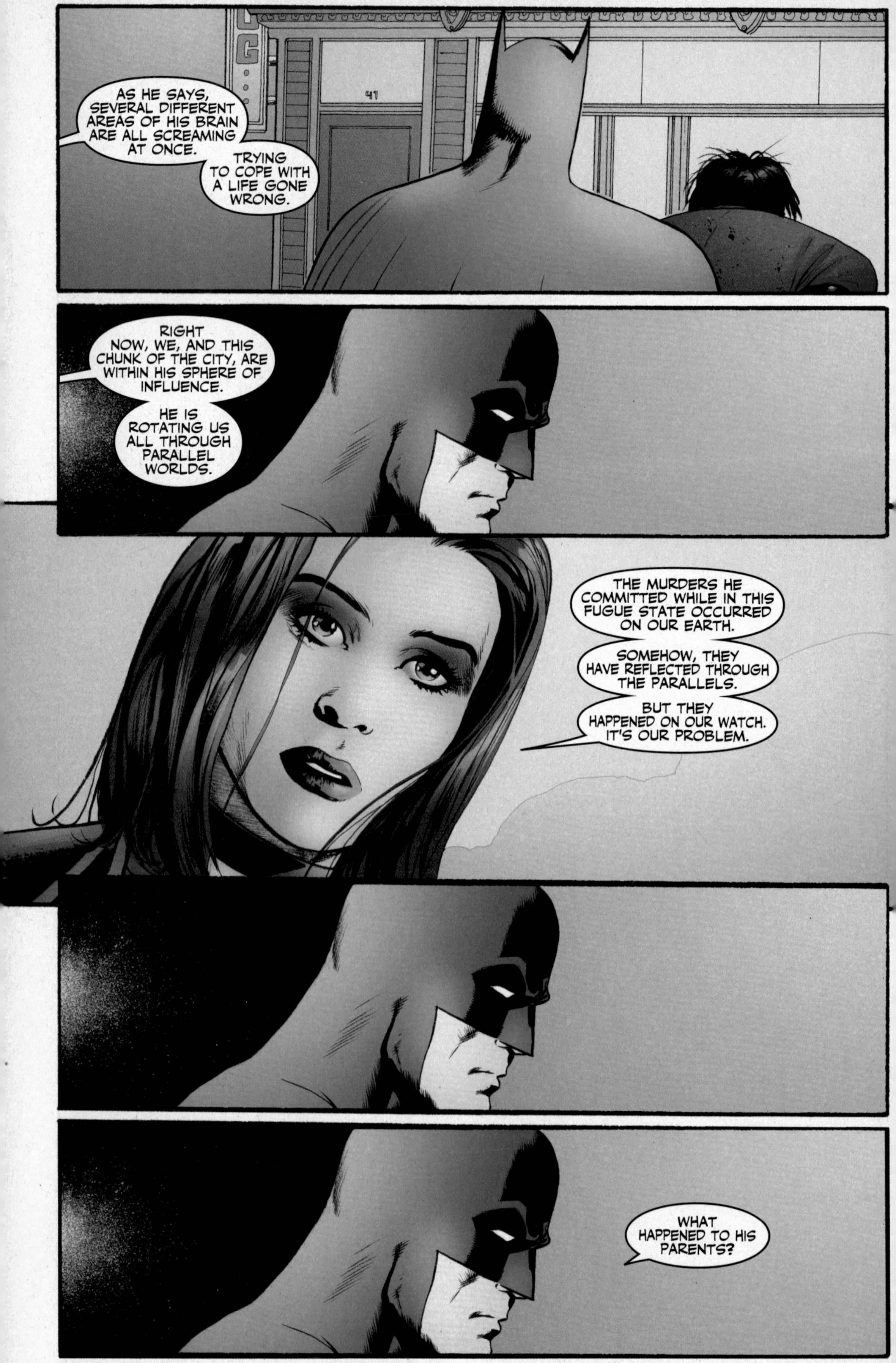
AS HE SAYS, SEVERAL DIFFERENT AREAS OF HIS BRAIN ARE ALL SCREAMING AT ONCE.
TRYING TO COPE WITH A LIFE GONE WRONG.
RIGHT NOW, WE, AND THIS CHUNK OF THE CITY, ARE WITHIN HIS SPHERE OF INFLUENCE.
HE IS ROTATING US ALL THROUGH PARALLEL WORLDS.
THE MURDERS HE COMMITTED WHILE IN THIS FUGUE STATE OCCURRED ON OUR EARTH.
SOMEHOW, THEY HAVE REFLECTED THROUGH THE PARALLELS.
BUT THEY HAPPENED ON OUR WATCH. IT'S OUR PROBLEM.
WHAT HAPPENED TO HIS PARENTS?

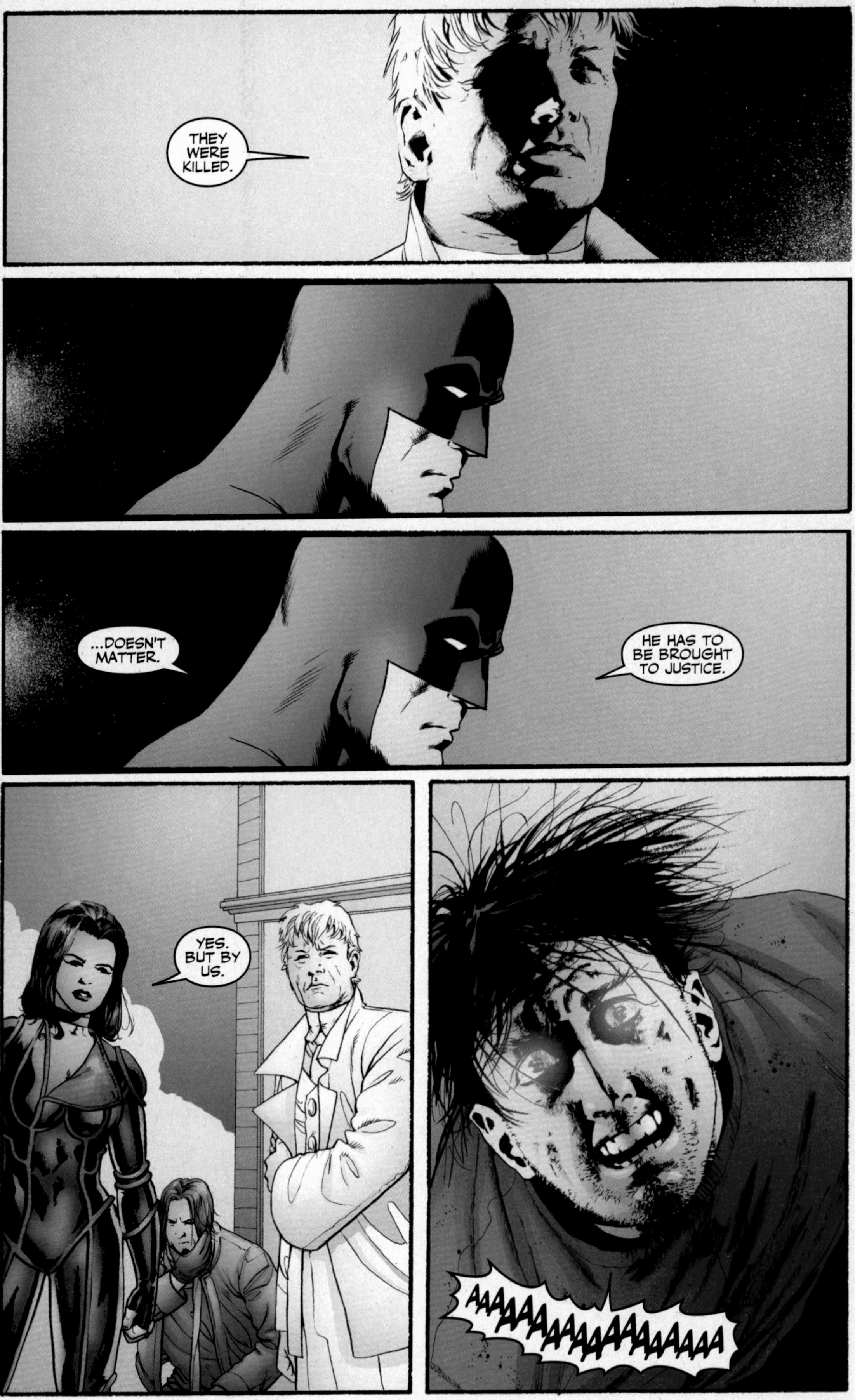
THEY WERE KILLED.
...DOESN'T MATTER.
HE HAS TO BE BROUGHT TO JUSTICE.
YES. BUT BY US.
AAAAAAAAAAAAAAAAAAAA

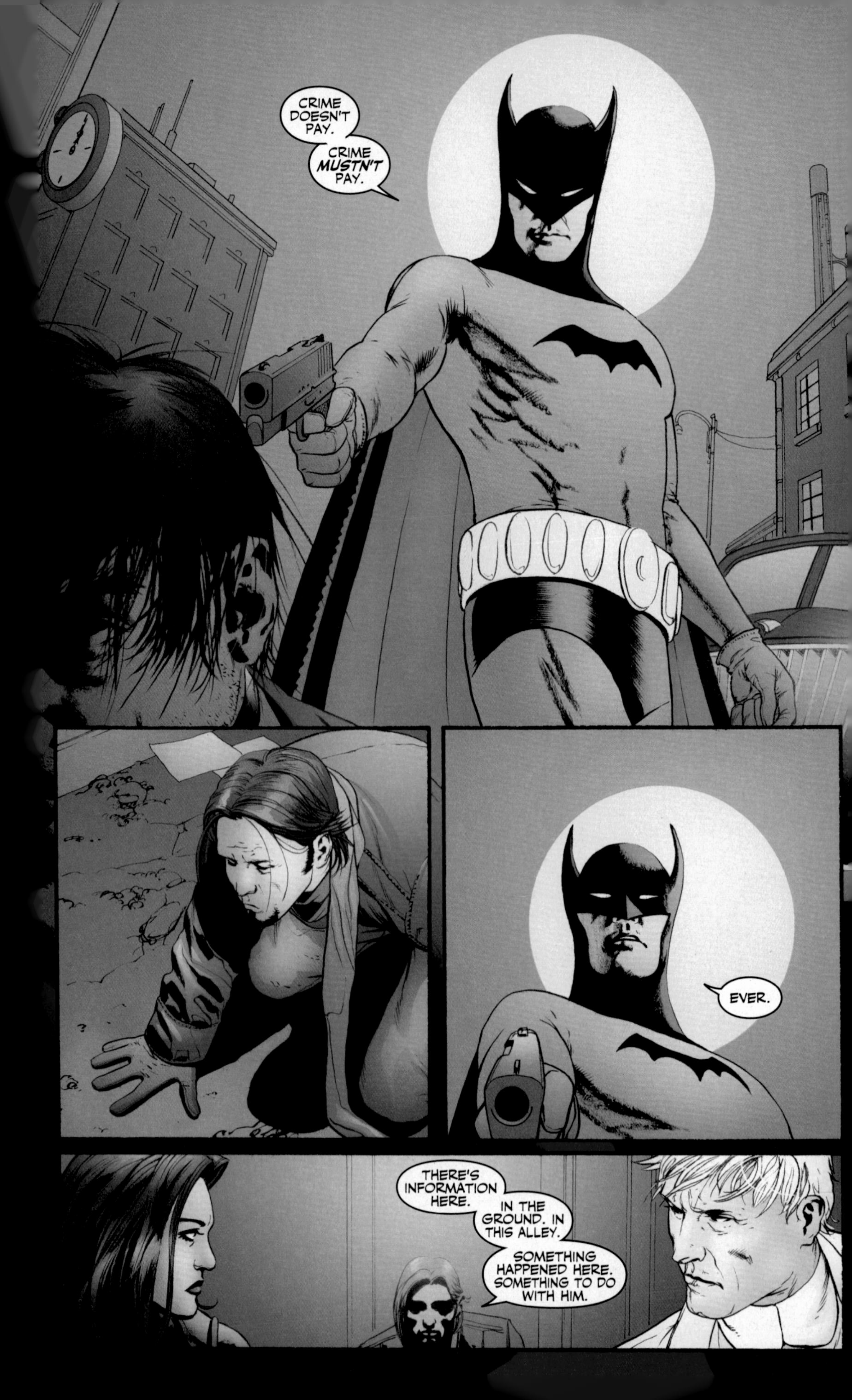
CRIME DOESN'T PAY.
CRIME *MUSTN'T* PAY.
EVER.
THERE'S INFORMATION HERE.
IN THE GROUND. IN THIS ALLEY.
SOMETHING HAPPENED HERE. SOMETHING TO DO WITH HIM.

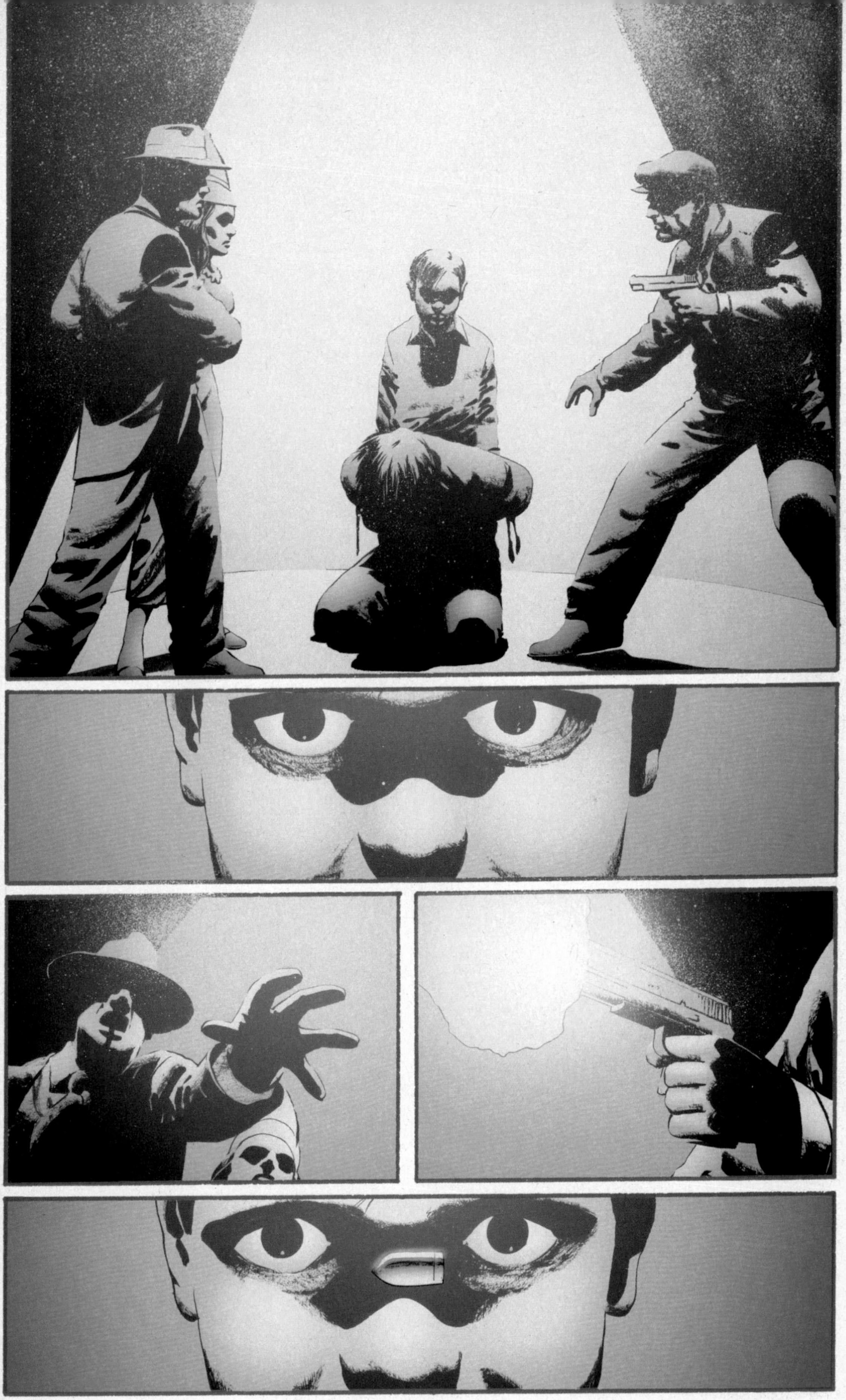

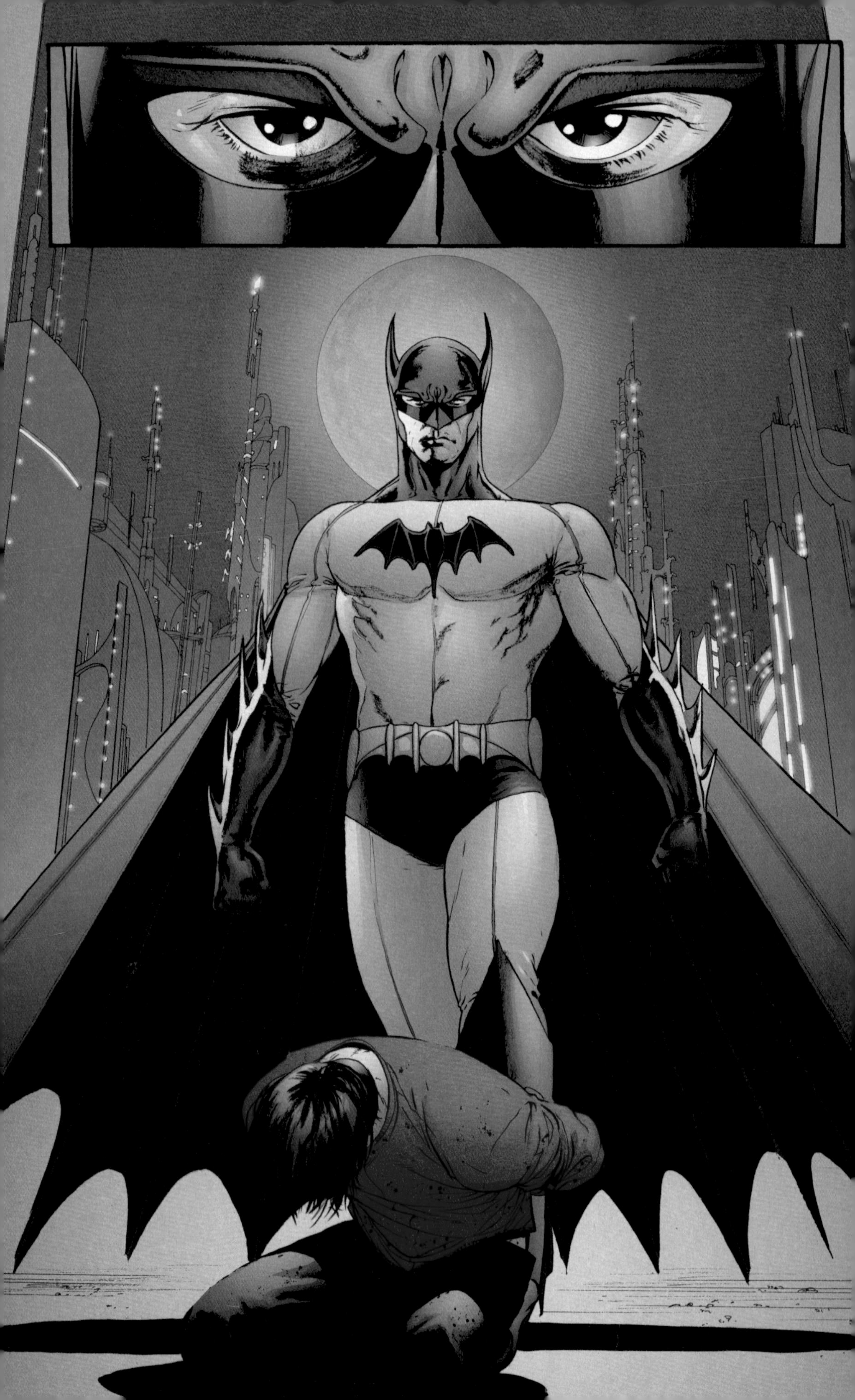

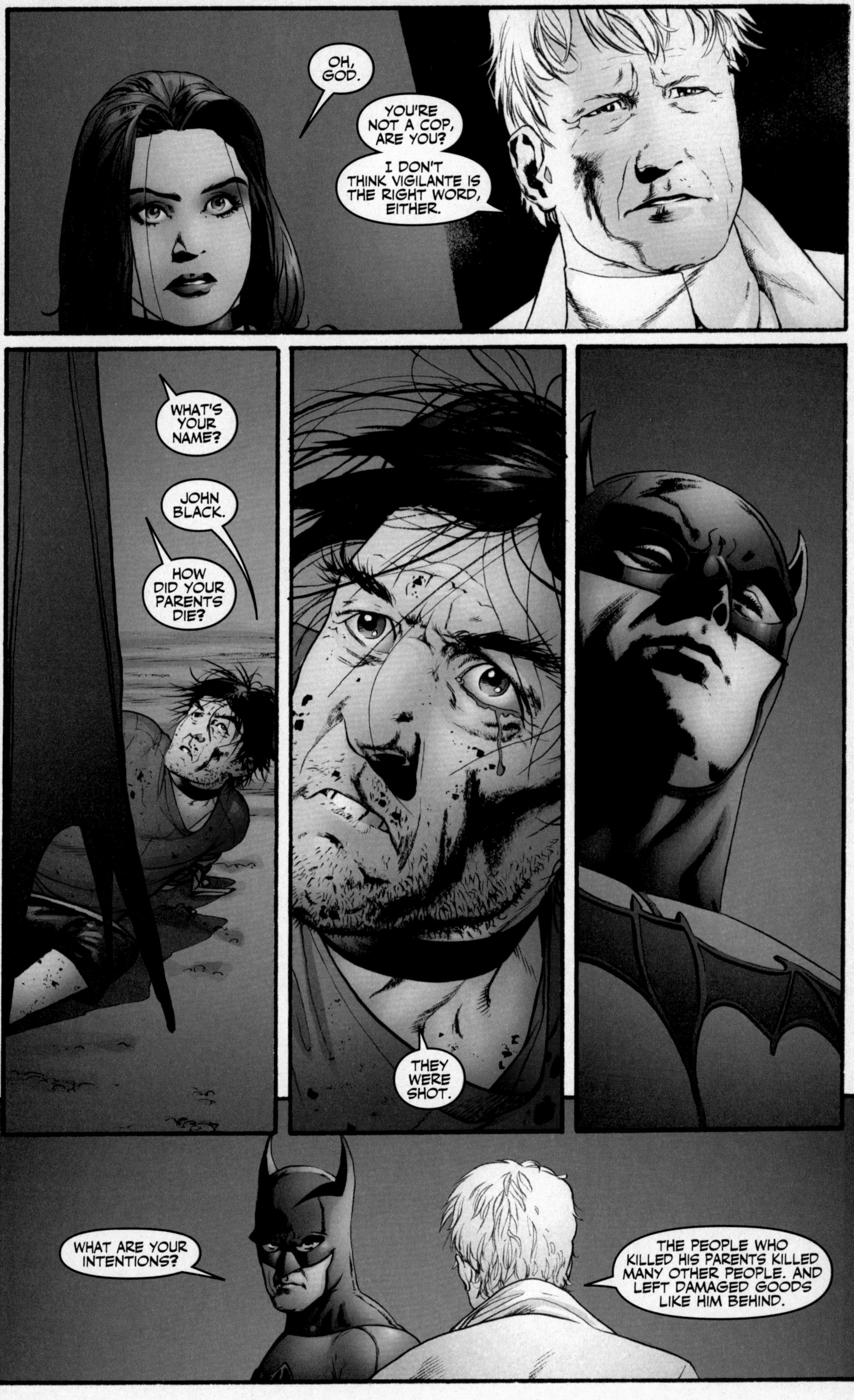
OH, GOD.
YOU'RE NOT A COP, ARE YOU?
I DON'T THINK VIGILANTE IS THE RIGHT WORD, EITHER.
WHAT'S YOUR NAME?
JOHN BLACK.
HOW DID YOUR PARENTS DIE?
THEY WERE SHOT.
WHAT ARE YOUR INTENTIONS?
THE PEOPLE WHO KILLED HIS PARENTS KILLED MANY OTHER PEOPLE. AND LEFT DAMAGED GOODS LIKE HIM BEHIND.

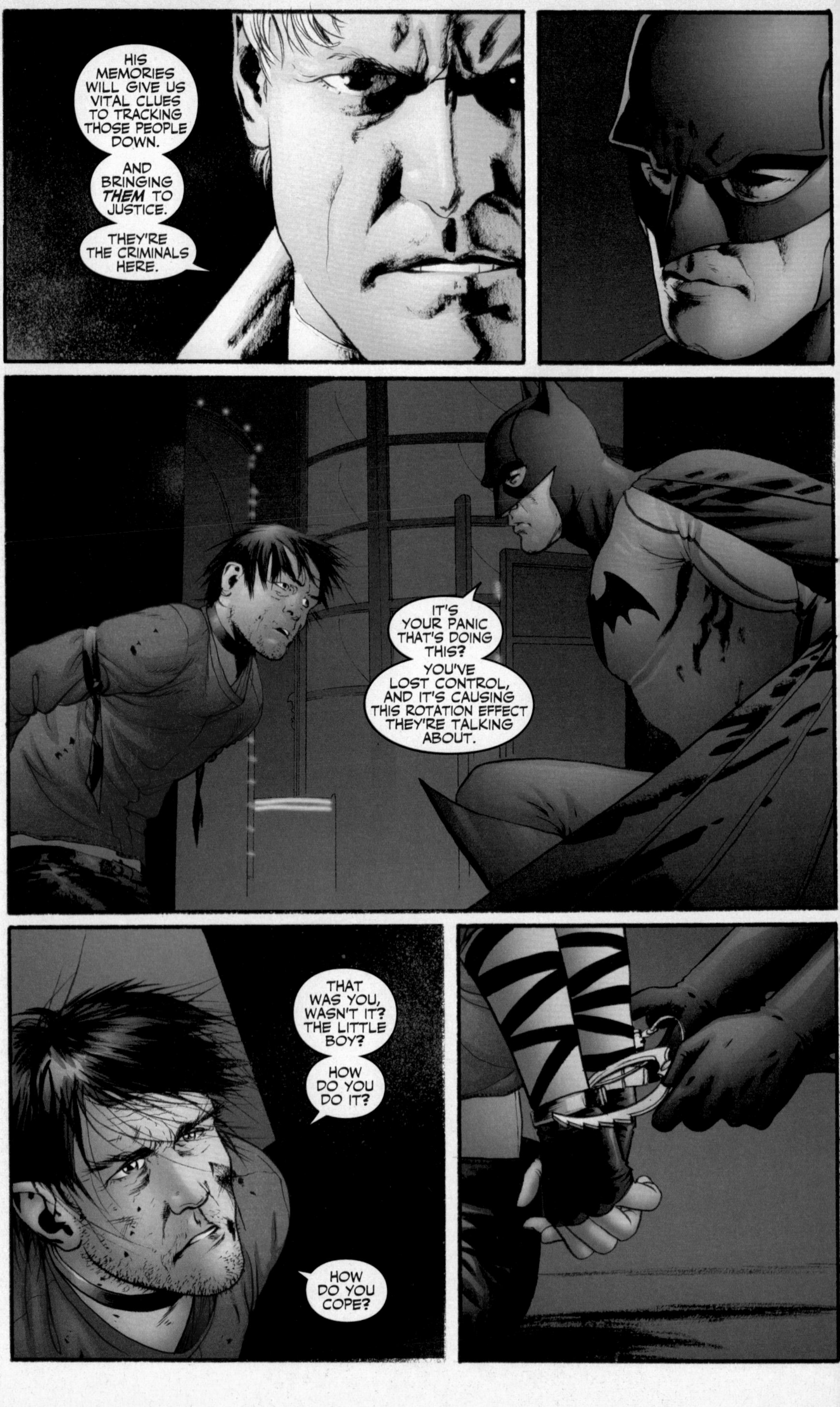
HIS MEMORIES WILL GIVE US VITAL CLUES TO TRACKING THOSE PEOPLE DOWN.
AND BRINGING *THEM* TO JUSTICE.
THEY'RE THE CRIMINALS HERE.
IT'S YOUR PANIC THAT'S DOING THIS?
YOU'VE LOST CONTROL, AND IT'S CAUSING THIS ROTATION EFFECT THEY'RE TALKING ABOUT.
THAT WAS YOU, WASN'T IT? THE LITTLE BOY?
HOW DO YOU DO IT?
HOW DO YOU COPE?

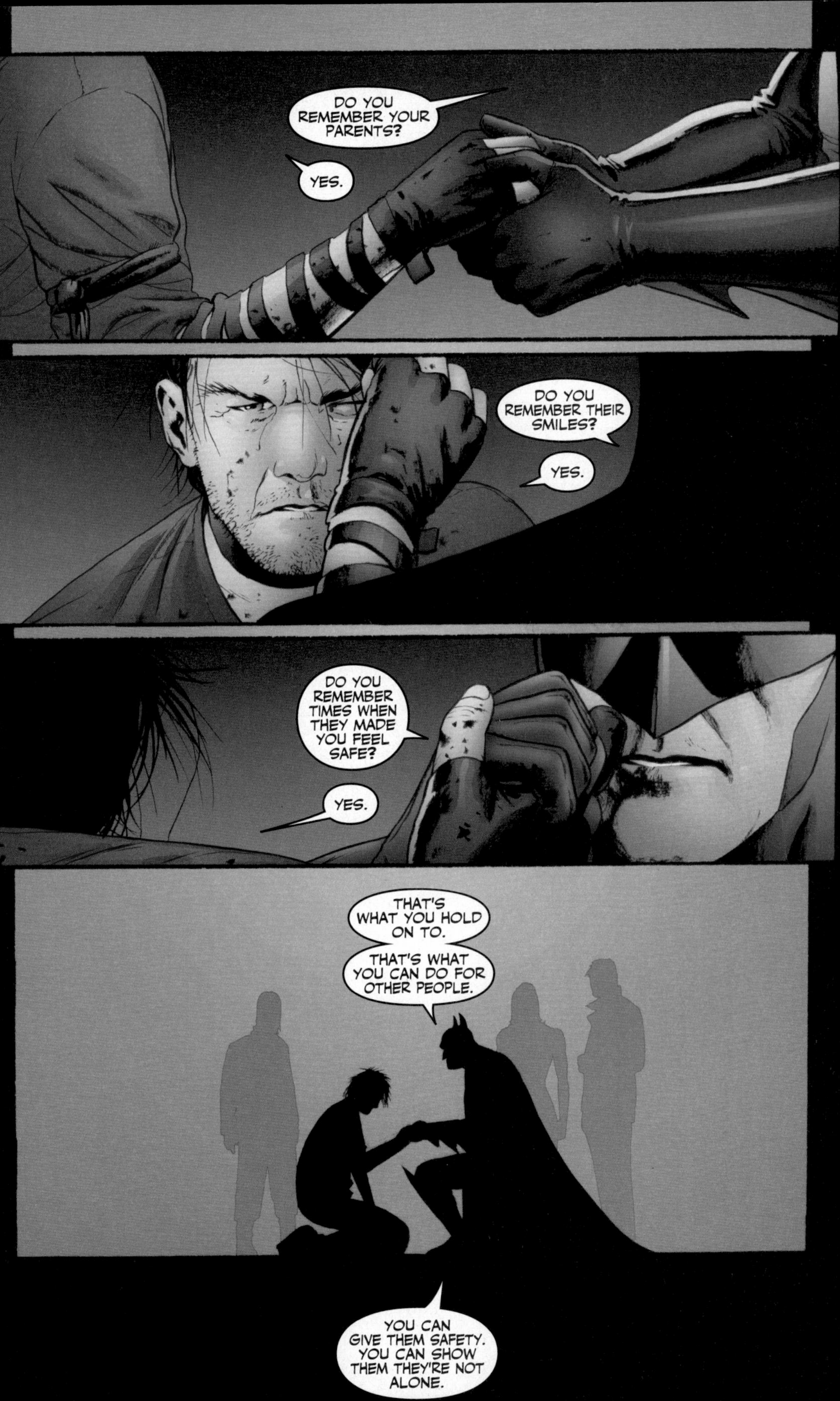
DO YOU REMEMBER YOUR PARENTS?
YES.
DO YOU REMEMBER THEIR SMILES?
YES.
DO YOU REMEMBER TIMES WHEN THEY MADE YOU FEEL SAFE?
YES.
THAT'S WHAT YOU HOLD ON TO.
THAT'S WHAT YOU CAN DO FOR OTHER PEOPLE.
YOU CAN GIVE THEM SAFETY. YOU CAN SHOW THEM THEY'RE NOT ALONE.

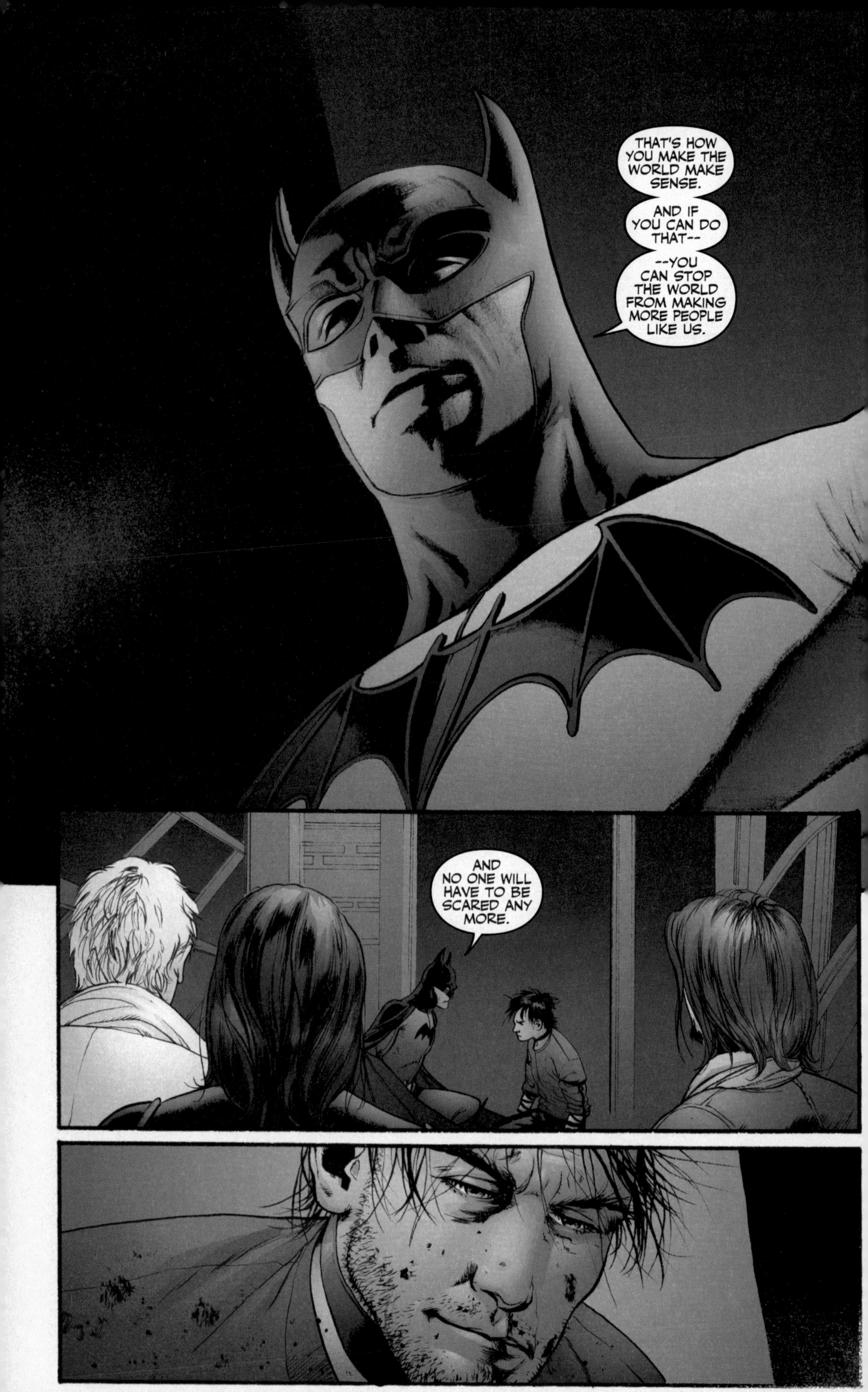
THAT'S HOW YOU MAKE THE WORLD MAKE SENSE.
AND IF YOU CAN DO THAT--
--YOU CAN STOP THE WORLD FROM MAKING MORE PEOPLE LIKE US.
AND NO ONE WILL HAVE TO BE SCARED ANY MORE.

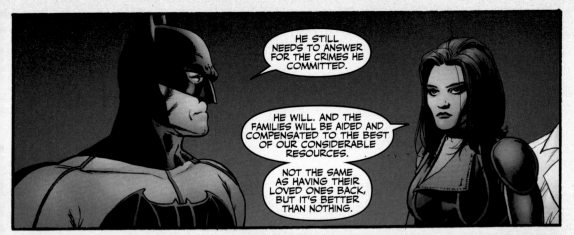

HE STILL NEEDS TO ANSWER FOR THE CRIMES HE COMMITTED.

HE WILL. AND THE FAMILIES WILL BE AIDED AND COMPENSATED TO THE BEST OF OUR CONSIDERABLE RESOURCES.

NOT THE SAME AS HAVING THEIR LOVED ONES BACK, BUT IT'S BETTER THAN NOTHING.

WE'RE ROTATING BACK. HE'S RELAXED.

I'M TRUSTING YOU TO DO THE RIGHT THING.

I DON'T CARE IF YOU'RE FROM MY "REALITY" OR NOT--THIS IS STILL MY CITY.

AND I'LL FIND YOU IF I HAVE TO.

I TOTALLY BEAT YOU UP, YOU KNOW.

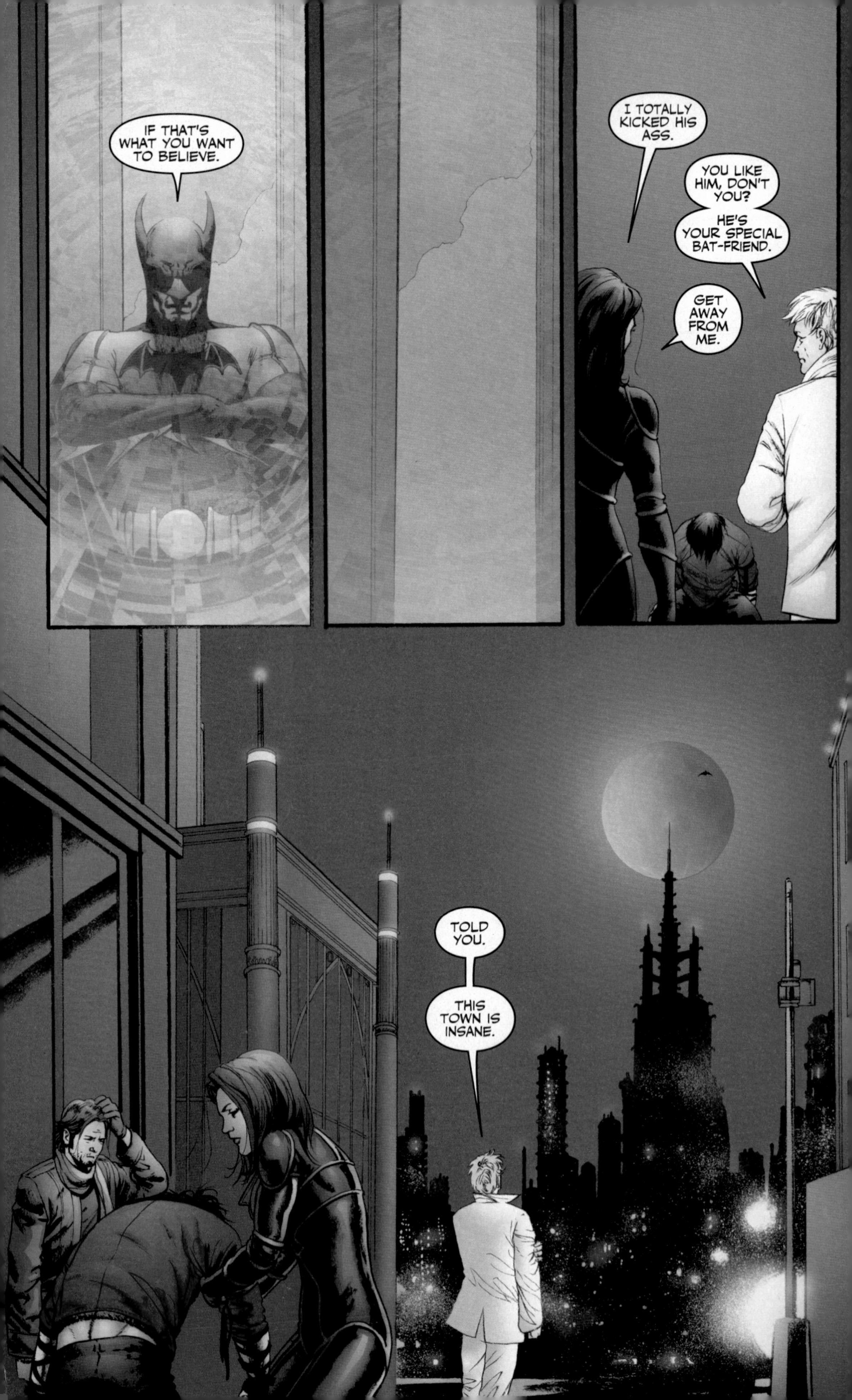
IF THAT'S WHAT YOU WANT TO BELIEVE.
I TOTALLY KICKED HIS ASS.
YOU LIKE HIM, DON'T YOU?
HE'S YOUR SPECIAL BAT-FRIEND.
GET AWAY FROM ME.
TOLD YOU.
THIS TOWN IS INSANE.

PLANETARY / JLA

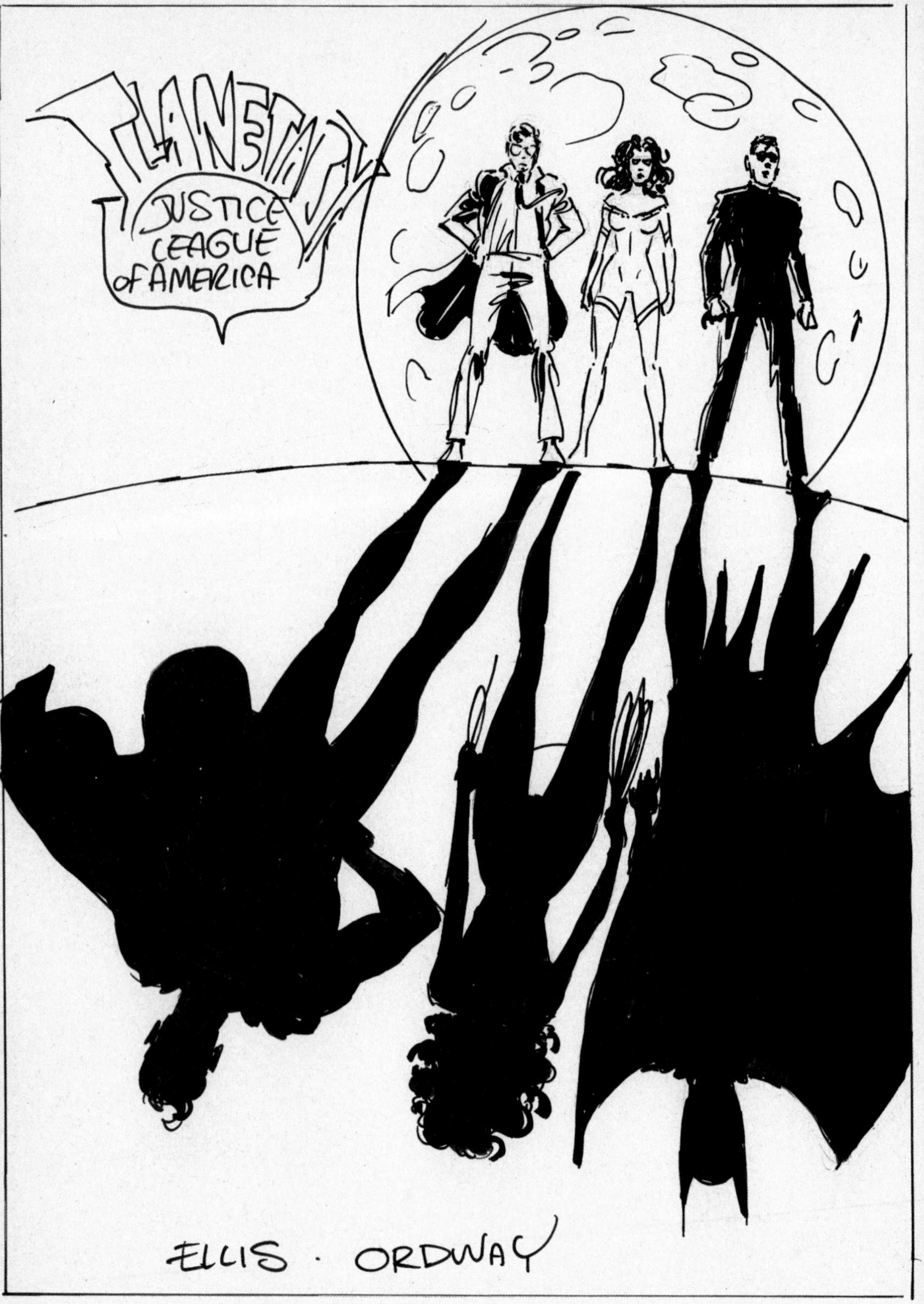
PLANETARY
JUSTICE LEAGUE of AMERICA
ELLIS · ORDWAY

SKETCH #2 FROM ORDWAY

ORIGINAL COVER CONCEPTS FOR TERRA OCCULTA

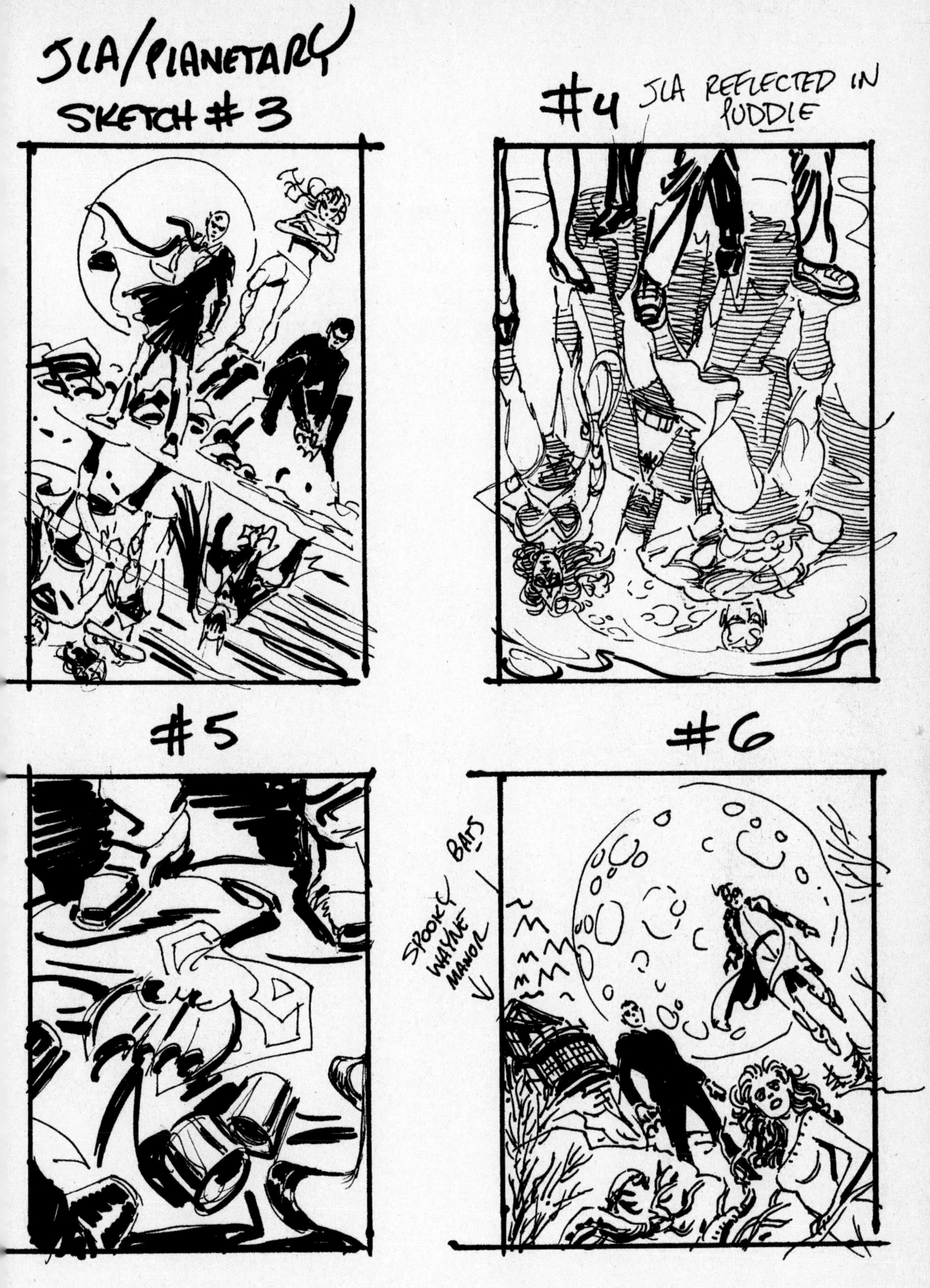
JLA/PLANETARY
SKETCH #3
#4
JLA REFLECTED IN PUDDLE
#5
#6
BATS
SPOOKY WAYNE MANOR

BY JERRY ORDWAY

IT'S A STRANGE WORLD, LET'S KEEP IT THAT WAY.

PLANETARY

BY WARREN ELLIS AND JOHN CASSADAY

Planetary is a globe-spanning organization dedicated to unearthing the fantastic secret history of the world we live in; they are the archaeologists of the unknown. From the deepest crevices where monsters dwell to the neon-lit streets where ghosts tread the Earth, Elijah Snow, Jakita Wagner and The Drummer will be there.

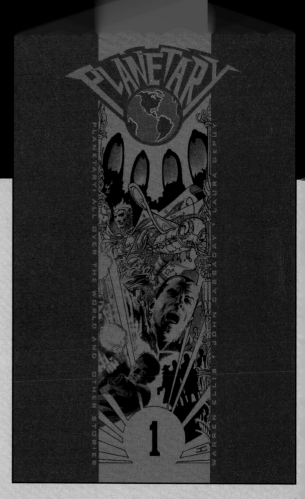

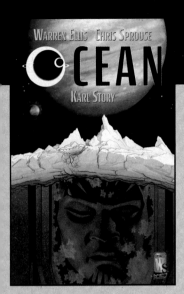

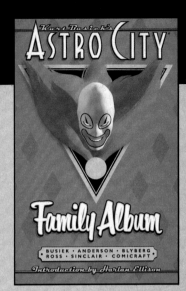

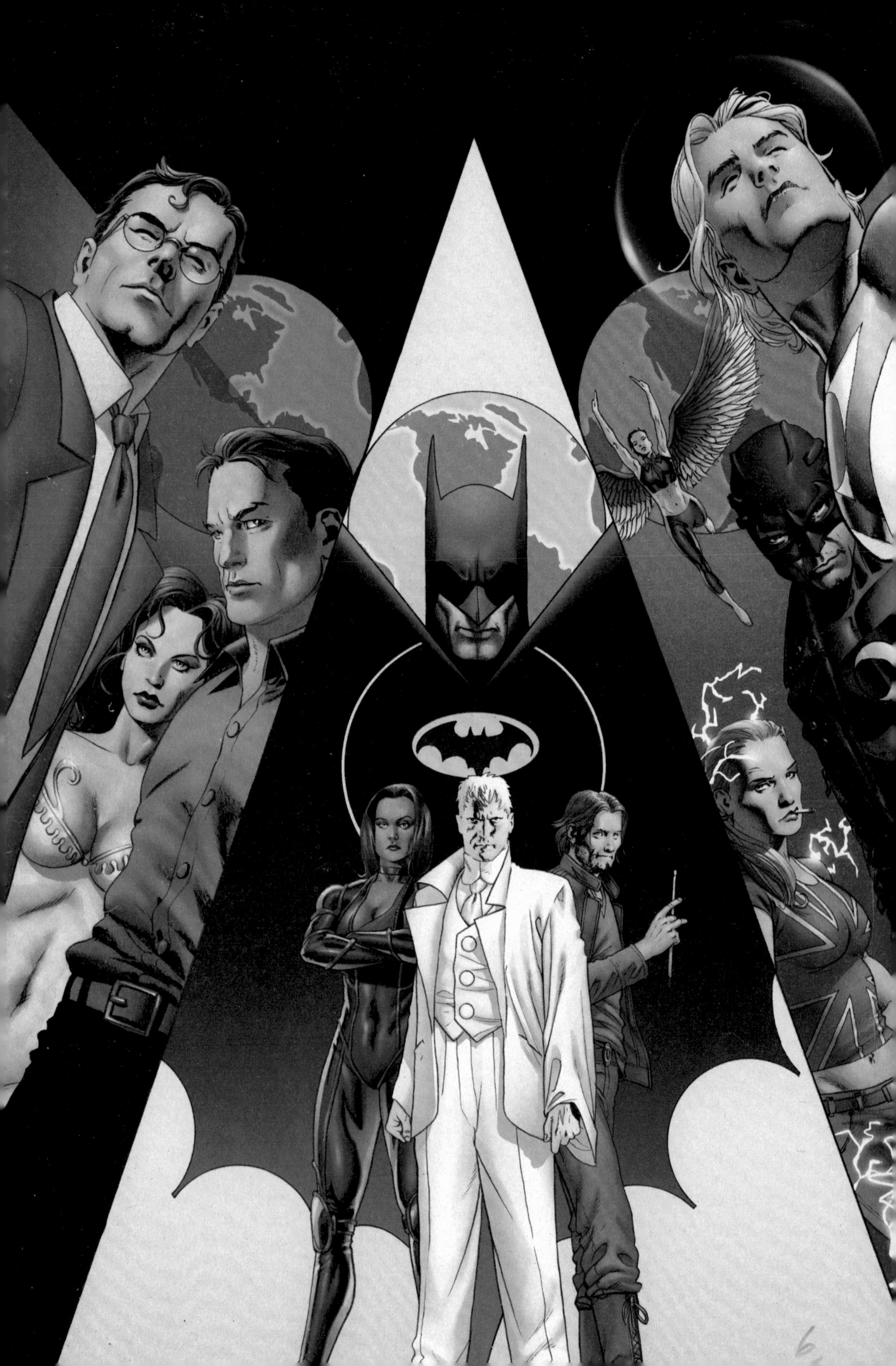